Collins

AS BUSINESS STUDIES

Andrew Ashwin • Stuart Merrills • Richard Thompson
and Denry Machin

www.collins.bized.co.uk

Published by Collins
An imprint of HarperCollinsPublishers
77 – 85 Fulham Palace Road
Hammersmith
London
W6 8JB

Browse the complete Collins catalogue at
www.collinseducation.com

© HarperCollinsPublishers Limited 2008
First published 2008

10 9 8 7 6 5 4 3 2 1

ISBN-13 978 0 00 727037 8

Andrew Ashwin, Stuart Merrills and Richard Thompson
assert the moral right to be identified as the authors of
this work.

British Library Cataloguing in Publication Data
A Catalogue record for this publication is available from
the British Library

Commissioned and project managed by Michael
Upchurch
Edited by Jenny Draine
Design by Newgen Imaging, India
Cover design by Oculus Design & Communications
Limited
Indexed by Derek Caudwell
Picture research by Michael Upchurch
Production by Simon Moore
Printed and bound by Printing Express, Hong Kong

DEDICATIONS

I would like to thank my colleagues at Biz/ed, Gareth
Bish, Will Scott, John Yates, Andy Hargrave and Stewart
Perrygrove for their support and professionalism
throughout the project.
I would like to dedicate the book to Richard Collishaw who
provided as much help as any book to get me through my
A' levels many years ago. Economic's loss is farming's gain.
Andrew Ashwin

Thanks to Claire Chappell for her help and support
throughout.
Stuart Merrills

For Sara, Joanna, William and Emily.
Richard Thompson

ACKNOWLEDGEMENTS

The authors would like to thank the following people for
their contribution to this book:

Rob Bircher, Malcolm Surridge and Denry Machin.

Every effort had been made to contact the holders of
copyright material, but if any have been inadvertently
overlooked the publishers will be pleased to make the
necessary arrangements at the first opportunity.

The publishers would like to thank the following for
permission to reproduce pictures on these pages.
T=Top, B=Bottom, L=Left, R=Right, C=Centre

© vario images GmbH & Co.KG / Alamy 97, 166;
© RF@PPS / Alamy 101; © Mary-Ella Keith / Alamy 105;
© Andrew Butterton / Alamy 14 (B); © Tim Hill / Alamy
113; © Niall McDiarmid / Alamy 123, 164, 369 (B);
© Emilio Ereza / Alamy 131; © V1 / Alamy 139;
© snappdragon / Alamy 145; © K-PHOTOS / Alamy 149;
© numb / Alamy 157 (L); © I. Glory / Alamy (R);
© guy harrop / Alamy 158; © Alex Segre / Alamy 163;
© Mike Harrington / Alamy 176; © Brownstock Inc. /
Alamy 183; © Mint Photography / Alamy 194, 247;
© David Levenson / Alamy 200; © Jeff Greenberg / Alamy
202; © David J. Green - Lifestyle / Alamy 205;
© ABN Stock Images / Alamy 221; © Markus Spiske /
Alamy 237; © William Nicklin / Alamy 239;
© Gary Roebuck / Alamy 240; © Steve Nichols / Alamy
243; © JUPITERIMAGES/ Creatas / Alamy 250;
© Steve Skjold / Alamy 259; © JUPITERIMAGES/ Think-
stock / Alamy 261; © Bernie Pearson / Alamy 267;
© MAX EAREY / Alamy 271; © Kitt Cooper-Smith /
Alamy 273; © D. Hurst / Alamy 274; © Digital Vision /
Alamy 279, 287; © ImageDJ / Alamy 282; © Kevin Foy /
Alamy 291; © David J. Green - studio / Alamy 295 (B);
© Tetra Images / Alamy 296 (C); © PSL Images / Alamy
296 (B); © Chris Howes/Wild Places Photography / Alamy
297 (B); © Nick Cobbing / Alamy 313; © Chloe Johnson /
Alamy 369 (T); © 2007 Apple Inc. 302 (L); © BBC 135;
© 2007 Caterham Cars 296 (T); ©2007 Caterpillar 294;
© Bettmann/ CORBIS 223, 226; Jake Wyman/Getty Im-
ages 3; Getty Images 9, 14 (T), 36, 50, 70, 71, 343;
AFP/Getty Images 299, 333; © Handirack UK Ltd 2007
359; Jim McAdam/Maria Difolco 6, 361; © 2007 WM
Magner of Clonmel 329; Alma Robinson/ allactiondigi-
tal.com/ EMPICS Entertainment/ PA Photos 16; Jon
Buckle/EMPICS Sport/PA Photos 24; Suzan/EMPICS
Entertainment/PA Photos 67; Paul Sakuma/AP/PA Photos
5, 302 (R); VINCENT YU/AP/PA Photos 354; Western
Counties Air Operations/PA Wire/PA Photos 372;
© National Pictures / TopFoto 310; ©TopFoto 342; Michael
Upchurch 13, 297 (T), 297 (C), 340; © UpMyStreet 2007
295 (T)

AS BUSINESS STUDIES

Andrew Ashwin • Stuart Merrills • Richard Thompson
and Denry Machin

www.collins.bized.co.uk

Contents

Unit 2 Managing a Business

The AQA Examiner speaks to the student

Stuart Merrills, AQA Business Studies Assistant Principal Examiner,
Head of Economics and Accounting, Hyde Clarendon Sixth Form College

The AQA AS specification has been designed to introduce and develop Business Studies in a practical and active manner. Initially it focuses on the contemporary business world and covers topics such as entrepreneurship, issues involved in starting a new business venture and factors influencing the success of new start-up businesses. Your studies will then move on to consider how established businesses might measure and improve their effectiveness. The course explores the major factors that influence the internal functions of differing types of organisation, whilst appreciating and examining that the business environment is a dynamic and active market.

What you have to study

The AQA AS specification consists of two units:

- **Unit 1** Planning and Financing a Business, worth 40% of the overall AS award.
- **Unit 2** Managing a Business, worth 60% of the overall AS award.

Assessment method

For the AQA Business Studies exam, you have to sit two papers. Each paper examines one of the units of study. These exams are:

Unit 1 – BUSS1

Planning and Financing a Business	Short answer and extended responses based on a mini case study.
1 hour 15 minutes examination	Total 60 marks

Unit 2 – BUSS2

Managing a Business	Compulsory multi-part data responses questions.
1 hour 30 minutes examination	Total 80 marks

Mini case studies and data response items

These consist of some initial background information that provides a scenario on which the examination questions will be set. These questions can be based on newspaper or magazine extracts or be entirely fictitious. They may well contain data in the form of tables, charts, graphs or diagrams. It is important that you remember that the information given in the scenario is there to help you. Case studies will often require you to offer solutions to business problems or analyse situations and propose business actions, so in order to gain high marks you must contextualise your answers; i.e. respond to the circumstances in the situation given. **So unless you want to throw marks away, make sure you do use the information given.**

Types of question

SHORT ANSWER QUESTIONS

These are usually quite straightforward and require you to give a formal definition of a business term, with perhaps a valid example or description of how it may be applied by a business.

EXPLANATORY QUESTIONS

These need slightly more development and require you to offer a description of relevant subject knowledge and an explanation of how this might apply to the scenario given. I.e. you need to expand upon a relevant point or influential factor to demonstrate your understanding of the term or theory presented and how it applies to the business situation given in the scenario.

ANALYTICAL QUESTIONS

These need much more depth. They often ask you to look at advantages and/or disadvantages of business actions or situations and require you to demonstrate knowledge, explain how it might affect the scenario or situation and then consider further implications; knock-on effects or cause and effect relationships. The main focus is for you to explain in detail the process whereby cause brings about the end effect. To answer these well you need to use a continuous prose style of writing in well-structured and developed paragraphs. One of the key areas here is to remember that in Business Studies there are two sides to every situation.

EVALUATIVE QUESTIONS

These types of questions require you to reach a judgement. This can be in the form of weighing up the relative strengths (pros and cons) of your arguments in order to reach a conclusion or a discussion. Or it could be involving the likelihood of factors occurring or the timescale involved, to develop a judgement of which factors may be considered the most important or influential. Again, remember to put your answers in the context of the scenario presented; this will help you make an informed judgement given the circumstances.

Command words

The key to understanding command words and the depth of response needed is to look at the command word given **and the mark allocation of the question**. This should then help you formulate the amount of detail you need to go in your answer: i.e. the length and depth of your response, **and the amount of time you should allocate for your response**. By far the most common mistakes in exam technique that I see are when students fail to develop arguments sufficiently or conversely develop questions that require only simple responses in too much detail and then run out of time on the later questions.

QUESTIONS THAT REQUIRE A SHORT ANSWER

These are usually characterised by the words or phrases:

- Define
- What is meant by
- State/identify.

WORDS THAT REQUIRE AN EXPLANATORY ANSWER

These are identified by the words or phrases:

- Explain
- Outline
- Distinguish between
- Or may require calculations.

WORDS THAT REQUIRE AN ANALYTICAL ANSWER

These can be distinguished by the words or phrases:

- Examine
- Analyse
- Consider.

WORDS THAT REQUIRE AN EVALUATIVE ANSWER

These can be recognised by the words or phrases:

- Evaluate
- Discuss
- To what extent
- Recommend.

What the examiners are looking for – how to get a good grade

LEVELS OF RESPONSE MARKING

All Business Studies papers are now marked using levels of response marking. This type of marking uses a number or descriptors against which your work is assessed; these are based on the type of questions discussed earlier. An example level of response marking grid for a 15 mark evaluative question is shown on the next page.

	Content (2 marks)	Application (4 marks)	Analysis (4 marks)
Level 2	**2 marks**	**4-3 marks**	**4-3 marks**
	Candidate shows good understanding of relevant terms or identifies two relevant points or a combination of both	Candidate applies knowledge effectively to issues in the case	Sound analysis of issues to the case
Level 1	**1 mark**	**2-1 marks**	**2-1 marks**
	Candidate shows some understanding of relevant terms or identifies one relevant point	Candidate attempts to apply knowledge to the business's circumstances	Limited analysis of issues

Evaluation is marked using a separate grid like the one given below

Level	Descriptor	Marks
E3	Candidate offers judgement plus full justification. Ideas are communicated using a logical structure, with some appropriate use of technical terms. There are occasional errors in accepted conventions of written communications.	5-4
E2	Candidate offers judgement plus limited justification. Ideas are communicated with some structure evident, with occasional use of technical terms. There are some errors in accepted conventions of written communications.	3-2
E1	Candidate offers undeveloped judgement based on evidence. Ideas are communicated in a simplistic way with limited use of technical terms. There are noticeable errors in accepted conventions of written communications.	1

To attain full marks for a question you must demonstrate all the different skills shown; content, application, analysis and evaluation and move through the levels of each skill. For example, a student who just provided a bullet point list would only be showing **limited content/knowledge** and thus only receive 1 or 2 marks.

A single paragraph of continuous prose that develops an argument may well show level 2 application (3 marks) as well as limited or sound analysis (1 or 2 marks), making a total of 4 or 5 marks.

A considered approach that offered good analysis of several points, applied to the context of the business scenario given, that shows reasoned arguments, drawing to logical conclusion would receive top level marks for each skill area and hence a maximum 15.

Important note. You can reach the top of each level independently, e.g. it is possible to get level 2 application and analysis but include no evaluation in your answer thus getting: content (2 marks), application (4 marks), analysis (4 marks) and evaluation (0 marks). Making a total of 10 marks.

It is therefore, very important that you understand the key command words so that you know what skills to demonstrate, and practise developing these skills so that you can move through the levels of each assessment objective. Another important issue is to note that to obtain level two application your answer must be relevant to the case. **I.e. you must put you answers in context and make them relevant to the scenario given.**

Quality of written communication

All exam papers now carry marks for the assessment of candidates' quality of written communication. For AS Business Studies these marks are embedded (included) in the marking grid for questions requiring you to demonstrate evaluation. These marks allocated to each question assess your ability to write in continuous prose, expressing ideas clearly and fluently, through well-linked sentences and paragraphs and using appropriate language and terminology.

You must therefore try to use a fluid, well-structured style to answer your questions and if you do have any time left at the end it is therefore wise to proof read and check your work.

Exam tips

- Be prepared; make sure you have all the required equipment. For example, Business Studies exams frequently require you to do calculations so a calculator is handy.
- Read the paper carefully and absorb the material. Remember to use the information in the articles to help you; if you don't use them when the question tells you to you will be throwing marks away. A good idea is to underline key points as you read through.
- Allocate time sensibly. Use the marks available and the command words as a guide to how much to write and at what level.
- A simple point, but read the questions. If the question says advantages or benefits just write about these aspects – writing about disadvantages will gain you no marks. If it says give two reasons, then give two. Make sure you're doing what the question asks, not what you think it asks.
- Use paragraphs to show the examiner when you are starting a new point or demonstrating a new skill. This makes it easy for them to follow your style, structure, arguments and logic.
- Always show your working fully for numerical questions. Then even if you've got it wrong you can receive some marks for method.
- Play the game. Understand what the examiners are looking for and provide it. Use proper terminology and avoid slang and jargon. Stay focused and don't use sweeping statements such as 'all business will'. There are usually two sides to any business action and things 'may' or 'might' happen.

Edexcel and OCR matching grids

Edexcel Specification	Collins Biz/ed AS Business Studies chapter reference
Unit 1 Developing New Business Ideas	
1.3.1 Characteristics of successful entrepreneurs	1
1.3.2 Identifying a business opportunity	2, 6
1.3.3 Evaluating a business opportunity	3, 5
1.3.4 Economic considerations	-
1.3.5 Financing the new business idea	8
1.3.6 Measuring the potential success of a business idea	11, 12, 18
1.3.7 Putting a business idea into practice	4, 15
Unit 2a Managing the Business	
2.3.1a Marketing plan	28, 29, 30, 31, 32, 33, 34
2.3.2a Managing the provision process	23, 24, 25, 26, 27, 30
2.3.3a How does a company budget efficiently?	13, 14, 15, 16, 17
2.3.4a Managing other people	10, 19, 20, 21, 22

OCR Specification	Collins Biz/ed AS Business Studies chapter reference
Unit F291: An Introduction to Business	
The nature of business	1, 2, 3, 5, 6, 8, 13, 19, 26
Classification of business	2, 6, 7
Objectives	1, 7, 15
The market	6, 34
Other influences	6, 10, 27
Unit F292: Business Functions	
Marketing	28, 29, 30, 31, 32, 33, 34
Accounting and finance	11, 12, 13, 14, 16, 17, 18
People in organisations	19, 20, 21, 22
Operations management	23, 24, 25, 26, 27

About www.collins.bized.co.uk

Instead of just providing the obligatory Teacher's Guide, Collins and Biz/ed are providing true added value by giving you the opportunity to access many more resources to support the book through a **subscription website**. The website is suitable for teachers and students alike and subscription is no more expensive than many existing Teacher's Guides but offers you so much more!

This unique new site enables you to:

- **Get the best exam results** - with a huge range of exam style questions plus mark schemes based on the sample assessment material produced by AQA, including student responses with examiner commentary
- **Raise standards** - using constantly updated case studies to reinforce understanding of business concepts in a range of different contexts
- **Engage students in the subject** - with activities to liven up your lessons and engage students in active learning, including role plays, presentations, games, group work, research and investigation and written reports
- **Help students to enjoy and achieve** - with video clips of the latest news items relating to the world of business from Sky News that can be integrated into lessons and help students to build on their knowledge and understanding.
- **Be part of a community** - download, review, comment on and share a variety of resources.

About Biz/ed

Since its launch in January 1996, Biz/ed has established itself as the primary provider of Internet-based learning materials for the economics and business education community.

Biz/ed is targeted at students and teachers in the post-16 education sector, covering schools, FE colleges, universities and beyond. The site offers support for economics, business, accounting, leisure and recreation and travel and tourism at many different levels including AVCE, AS and A2 level, International Baccalaureate, HNC, HND and MBA.

How to use this book

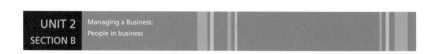

At the start of each **section** there is an overview presented as a **mind map** and discussion of a **Key concept** relevant to the section.

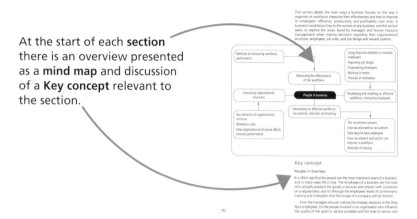

Activity
Suggestions for **activities** for use in the classroom, to reinforce information and concepts presented and for further research.

Activity

A juicy business

Nature's Bounty Ltd manufactures a range of organic fruit juices for sale in supermarkets and health food stores. It has set sales and expenditure budgets for each of the different fruit juices it makes. Information for the last year of trading has been collated in the table below to show the budgeted and actual performance of each type of fruit juice.

Fruit juice	Sales variances (£'000)			Expenditure variances (£'000)		
	Budget	Actual	Variance	Budget	Actual	Variance
Sunshine Orange	450	400	50 adverse	200	180	
Orchard Apple	350	380		180		30 adverse
Tangy Tropical	400	480			240	40 adverse
Morning Grapefruit	120		30 adverse	100	120	

1 Complete the missing information in the table.
2 Calculate the total profit variance for Nature's Bounty Ltd.
3 Of what value is the information in the table to Nature's Bounty Ltd?

Key terms

Enterprise A business organisation that is characterised by particular goals shared by a group of people, and with a responsibility for the control of its own performance.

Enterprise (*alternative interpretation*) The demonstration of initiative, risk, flair, dedication and skill in setting up a business.

Entrepreneur A person who organises factors of production, such as people, finance, land and equipment, in a business. In so doing, the individual demonstrates initiative, flair and skill, combined with an appreciation of risk.

Opportunity cost Cost expressed in terms of the next best alternative sacrificed in making a decision.

Profit The reward for enterprise. Profit is the difference between the total revenue generated and the total costs of production.

Risk The degree of chance of failure resulting in a loss of some sort.

Key terms
These are simple definitions of important terms and concepts used in each chapter. Each key term is printed in bold type the first time it appears in the main text.

Guru's views

'How do I motivate someone to play the piano? First, I teach them how to play it.'
– Frederick Herzberg

Guru's views
Inspiring and influential quotes relating to the world of business.

For example...

Kraft Foods were reported to the ASA for an advert for its 'Lunchables' product which had the strapline 'Packed with good stuff'. The ASA received complaints that the product contained high levels of salt, and after investigation, the ASA concluded that the product implied it was healthy and nutritious when in fact it contained high levels of saturated fat and sodium. The complaint was upheld and the ad deemed misleading. The relevant part of the CAP code in this case was truthfulness and substance.

For example...
Relevant case studies draw upon real examples and fictional scenarios to develop understanding and analysis.

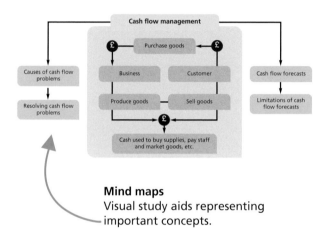

Mind maps
Visual study aids representing important concepts.

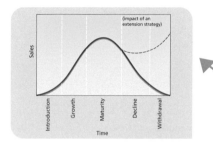

A variety of charts, graphs and tables illustrate important concepts and help students gain confidence with different presentation methods.

Summary spreads consolidate knowledge from the chapter. They include:

A brief **summary** of the key points of the chapter.

Summary questions to help students build key points for their notes

Tasks/ Points for discussion help extend understanding of material in the chapter.

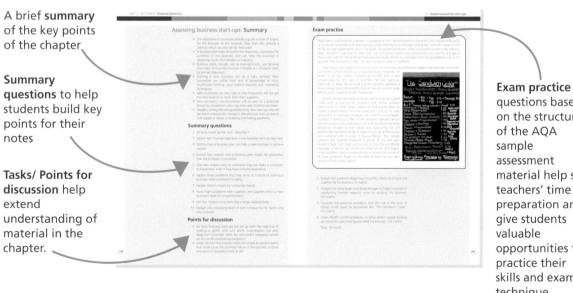

Exam practice questions based on the structure of the AQA sample assessment material help save teachers' time in preparation and give students valuable opportunities to practice their skills and exam technique.

UNIT 1
SECTION A

Planning and Financing a Business:
Starting a business

Section overview

1 Enterprise

2 Generating and protecting business ideas

3 Transforming resources into goods and services

4 Developing business plans

5 Conducting start-up market research

6 Understanding markets

7 Choosing the right legal structure for the business

8 Raising finance

9 Locating the business

10 Employing people

This section will introduce you to what Business Studies is all about and in particular, the process of how new businesses are set up. You will learn about the nature of entrepreneurship, how business ideas can be developed, the different types of business organisations and the different ways a business can raise finance in order to set up.

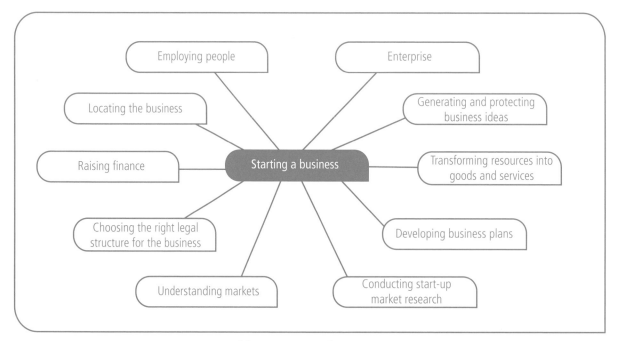

Key concept

Risk

Risk is a feature of our lives. When we cross the road we are taking a risk. When we drive a car, fly in an aeroplane, get onto a bus or a train, go out for the evening, walk down the stairs at home, climb a ladder, play a sport – whatever we do there will be some risk involved. Most of the time we do not think about it or consider what risk actually means.

Risk is all about the exposure to hazard, injury or a loss. Whenever we take a risk we expose ourselves to the chance of some loss, hazard or injury. Our behaviour is affected by the size of the chance of experiencing that loss, hazard or injury. We know, for example, that walking across a busy motorway means that there is a high chance that we might be killed. The vast majority of people, therefore, avoid such a risk by not walking on a busy motorway!

As we go about our daily lives we are constantly – albeit subconsciously – assessing risk and taking decisions based on that subconscious assessment. How many times have you stood waiting at the side of a road and taken a decision to cross when there are cars coming? You think you can get across and save yourself a precious second. If you slipped or stumbled then you might not make it. The risk of that happening, however, is computed to be small and many of us will cross when there is a relatively high risk.

In business, risk is central to decision-making. In this section we will look at starting up a new business. In so doing, people are putting themselves at risk – the risk of a loss. This loss might be money, it might be a house, it might be reputation – it might be lots of things.

There is an increasing interest in the role of risk in business decision-making. Some people may be classed as risk-seeking – they enjoy pitting themselves against the chance of the hazard, loss or injury. People who enjoy extreme sports like bungee jumping might be in this class of people. Then there are people classed as 'risk averse'. Such people tend to err on the side of caution, avoiding situations where the chance of hazard, loss or injury is high.

It may be that risk-seeking individuals are more likely to be successful entrepreneurs and willing to take the chance of setting up in business. The chance of failure in business is high. Some reports suggest that the number of new businesses failing in the first two years is around 66%. The risk of starting a business, therefore, is very high. It does seem, however, that many people are prepared to take this risk.

One of the reasons is that, whilst the chance of hazard, injury or loss may arise, there is also a chance that success could bring a host of rewards. These might include self-confidence, self-esteem, a feeling of self-worth, a feeling of control over your life, satisfaction at meeting a challenge, not to mention the prospect of financial rewards – the profit; that is the reward to enterprise.

Risk, therefore, is about balancing the cost of a decision (the potential hazard, loss or injury) against the benefits (the rewards).

Chapter 1   Enterprise

This chapter will look at the nature of **enterprise** and entrepreneurship. Entrepreneurship is not just about setting up a new business, but also refers to how existing businesses might go about developing new or innovative products. You will learn about the balance between **risk** and reward in decision-making and the motives of individuals in setting up a business.

Key terms

Enterprise A business organisation that is characterised by particular goals shared by a group of people, and with a responsibility for the control of its own performance.

Enterprise (*alternative interpretation*) The demonstration of initiative, risk, flair, dedication and skill in setting up a business.

Entrepreneur A person who organises factors of production, such as people, finance, land and equipment, in a business. In so doing, the individual demonstrates initiative, flair and skill, combined with an appreciation of risk.

Opportunity cost Cost expressed in terms of the next best alternative sacrificed in making a decision.

Profit The reward for enterprise. Profit is the difference between the total revenue generated and the total costs of production.

Risk The degree of chance of failure resulting in a loss of some sort.

Enterprise and entrepreneurs

In recent years there has been a great emphasis on the 'enterprise culture'. Being enterprising is seen as being a desirable quality. TV programmes celebrate enterprise and the enterprise culture with programmes such as *Dragon's Den* and *The Apprentice* drawing high viewing figures. In schools, the government has made enterprise education a key feature of entitlement to every child.

The emphasis on enterprise comes because enterprise and entrepreneurship are important factors in creating a healthy and vibrant economy. The term 'the economy' refers to the level of economic activity over a period of time, and this economic activity is the amount of buying and selling that goes on. Enterprise and entrepreneurship provide the impetus for change and the dynamism that helps the economy grow.

If there are plenty of people who demonstrate the skills of entrepreneurship this can have lots of advantages for everyone in society – that is why the government is so keen to encourage enterprise.

What is enterprise?

Enterprise includes the following characteristics:

- innovation – coming up with an idea, a product or a service that is new or different
- initiative – the willingness to take action and to take the lead
- risk-taking – the willingness to take risks in the search for rewards and at the same time weighing up the impact of failure; taking calculated risks
- thinking creatively – looking for solutions to problems and seeking out opportunities
- Asking important questions like 'why not?'
- Being willing to not only have ideas but to take action to realise them
- Being systematic – thinking through ideas, planning moves to help minimise risk and paying attention to detail.

Entrepreneurs

In setting up a new business, all of these characteristics are likely to be required to some extent. **Entrepreneurs** invariably have these qualities and are prepared to take the risk to organise factors of production – land, labour and capital – in production. They take risks to set up in

Facebook founder and entrepreneur Mark Zuckerberg

business. In addition, many entrepreneurs possess the following qualities:

- a high level of personal motivation – a willingness to succeed
- a willingness to work hard, and have energy and drive
- flair and initiative
- high-level organisation and leadership skills
- able to work with others and motivate people
- have a clear vision of where they want to be and able to share this with others.

You are very likely to have heard of many celebrated entrepreneurs who are able to tell stories of how they started their business from very small beginnings and are now multi-millionaires. The reality for many entrepreneurs is that they will not end up as millionaires. Even those people who have many of the characteristics outlined above still face huge challenges to make their business successful. Business success might not be a case of making a million, but might be as simple as surviving the first two years!

The examples below highlight two small businesses that are in the early stages of trying to make it. The reality of business is that, whilst at the time of writing things are going well for both, by the time you read this it may not still be the case and both entrepreneurs are very aware of this fact.

For example...

Lings Cars

Ling Valentine is a Chinese woman who lives in the North East of England with her husband Jon. In 2000, she set up a business providing contract hire finance for new cars – a sort of long-term rental with mileage restrictions. Ling has many of the characteristics in the bullet points above – she is certainly not afraid to ask 'why not?', she takes risks, has flair and uses her initiative, works very hard and has a clear idea of what she wants to achieve. Faced with real difficulties in breaking the

dominance of traditional car dealerships, Ling has managed to establish a growing and increasingly successful business. Her methods are often unorthodox but certainly get her noticed. One of the trade magazines for the motor industry said of her:

'She's been called a parasite, a deranged Internet freak and a blatant publicist, but she's also the north-east woman entrepreneur of 2006. And one look at her accounts reveals that Ling Valentine is enjoying levels of profit that no dealer can match.'

Source: *Automotive Management*, May 2007

For example...

Stupid Bags

Laid up in a hospital after an accident at work, Maria Difolco developed an idea to create gift bags for wine. The bags had a variety of messages on them suitable for giving as a gift in a variety of different situations – birthdays, anniversaries, to apologise for forgetting, for being insensitive, to offer congratulations and a host of other ideas. The bags all had a cartoon character that she had doodled in her hospital bed who she called Squiffy. Maria is into her second year of trading and, despite the hard work, is starting to see some signs of success and growth in her business. Maria has demonstrated high levels of personal motivation, has taken risks, is determined, has energy and drive and is systematic in planning her business (see Chapter 4 for more on business planning and page 361 for more about Stupid Bags).

Without enterprise and entrepreneurs willing to take risks, our lives would not be as rich and interesting as they can be. Virtually all the gadgets, labour-saving devices, products and services that we use in our lives have come about because of the initiative and drive shown by an entrepreneur.

The importance of risk and rewards

For any entrepreneur thinking of setting up a new business, being aware of the risk and the potential rewards is essential. The reward for enterprise is **profit**. This is the difference between the revenue generated and the total costs of running the business.

Starting up a new business requires massive commitment in time, effort and often money. The risk involved is high. Many individuals have a desire to be in business and see examples like Sir Alan Sugar, Sir Richard Branson, Michael Dell, Simon Cowell, Bill Gates, Gordon Ramsay and Jeff Bezos, all of whom are successful entrepreneurs in different businesses. The rewards for demonstrating enterprise can be considerable.

However, as we have pointed out, the success rate of new businesses is not high. Every year, the dreams of thousands of people to run their own successful businesses and reap the rewards of high profits and a more luxurious lifestyle are dashed as their businesses are forced to close.

What entrepreneurs do have to consider, therefore, is the balance between the risks and the rewards of setting up in business. When considering the risks the following questions may be important:

- What is the chance of the business being a success?
- What is the chance of it not being a success?
- If it is not a success, what are the costs involved?
- How is 'success' to be defined?

The risk to reward ratio

If the statistics show that only one in three businesses are likely to make it beyond the first two years, then that gives a clear idea of what the chances of success are. This, in turn, means that there is a 66% chance that the business might fail. If it does fail, what is the extent of the losses that the entrepreneur might incur? It might be that they lose the initial money they put into the business. They might lose their house if it was used as security on a loan to get the business going. They might have to sell personal possessions like their car to pay off the debts they owe. Entrepreneurs must have some awareness of the extent of the losses they might make.

The business might, however, be a success. The entrepreneur might regard success as surviving past the first two years, or breaking even after 18 months, or generating a small operating profit after the second year. (These terms will become more familiar to you as you work through the book.)

Any entrepreneur has to balance out the potential risks with the potential rewards. If the extent of the potential losses is considered too great in relation to the rewards, then the entrepreneur might choose not to take that course of action. Larger businesses appreciate this very well. Pharmaceutical companies might invest millions of pounds in developing new drugs and at any one time might have five to ten products in development. The chances are that only one or two of these products will ever make it. However, it may be that the potential rewards in terms of revenue generated by these two successes more than compensates for the losses made by the flops!

What entrepreneurs are doing, therefore, is spotting potential gaps in a market – identifying consumer needs that are not currently being met – and researching and developing new products or processes to meet those needs. They will be prepared to take risks following the identification of these gaps – and to take action.

The notion of opportunity cost

Opportunity cost is one of the most important concepts in business. It underpins every decision that is taken. The opportunity cost of any decision is what had to be given up by not being chosen – the next best alternative sacrificed.

Business is all about decision-making and in making decisions we have to consider the following:

- We all have unlimited wants and needs.
- We have limited resources to satisfy those wants and needs.
- This means we have to make choices.
- In making choices we have to accept that there are sacrifices.
- Making a choice involves sacrificing alternatives.

Making choices reflects the value we place or the benefits received on the outcome of that choice. It also says something about the value we place and the benefits received on those things we have to sacrifice. Opportunity cost provides us with a means of understanding the real nature of decision-making.

For example...

For example, an entrepreneur is considering possible locations for a new business venture. She has identified three possible sites. Site A is on a business and enterprise park. It has excellent IT links, is modern and bright and reflects the dynamic nature of her business, but is expensive to rent.

Site B is in the middle of a busy town. It would provide the business with some credibility and there would be easy access to the clients she is targeting. The location does mean that congestion is often a problem, however.

Site C is on the outskirts of a small village in a rural development unit. It is very cheap to rent in comparison to the other two sites but is quite remote and may not reflect what she wants the business to be.

Each site has its costs and benefits and our entrepreneur must make a decision between the three. If she chooses to go with site B, then she is sacrificing the benefits that sites A and C could provide. She might consider site A the next best alternative. The opportunity cost of choosing site B is that she cannot gain the benefits that site A would offer. We would assume that the value of the benefits provided by site B would be greater than the value of the benefits that site A would provide.

As we go through the whole of this book, you need to remember opportunity cost at all times. Opportunity cost is not a topic to cover in the first week of your course and then forget. It is fundamental to thinking in the subject – to be able to understand the methods and approaches of business as a discipline.

Motives for becoming an entrepreneur

There are many reasons why individuals choose to set up in business. The main reasons are included below:

- Personal circumstances – the need to find employment combined with the funds from redundancy payment provide the ideal opportunity to strike out on your own.
- Dissatisfaction or boredom with working for someone else's business.
- Profit – an opportunity to make your own profit rather than being paid a wage by someone else is a great motivator!
- Invention – a new product idea may be developed and setting up a business may be the best way to produce and sell it.
- Personal satisfaction – seeing if you can measure up to the challenge of running your own business.
- Independence – the opportunity of making your own decisions and taking control of your own future.
- A belief in a particular cause, mission or purpose – it might be environmental, humanitarian, ethical or social, or simply that people ought to have access to the wonderful idea you have generated!

Whilst many people who become entrepreneurs will have more than one of these in their mind, it may be particular things that drive the business. Ben Cohen and Jerry Greenfield started the Ben and Jerry's chain because they liked eating; Dr Paul Moller has spent many years trying to perfect the Skycar, a personal transport vehicle that flies ten

The Skycar

feet off the ground and does not require the operator to have a pilot's licence; Steve Parks used his expertise in audio and business to develop a series of programmes that other businesses could use to train their staff.

Every individual is likely to have different motives, but a passion allied to the qualities and characteristics we have outlined earlier is crucial in getting a business idea off the ground and into production.

Government support for enterprise and entrepreneurs

For new businesses starting up, getting help and advice is very important. The government is keen to promote enterprise and entrepreneurship because new businesses represent growing businesses of the future and these businesses will not only employ people but also contribute to tax revenue.

The main forms of help provided by government are listed below.

Grants

A grant is a sum of money given to a business for a specific reason. Grants are awarded on the basis of certain conditions and will normally cover only some of the costs of the project concerned. Grants may be awarded on the basis of where the business is located (it may be that the government want to encourage business development in certain areas of the country), what size the business is, what impact it might have on employment and the type of industry. Grants are available from a variety of government sources which include the national government, the European Union, Regional Development Agencies, local authorities and Chambers of Commerce.

Grants may be awarded for the following areas:

- innovation, research and development
- training and education
- economic regeneration in areas where old industries may have closed down or where employment levels are low and economic development stagnant

- employment – grants can be given for businesses embracing the government's New Deal scheme
- young entrepreneurs – if you are aged between 18 and 30 you can apply for grants under the Prince's Trust.

Support for new ideas

Many people have good ideas but have difficulty translating that into a working business operating on commercial lines. There are support networks available to help businesses make that leap between an idea and a full-blown business. These networks include Chambers of Commerce, Innovation Relay Centres, Business Innovation Centres, Development Agencies and Science Parks. The aim of many of these is to share expertise and offer advice to help businesses get off the ground.

Links with universities and colleges

There are systems in place to link up businesses and people with new ideas to institutions of further and higher education. Some of the organisations associated with this include Knowledge Transfer Partnerships, Knowledge Transfer Networks, the Shell Step Programme and Research Councils.

Tax

There are a number of schemes that provide various tax advantages to people looking to start up a new business or who have set up a new small business. This might include: tax allowances and tax relief for research and development; relief on stamp duty in certain areas of the country; capital allowances which reduce the tax which has to be paid if the spending is on investment in equipment, buildings and machinery; an allowance for renovation of business premises; the Enterprise Investment scheme which offers help to small business in raising capital by providing tax relief on those investing in the business.

Further material and resources relating to this section can be found at **www.collins.bized.co.uk**. Keep checking for updates.

Enterprise: Summary

- Enterprise is about having the flair, skills and initiative to take risks in the pursuit of an objective.
- Entrepreneurs take the responsibility of organising factors of production (land, labour and capital) to create production.
- The reward for enterprise is profit.
- Entrepreneurs will take calculated risks which balance out the risk versus the reward.
- The concept of opportunity cost is an important one in business. It takes into account the value of the benefits foregone when a decision is made.
- There are a variety of reasons why an individual might want to set up their own business – not just to earn money!
- There are a variety of ways in which government tries to support new businesses, including the provision of grants, networks and advice and tax breaks.

Summary questions

1 Using an example, give a definition of the term 'enterprise'.

2 Identify five possible qualities of an entrepreneur.

3 Explain the role of risk in enterprise.

4 Explain why profit is the reward to enterprise.

5 Explain the risk to reward ratio, using an example.

6 Give a definition of 'opportunity cost'.

7 What might be the opportunity cost of a decision by a business to invest in a new piece of software to manage their accounts?

8 Identify five motives for becoming an entrepreneur.

9 List four ways that governments might support a new business.

10 Will an entrepreneur who is not prepared to take a risk ever succeed? Explain your answer.

Points for discussion

Using a search engine, type in the phrase 'famous entrepreneurs'. From the search results find some details about five entrepreneurs and write a short summary of their business and how they developed it. From your research, what qualities do you think they possess that have made them successful?

Exam practice

The life of a hill farmer might look idyllic in some respects – peaceful, quiet, away from the hustle and bustle of city life with just sheep for company – but the economic reality for many hill farmers has been as bleak as the weather on the moors and fells for many years. Two enterprising farmers have found a way of helping to supplement their incomes by developing new products.

One farmer has been looking at utilising the wool in compost. This particular farm has a lot of bracken on it and the farmer has managed to use this to produce a range of peat-free compost. Now he is using the wool to add to the mixture and in doing so is able to improve the range of nutrients in it. Wool provides sources of nitrogen that complement the potash produced by the bracken. The bags of *Lakeland Gold* are proving popular with over 6,000 bags having been sold. The batch of 50,000 bags has used up 50 tonnes of wool. The farmer got the idea from reading an old gardening book that explained how fleeces were laid in the bottom of pits that were used for planting. From such a simple idea has developed a new business!

The other use for wool that has been developed came from a farmer's daughter who has investigated the use of wool for insulating properties. The product is called *Thermafleece* and is made from 85% wool and 15% polyester. *Thermafleece* has increased its turnover rapidly since it was first launched in 2001. The entrepreneur concerned, Christine Armstrong, was an interior designer and hit upon the idea when she was renovating an old farmhouse and discovered that sheep's wool had been used as an insulating material in days gone by.

She has had to do a great deal of research and invest time and money into developing the product from the initial idea but it seems that the hard work and investment is now paying off.

Source: adapted from Biz/ed In the News, http://www.bized.co.uk/cgi-bin/chron/chron.pl?id=2694

1 What is meant by the term 'enterprising'? (2 marks)

2 What is meant by the term 'investment'? (2 marks)

3 State two possible motives that either farmer might have had in developing their new business idea. (2 marks)

4 Explain two possible sources of help from government that new ventures like those in the article might be able to access. (4 marks)

5 Explain how Christine Armstrong might have assessed the risk to reward ratio in relation to the setting up of *Thermafleece*. (4 marks)

6 Discuss the relevance of opportunity cost to the situation facing hill farmers such as those in the article. (6 marks)

Total: 20 marks

Chapter 2   Generating and protecting business ideas

In this chapter you will learn about the ways in which new business ideas can come about and how businesses can be developed based on existing markets but meeting specific needs. You will learn that one way of reducing the risk of setting up in business is to operate a franchise, but that there are advantages and disadvantages in so doing. Finally, you will learn how businesses can seek to protect their business ideas.

Sources of business ideas

Business is basically very simple; think of something someone else wants to buy at a price, which covers the cost of providing it and which enables the entrepreneur to make a profit, and you have the recipe for success. The difficult thing is really identifying what it is that people might want!

Many of the world's best-known products have come about through a mixture of accident and design. In some cases individuals have found a use for a product that someone else has developed or have been curious, and in satisfying that curiosity have hit upon an idea that has become a winner.

These three examples show how three popular products originated. Sources of ideas do not just come about by accident, however; they can be developed through the following methods.

Brainstorming

Brainstorming is a way of coming up with ideas by suggesting anything that seems possible and relevant – however ridiculous it might be. The atmosphere in which brainstorming occurs has to be mutually supportive and based on trust. Once ideas have been generated, the process then develops in whittling down the ideas to those that might have some possible prospects for further analysis and those that really are not going to work!

Key terms

Copyright The legal right provided by an Act of Parliament to produce copies and to control an original literary, musical or artistic work for a specified time.

Franchise The sale of the right to use a business idea by an existing business.

Franchisee The individual buying the right to use the franchise.

Franchisor The business organisation selling the licence to use their business model.

Market niche A clearly defined part of an existing market where customer needs are not currently being met.

Patent A government grant of ownership conferring rights to a person or business assuring sole rights to make, use and sell a new invention or manufacturing process for a limited period.

Trademarks Names or symbols used by businesses to represent a particular good or service that they provide, and to distinguish it from competing manufacturers.

For example...

Art Fry was a new product development engineer at 3M. He was singing in a church choir when he wished that there was a way of being able to bookmark his hymn book with something which would stick without damaging the book. One of Fry's 3M colleagues, Dr Spencer Silver, worked on adhesives for the firm. He had developed an adhesive that formed clear spheres instead of a film. What he didn't know was how it could be used. Fry found a use for it by putting it onto a piece of paper – the *Post-it* note was born.

cont...

For example…

Ruth Wakefield was an innkeeper. In the 1930s she was baking cookies. She decided to chop up a chocolate bar and added it to the biscuit mixture. She thought the chocolate would melt – but it didn't. What she ended up with was not a chocolate flavoured cookie but chocolate chip cookies. The biscuit went on to become one of the most popular biscuits of all time.

In 1886 a pharmacist named John Pemberton cooked up medicinal syrup in a large container with the aim of creating a herbal medicine. The mixture was diluted with ice water and Pemberton and his assistant agreed that it was a pleasant drink. When they made the next batch they accidentally added carbonated water. The result was *Coca-Cola*, the most popular soft drink in the world.

Personal experience

The case of Art Fry above is a perfect example of how personal experience can lead to new business ideas. There are other examples which include James Dyson's bagless vacuum cleaner and the wind-up clockwork radio developed by Trevor Baylis. James Dyson was frustrated by the limitation of the vacuum cleaners he was using and thought 'I could have designed this better myself'. Trevor Baylis watched a TV programme about AIDs in Africa in 1993. In those regions radios were the only means of broadcasting health information but many could not use one because of the shortage of batteries and electricity. He identified a need and acted upon it. In many cases, ideas will develop by the individual concerned experiencing the situation and then asking 'what if?' or 'why not?' This may be the start of a journey that takes the individual to success or it might be the start of many frustrations before the idea becomes a commercial reality.

Business experience

Having worked in business and made lots of contacts, many people spot a business opportunity and decide to try their hand at setting up their own business. John Saunders worked for many years for a major footwear distributor. When he was made redundant following a business reorganisation, he was able to use contacts to set up an agency in the UK selling footwear for a US company. His knowledge of the market, ability to deal with people effectively, reputation, business acumen and skills were all highly valued by his American colleagues, and John was able to begin the first stages of a new business.

James Dyson and his bagless vacuum cleaner

The identification of a product or market niche

A **market niche** is a small gap in an existing market where consumer needs are currently not being met. It is an opportunity to offer consumers a product that currently does not exist. Many market niches, by definition, are linked to existing products, but in some way an individual might see the opportunity of expanding or developing that product in a different way. Restaurants serving food was not a new idea, but McDonald's saw the opportunity to meet a customer need by serving food quickly; Starbucks saw the chance to make coffee more than just a drink – it has become much more than this – a meeting place, a culture!

Trevor Baylis – inventor of the clockwork radio

Some individuals specialise in providing particular cleaning services – just dealing with carpets or blinds, offices, hand-washing cars, and so on. Others see the need for specialities in other types of businesses, for example, Frank Kern set up a website providing information for parrot lovers on how to make their parrot talk. He discovered that this was a market need and developed an idea to fill that need.

All of these examples initially started out as small businesses with limited capital, but with ideas and an identified market niche. In thinking about developing a market niche, the entrepreneur will have to consider the following:

- What type of product or service are you offering to customers?
- What are the needs that the product or service fulfil?
- Who are the potential customers for your product?
- What sorts of financial resources will you need and how will you get hold of the finance for the project?
- How will you make your product/service known to your potential customers?

Franchises

For many people, the idea of setting up their own business is very appealing. However, the risk involved often puts off potential entrepreneurs from taking the plunge. If that risk can be reduced then people can be persuaded to set up their own business. A **franchise** is one way that the risk of setting up in business can be reduced.

The term 'franchise' can refer to a variety of different types of business relationship. These might include licensing, arrangements for distribution, agency agreements and so on. We will look at it as an opportunity to buy a business 'off the peg' as opposed to the greater risks involved in setting up a completely new business enterprise. In this context, a franchise is an opportunity to buy the right to use the template of an existing business. The existing business could be a well-established name or could be a relatively new business idea which the owner wants to expand to counter threats of other people using the business idea.

A franchise involves two parties. The **franchisee** buys the right to use the trademark or trade name of the **franchisor** – the business that owns the right to use that trademark or name. The franchisee is thus buying into a business model that has been developed by someone else. For the franchisee, there is the chance to run their own business, but to have the finance and experience of the franchisor behind them. The franchisor is the individual or group who own the trademark, name and or business model.

Franchising has become an increasingly important way of businesses expanding their brand, as well as helping individuals to take the often scary step into running their own business. In the UK there are around 327,000 people involved in franchised business activities. In April 2007, it was reported that there were 781 franchise systems operating in the UK with around 34,000 outlets.* This represents a rise of 44% in 10 years.

In the UK many popular names operate either wholly or in part as franchises, for example, McDonald's, Prontaprint, Domino's Pizza, Cash Generator, Costa Coffee, Kall Kwik, Timpson, Lasertech, Interlink, Toni & Guy and Drain Doctor.

*Source of data: NatWest/British Franchise Association Survey 2007

How does a franchise work?

The franchisee puts up a sum of money to buy the right to trade under the franchisor's name. Some franchises will also have an arrangement where the franchisee pays an annual fee for various services provided by the franchisor, such as training and equipment supplies, and may also involve the payment of a proportion of the annual profits or turnover generated by the business.

The franchisor, apart from granting the right of the franchisee to use the tradename, also provides a range of different services including training, but also equipment – for example, point-of-sale display stands, logos, advertising packages, fittings, and so on.

The franchisor has an overall say in the marketing of products and over the quality control processes, but other than that it is up to the franchisee how they conduct the business. The relationship between the two parties is vital to the success of the franchise. The relationship can mean that the franchisee not only benefits from the name, but also other aspects of the business model, such as supplier relationships, insurance cover and supply chain management.

Franchises do have some advantages and also some disadvantages. The average cost, for example, of buying into a franchise in the UK is £42,200; it is important, therefore, that any potential franchisee is aware of these advantages and disadvantages. These are shown in the table on the opposite page.

For example…

Kerry Katona helps launch the Pink Ladies taxi firm in 2006

Pink Ladies is a unique taxi service that originated in Warrington, Cheshire. The business provides taxi services exclusively for women. Women drive the vehicles and they will only pick up women customers. The primary aim of the service is to provide a safe and secure means of transport for women. The drivers are all fully qualified, have distinctive uniforms and are trained in self defence, first aid, customer care and working with the disabled. Pink Ladies do not accept cash but provide a flexible means of payment methods that customers can use. Their service means that women are not standing around waiting for cabs in the streets and the drivers will ensure that their customers are safely in their homes after dropping them off.

Having got established, the owners, Tina Dutton and Andrea Winders, are planning on expanding the business to other areas through franchises. Individuals can buy the licence for the Pink Ladies business model and set up their own Pink Ladies service in other localities around the UK. Tina and Andrea see this as an important way in which the high quality service they offer can be expanded quickly and provide budding entrepreneurs with the opportunity of running their own business.

Franchises

Advantages	Disadvantages
• Franchisee gets to run a business with less 'risk'.	• The franchisee is responsible for debts and pays a royalty to owners of the brand before keeping any remaining profit. This may be less than if they were independent.
• Franchisee buys the right to use the established company's name, format, products, logos, display units, methods, and so on. This can be much cheaper than setting up an independent business.	• The franchisor might have difficulties in maintaining relationships and standards in franchised operations – especially if the franchise has expanded quickly.
• The franchisee has ready access to the opportunities provided by the franchisor in advertising and marketing, which reduces average costs.	• The initial cost of setting up a franchise can be high and may exclude some individuals.
• The chance of failure is reduced since in many cases the business model is already proven.	• There is a lack of freedom in operating a franchise. The franchisor will expect standards and certain rules to be adhered to and this can put a strain on relationships.
• It may be easier for an individual to raise finance to set up in a franchise operation because lenders will see that there is less risk.	• Royalty payments can be relatively high and have to be paid. If the business has a bad year this can cause financial difficulties.
• For the franchisor, it can be a speedy way for business to expand.	• The franchisee must investigate the franchise carefully. The franchisee must be aware of what obligations they are entering into and whether they can really afford to lose their investment.
• Larger franchises offer a range of training and support services for the franchisee.	• Many franchises belong to the British Franchise Association where a code of conduct is in operation. That does not mean that all franchises are 'good' or 100% safe. The franchisee must be aware of the risks and the financial stability of the franchisor.

Copyright, patents and trademarks

If a business develops an innovative product idea, it could become a valuable asset in the years ahead and therefore needs protection. **Patents**, **trademarks** and **copyrights** offer important protection for a new business, giving it the right to reap the rewards for its innovation.

PATENTS

A patent ensures that no other business or individual can make, use, sell or offer for sale a patented product, machine, invention or production process, for up to 20 years. To be awarded a patent, the business will need to prove that its product is its own distinctive and original work.

COPYRIGHT

A copyright is the equivalent protection offered to authors, artists and composers. In this respect it refers not to a product but to the creation of an idea, expression or information.

TRADEMARKS

A **trademark** is a sign or logo that is used by an individual or a business organisation (in both the private and the public sector) that in some way identifies and distinguishes the individual or organisation from others. Once registered, other individuals or organisations are not allowed to use that trademark.

These three methods are all ways a business might use to protect a new business idea or a new business. If others breach the copyright, breach the patent or use the trademark, then the owner has the right to take legal action to defend themselves. However, in some cases, the legal costs involved in bringing a case to court to enforce the patent, trademark or copyright would be very expensive – something a small business is unlikely to be able to afford. In addition, the law relating to these areas is very complex and it is not always easy to prove such a breach.

Further material and resources relating to this section can be found at **www.collins.bized.co.uk**. Keep checking for updates.

Generating and protecting business ideas: Summary

- New business ideas can arise by design, accident, brainstorming and personal experience.
- Business ideas might involve the exploitation of a market niche to meet customer needs that are not currently being provided for.
- One way of reducing the risk of setting up in business is to buy into a franchise.
- Franchises are certainly not risk-free – there are advantages and disadvantages.
- There are legal ways to protect new business ideas which include patents, copyright and trademarks.

Summary questions

1 Provide a simple definition of what a business does.

2 Choose two well-known products and examine how they might have been developed.

3 Define the term 'market niche'.

4 Identify a possible market niche in each of the three following markets:
- the motor industry
- the music industry
- the perfume industry.

5 Identify three factors that an individual might need to consider in developing a market niche.

6 Using examples, explain what is meant by the term 'franchise'.

7 Explain the difference between a 'franchisor' and a 'franchisee'.

8 Outline two advantages to a franchisee of taking out a franchise.

9 Outline two advantages to a franchisor of operating a franchise.

10 Explain two possible disadvantages to a franchisee of this type of business organisation.

Points for discussion

Go to the website of the British Franchise Association (http://www.thebfa.org/index.asp). Using the information available on that site, write a short (300-word) report giving advice to an individual who might be thinking of taking on a franchise. You could also present the information through a PowerPoint® presentation to your class.

Exam practice

A former bank employee in New York, Arshad Chowdhury, and a friend who was a health economist, Christopher Lindholst, noticed that colleagues were working longer hours but that this did not always mean that they were more effective in terms of productivity. The afternoon period, in particular, was a time where productivity levels dipped.

Arshad noticed that some employees went to the toilet and spent time having a short nap; in doing so, they were able to approach their work with renewed zest. Arshad thought: why not set up a place other than the toilet where busy people can retreat for a short period of time to relax and catch up on some sleep? This place would be comfortable and accessible. It would provide people with the peace and quiet that can help to provide that important nap and wake them up gently with a gentle vibration movement around the legs after 20 minutes.

The result was the sleep pod. They called the business *MetroNaps* and set themselves up in the heart of the financial district in Nassau Street, New York. Customers can buy a membership at $55 a month that gives them unlimited access to the *MetroNaps* pods. Not only that but firms can lease the pods to place in their offices to help staff stay focused and boost productivity as well as improve motivation and a healthy work–life balance.

Now *MetroNaps* are planning to expand by offering franchises in other parts of the US and in the rest of the world.

Source: adapted from Biz/ed 'In the News' http://www.bized.co.uk/cgi-bin/chron/chron.pl?id=2577

1 To what extent would you consider this case study to be an example of the identification and exploitation of a market niche? (10 marks)

2 Examine the source of this particular business idea. What would Arshad and his partner have had to consider in developing the idea? (15 marks)

3 Assess the decision to use a franchise as a means of expanding the business model for *MetroNaps*. (15 marks)

Total: 40 marks

Chapter 3   Transforming resources into goods and services

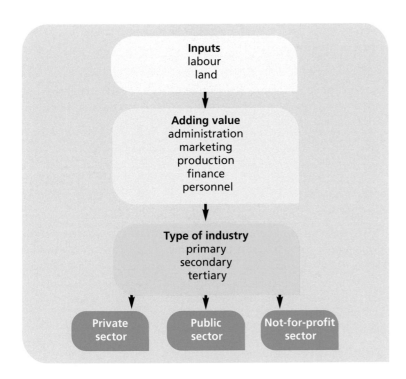

In this chapter you will learn about the way in which a business takes factors of production and uses them to produce a product. You will learn about the concept of 'value added' and how value can be added by a business.

Inputs, outputs and the nature of the transformation of resources into finished products

The sectors of production

Business activity is classified into a number of different sectors:

Primary sector: extraction of raw materials from the earth – mining, quarrying, fishing, agriculture, forestry.

Secondary sector: processing of raw materials into finished or semi-finished products – manufacturing.

Tertiary sector: service industries – leisure, transport, finance, distribution, retailing, wholesaling, communications.

Quaternary sector: hi-tech industries, training, health, education.

Key terms

Adding value A process whereby the value placed on the product is higher than the material or bought-in costs.

Factors of production The resources used in production. These resources are classified as land, labour, capital and enterprise.

Primary production Businesses involved in the extraction of raw materials from land or sea.

Secondary production Businesses involved in turning raw materials into finished products.

Tertiary production Businesses that provide a service to consumers or to other businesses.

In the last chapter it was mentioned that business is essentially very simple – think of something someone is prepared to pay for at a price that more than covers the costs of getting the product or service to the consumer. Every product or service requires some form of input into production. These inputs will include things like buildings, machinery, equipment, people, raw materials, and so on. These are collectively referred to as the **factors of production** – the things every business needs to be able to carry out business. The skill is in combining these factor inputs effectively to create the product that people are going to be prepared to pay for. It is usual to classify these so-called factor inputs into four groups:

Land: all the natural resources of the earth including the sea.

Labour: all the human mental and physical effort that goes into production. This includes those in managerial positions, labourers, programmers, supervisors, maintenance, and so on.

Capital: anything that is not used for its own sake but which contributes in some way to production. This will include offices, computer equipment, tools, machinery, vehicles, and so on.

Enterprise: the risk taken in organising factors of production for which the reward is profit.

These factor inputs can be combined in different ways to generate production. In some cases, a business might rely more on labour than capital, whilst a similar business might use more capital than labour. Whatever the combinations of these factors used in production, acquiring these factors incurs a cost. These costs of production are in turn divided into two broad categories: fixed costs and variable costs (see also pages 92–94).

FIXED COSTS

Fixed costs do not change in relation to the amount produced or to the level of trade. This does not mean they never change at all – they do. Examples of fixed costs are: insurance, rent, rates, salaries, security, maintenance, administration costs, and so on.

VARIABLE COSTS

Variable costs change in direct proportion to the amount produced or the level of trade. Examples of variable costs are: raw materials, component parts, packaging, wages (where payment is related to the number of hours worked) and some types of energy costs where these are associated directly with production.

The diagram opposite (Figure 3.1) outlines what a business does.

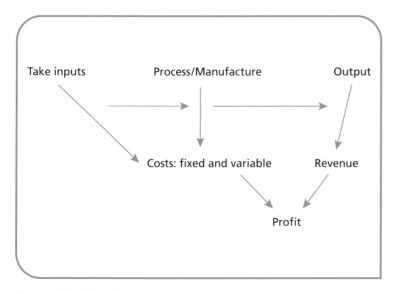

Figure 3.1 What businesses do

Different businesses will combine these factor inputs in different ways. A business operating as a sandwich bar will take its raw materials of bread, butter and various fillings to produce the product for the consumer. A chemical firm might use a combination of different chemicals and carry out several different processes to get the molecule they require for their customer. The complexity of the process might require much more capital equipment and highly skilled individuals.

Every business will have to organise the factors of production. In a very small business the number of factors might be limited, but in a large business the process of organising the factors can be very complex. The work done in transforming factor inputs into the finished product is what a business does. When the factor inputs have combined to produce an output, the business sells that output and receives revenue. The business not only has to consider the cost of production but, in addition, must also be aware of the price that consumers are prepared to pay to acquire the product. This is the subject matter of **adding value**.

For a business offering a service, factor inputs still have to be organised. A travel agency, for example, has labour and capital and premises. These have to be organised to ensure that consumers get the right information and the right product. In this case the product is the right holiday for the customer. Staff have to know their jobs, the equipment has to be organised so that it finds information quickly, the premises have to be welcoming and comfortable as well as having access to information. The customer leaves with the holiday booking – not a physical product – but the factors of production still have to be organised.

Adding value

Added value refers to the process by which a business is able to create a product that customers value more highly than the material or bought-in costs used in its production. By combining inputs to produce a good or service that customers want, a business aims to create a product that is worth more than the total cost of the inputs. This is known as adding value. By creating willingness, in the mind of the consumer to pay more for a product than the total cost of the inputs, the business is able to make a profit – the selling price is higher than the cost of production. In order for an action or a process to be considered value added, certain criteria must be met, which include the simple fact that the consumer must be prepared to pay for the action or process, and the action or process must change the product in some way. You might be reluctant to buy a *Mars* bar from a friend for a higher price than they bought it for unless in some way the delivery of the bar to you warranted the additional price charged.

For example...

Trainers are a good example of this. Millions of pairs of trainers are on sale around the world. Many of them will be made in factories in countries like Vietnam and Indonesia. The material costs will include canvas, leather, rubber, metal, the machinery that is used in production and the human effort that is expended. Let us assume that these material costs total £15 per pair. The sale price of these trainers might vary enormously. A company like Nike is able to charge £80 or £90 for a pair of trainers, but other companies might only be able to charge £30. What is the difference, given that they are essentially the same product? The difference is that Nike has been able to create a brand image and reputation that customers are prepared to pay for. The addition of the Nike 'swoosh' to the side of a pair of trainers means they are able to set a price that is much higher but which consumers are still prepared to pay for.

A pair of Nike trainers

Figure 3.2 The value added in CD production and sales

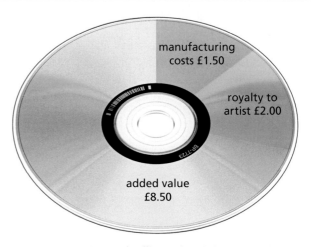

manufacturing costs £1.50

royalty to artist £2.00

added value £8.50

CD total selling price: £12

Figure 3.2 illustrates the value that is added in making and selling a CD. You can see that manufacturing costs are only small and even after royalty payments to the artist, the added value is significant. However, this is not all profit for the music company, which must cover its overheads, the costs of marketing and the retailer's share of the profits.

A business can seek to add value in a variety of ways.

DESIGN

It can develop new technology or add new design features to make its product unique. James Dyson's 'dual cyclone' technology allows Dyson vacuum cleaners to be sold at a price well above the costs of production.

Apple has a reputation for high quality design. One of their more recent innovations is a laptop called the MacBook Air. The product's main attraction is that it is 'ultra-thin' - only 0.76 inches (1.93 cm) at its thickest point. Apple hoped that the advantages that the design provides to users are sufficient to encourage them to pay the starting £1,200 price tag on the machine.

PRODUCTION

Achieving quality and efficiency in production creates added value. Quality will help ensure a higher price for the output, while efficiency helps to cut the costs of the inputs. The gap between the two is added value.

The main job of the fishing industry is to catch fish. However, many customers do not want to gut the fish and carry out other preparation tasks to enable them to be able to cook and enjoy the fish. As a result, part of the production process will involve specialists carrying out such tasks. The additional price that people are prepared to pay for fish that is ready to cook represents the added value provided by the firm in preparing the fish in this way.

MARKETING

Finding ways of increasing the customer's willingness to pay can be done through clever marketing – creating an image that makes the product more desirable. People are often willing to pay quite a bit more for a branded product, such as Gap clothing, or for a product that has a unique selling point (USP).

In 2008, Unilever - producers of the savoury spread Marmite - carried out a value added marketing exercise when it released a limited edition jar of Marmite which was made with a small amount of champagne and which had a heart shaped label with the words 'I Love You' and 'For My Lovely Marmite Lover' on the label. The limited edition jars – 600,000 of them – were designed to tap in to the Valentine's Day market. The price of a normal 250g jar is around £2.10; these special edition jars were retailing at £2.99.

Further material and resources relating to this section can be found at **www.collins.bized.co.uk**. Keep checking for updates.

Transforming resources into goods and services: Summary

- Production is categorised into three or four sectors – primary, secondary, tertiary and quaternary.
- Businesses employ factor inputs to produce products.
- The factors of production are land, labour and capital.
- Factor inputs have costs usually classified as fixed costs and variable costs.
- In the process of production a business will seek to add value.

Summary questions

1 List six businesses in your local area and categorise each into the primary, secondary, tertiary or quaternary sectors.

2 State three business inputs. Give an example of how each is used within business.

3 What do you think is meant by a business that is described as labour intensive and capital intensive?

4 Explain the meaning of the term 'fixed costs', using examples to illustrate your answer.

5 Explain the meaning of the term 'variable costs', using examples to illustrate your answer.

6 Describe the transformation process for a loaf of bread, or any other product with which you might be familiar.

7 Explain the meaning of the term 'value added'.

8 Describe three ways in which a business might add value.

9 Does the fact that a business can add value mean that it is always making a profit?

10 Explain how the following businesses might add value:
- British Airways
- a business selling hobby or special interest magazines
- a supermarket like Sainsbury's or Tesco
- a business selling sports equipment in a high-street store.

Points for discussion

Identify which sector or sectors of production the following businesses are in. Explain your answer:
- an insurance company
- Shell (multinational energy providers)
- a double-glazing manufacturer
- an auto electrician
- Eidos (computer games publisher)
- Nike (sportswear).

Exam practice

The average dessert in an average restaurant might be priced around £4. This price reflects the cost of the ingredients, the work put into creating the dessert, presenting it and serving it to you. In some cases, the work of the chef can be considerable, as well as the skill level in blending ingredients and presenting a 'work of art'. In such a case the price may be much higher.

One restaurant in Sri Lanka has gone a little further than this, though. The Fortress Hotel in Galle in the south of the country created a dessert which claimed to be the most expensive in the world. At $14,500 you might wonder just what the chef could have done to create such an expensive pudding.

The pudding has caramelised sugar formed into a sail of a traditional fishing boat. This is accompanied by a sculpture in chocolate of a fisherman on a stilt plus various fruits and champagne. The dessert is called 'The Fortress Stilt Fisherman Indulgence'.

What actually pushes the price up is the inclusion in the pudding of an 80 carat aquamarine gem stone. The dessert, needless to say, has to be specially ordered. The dessert was created to reflect the tastes and clientele at the hotel. It is one of the most luxurious in Sri Lanka.

'The Fortress Stilt Fisherman Indulgence'

Source: adapted from Biz/ed 'In the News' http://www.bized.co.uk/cgi-bin/chron/chron.pl?id=2941

1 Using an example, explain the meaning of the term 'added value'. (4 marks)

2 Consider the fixed and variable costs that the hotel in the case study might incur in the production of dessert. (6 marks)

3 How important is added value to a business? Explain your answer. (8 marks)

4 Which sector of production is a hotel in? Describe the main factor inputs and how these are processed to provide the 'product'. (10 marks)

5 To what extent do you think the hotel adds value by providing an expensive pudding like the one in the case study? (12 marks)

Total: 40 marks

Chapter 4   Developing business plans

Key terms

Business plan A document that provides important details about different aspects of a business that may be used by an individual in setting up a business or required by a bank when considering a request for a loan. It is the process of setting objectives, researching the market, deciding on a strategy, planning and implementing actions, and monitoring and reviewing the business.

Competitive advantage The ways in which a firm appeals to its consumers through adding value which makes the firm unique in some way. This uniqueness can be both defended and is distinctive in a way that means that it is difficult for its rivals to be able to imitate or replicate these features.

In this chapter you will learn about the importance of planning for a new business start-up. You will learn that careful thought and effective planning at the early stage in the life of a business will help to identify potential problems and prepare the business for these, and will also tell an individual whether a business is likely to be viable.

The purpose and contents of business plans

However good the business idea and however skilled the entrepreneur, without effective business planning a new business will quickly lose its way. A **business plan** is designed to help an entrepreneur in setting objectives, researching the market, planning strategy, and monitoring and evaluating finance and progress. A well-researched business plan that is regularly reviewed and updated can make the difference between success and failure.

A business plan is a document that sets out how the business will operate and what it hopes to achieve. One of the important points about such a business plan is that it serves to help the prospective business identify whether it will be viable or not. There is always a tendency to ignore the evidence collected and assume the business will be a roaring success, even if everything you have collected suggests it will not!

THE BUSINESS PLAN

1 Introduction
a Basic business details.
b The type of legal ownership.
c The goals of the business.

2 The business idea
a The product/service to be provided.
b Summary of its key selling points.

3 Management and personnel
a The roles of managers.
b The experience and skills of the workforce.

4 The marketing plan
a Market analysis showing level of demand.
b Who customers are and what they want.
c The strengths and weaknesses of competitors.
d The marketing mix – product, price, promotion and place.

5 The production plan
a The methods and stages of production.
b The premises and equipment needed.
c Ways of ensuring quality.

6 The financial plan
a Sources of finance required.
b Profit forecast/break-even analysis.
c Cash flow forecast.

Figure 4.1   The business plan

A business plan is an essential business tool, providing the framework within which a business can develop. It brings a number of benefits:

- Providing focus and direction for the ideas that lie behind the new business venture. The business plan forces an entrepreneur to consider all the key aspects of running the business, and whether it has a good chance of success.
- Testing the viability of the business proposal through financial forecasts that show whether the business has a good chance of success before committing any money. Potential problems can be identified at an early stage and action taken to avoid them.
- Convincing potential investors or lenders such as the high-street banks that this is a business idea they should be willing to support.
- Planning and reviewing the business strategy through the targets and forecasts in the plan provides a way of measuring the actual performance of the business over time.

There are also drawbacks to business planning. These include:

- Planning can lead to a lack of flexibility – there is a desire to stick to the plan regardless of the situation.
- Getting accurate information to help develop a business plan is not easy – especially forecasting future sales and costs.
- Business plans take time and commitment – it is not a task to be undertaken lightly.
- If your business plan is based on faulty or inaccurate data, the whole plan can be rendered useless.
- The planner might not have the skills or expertise to analyse and report on every aspect of a business plan.
- Unrealistic financial projections can lead to misplaced confidence in the likely success of a business venture.

Guru's views

'It is not the plan that is important, it's the planning.'

–Dr Graeme Edwards

The plan

In the early stages a business idea may only be fairly sketchy without much detail. For example, if you were considering setting yourself up in business as a window cleaner, you might be able to identify a local need and be thinking of targeting home owners. You might also have worked out what you need to run the business – a van, ladders, bucket, squeegee, and so on – but do not have much in the way of details about how much these things cost or the precise nature of the local market. The next stage, therefore, is to try to get more detail.

Business plans can be difficult to draw up because getting accurate information about the range of things that are included in the plan might not be easy, but it can also be due to a lack of care in the gathering of information.

We will look at a typical business plan based around a decision by an individual to set up as a window cleaner. The case will go through the main sections of a business plan and briefly outline what the individual in this example might include.

1 INTRODUCTION

This section will contain the basic business details – name and address, what the business function will be, the type of legal ownership and the goals of the business. In the case of a window cleaner, the business function will be to provide high quality window-cleaning services. The legal ownership is likely to be a partnership, sole trader or private limited company (see Chapter 7). The goals of the business might include some comment on the business philosophy – to provide high quality window-cleaning services, and about the expectation about the returns for the entrepreneur. This area of the plan might also consider the following areas: legal requirements of the business (health and safety, employment legislation, and so on) and tax liabilities – Value Added Tax (VAT), Income Tax and National Insurance Contributions (NICs).

2 THE BUSINESS IDEA

This section will provide more details about the nature of the business and the product or service to be provided. This might include more details on exactly what the business proposition is going to be. This might detail whether the service will cover residential accommodation, shops and offices, skyscrapers, city centre buildings, rural areas, and so on. If the aim is to provide window-cleaning services for businesses in city centres, then that might well be a different proposition from someone planning to offer window-cleaning services to a new residential development on the outskirts of a town.

Further material and resources relating to this section can be found at **www.collins.bized.co.uk**. Keep checking for updates.

This section will also include some details about the key selling points – what will this business offer that is different from any other window-cleaning service that already exists? This is where the entrepreneur has to think about the market they are targeting and what its needs might be and how they might add value. In addition, this is where the entrepreneur will have to think carefully about what it is about this business that offers **competitive advantage**.

3 MANAGEMENT AND PERSONNEL

This section will outline the role of management and personnel in the organisation. A sole trader may only have themselves to worry about, but many sole traders employ other people and it needs to be clear what the relationship is between the people in the business and what their roles and responsibilities will be.

As a means of giving further information to prospective lenders, as well as identifying constraints for the business, the experience and skills of the workforce will be included. This helps the business to identify areas where they may have skill deficiencies, for example, in accounting or in administration.

This section might also include information about the insurance that is required.

4 THE MARKETING PLAN

Marketing is about identifying consumer needs, seeking to satisfy those needs profitably and gaining a competitive advantage over rivals. In a window-cleaning business, you might want to specify a particular unique selling point (USP), such as time of day or special kind of service which might persuade customers to use your service. You will also need to identify the level of demand for such a service and the type of market you will be targeting. If you plan to focus on a new housing estate, you will need to think about how many potential customers there are, how often they might want your service – every week, every month? – what the level of competition is, what the opportunity for market expansion is, and so on.

This section might also include some detail on networking. This involves the contacts that businesses might need to help develop, and may include building relationships with local trade associations, such as the local Chambers of Commerce and trade associations.

Networking is becoming increasingly important for many small businesses as a means of building contacts that help to develop the business, and can be a key part of the marketing process.

5 THE PRODUCTION PLAN

Because the example we are using is a service, the details of the production plan might be different from when a business is manufacturing a product. This is concerned with the day-to-day activities of the business referred to as operational planning. If you are considering a business that is actually making something, you will need to consider how this will work in practice and what you will need to be able to produce effectively and efficiently.

Some of the issues to think about in this section will be:

- Where will you get your supplies/raw materials?
- How reliable and secure are these supplies? (You do not want to let customers down!)
- Will you need to have a website? Will you need to sell online?
- What security arrangements might you need to make with regard to your business?
- How might you expand the business in the future?

The window-cleaning business, for example, might involve consideration about where the equipment will be stored when not in use to prevent theft or vandalism, and whether an online presence is really required for this type of business. How many employees do you need now, and, if the business is a success, in the next 12 months? Where will you get these employees from and what will you require of them in terms of qualifications, training, personality, and so on?

Details of the production process, in this case, might involve the equipment needed to make production levels efficient. In the case of a window cleaner, thought needs to be given to the equipment needed. In addition, the business might think about how to actually go about the job of cleaning windows – is there a routine, a way of cleaning the windows on a house that maximises productivity (number of windows cleaned per hour)? The business will also need to consider how it is going to provide and maintain quality and what it will do if it receives complaints about quality.

6   THE FINANCIAL PLAN

The financial planning section requires you to consider the following issues:

- costs and prices
- cash flow monitoring
- record-keeping
- setting up financial reserves and contingency plans
- availability of long-term or emergency finance.

In the case of a window cleaner, the production plan will have identified the equipment needed to be able to run the business. Checking on the costs involved, therefore, needs some further research. Examples are given below:

- Transport – what type is appropriate, how much will it cost, what are the insurance and tax costs? How much will the petrol costs be?
- Ladders – how many and what type? If the round is likely to be residential properties only (as opposed to high-rise office blocks, for example) then a ladder that can reach relevant heights is essential. Also needed is a ladder that is able to reach lower levels but is not so bulky to carry around.
- Basic equipment – cloths, leathers, buckets, squeegees, and so on.
- Business cards to advertise the service.
- Invoices to record payments and money owing for services carried out.

Having detailed the costs, some consideration will need to be given about how the finance to pay for the start-up will be raised. There will need to be detail of prices. This, along with the market information from the section above, helps the business to be able to produce a forecast profit and loss account, a break-even forecast and a cash flow forecast.

Sources of information and guidance

New businesses can get advice from a range of different sources. The business plan is going to be an important source of information about the business and is often used as the basis for advice. It helps pinpoint particular areas of concern.

The main sources of help are listed below.

Banks

Many businesses will use a high-street bank as a source of funds for their business, as well as holding a business account with them. For the bank, it is important that the business flourishes, so they do provide support services and advice for small businesses.

Accountants

Most small businesses will employ an accountant to prepare and check their accounts each year. Many accountants will also offer the benefit of their experience and expertise to the business. They might be able to see particular problems or potential problems facing the business, and as a result, be able to offer valuable advice to the business.

The Small Business Advice Service

This is a body managed by the National Federation for Enterprise Agencies (NFEA) and is funded by sponsors who offer free and independent information for small businesses. It has a website with a series of frequently asked questions and will also provide individual advice to particular questions. It also has a number of resources available from the site to help those thinking of starting up or who have just started up their business.

www.smallbusiness.co.uk

The website www.smallbusiness.co.uk is a source of online-only advice which covers all the main areas of advice for start-ups and new businesses including finance, market research, business formation, sales and marketing, legal advice, business technology and operating abroad.

Small business advisors

There are a host of small business advisors providing advice and consultancy services to small businesses. They are represented by the Institute of Business Consulting (IBC). The IBC is dedicated to increasing the standard of advice provided by its members in helping improve the performance and standards of new and small businesses. There is a directory to find a local business advisor but the business will have to pay for the advice received.

Government agencies

One of the main sources of government-sponsored help is Business Link. Business Link is financed by the Department for Trade and Industry and has nine main regional offices in England representing different parts of the country. It also has a website that contains large amounts of information for small businesses and those thinking of starting up a business. It also has affiliated organisations elsewhere in the United Kingdom (as a result of devolution) which include Business Eye in Wales, Invest NI for Northern Ireland, The Highlands and Islands Enterprise in Scotland and Business Gateway which is based in Glasgow.

In addition to this, various government departments will provide some form of advice and Her Majesty's Revenue and Customs will also offer advice to small businesses in relation to tax and national insurance matters.

Further material and resources relating to this section can be found at **www.collins.bized.co.uk**. Keep checking for updates.

Developing business plans: Summary

- Planning at the outset of a new business venture is seen as being an essential part of starting up a new business.
- A formal business plan is not only useful for prospective investors, but also for the entrepreneur themself.
- A formal business plan covers key areas of the business, such as marketing, finance and legal structure.
- There are a range of independent and government-run sources of advice to help small businesses and entrepreneurs setting up a business.

Summary questions

1   Explain what is meant by a 'business plan'.

2   What is the purpose of a business plan?

3   Identify three benefits that effective planning might provide to a start-up business.

4   State three items that would appear in a business plan.

5   What element of the business plan do you think is the most important and why?

6   What help do banks provide to new business start-ups?

7   What help might the government provide to start-ups?

8   Evaluate the different sources of help available to an entrepreneur.

9   Is good business planning the key to a successful business?

10   Explain three problems a start-up is likely to face.

Points for discussion

Look at the websites of the major high-street banks (links given below). What kinds of help and guidance do the banks give to small businesses?

NatWest: http://www.natwest.com/business.asp

Lloyds TSB: http://www.lloydstsbbusiness.com/home.asp

HSBC: http://www.hsbc.co.uk/1/2/business/home

Barclays: http://www.business.barclays.co.uk

Up-to-date links to these websites can be found at **www.collins.bized.co.uk**.

Exam practice

Alex Tew was a 21-year-old student who was contemplating what to do to reduce the debts he had run up. His answer was to come up with a website offering advertising space for companies around the world.

Like many good business ideas it is very simple – almost too simple to be true! His site, **www.milliondollarhomepage.com/** consists of a grid with a million pixels. Each pixel can be bought for $1. Firms around the world can buy as many pixels as they like and place a logo in the boxes linking their webpage with the world.

When you select any of the logos or text-based ads you are sent direct to that firm's website. So far there is a wide range of companies who have made use of this service – including companies selling ringtones, web hosting, online poker, loan finance, magazines and advice on quitting smoking.

Tew has sold all the million pixels. The success of the project has encouraged him to look at other projects and he is busy working on developing them.

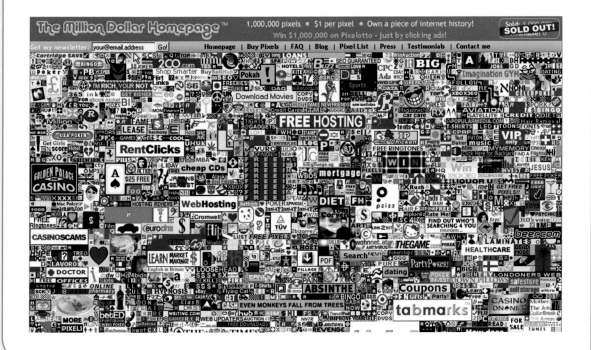

1 If a individual spent time preparing a business plan but discovered that the venture would not be viable, should the individual make a decision to abandon the business idea? (10 marks)

2 Alex did not produce a business plan. Does his success mean that a business plan is a waste of time? (15 marks)

Total: 25 marks

Chapter 5   Conducting start-up market research

In this chapter you will learn about how a business finds out information to help it to get started. Information about the potential market can come from a variety of sources.

Uses of market research

Market research is the process of collecting and interpreting data about customers and competitors. This research is the key both to understanding the needs of customers and to making more reliable business decisions.

New and existing businesses use market research to investigate the following.

MARKET TRENDS
- Market size and trends.
- Potential size of the market in the future.
- Actual and potential sales and market share.

CUSTOMERS
- Number of customers and whether their spending is growing.
- Market segments.
- Actual and potential customers.
- The needs, habits and lifestyles of different groups of consumers.
- Customer preferences.
- What customers want from the product.
- What price they are prepared to pay.
- How customers wish to buy the product.
- What methods of promotion will be most effective.

COMPETITION
- Who are the main competitors?
- What is the market share of these competitors?
- Strengths and weaknesses of each competitor.

Key terms

Desk research The process of gathering secondary data.

Field research The process of gathering primary data, using observation, experimentation or asking questions.

Market research The process of collecting and interpreting data about customers and competitors.

Primary research Involves information collected first hand, which did not previously exist.

Qualitative data Information gathered from a small group of people, using detailed discussions and interviews (quality information) to explore the attitudes of consumers in depth.

Quantitative data Data from a large group (quantity) of respondents showing numbers, proportions or trends within a market, such as how many people buy a particular product.

Sample A smaller group selected from a larger total in order to be representative of the attitudes and characteristics of the total population.

Secondary research Involves information that has already been collected or published.

MARKET RESEARCH – A SUMMARY

Benefits	Drawbacks
• Helps to identify the wants and needs of customers.	• Without clear objectives, research may produce irrelevant information or leave important questions unanswered.
• Allows the business to design and vary its marketing mix (product, price, place and promotion) to target the needs of different market segments.	• The sample may be unrepresentative of the total population due to a small sample size, bias in the method of choosing respondents or poorly constructed questions.
• Enables a swifter response to changes in customer needs, allowing the business to stay a step ahead of its competitors.	• Even with a carefully constructed **sample**, the results cannot provide 100% accuracy – if the business relies on the results, costly mistakes could possibly be made.
• Research into existing competition allows a business to spot a 'gap in the market' that it can profitably fill.	• Respondents may provide answers they think the interviewer wants to hear rather than their true views.
• A new product can be developed and launched with greater confidence in its future success.	• Secondary data is often out of date while primary data can be expensive to collect and analyse.
• The wasted expense of failed products or promotions can be reduced or eliminated.	

Methods of primary and secondary market research

Market research can be carried out in two ways – **primary research** and **secondary research**. Neither one is necessarily better than the other but they do have different advantages and disadvantages and, for a business about to start up, not all methods included in both may be appropriate. The entrepreneur has to select what is appropriate for their circumstances.

Primary research refers to information that is gathered first hand by the entrepreneur or the business. It is unique in that it did not exist previously. Primary research is sometimes referred to as **field research**.

Secondary research uses information that has been gathered by someone else and which already exists. Secondary research is sometimes referred to as **desk research**.

Primary or field research

Field research involves gathering new and original, first-hand information or primary data. Field research can be carried out through observation, experimentation, surveys and interviews. For a business just setting up, some of these methods may be more appropriate than others. It will depend on the type of business and the funds available to the entrepreneur.

OBSERVATION

Observation involves, among other things, watching consumers as they shop, measuring pedestrian flows in a town centre or looking at how rival products are packaged and displayed. Market researchers try to draw conclusions about shoppers from observing their behaviour – such as where they go when they enter a store or how long they spend selecting a product from the shelves. This information can be used to improve store and shelf layout or point-of-sale promotions. In itself, though, observation of consumer behaviour cannot answer questions about *why* customers act in certain ways.

EXPERIMENTATION

A crucial stage in the development and launch of a new product is to assess the reaction of potential consumers. It is vital to test and experiment with new product ideas. Manufacturing companies may build a prototype for testing and showing to prospective customers. This will be an essential part of the development and marketing process.

Some businesses use consumer panels. These are groups of consumers who are asked to give their opinions on ideas or products over a period of time. They may be used by marketeers to comment on a range of product ideas or samples.

Alternatively, a product may be launched in a small part of the market – such as one region or just a few stores in a chain – in order to test how actual consumers react to it. This is known as test marketing.

Experimentation and testing may seem like an additional cost or time delay, but without it a much greater loss of time and money may be suffered if a new product proves unsuccessful in the market. In addition, if the test marketing is very successful then the business can use this to market the product when it goes 'live' nationally.

SURVEYS

Questionnaires can be used to ask a large number of people pre-set questions. Before carrying out a questionnaire-based survey, a business must decide the following.

Objectives for the survey – what it is trying to find out?

A business is better able to collect the data it needs if the objectives are clear. Some objectives may be:

- to describe the current habits of customers
- to explain why they act as they do
- to help predict future trends in the market
- to explore how customers might react to a new product.

How to write the questionnaire to gain this information

In order to get information that is accurate and unbiased, careful attention must be paid to the way questions are phrased:

- The meaning of each question must be clear – the way the question is worded must not lead the respondent towards a particular answer.
- A balance must be struck between closed questions, which offer a limited choice of pre-set responses, and open questions, which allow respondents to offer their own views. Closed questions make it easier to collate and analyse data, while open questions allow for a more detailed insight.

The most effective method of carrying out the survey

Surveys may be face to face, by telephone or by post.

- Face-to-face surveys allow an interviewer to explain questions that the respondent does not understand, but introduce the possibility of bias in the way the interviewer presents the questions.
- Telephone surveys are quicker and cheaper than face-to-face surveys, but may generate resentment among customers.
- Postal surveys rely on customers completing and returning the questionnaire. It is a cheap method that may avoid interviewer bias, but suffers from low response rates.
- Online surveys can use web or e-mail. Web is often preferred over e-mail because interactive HTML forms can be used. They are inexpensive to administer and can produce results quickly.

How many people to question?

To question every actual and potential customer would be both expensive and time-consuming. To avoid this problem, a sample is chosen. A sample is a smaller group selected from a larger total group.

However, the sample should be large enough to provide data that is reliable and representative of the attitudes and characteristics of the total population. The more people who are asked, the greater the degree of confidence the business can have in the accuracy of the results. If everyone in the population were asked, there would be a 100% confidence level. If a sample can provide a 95% confidence level, the results can be considered statistically reliable. There is a small margin of error, but nothing that makes the results unusable.

Sampling: who to question?

If a business questions a sample of consumers, it must select a group of people representative of the whole population. Businesses will approach this in different ways. See page 42 for more information on sampling.

INTERVIEWS

To gain more detailed, qualitative information from a smaller group of people, personal interviewing will be much more useful than a survey. In a personal interview, the interviewer spends longer with each respondent, asking them a wide range of questions and exploring their responses more deeply. The interview is often led by the customer's (interviewee's) comments and will not necessarily follow set questions. The interviewer must be well trained, and the information gained must be properly recorded and analysed.

The results will not be statistically representative of the whole population because of the small sample size. However, when carried out professionally, this method may generate information that explains and explores issues far more effectively than any other market research method.

Secondary or desk research

Desk research is the process of gathering information that has already been collected or published. This type of information is known as secondary data.

Secondary data may exist within the business in the following forms.

SALES RECORDS

These identify trends in sales over time or sales patterns around the country.

CUSTOMER INFORMATION

There may be customer records of purchases, or what their future needs might be. The use of EPOS (electronic point of sale – where your goods are read by a bar code reader and the information collected) and loyalty cards allows many large retailers to identify customers' shopping habits and to use this information to target promotions. For a business just setting out, this type of technology is unlikely to be available, but records can be kept by a small business of sales and customer types.

SURVEY DATA

The results of previous market research surveys may still be of value. There will also be external sources from where existing, valuable information can be gained. The growth of the Internet has made an immense volume of secondary information easily accessible to firms. Such sources include:

Commercial data

Organisations such as Mintel or the Economist Intelligence Unit specialise in gathering market research data about a wide range of markets. Their reports can be purchased to provide detailed, up-to-date information about a specific market. For a small business this might not be a source of information because some of the reports can be very expensive.

Government data

Government departments collect and publish a wide variety of information about all aspects of the economy and society. The Office for National Statistics produces up to date data about social, economic and labour market trends, whilst the Census of Population provides a valuable snapshot of the country every 10 years. The ONS also produces a document called 'Social Trends' containing a wealth of information that can be very useful for a new or existing business.

INFORMATION ABOUT COMPETITORS

Examining rivals' websites reveals much about their products and prices. Competitors' annual reports and accounts can help to build up a valuable picture of their strategy. For a small business, getting information about competitors is no less important. Just because the business is small does not mean it is immune from competition from very large organisations, and in many cases such organisations may be the main source of competition.

OTHER PUBLICATIONS

Local libraries, Business Link or high-street banks help by providing access to a wide variety of other secondary sources, such as market profiles or journal articles.

Desk research can gather large quantities of data without great expense. Extracting useful information, however, can be difficult and time-consuming – whilst the data itself may be neither reliable nor up to date!

For a business just setting up, care will have to be taken in choosing the right type of method to gather market data. However, as we have seen in the section on business plans, potential investors will be expecting to see some evidence that market research has been carried out. In addition, for the entrepreneur, it will be an important exercise in assessing the likely success and viability of the business. The box below summarises some of the ways that businesses with a limited budget can use to gather market research.

MARKET RESEARCH ON A SMALL BUDGET

Primary research	Secondary research
• Approaching local business people to find out more about the area and its potential.	• Look up competitors in the *Yellow Pages* or local newspapers.
• Conducting in-depth interviews with a small group of consumers to identify what really matters to them.	• Obtain competitors' brochures and price lists by post, from exhibitions or from the Internet.
• Observing competitor products – their packaging, prices and promotions.	• Find trends and developments in the market through trade publications such as *The Grocer*.
• Pedestrian and traffic flow counts to identify the most desirable location for passing trade.	• Local Business Link organisations or banks provide free information about specific product markets.
• Discuss consumers' preferences, new products and trends in the market with suppliers or retailers.	• Government facts and figures about society and the economy are available on the Internet or from local libraries. These help a new business to identify the threats and opportunities it faces from its external environment.

Qualitative and quantitative research

The information that an entrepreneur gathers about the market can be classified into two categories: **qualitative** and **quantitative** research.

Quantitative data

Quantitative data is information acquired from a large group of respondents showing numbers, proportions or trends within a market, such as how many people buy a particular product. This is particularly useful when a firm is using research to describe its market. The quantity of data makes it accurate and representative of the whole market. Analysis of statistics helps a firm to understand its market. However, on its own, quantitative data is unlikely to help explain why the market is as it is. To understand why, qualitative data is needed.

Qualitative data

Qualitative data is information gathered from a small group of people, using in-depth discussions and interviews to explore their attitudes. This gives detailed information about the reasons why consumers act as they do, why they buy what they do, when they buy it and, in some cases, why they do not buy a particular product. The information provides an opportunity to respond more fully to customers' ideas. However, the few who are interviewed may not be representative of the whole market. This information is also more difficult to quantify and analyse so conclusions will be less scientific than with quantitative research. In addition, gathering qualitative data may be an expensive task as interviewers need to be trained and interviews can be lengthy.

Size and types of samples

A start-up business might be in a position where it decides to carry out some primary research. Having chosen an appropriate method, it then has to decide on a sample size and the type of sampling technique to use. Larger businesses might have a number of very sophisticated devices available to them to try and make the data collected as accurate and representative as possible, but for a start-up the methods generally include just three types: random, quota and stratified.

Random sampling

Random sampling involves selecting individuals in such a way that anyone in the total population has an equal chance of being chosen. To achieve a truly random sample involves careful planning, otherwise the location or time of day could lead to an unrepresentative sample. For example, a random survey outside a secondary school at 3.30 p.m. may lead to an over-representation of teenagers! A systematic method of random sampling, such as choosing every 100th name from a census list or from the register of electors (which is available at local council offices), is more likely to be successful. Small random samples are more likely to be unrepresentative as they probably will not include all types of people.

Quota sampling

Quota sampling involves identifying the exact sample proportions that the business wants to draw from each market segment. This may be done to build a sample that reflects the proportions of different groups within the total population. For example, if 60% of cola drinkers are male, 60% of the sample questioned should be male. If half of that 60% is under 25, the final sample selected should also reflect this. As long as the original information was accurate, this method has the benefit of producing a sample that reflects the make-up of the market.

Stratified random sampling

Stratified random sampling is used when a business is specifically interested in the views of a particular market segment, such as females in their 20s. The business first selects its market segment, the types of people it wants to include in its sample, then it chooses people within this group at random in the way described above.

Factors influencing the choice of sampling methods

For a small business, the options open to them in conducting market research are more limited than in a larger business. However, as mentioned above, it is essential that an understanding of the market is generated for the entrepreneur to be able to plan effectively and meet customer needs. There are a number of factors that will affect the choice of sampling method that a small or start-up business might employ.

The nature of the product

If the product or service is planned to meet a very local market or a specific market segment, then quota or stratified sampling might be more appropriate than random sampling. A product or service aimed at a much wider market might be more appropriate to random sampling where large amounts of customers might be involved. Specialist products or services that meet individual needs might require qualitative information to be gathered and in such cases, more in-depth data may be required, meaning a stratified sample is the choice.

The risk involved

If the project is a highly risky one with a very high chance of failure then the requirement for more detailed market research might be more pressing. In such a situation there might be a case for not only choosing a random sample but also to carry out some additional qualitative research via a quota or stratified sample. This might give a more rounded picture of the views and needs of the market and help the business in its decision-making.

Available finance

Conducting any market research requires some cash outlay. The size of a sample and the method used, as well as the way in which the results can be processed, might all be limited by the amount of cash available. For a small business this might be very limited.

The target market

As mentioned above, the type of product might be aimed at a particular target market – young people aged between 15 and 19, people living in three-bedroomed detached houses, people who watch more than 48 hours of TV per week, people with an interest in jazz guitar, and so on. These types of people will have specific requirements and it might be far more appropriate to find out what those requirements are through a quota or stratified sample than a random sample.

Further material and resources relating to this section can be found at **www.collins.bized.co.uk**. Keep checking for updates.

Conducting start-up market research: Summary

- Market research is important in helping a business to understand the market it is planning to operate in more effectively.
- Market research can be either primary (or field) research, or secondary (or desk) research.
- Market research can be quantitative – which provides numbers – or qualitative – which can explain how people behave and why they behave in those ways.
- In conducting primary research, a business will have to think about sample size and the type of sampling to use.
- Samples can be random, quota or stratified.

Summary questions

1   What is market research?

2   Explain the four different types of question that market research can seek answers to, giving an example of each.

3   State three benefits and three drawbacks of market research.

4   What is the difference between quantitative and qualitative data?

5   Give three examples of secondary data that may exist:

(a) within the business

(b) outside the business.

6   What is primary data?

7   Explain why observation and experimentation can be useful types of field research.

8   What does a business need to consider before conducting a survey?

9   Describe three factors that might influence the sample size and the method of sampling a small business might use

10   What is the difference between random sampling and quota sampling?

Points for discussion

What methods of primary research would you use to collect information about the following products? Justify your choices.

The products

- An MP3 player.
- A new first-person shooter computer game.
- A new business offering home painting and decorating.
- A device for plasterers that helps improve the consistency of the plaster mix.
- A business offering a photo-framing service.
- A florist.

Think about:

(a) The method you would use and how you would you carry this out.

(b) What type of person you might ask.

(c) Why you would ask those particular people.

Exam practice

The man responsible for inventing the C5 battery-powered one-seater tricycle launched in 1985 has tried to launch a new product. The C5 was a disaster – the market research was simply wrong and it did not meet consumer needs; it flopped badly.

Sir Clive Sinclair's latest attempt at personal transport is the A-bike. Sir Clive has teamed up with a Chinese firm called Daka to develop the bike – it has taken almost twenty years to get to this stage. The bike is called the A-bike because it has the shape of an A when opened out. It is light, weighing in at only twelve pounds, and is likely to be sold for around £200. When folded, it is half the size of current folding bikes on the market and is considerably lighter. Sir Clive anticipates marketing the product around the world and points to the fact that 'many thousands' have already been ordered.

At the moment there are some limitations as to who can use the bike. There is a weight limit of 13 stones and people over six feet four might find the riding experience a little uncomfortable, given the position of the handlebars in relation to leg space. The design of the bike does allow people up to 17 stones to ride it but Sir Clive is suggesting that until they have more experience with sales and the use of the bike, the 13 stone limit will apply. It may be that the experience of the C5 has helped Sir Clive and Daka in developing and marketing this product.

Source: adapted from Biz/ed 'In the News' http://www.bized.co.uk/cgi-bin/chron/chron.pl?id=2643

1 Explain what method of market research Sir Clive might have used in developing the A-bike. (6 marks)

2 Explain one reason why Sir Clive might have used the method you have selected. (4 marks)

3 Consider the factors that might have influenced the type and size of sample that Sir Clive might have used in any field research conducted. (8 marks)

4 Examine TWO benefits and TWO drawbacks of market research for a product like the A-bike. (12 marks)

5 To what extent will careful market research result in success for the A-bike when the C5 failed so miserably? (10 marks)

Total: 40 marks

Chapter 6   Understanding markets

Key terms

Demand The amount consumers are willing and able to buy at different prices.

Market Any place that brings together buyers and sellers to agree a price.

Market growth The rate at which sales of a product in a particular market are growing and at which the market is expanding or contracting.

Market segment The division of larger markets into smaller sections, each with similar needs and/or characteristics.

Market share The proportion of total sales in a market accounted for by any one business.

Market size The total potential or actual sales/customers in a market.

Supply The amount producers are willing to offer for sale at different prices.

In this chapter you will learn that whilst there are different types of markets – local and national, physical and electronic – they all have one thing in common – they are made up of **demand** from buyers and **supply** from producers. The demand for any one firm's products will depend not only on their own decisions – such as their price or promotion – but also the actions of their competitors and other external factors beyond their control.

The nature and types of markets

A **market** is any place that brings together buyers and sellers to agree a price. Buyers might be looking for a particular product and are likely to have some idea of the price they are willing and able to pay to acquire that product. On the other side, producers may have such products for sale but will also have a price in mind that they would like to receive. The market is made when both are able to agree on the price.

If you go to a supermarket there are lots of products for sale – each one is provided by a producer and is on the shelf screaming at you to choose it. You scan the shelves and make a decision to select a particular product – that is the point where the buyer and seller are brought together to agree the price.

Markets exist in thousands of different forms. Some of these are listed below.

Local markets

Local markets are where the buyer and seller exist and are brought together from within a small area, for example, the market for hairdressing services, an off-licence, a pub, restaurants and a hardware store. Each of these will tend to draw their custom from a limited area and are set up to provide a service or products to that limited area. It is unlikely, for example, that many people would travel 300 miles to visit a small town hairdresser or restaurant, and it is unlikely that a hardware store will be keen on supplying goods to places outside a 50-mile radius of the shop.

National markets

National markets exist where there tends to be a buyer purchasing on behalf of the country as a whole. For example, the government buy various services for health, defence, education and justice, and may buy those services or products from a particular country (including, of course, the UK).

Physical markets

Physical markets tend to be markets that are specifically designed to bring together buyers and sellers of particular items. These items might be commodities like oil, sugar beet, pork bellies, soya beans and zinc, and financial products such as stocks, shares, bonds and currencies. These markets tend to be highly organised and highly regulated to protect both buyers and sellers, and are also likely to be global in nature – anyone, anywhere in the world can enter the market (although the money needed might preclude many ordinary people!).

Electronic

Increasingly markets are becoming virtual – buyers and sellers are linked by some form of electronic infrastructure that enables them to engage in trade. The buyer and seller might never meet each other, have no idea who each other are and be from anywhere in the world. Examples include Amazon and eBay.

The importance of demand

Buyers of products and services represent demand. Demand is the amount buyers are willing and able to purchase at different prices. It is not sufficient for a buyer to want to buy something – they must have the means to be able to buy it. This is called effective demand.

The level of demand for any good or service depends on a variety of factors. These can be summarised as follows.

Price

The higher the price, the lower the demand is likely to be – the reverse is also likely to be the case.

Prices of other goods – substitutes and complements

Many products and services are linked together, and changes in the price of one might affect the demand for another. If taxi prices rise, for example, then it might lead to a rise in the demand for other forms of public transport like buses, trams and tube systems. These products would be classed as substitutes. DVDs and DVD players are called complementary goods. If the price of DVD players falls then it might be expected that the demand for DVDs would rise.

Incomes – the level and distribution of income

The amount of money that people have at their disposal for consumption is going to have a large effect on the level of demand. If incomes rise, then we might expect the demand for most goods and services to also increase. The distribution of income refers to the fact that in most countries the way income is distributed amongst the population can vary enormously. There are always going to be rich and poor, but the proportion of rich and poor can affect demand for some types of goods disproportionately. For example, the demand for champagne in the UK has changed dramatically in recent years, no longer is it seen as being the preserve of the very rich. Changes in income distribution have been partly responsible for this.

Tastes and fashions

Tastes and fashions have a major impact on demand. What determines what is fashionable and how tastes are determined is never clear but most businesses know that tastes and fashions can change very quickly. What appears to be cool, hip, trendy, in – or whatever term is used – one week, can become 'out' the next and businesses have to be flexible enough and conduct market research to keep abreast of such changes in the market.

The level and structure of the population

The higher the level of population, the higher the demand for a product is likely to be. In addition, the structure of the population is also an important determinant of demand. In the UK we have an ageing population which means that there is an increasing proportion of the population that is over 65. People in this age bracket have different needs from those in the (say) 18–25 age group, and there may be new market opportunities to satisfy these needs.

Advertising

Advertising can and does influence the demand for a product. This might not be simply obvious forms of advertising like that on the TV or billboard, but advertising through people wearing branded clothing, sponsorship of sports clubs, people carrying branded shopping bags, and so on. The more aware we are of products, the more likely we are to choose those products when making buying decisions.

Expectations of consumers

The existence of high levels of information these days means that consumers are more aware of events and issues than ever before. This information can serve to heighten demand, but it might also depress demand. For example, if there is constant talk of falling house prices in the press, then buyers may well defer plans to move house and this affects the demand for housing. If people feel that the economy is doing well they might be more inclined to borrow money to buy material things or holidays. Equally, if they expect the economy to do worse in the future, they may fear losing their jobs and put off planned spending.

The seasons

The time of year can have an effect on the demand for a variety of goods and services. Housing demand rises in the spring, ice creams tend to be in higher demand in the summer than winter, skiing holidays are very popular during the Christmas holiday and the winter half-terms, and so on.

Types of market segmentation

One of the most widely used methods of identifying particular markets is to break down a market into different **market segments**. In this context the term 'market' is used to describe all the potential customers that might be interested in purchasing a good or service. Let us take an example. The market for drinks contains a very wide range of different products and customers. Within that broad definition of the market there will also be many different types of customers. A small carton of orange juice might be drunk by small children aged between 3 and 5; a *Bacardi Breezer* is not going to be drunk by small children between the ages of 3 and 5!

Many companies will find that customers in a market have certain habits and preferences and types of behaviour. These buying habits and preferences can be grouped together to identify particular market segments.

The sports energy drink market is a segment of the much larger drinks market. Most markets, therefore, can be divided up to meet the needs of certain groups of people with similar buying habits and characteristics. For example, young males aged between 18 and 25 are likely to have different buying habits and tastes from males aged between 45 and 55; people who live in built-up urban environments will tend to have different buying habits from those who live in predominantly rural areas. This does not mean that a market consists *only* of a certain type of person; a young male aged 18 might buy a CD by Led Zeppelin and so might a male aged 54! Anyone can be part of a market, but the business will be interested in what their *typical* customer is like.

Smaller businesses will also be interested in market segments. In a small town hairdressing salon, for example, women over 65 may well come into the salon predominantly on Thursdays and Fridays to get their hair done – these types of customers are sometimes referred to as the 'blue rinse brigade'.

Many market segments have almost passed into common language use – yuppies, the grey market, dinkies (dual-income-no-kids-yet) and the hunting set. When we use these terms we might immediately conjure up an image of what someone who is identified as belonging to this segment looks like!

Through market research, businesses try to discover a huge range of information about customers (and potential customers). They might find out things such as:

- what TV programmes they watch
- what magazines they read
- how much they earn
- where they do their shopping
- who in the household tends to do the shopping and when
- what products they use and why they use them
- how regularly they buy particular products
- whether they tend to buy online or in stores
- whether they tend to buy when there are promotions on or if these are more regular purchases.

This information can then be used to discover more about the needs of this group and to develop products and marketing strategies that appeal directly to these specific consumer groups. Actors and actresses used in TV adverts might be specifically chosen because they represent (or will appeal to) the market segment that the advertisement is aimed at. For example, the market segment interested in the BMW *Mini* tends to be young, fun-loving and in search of something a little different – any

promotional strategy will reflect this and the people used in advertisements will be of a similar age to the target customers. Knowing and understanding market segments, or target markets, makes marketing activities more likely to succeed.

Ways of segmenting the market

The main ways of segmenting a market are listed below.

GEOGRAPHICAL SEGMENTATION

This means identifying consumers according to the area where they live. This could be fairly broad – for example, Waitrose supermarkets are located predominantly in the south of England. Or, it may be quite specific – many insurance companies target customers according to crime rates in their locality.

DEMOGRAPHICAL SEGMENTATION

This relates to the population and is the broadest of all segmentation methods. It includes a wide range of different criteria (see the examples in Figure 6.1). Markets may also be segmented according to social class groupings (socio-demographic segmentation). Figure 6.2 shows one way that this is done within the UK. Products can then be aimed at specific groupings, such as ABs or DEs. (For example, hair salons such as Toni & Guy are aimed at ABs).

Type	Example
Age	Nightclubs aimed at over 21s
Gender	Hair products aimed at females
Ethnic group	Food products aimed at different religious groups (for example, kosher or halal meat)
Income	Credit cards aimed at people earning over certain amounts
Family characteristics	Products such as replacement furniture and foreign holidays aimed at 'empty nesters' (middle-aged parents whose children have left home)
Education	Courses aimed at those with few qualifications
Occupation	Magazines, such as *The Grocer* or *Management Today*, aimed at specific professions

Figure 6.1   Examples of demographic market segmentation

Group	Social status	Description
A	Upper middle class	Higher managerial, administrative or professional (doctors, solicitors, company directors)
B	Middle class	Middle management, administrative or professional (teachers, nurses, managers)
C^1	Lower middle class	Supervisory, clerical or junior management (shop assistants, clerks, police officers)
C^2	Skilled working class	Skilled manual workers (electricians, service engineers, technicians)
D	Working class	Semi and unskilled manual workers (farm hands, labourers)
E	The poorest in society	State pensioners, casual workers, unemployed

Source: Institute of Practitioners in Advertising

Figure 6.2   Social class groupings

BENEFIT SEGMENTATION

Here the market is segmented according to the benefit consumers seek or gain from the product. Car companies may develop a range of products related to the benefit that car users are looking for. For example, some people will be interested in safety, others in load space or performance. Hence, car companies develop ranges of products to appeal to these different segments (five-door, sports, estate, and so on) and usually promote the product in different ways to the different groups.

GROUP SOCIAL STATUS DESCRIPTION

Registrar General's grouping

Class 1 – Higher managerial and professional

Class 2 – Lower managerial and professional

Class 3 – Intermediate occupations

Class 4 – Small employers, self-employed

Class 5 – Lower supervisory

Class 6 – Semi-routine

Class 7 – Routine

Class 8 – Long-term unemployed/never employed.

BEHAVIOURAL SEGMENTATION

This involves segmenting consumers according to different behaviours. A supermarket might use its loyalty card scheme to track the spending habits of customers and identify that, for example, most over-50s tend to shop on Mondays. Having identified this, it may run special promotions every Monday to attract even more over-50s and to encourage them to spend a greater amount in the store.

BUYER-READINESS SEGMENTATION

This divides consumers according to how ready they are to buy a product. Will they buy regularly, occasionally, rarely? Are they keen on getting new products as soon as they are released or do they prefer to wait? Think about the queues that exist when new films or games consoles are released, or new editions of popular books like the *Harry Potter* series.

LIFESTYLE SEGMENTATION

This is based on how the opinions, interests, hobbies and activities of individuals affect spending habits. For example, 'experiencers' are considered to be young, frequently engaged in physical or social activities, and avid consumers of new products.

GEODEMOGRAPHIC SEGMENTATION

This is perhaps the most powerful of all the segmentation types. It combines both geographic and demographic data to build a detailed picture of different localities. The data can be used to pinpoint the best location for a new store or to identify where a mailshot might be most effective. A brief example of the type of information geodemographics can provide is given in Figure 6.3. Most businesses use a combination of methods to accurately describe their market segments.

- Segmentation is an essential part of the marketing process. It allows businesses to:
  - use marketing budgets effectively
  - target marketing campaigns accurately
  - spot gaps in the market and identify new opportunities
  - differentiate products from those of competitors (allowing higher prices to be charged or wider margins to be maintained).
- The basic foundation of marketing success – know your customer – is an integral part of segmentation.
- Segmentation involves clearly defining who these customers are and developing a detailed understanding of their needs, which, as we have seen, is essential to marketing success.

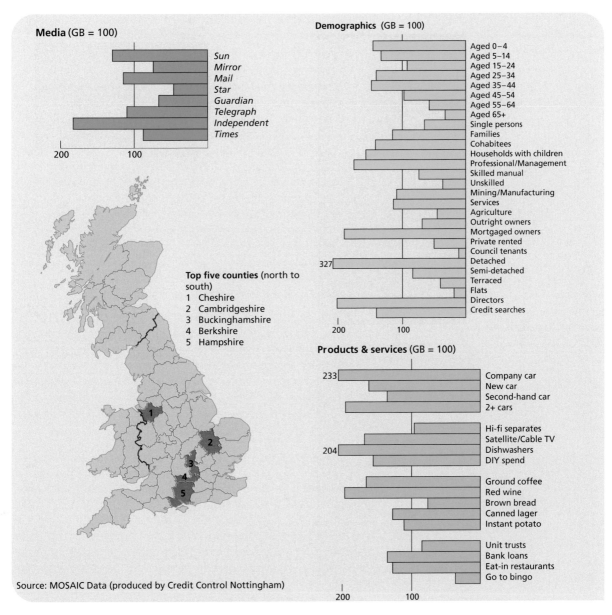

Media (GB = 100)

Sun
Mirror
Mail
Star
Guardian
Telegraph
Independent
Times

200   100

Top five counties (north to south)
1 Cheshire
2 Cambridgeshire
3 Buckinghamshire
4 Berkshire
5 Hampshire

Demographics (GB = 100)

Aged 0–4
Aged 5–14
Aged 15–24
Aged 25–34
Aged 35–44
Aged 45–54
Aged 55–64
Aged 65+
Single persons
Families
Cohabitees
Households with children
Professional/Management
Skilled manual
Unskilled
Mining/Manufacturing
Services
Agriculture
Outright owners
Mortgaged owners
Private rented
Council tenants
Detached   327
Semi-detached
Terraced
Flats
Directors
Credit searches

200   100

Products & services (GB = 100)

Company car   233
New car
Second-hand car
2+ cars

Hi-fi separates
Satellite/Cable TV
Dishwashers   204
DIY spend

Ground coffee
Red wine
Brown bread
Canned lager
Instant potato

Unit trusts
Bank loans
Eat-in restaurants
Go to bingo

200   100

Source: MOSAIC Data (produced by Credit Control Nottingham)

Figure 6.3 Geodemographic segmentation

Benefits and drawbacks of segmentation

The main benefits of segmentation are:

- It can help to increase sales through a better understanding of the market and its different needs.
- It can allow a business to identify potential gaps in the market and to develop new products and services to meet those needs.
- A greater understanding of the market(s) a business operates in helps in devising more efficient promotion strategies and distribution networks.
- Segmentation allows the business to target scarce resources at particular markets and can increase efficiency as a result.
- Segmentation can enable the business to increase revenue from sales, but reduce costs especially on promotion and advertising, thus widening margins.

The drawbacks that need to be considered include:

- Focusing on too narrow a market could expose the business to competition and also to changes in market needs – it can be like putting all your eggs in one basket!
- Research into market segments requires resources and can increase costs – the additional revenue generated must outweigh the costs involved. Increased costs could arise from:
  - research and development of new products to meet different market needs
  - costs of holding stock to meet different segments
  - producing different products or having different production processes to provide for different needs
  - expenditure on market research (many small businesses might not be able to afford this)
  - additional advertising and promotion costs to cover different segments.
- Segmentation relies on accurate information – if the information is not accurate, it can damage a business.

If a business is deciding the extent to which it might need to consider market segmentation, it will have to balance out the possible costs that arise and the benefits it expects to gain. This might be expressed simply as how much additional revenue it is expected to bring in. If the additional revenue is expected to be higher than the cost of segmenting the market and all that entails, then it is likely to be worth doing it. The business will have to make a decision on how far the benefits have to outweigh the cost to make it worthwhile!

Market share

Market share is the proportion of the total sales of a market accounted for by a particular brand or business. For example, in the supermarket industry, sales at Tesco account for around 29% of all sales in supermarkets. It is an important measure of business success. Many businesses will have a specific objective to try and increase their market share. Market segmentation can help in this process by allowing marketing departments to work more effectively, hopefully leading to increased sales and improved market share.

If a company is able to analyse its market, identify its main customer types and then build an understanding of their needs (and their changing needs), marketeers are better able to develop products and services to gain competitive advantage and thus capture market share. It can also help a business to branch out into a new market. If they know their customers' habits, hobbies, likes and dislikes, why not try and sell other products to them? *FHM* magazine, for instance, knew its readers were style-conscious and expanded its presence in the magazine segment by launching *FHM Collections* (a fashion magazine).

'In 2005, the global confectionery market was worth an estimated USD119.69bn, having risen by almost 19% in value terms compared with levels in 2001.

'In value terms, chocolate confectionery is the largest sector, accounting for almost 60% of total sales. By volume, however, sugar confectionery accounts for the majority of sales, with a share of just over half (51%).

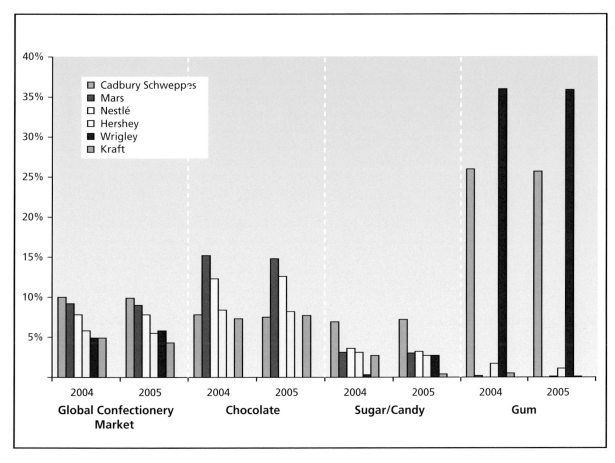

Figure 6.4 Market share in the global confectionery market 2004/5 (US dollar share)

'The global confectionery market remains relatively fragmented, with the top six manufacturers accounting for less than half (45%) of value sales.

'Between 2006 and 2010, the global confectionery market is forecast to increase by over 16% in value terms, reaching more than USD145bn.'

Sources: Euromonitor 2004/2005 and Leatherhead Food International

Market size, growth and share

It is important to distinguish between **market size**, market share and **market growth**.

Market size refers to the total number of sales in the market at a point in time or the potential number of sales that could be made. The latter is especially relevant when planning to introduce a new product. The market size for premier league football matches for Sky TV might be measured by the number of households in the UK with a television. The market size for a particular club, such as Portsmouth, might be the number of people willing to watch Portsmouth on a weekly basis. Knowing this type of information can help businesses to plan for capacity. For example, Manchester United knows that they could probably increase their ground capacity from 80,000 to 100,000 and still fill it every home game. Their market size is likely to be much higher than that of Portsmouth FC.

Market share refers to the proportion of the market held by one company (see Figure 6.3). For example, Cadbury Schweppes had a 10% share of the global confectionary market in 2004. By 2005 this had declined to 9.9% (see Figure 6.4).

Market growth refers to the whole market and looks at how sales in the market as a whole are growing. If the market is growing but a company's market share stays the same, then it may be that this is satisfactory, but it might also be that the company will be asking why it is not able to gain a larger proportion of a growing market. For example, look at the statements in Figure 6.4. The market as a whole is growing, but out of the top five companies only Wrigley has grown their market share for the global confectionery market between 2004 and 2005.

Further material and resources relating to this section can be found at **www.collins.bized.co.uk**. Keep checking for updates.

Understanding markets: Summary

- Markets bring together buyers and sellers.
- They can vary in nature – some are local, others national and others are international – and bring together buyers and sellers of commodities.
- Demand is a key part of any market.
- The level of demand is affected by a variety of factors such as price, incomes and advertising.
- Markets are broken down into sections called market segments, which group people with similar needs and buying behaviour.
- Markets can also be described by their size and the rate at which they are growing.
- The proportion of total sales accounted for by any one firm is called market share.

Summary questions

1 Give a definition of the term 'market'.

2 What type of market do the following activities belong to?

   (a) The purchase and sale of dollars by a multi-national corporation for international trade.

   (b) A farmers' market.

   (c) The purchase by Boeing of aircraft engines from Rolls Royce.

   (d) The purchase of a rare CD by a buyer on an Internet auction site.

3 Explain the meaning of the term 'demand'.

4 Identify and explain three factors that might affect the demand for tickets for a summer music festival such as Glastonbury or Reading.

5 Describe, using an example, what is meant by a 'market segment'.

6 State and explain three methods a firm might use to segment its market.

7 Outline the key advantages of market segmentation.

8 Segmentation is especially important in niche marketing. Explain why this is the case.

9 Tesco has a market share of around 29% in the UK supermarket industry and Microsoft has a market share of around 90% of operating systems on PCs. Explain what this means.

10 Explain how market growth can be slowing down even though market size is rising.

Points for discussion

Produce a segmentation statement outlining the typical consumer profile for each of the following products:

- *The Financial Times*
- *Stella Artois*
- A tube of *Smarties*.

Exam practice

Chocolate manufacturer Cadbury relaunched a product that it had withdrawn from sale in 2003. *Wispa* was originally launched in 1983 as a product to exploit the so-called 'countline bar' market. This is the sort of product that people can eat anywhere – especially when they are on the go – and which can be distributed to a wide variety of outlets.

Wispa was developed to compete with other bars in this market; in particular *Aero* made by then rivals Rowntree. *Aero* had been changed into a countline bar and had been gaining market share. Cadbury used its reputation for high-quality chocolate to produce a bar that would compete with such products and which moved away from the traditional block chocolate bar. *Wispa* was launched in the Tyne Tees area in 1981 in a test market. The product proved enormously successful. Cadbury withdrew it from sale and put into place plans to launch the bar nationwide. It had to construct a purpose-built plant costing £12 million. Once relaunched nationally in 1983 the product became enormously successful.

The 80s themed relaunch of the Wispa bar in 2007

The product was successful because it appealed to a wide range of different people. By using Cadbury chocolate and re-forming it into a small bar that was easy to eat and widely available, the company tapped into a growing market and market share grew. However, by early 2001, sales of the product had declined and Cadbury withdrew the product from sale in 2003.

Cadbury now say that the level of demand is such that it has been persuaded to re-issue the bar. Cadbury are pointing to the pressure it has been under from consumers who have advocated the 'Bring Back Wispa' campaign. Internet sites such as YouTube, Facebook, Bebo and MySpace have featured such campaigns, and amidst the fans' invasion of the stage during Iggy Pop's set at Glastonbury in 2007 was a banner bearing the legend 'Bring Back Wispa'.

Cadbury has said that they have produced around 23 million of the bars which will be made available at 42p. The relaunch appears to be for a limited amount of time. Whether there is any longer term future for the bar is another matter. Maybe it will need another demonstration of consumer power to persuade Cadbury to release the product again in the future but in the meantime it is encouraging consumers to try the bar once again. As they said back in the 1980s, once bitten, never forgotten. If the extent of the support for the bar is as high as Cadbury says then maybe it is true!

Source: Adapted from Biz/ed 'In the News' http://www.bized.co.uk/cgi-bin/chron/chron.pl?id=2949

1 Using an example, explain the meaning of the term 'market share'. (4 marks)

2 Using examples, explain the difference between the terms 'market size' and 'market growth'. (6 marks)

3 Using examples, explain the meaning of the term 'market segmentation'. (4 marks)

4 Analyse the possible market segments that Cadbury might have been seeking to target:

(a) with the original release of the bar in 1983 and

(b) with the re-launch of the bar in 2007. (10 marks)

5 What type of segmentation analysis do you think Cadbury would have been most likely to use when planning the marketing of a chocolate bar such as *Wispa*? Explain your reasoning. (6 marks)

6 Discuss the problems facing Cadbury in operating in a market which is highly competitive and is growing very slowly. (10 marks)

Total: 40 marks

Chapter 7   Choosing the right legal structure for the business

In this chapter you will learn about the main types of business ownership. In setting up a business an entrepreneur has to accept certain legal obligations which are different depending on the type of ownership. You will learn that business ownership is not just about making a profit, but that some businesses operate 'not-for-profit'.

Sole traders, partnerships, private limited companies and public limited companies

WH Smith, Marks & Spencer and Sainsbury's are big businesses now but, as their names suggest, they all began with the ideas and efforts of just one or two business owners. Trace the history of any large business and you are likely to find key moments when ownership and organisation changed. In the private sector of the economy, businesses are owned by individuals, not the government. There are four main types of business organisation within the private sector:

- sole traders
- partnerships
- private limited companies (Ltd)
- public limited companies (plc).

Limited liability

In choosing the ideal type of ownership, the first decision is what legal status to give the business.

UNINCORPORATED BUSINESSES WITH UNLIMITED LIABILITY

Unincorporated businesses tend to be small organisations, and include sole traders and partnerships. The law does not see these businesses as being separate from their owners. This means that if the business runs into financial trouble and cannot pay the money it owes, the owners are responsible for paying the debts. This is known as having **unlimited liability**.

INCORPORATED BUSINESSES WITH LIMITED LIABILITY

The alternative option is to incorporate the business by setting it up as a company that, in the eyes of the law, is separate from the business owners. **Incorporated businesses** are known as limited companies because they have **limited liability**. This means that the owners do not have to pay off any debts using their personal finances – all they would lose is the money they had originally invested in the business. If there was not enough money left in the business to pay all those to whom it owes money (its creditors), the debts would go unpaid. There are two types of limited company: a private limited company (Ltd) and a public limited company (plc).

Key terms

Flotation Becoming a plc by issuing shares for general sale on the stock market.

Incorporated business An organisation with a separate legal identity from its owner (a limited company).

Limited liability Where a business owner can only lose the amount of money invested into the business if it fails, and not their personal wealth.

Shareholders The joint owners of a limited company, whose investment entitles them to vote on major decisions and take a share of the profit.

Unincorporated business A business that is not legally separate from its owner (sole traders and partnerships).

Unlimited liability Where the business owner can lose personal wealth to pay off business debts.

Sole traders

A sole trader is a business owned by just one person. There are more sole trader businesses in the UK than any other type of business. The single owner of the business has full control over decision-making and receives all the business profits, although there may be a number of other employees working for the business. The popularity of the sole trader as a form of business ownership is largely down to its simplicity.

BEING A SOLE TRADER

Advantages	Disadvantages
• Easy to set up the business – few forms to complete, allowing the business to be set up swiftly and cheaply.	• Unlimited liability – if the business fails, debts must be paid by the owner; personal possessions may be at risk.
• Complete control – the single owner makes all decisions about running the business. This allows the business to adapt quickly to customers' needs. Many sole traders find the independence of self-employment crucial to job satisfaction.	• Shortage of finance – the owner's savings may be the only source of financial capital. A bank loan may be difficult (but not impossible) to get if the business idea is a risky one. Shortage of finance may prevent expansion.
• Keep all the profit – with no other owners, the sole trader will not have to share business profits or discuss with others how they should be used.	• Pressure of responsibility – running your own business can involve long hours, stress and difficulty during times of illness.
• Personal service – a business owned and run by the same person, the sole trader, can get to know customers well and ensure their needs are met. This quality of personal service can be an excellent tool for gaining customers and keeping them loyal.	• Lack of expertise – sole traders usually have an area of expertise that led them to set up the business; but they are unlikely to have all the skills needed to manage a business successfully.
• Privacy – the business's financial information does not have to be published (except to Her Majesty's Revenue and Customs for tax purposes).	• Lack of continuity – because the business is not legally separate from the owner, if the owner retires or dies the business must be wound up (closed down).
• There may be more of a chance of securing credit terms.	
• There may be some types of tax advantages to being a sole trader.	

Partnerships

A partnership is the joint ownership of a business by more than one owner. These joint owners will each:

- contribute their own financial capital to the business
- share the responsibility for decision-making and control
- share the business profits.

A partnership, like a sole trader, may have unlimited liability and so the personal finances of partners could be taken to pay off business debts. In 2001, a new law was passed that allowed Limited Partnerships to be established. There are certain rules and regulations that have to be adhered to if applying to be a limited partnership.

The workload and profits are shared between the partners, though not necessarily equally. The partners can draw up a Deed of Partnership when they set up the business. In this they can state:

- what share of the profits each partner receives
- the role each partner can play in decision-making
- rules and procedures for solving disagreements between partners.

The Deed of Partnership is a legal document that can help to prevent disputes over who is entitled to what. It is not required by law, but without it there is an assumption that all profits will be shared equally.

PARTNERSHIPS

Advantages	Disadvantages
• Extra financial capital – with more than one business owner contributing finance, the business has more capital with which to grow.	• Unlimited liability – the personal possessions of partners are at risk in the event of business failure. This will not apply if the business has successfully applied to become a Limited Partnership.
• Additional skills – partners may bring different skills to the business, allowing each to specialise in their own area of expertise.	• Shared profit – the downside of having partners to share the workload is that the profit has to be shared out as well!
• Shared workload – the running of the business and the decision-making is shared between the business owners.	• Disagreements – having more than one person making decisions can lead to conflict and slow down decision-making. The business could lose its flexibility.
	• Shortage of capital – although there may be more financial capital, the amount available is still limited to the owners' contributions and what can be borrowed from a bank.

Limited companies

The alternative to being a sole trader or partnership is to set up a limited company. A limited company has a separate legal identity from its owners and so brings the protection of limited liability. Capital is invested in a limited company through the purchase of shares. A share is a part-ownership of a business. The business owners are therefore known as **shareholders**.

Shareholders have a right to share in decision-making and in profits. The more shares owned by a shareholder, the greater their power in decision-making and the greater their share of the profits. A board of directors, headed by a chairperson, is elected by shareholders to carry out the day-to-day running of a limited company.

SETTING UP A LIMITED COMPANY

Setting up a limited company involves following the formal process of incorporation by registering the business with the Registrar of Companies.

> **Submit *Memorandum of Association* to Companies House –** sets out basic details of company, such as name, objectives and amount of initial capital.
>
> **Submit *Articles of Association* to Companies House –** sets out how the company is to be run, including the powers of shareholders and directors, and the frequency of shareholder meetings.
>
> Registrar of Companies issues *Certificate of Incorporation* allowing business to trade as a company.
>
> Each year, a copy of the company's accounts must be sent to the Registrar, as well as to all shareholders.
>
> Shareholders must also be told annually about the date of the annual general meeting, which they are entitled to attend.

Figure 7.1   Limited company legal requirements

Private limited companies

A private limited company (Ltd) is the smaller of the two types of limited company. It is suitable for a new business start-up or for an existing sole trader or partnership seeking the benefits of limited liability. The shares it issues cannot be advertised for sale or traded on the stock market. This is why it is a private limited company – any transfer of shares must be done privately and with the agreement of all shareholders. Many Ltds are family businesses, with the family members being directors and shareholders.

PRIVATE LIMITED COMPANIES

Advantages	Disadvantages
• Limited liability – the key benefit over a sole trader or partnership. If the business fails, shareholders lose only the value of their share capital.	• Legal requirements – the added burden of legal duties (see Figure 7.1) takes time and money.
• Sources of finance – the security of limited liability makes it easier to attract investors and so raise finance.	• Loss of privacy – the need to declare business accounts to Companies House means that anyone (including competitors) can find out about a company's financial position.
• Continuity – the separate legal identity of the business means that it continues to exist even if one of the owners dies.	• Limited growth – the restriction of share capital to a maximum of £50,000, and the inability to sell shares to the public, limits the opportunities to raise finance and expand.
	• Some limited companies find it harder to secure loans and credit terms because of their limited liability status.

Public limited companies

A public limited company (plc) is a much larger type of company that must have at least £50,000 of share capital and has its shares traded on the stock market. The majority of the big and famous high-street names are either plcs or are owned by plcs. When a company decides to become a plc, it must be floated on the Stock Exchange. This involves publishing a prospectus to advertise the company to potential shareholders and can be an expensive process. Once a plc has a listing on the stock market, any member of the general public can buy and sell shares in the company.

PUBLIC LIMITED COMPANIES

Advantages	Disadvantages
• Sources of finance – the key benefit compared to a Ltd. Enormous potential to raise large amounts of capital as shares can be advertised to the general public, and bought and sold with ease.	• Costs – initial **flotation** on the stock market is expensive, as are the requirements to publish detailed accounts and to keep large numbers of shareholders informed each year.
• Expansion – the capital available to a plc allows it to expand and benefit from the increased business size and market power.	• Loss of control – by selling shares on the stock market, the original owners' control of the company can be lost. Other individuals or businesses could take major shareholdings in a plc and maybe influence key decisions, even launching a takeover.
• Credibility – plc status is likely to give the business more credibility with lenders, suppliers and customers.	• Business size – the growth of a plc could lead to problems, such as a lack of flexibility or loss of personal touch with customers or employees.

DIVORCE OF OWNERSHIP AND CONTROL

This can introduce a divide between those who own the company (the shareholders) and those who are controlling it on a day-to-day basis (the board of directors). This divorce (separation) of ownership and control can have important effects on the business. Decisions could be taken that meet the needs of the directors – for example, greater financial bonuses – but are not in the best interest of the business owners. Shareholders can, in theory, use their power at the annual general meeting to overrule or remove directors, but these meetings occur only once a year and are often poorly attended. In addition, many shareholders are very large so-called 'institutional investors'. These are insurance companies, other companies and pension funds who are often the largest group of owners of shares in plcs.

The effects of business ownership

The important effects that business ownership has on the way businesses operate and develop include:

- The ability to expand – a successful business might want to grow and limited company status will allow this to happen.

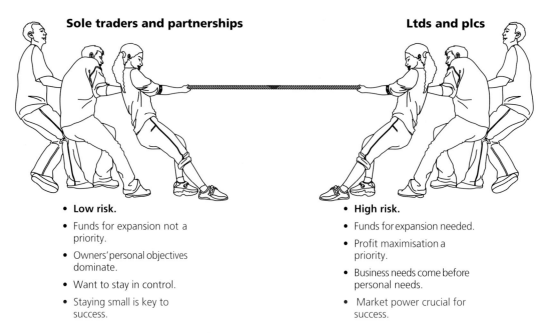

Sole traders and partnerships

- **Low risk.**
- Funds for expansion not a priority.
- Owners' personal objectives dominate.
- Want to stay in control.
- Staying small is key to success.

Ltds and plcs

- **High risk.**
- Funds for expansion needed.
- Profit maximisation a priority.
- Business needs come before personal needs.
- Market power crucial for success.

Figure 7.2 The business ownership tug-of-war

- Who is in control – from the sole trader, where a single owner is in complete control of decision-making, to a plc, where shareholders play a limited role in decision-making, business ownership determines who is in charge.
- The effects of business failure – for a sole trader or partnership, business failure can mean personal ruin. The owners of a failed limited company, on the other hand, could be back in business with a new company almost instantly. These consequences of limited liability, however, also mean that anyone who is owed money (a creditor) by a failed limited company may never be paid.

Not-for-profit businesses

A not-for-profit business is one which is formed for reasons other than generating profit. This does not mean that such an organisation does no more than cover costs – they do. However, rather than describing this as 'profit' it is more generally referred to as 'surplus'. Not-for-profit organisations can be set up for charitable, educational, scientific, research and religious purposes. As such, any surpluses that the organisation does make are ploughed back into the organisation rather than going to shareholders or the owners.

Most not-for-profit organisations share similar features with normal business organisations that exist to make profit. They have unlimited liability and are separate legal entities which can sue and be sued. However, if the organisation folds then any assets it possesses must be distributed to other similar non-profit organisations. In addition, no individual in the organisation should get any specific personal gain from the organisation.

Not-for-profit organisations are not just charities; in many respects they operate differently from charities and some of the entrepreneurs who set them up look at specific problems and apply their skills to solving those problems. When the problem is solved they move onto other problems. Not-for-profit organisations are often referred to as social entrepreneurship and the idea is becoming increasingly popular. There may be tax advantages for such organisations. Examples of these types of organisation include the Grameen Bank which offers small, largely unsecured loans to people in poor countries, the Aravind Eye Hospital in India which carries out over 200,000 cataract operations every year, and possible plans for nurses in the NHS to form a not-for-profit organisation to sell services to primary care trusts and the National Health Service.

Further material and resources relating to this section can be found at **www.collins.bized.co.uk**. Keep checking for updates.

Choosing the right legal structure for the business: Summary

- There are a number of different types of business ownership ranging from small one-person organisations to very large multi-national businesses.
- One of the key aspects of deciding the type of business ownership is the question of liability.
- Limited liability means the owner only risks losing what they have agreed to put into the business.
- Unlimited liability means the owner might risk losing all their personal possessions to pay off any debts of a company.
- The type of business ownership has an effect on:
    - the ease and method of expansion
    - the degree of control exercised by the owner
    - the owner if the business fails.
- Not-for-profit businesses exist for purposes other than making profit – but they do make surpluses.

Summary questions

1 Why might an entrepreneur choose to set up as a sole trader rather than as a partnership?

2 Identify TWO advantages that a private limited company might have that a sole trader or partnership does not have.

3 What are the main advantages of a partnership?

4 Why might a business that has limited liability find it harder to raise loans and/or credit?

5 What is limited liability?

6 Why might a growing partnership wish to incorporate?

7 Compare and contrast public limited ownership and private limited ownership.

8 Compare the options available to sole traders and plcs for raising finance.

9 In choosing a type of ownership, identify three considerations that need to be made.

10 Explain the principles behind not-for-profit organisations.

Points for discussion

Using a copy of the *Yellow Pages* or the Internet, find five examples of each of the four types of business ownership and not-for-profit organisations.

Exam practice

The music business is changing rapidly and as it does, businesses in the industry are having to adapt quickly or face closure. The Fopp chain of retail music stores began as a market stall in Glasgow and grew into a major unlimited-liability incorporated retail chain with 105 stores. Its main competitive advantage was in selling CDs at cheap prices. Many retailed for either £5 or £10; the store also sold books. With clear prices you knew just where you stood. However, when using price as a main source of competing one also has to consider the costs of production – CDs have to be purchased from the distributors and the cost of purchasing may not be wildly different for a firm like Fopp from that of a group like HMV. This immediately puts a squeeze on margins and to generate profits, Fopp would have had to rely on selling volume.

Nerina Pallot performs during an instore gig at Fopp

Fopp had been subject to a number of competitive pressures and as a relatively small company the pressures were felt more keenly. In July 2007, Fopp announced that it would be closing its 105 stores.

Source: Adapted from Biz/ed 'in the News' http://www.bized.co.uk/cgi-bin/chron/chron.pl?id=2880

1 Distinguish between the terms 'limited' and 'unlimited' liability. (4 marks)

2 Distinguish between the terms 'incorporated' and 'unincorporated' business. (4 marks)

3 Explain how the business ownership and organisation of Fopp may have changed during its growth and why. (10 marks)

4 The Fopp business began in 1981. Discuss the problems that its owner, Gordon Montgomery, might have faced in seeking to expand his business. (10 marks)

5 Is there such a thing as one 'right' form of business ownership? (12 marks)

Total: 40 marks

Chapter 8   Raising finance

Key terms

Capital expenditure Money spent on purchasing fixed assets (buildings, machinery, and so on).

Equity Money generated through the sale of shares; another term for share capital.

Overdraft An agreement with a bank to allow a business to exceed the balance in the account. Interest is charged on the amount overdrawn only.

Revenue expenditure Money used to help generate sales (stock purchases, wages, and so on).

Share capital Finance raised through the issue of shares; a part ownership in a company.

Venture capital Specialist finance providers who are prepared to invest in risky business ideas with little or no requirement for security. Venture capitalists will expect to have a share in the ownership of the business.

In this chapter you will learn about the different ways in which a business can raise finance to start up. All businesses will need money to start a business in the first place and when they have set up will also need to raise money to expand. You will learn that there are different means of doing so depending on the time period involved and the type of business organisation.

Sources of finance available to start businesses

A significant practical problem for a new business is raising sufficient initial finance to successfully launch the business. Even with a convincing business plan, the risk attached to new business start-ups make potential investors very wary of committing their funds. This can make it especially difficult for a new business to get the funds needed to get started.

A new business requires finance for two main purposes:

- Purchase of premises and equipment. Any business, whatever its size, will need to have some equipment and a base to begin trading. There has to be money available for acquiring these things.
- Working capital – the cash needed to keep the business working day to day, pay bills, and so on, in its early months of trading. Many new businesses underestimate the importance of having sufficient cash for working capital and quickly find themselves short of cash when revenues are slow to come in. In some cases, it might be many months from the original set-up to the time when cash in the form of revenue starts to come into the business from sales.

A new business might be an individual having an idea and wanting to set up as a sole trader. Equally, it might be an existing business looking to set up a new business idea. In this case the amount of finance needed may be much greater but the principle and the difficulties are similar.

We can broadly classify the way in which a business will use finance it manages to raise in two ways:

- **Capital expenditure** – money spent on purchasing fixed assets such as buildings, machinery and vehicles. Capital expenditure adds to the value of the company.
- **Revenue expenditure** – money used to help generate sales such as stock purchases, wages, and so on. Revenue expenditure does not add fixed value to the company.

We will look at the main ways in which a business can raise money and give an example in each case to highlight the advantages and disadvantages.

Ordinary share capital

Private and public limited companies are able to raise finance through the sale of shares in the business. A share is a legal right to part ownership of the business. For a private limited company, there might be only two shareholders, a husband and wife, for example, who hold the shares in the business, but it can be more. Note from Chapter 7 the limitations on the sale and transfer of shares in this form of business ownership.

Public limited companies can issue shares to the general public. This allows them to be able to raise large sums of money – **share capital**. If a member of the general public owns shares in a plc then they are able to trade them on the Stock Exchange, which provides the facility for the purchase and sale of shares. When share ownership is transferred through the Stock Exchange, the company whose shares are being traded are not directly affected – the role of the Stock Exchange is to bring together those who wish to sell shares and those who wish to buy shares.

Whilst raising finance in this way does give access to greater amounts of money, there are some drawbacks. The cost of planning and implementing a share issue can be expensive and time-consuming. Specialist organisations such as merchant banks might handle such a share issue on behalf of the company but using their specialist services does not come cheap. There are a number of legal requirements to be fulfilled and this can make such a method difficult.

> ### Guru's views
>
> 'A bank is a place that will lend you money if you can prove that you don't need it.'
>
> –*Bob Hope, American comedian*

For example…

Typical plc is planning on setting up a new business venture in a related but different market from its existing one. The business plan and market research have all been carried out, and the sum needed to finance the new venture is £150 million. The company has decided to raise the funds through a new share issue. It has offered existing ordinary shareholders the opportunity of buying additional shares and it will also be offering the shares on the Stock Exchange. They have hired an investment bank, to organise the share sale for them. In addition, the company's solicitors have been working hard drafting the agreements, contracts and attending to the regulations that govern new share issues. Typical had to produce a prospectus to outline details of the share offer to give information to prospective investors and have had to give notice in the national press. The whole project has taken two years to plan and has cost the firm over £1 million. However, Typical is confident that it will be able to sell all the shares it is planning to issue. Even if it does not, the advantage in hiring an investment company is that they will underwrite the issue. That means that they will agree to buy any unsold shares. This makes it pretty certain that Typical will be able to raise the money it needs on time to get the business started as planned.

Loan capital

Businesses, large and small, will borrow money from banks in order to finance a start-up. In many cases, the loan will form part of the finance raised, but not all of it. The reason for this will become clearer later. We will look at two main types of loan capital: bank loans and **overdrafts**.

Bank loans

A bank loan is a common form of start-up business finance. Most of the main high-street banks, such as HSBC, Lloyds TSB, NatWest, and The Royal Bank of Scotland, will have a team of people working specifically on supporting businesses and managing business accounts.

The size of a bank loan will be dependent on a variety of factors. The bank will want to consider the risk involved. This will involve the likelihood that the borrower will be able to pay it back, the type of business venture the loan is for, the quality of the planning that has gone into the application and the client's banking history.

A bank loan is usually repaid on a monthly basis over a number of years. It can be medium- or long-term and incurs interest charges. The interest payable can be either fixed or variable. With a variable rate loan, the interest rate may change in line with decisions made by the Monetary Policy Committee of the Bank of England. If they change the rate at which they are prepared to lend to the banking system, it affects the structure of interest rates throughout the system.

This might mean that if the Bank of England raises interest rates, a business's interest payments will also rise – usually about a month after the announcement by the Bank. If rates are rising steadily over a period of time, this can make a significant difference to the costs of a business. This is something it will have to consider when taking out the loan. In the same way, the business might find its costs falling if there is a period where the Bank is reducing interest rates.

For businesses who negotiate fixed interest loans, there is usually a period of time which the rate is fixed for. This helps businesses plan more effectively and they will have a greater degree of certainty about their on-going costs. However, it might also be that when the fixed rate ceases and reverts to a new interest rate, it could be quite a different rate from that which the business has been experiencing. This could be a major shock to the cash flow of the business.

Bank loans are relatively popular and easy to access. However, banks usually require some form of security on the loan. This is some asset which shows the bank that the borrower is serious about the loan and understands the consequences. Assets which might be put up as security against the loan might be a building or, in the case of a sole trader, a personal asset such as a house. If the business is unable to repay the loan, the bank will seize this asset to cover its loan. This means that sole traders, who have unlimited liability, do have to think very carefully before committing themselves. Now can you see why Bob Hope made the comment he did (see 'Guru's views' on page 69)?

Overdraft

An overdraft is effectively a short-term bank loan. A bank will allow a business to withdraw from its account more money than it has deposited. Overdrafts are often used to cover cash shortages, so a business may be overdrawn only for a matter of days. Interest is paid only when the account is overdrawn. An overdraft is a flexible way for businesses to borrow small sums of money as and when required. The bank will usually agree a limit for the overdraft above which the business should not go. Businesses that do breach this limit are not penalised immediately (they are likely to be charged a hefty fee and also higher interest on the excess), but over a period of time if the business cannot show that it can control its cash flow and keep within the overdraft, the bank may well withdraw the facility or, at the very least, want to have some serious discussions with the business.

Both loans and overdrafts tend to attract higher rates of interest. In many cases, small businesses might face very high rates of interest for loans and overdrafts. The more risky the business proposition is in the eyes of the bank, the higher the interest rate is likely to be.

For example...

Diane is thinking of starting a business providing manicures and nail art. She has found a small shop in a town centre that is available for rent and one which would provide the ideal accommodation for her business. She has prepared a business plan and has approached her bank's business manager for a loan of £40,000 to help pay for some of the fixtures and fittings she requires for the shop. She has also asked for an overdraft facility to be arranged for £5,000. The bank has looked closely at her business plan and especially her projected cash flow figures. They are a little concerned that she has been rather over-confident in her revenue projections, although they believe the basic business idea is sound. Diane knows that the normal interest rate on loans for things like cars is 7.5% and she has based her cost projections for the loan on this figure.

She had a bit of a shock when she had her meeting with the bank. They said that they would only be prepared to lend her £30,000 and that the interest rate would be 12.5%. In addition, they were only prepared to offer an overdraft of £2,500 and the interest rate on this would be 15%. That was very different from what she had expected. Diane had to go away and rethink and rework her projections as well as work out how to raise the additional £10,000 she needed. The bank had told her that if she could put up some form of security for at least £50,000 then they might be able to accommodate her original request. Having only just bought a ground floor flat, and getting sorted out in life, Diane was not keen to risk losing her home. Not only that, she was advised by the bank that she could also risk losing her business assets to the bank if she was not able to repay her debt. She had some hard thinking to do over the next few weeks!

Venture capital

Venture capitalists are specialist finance providers. If a business is unable to raise sufficient funds, **venture capital** is often used. Venture capitalists usually invest in smaller, risky ventures and do not ask for security. Rather, they will loan a business money in return for a share of business ownership or of any eventual profits.

Venture capital has become an increasingly important source of finance over the last 10 to 15 years. Venture capital can be defined as capital contributed at an early stage in the development of a new enterprise, which may have a significant chance of failure but also a significant chance of providing above-average returns and especially where the provider of the capital expects to have some influence over the direction of the enterprise. Venture capital can be a high-risk strategy.

With over 400 members, the British Venture Capital Association (BVCA) represents the majority of UK-based private **equity** and venture capital firms. Since 1983, additional private equity invested in UK industry has amounted to over £60 billion with a further £20 billion invested in the rest of Europe. Those funds have gone to assist 29,500 UK companies. In 2005 alone over £6.8 billion was invested in more than 1,300 companies in the UK.

Source of data: BVCA

Business angels

Business angels are informal investors who are wealthy and entrepreneurial individuals looking to invest in new and growing businesses in return for a share of the **equity**. They usually have considerable experience of running businesses that they can place at the disposal of the companies in which they invest. Business angels invest at all stages of business development, but predominantly in start-up and early-stage businesses. The majority of them tend to invest in businesses located within a reasonable distance from where they live.

The general profile of a business angel style of relationship is that:
- you are looking to raise between £10,000 and as much as £600,000
- you are prepared to give up some of the equity in your business and allow an investor to take a 'hands-on' role
- your business has the potential to grow sufficiently over the next few years to provide the business angel with a return on investment
- you can offer the business angel an 'exit' (for example, through a trade sale or the repurchase of their equity stake) at some future date.

Business angels, then, are small business-related investors who can have a major impact on the success of a start-up company.

For example...

Devon Adams had an idea for a new business. He had prepared a business plan and visited his bank to get a loan to help start-up. He was prepared to put in £40,000 of his own money but needed another £120,000. He thought he had everything planned out and had offered his three-bedroom house as security. He was therefore staggered when he read the bank's letter refusing to grant him a loan. The reason, they said, was that they felt the risk was too great that the business would not be a success. He tried three other banks but they all gave the same response.

His Business Link advisor explained that his idea was indeed risky but that he might try contacting the British Venture Capital Association. Through their website he identified a member and made an appointment to see them. The meeting was very productive. They pointed out that they were not a last resort of finance for a new business but simply a different way of securing finance. They identified a number of advantages. If an agreement was reached they did not always require security and therefore took on the same risk as he did.

They were in it for the long term – a bank's interest might be limited to the period of the loan. The return to the venture capitalist was not interest payments but the success and profitability of the business and therefore they had an interest in making sure Devon had all the support he needed. Devon did have to accept that the venture capitalist would expect to have some say in the running of the business. This did reduce the amount of independence he had but at the same time provided Devon with experience, skills and expertise that could be a real benefit to him in making sure the business was a success. Devon was also told that he would have to convince the venture capitalist that there would be some form of exit for them. This might be in the form of a future management buyout, the ability to sell shares to another investor or another business, or possibly a future stock market listing.

Devon was impressed with the quality of the advice he was given and the professionalism of the venture capitalist. This might be the ideal route for him!

Personal sources

Many people will start up a business using their own money as the source of finance or at least as part of the financing of the start-up. Such sources can range from the personal savings of an individual – it might be that someone has received a sum of money through an inheritance – through selling another business and even through redundancy.

Individuals might also ask friends and family if they wish to invest in the business. In such cases it is important that the individual makes it very clear to the investor what they are letting themselves in for, what the risks are and what the terms and conditions of the investment would be.

Guru's views

'Out of debt, out of danger.'

– *Proverb*

	Time frame	Possible usage
Short term	Under 1 year	Working capital
Medium term	1–5 years	Capital expenditure (vehicles, refurbishment, etc.)
Long term	Over 5 years	Major capital expenditure (buildings, land, etc.)

Figure 8.1 Borrowing money: time frames and possible uses

For example...

Mike had been working as a technical engineer for a motor manufacturer for 25 years. He had built up a considerable expertise in his field and was widely respected. However, when the business had to close due to the pressure of competition from China and Japan, Mike found himself redundant. Due to the number of years he had been with the company and the generous redundancy package they had offered, Mike had some time to be able to consider his next step. At 45, he knew that this was an important decision in his life. He looked around for jobs but many of them paid him less than he was earning before and did not fully make use of his skills. The more he looked, the more he felt that he could set himself up in business acting as a consultant for other engineering firms. He decided to use the £25,000 lump sum payment from his redundancy, which he had initially put into a savings account, as the main source of funds for the new venture. He was also able to get a further £15,000 backing from three contacts he had from his previous work. They knew how good Mike was at his job and believed he could make a success from his idea. The £40,000 was sufficient to be able to rent a small office and to equip himself to begin his new life.

Further material and resources relating to this section can be found at **www.collins.bized.co.uk**. Keep checking for updates.

Raising finance: Summary

- Start-up finance is required for two main reasons:
  - purchase of premises and equipment
  - for working capital.
- A start-up business can be a completely new business idea developed by an individual, a small group of individuals or an existing business moving into a new market.
- There are several main ways in which a start-up might raise finance – each has its own advantages and disadvantages and depends on the particular business context:
  - ordinary share capital
  - loan capital (loans and overdrafts)
  - venture capital
  - personal sources.

Summary questions

1 What are the two main reasons why a start-up business would require finance?

2 What is meant by the term 'working capital'? Give an example to illustrate your answer.

3 Distinguish between capital expenditure and revenue expenditure.

4 Explain why working capital is so important to a start-up business.

5 Identify two advantages and two disadvantages of the use of ordinary shares as a source of start-up finance.

6 Identify two advantages and two disadvantages of the use of using loans as a source of start-up finance.

7 Distinguish between a loan and an overdraft as a source of finance.

8 Identify two advantages and two disadvantages of the use of venture capital as a source of start-up finance.

9 Identify two advantages and two disadvantages of the use of personal sources of money as a source of start-up finance.

10 Why might a business prefer a bank overdraft to a bank loan?

Points for discussion

Investigate the activities of several venture capital companies. Using the Internet, research the following:

- what services are offered
- what recent loans have been made
- what criteria have to be met for a loan to be made.

The following websites might be useful:

- http://www.bvca.co.uk
- http://www.3i.com/

Up-to-date links to these websites can be found at **www.collins.bized.co.uk**.

Exam practice

If your house is anything like the author's, there are miles of cables and dozens of plugs seemingly dominating every room. The family collection of mobile phones brings with it different plugs, then take into consideration the MP3 players, cameras, games consoles, TVs, laptops, CD players, etc. Is the situation just going to get worse in the future? Possibly not; researchers at the Massachusetts Institute of Technology (MIT) have been conducting experiments that could see a number of smaller items being capable of being charged without the use of a plug.

The researchers have dubbed the development 'WiTricity'. The experiments centred around two copper coiled antennas – one connected to the electrical device and the other housed inside a wall. The antenna resonates and produces electromagnetic waves. These are picked up by the antenna connected to the device and charges it. It is suggested that the efficiency rate of electricity transfer is around 96%.

One UK-based business that is looking into this type of system suggests that wireless electricity transfer could be available in a little as two years. The researchers at MIT, however, having proved that energy transfer can work in this way, will now be turning their attention to looking at how their ideas can be turned into a commercial proposition – one that will make the antenna smaller, improve the efficiency and range of operation as well as making sure that the system is safe.

Source: adapted from Biz/ed in the News. http://www.bized.co.uk/cgi-bin/chron/chron.pl?id=2865

1 Using examples, explain the difference between 'revenue expenditure' and 'capital expenditure'. (6 marks)

2 Explain the importance of working capital to a start-up business. (8 marks)

3 Evaluate possible sources of finance for a business like the one in the UK that is thinking of setting up to develop and sell 'WiTricity'. (16 marks)

Total: 30 marks

Chapter 9   Locating the business

In this chapter you will learn about some of the factors that a business will have to take into account when considering setting up, in terms of where to locate the business. Such a decision will depend on a variety of factors and the nature of the business.

Factors influencing start-up location decisions

Many new businesses depend on the right location for their success. Manufacturing businesses need to balance accessibility to suppliers with closeness to their market. For retailers and other service-based businesses, location at the heart of their market is the key to maximising sales.

Most new small businesses do not have sufficient finance to fund an ideal location. Their priority is to keep start-up costs down and overheads low, but in so doing they may be stuck with a location that makes it very difficult for them to succeed.

The main factors affecting the decision of where to start up a business are listed below.

Technology

If a business is setting up and requires the use of technology, then it might look to secure premises near to suppliers of that technology or where that technology exists. For example, a business looking to set up as an Internet-based retailer will need to ensure that the area it locates has access to fast broadband technology with appropriate bandwidths being available. This is because it is likely to have to transmit a lot of data across its network and so needs the capacity to be able to do this.

Costs

Virtually every factor will have some form of influence on cost. In general, a business will look to set up where the cost of production is lowest, but for a start-up business this is not always possible. The costs of setting up might be influenced by the following:

- Site costs – different areas of the country have different land costs, office costs, rents, and so on. Some business parks may offer low-cost accommodation compared to sites in the city centre, and businesses will have to consider such factors.
- Availability of grants/subsidies – government and EU grants are available for businesses especially if they are setting up in areas that are designated for regeneration.
- Cost of loans associated with set-up – loan capital from banks, and so on, can be affected by the perceived risk of the venture.

Key terms

External economies of scale The advantages of large-scale production that result in lower cost per unit produced (average cost) due to the concentration of industry in a particular area.

Infrastructure The structural elements that make up a country which provide the ability for businesses and people to be able to carry out their normal lives. It includes such things as bridges, road networks, other transport networks and communications systems.

- Cost of utilities – gas, water, electricity.
- Cost of hiring fixed salaried staff – some areas may have a supply of skilled labour that might help to reduce costs. In addition, the business will have to consider other hiring costs such as National Insurance contributions and pension schemes.
- Cost/availability of technology – locating in an area that has a reputation for technology might reduce costs – 'Silicon Valley' along the M4 corridor outside London, for example.
- Nearness to market.
- Cost of raw materials.
- Cost of sourcing supplies.
- Transportation costs.
- Tax advantages.
- Bulk increasing – where the finished product is more expensive to transport than the raw materials/components used in production. It might then be cheaper to locate nearer to the market.
- Bulk reducing – where the finished product is cheaper to transport than the raw materials/components used in production. It might be cheaper to locate near the supply of raw materials/components.
- Nearness to a supply of skilled/unskilled labour.

Infrastructure

Infrastructure refers to the ports, motorways, bridges, communications systems, airports, railway networks, energy systems, sewage and waste disposal systems, and so on, that exist within a country or a region. These might all be important considerations for a new business. Once again, it will depend on the type of business it is as to what is really important. For example, a business that starts up a new chemical plant may look for a location that has sufficient energy supplies to be able to cope with its needs as well as facilities for dealing with waste products; an individual looking to set themselves up as a courier service might need to look for a location that is conveniently placed for the motorway network; a business setting up in import/export is likely to look at port facilities and the ease of access to and from these ports.

The market

Any business will need to consider its market – who it actually sells products or services to. However, some businesses need to consider this more than others. Retail businesses, for example, must think carefully about their location. The ideal location for a new shop selling greetings cards, for example, would be in a city centre location where there are lots of people passing by the shop – being tucked away in a side street may not be the most appropriate location, although it might be cheaper! The development of Internet-based businesses can mean that some businesses can have more flexibility in where they locate, but at the same time meet their customers' needs effectively. In such a case, infrastructure factors may be seen as being more important.

For other firms, the nearness to market might be linked to cost factors. A bulk increasing firm, where the finished product is more bulky than the raw materials, might need to be located as near to the market as possible to avoid excessive transport costs.

Qualitative factors

These are factors that cannot be quantified but which may have a significant impact on the location decision. They will include such things as the following.

WORKING ENVIRONMENT

Working in a busy city centre, for example, might be more stressful than in a more rural environment. This factor might also include how light and spacious the premises are, how modern or old they are, the ease and cost of heating, and so on.

EASE OF ACCESS FOR EMPLOYEES

If the business is contemplating employing staff then it has to consider how easy it will be for staff to get to work. Will they need a car, are there good rail and/or public transport links to the business?

HEALTH AND SAFETY CONSIDERATIONS

This might relate to the actual premises themselves or to the area in which the business is located. Some land, for example, might be reclaimed or former landfill, some might have had toxic waste on it, some buildings might not be suitable for the sort of health and safety regulations that certain businesses have to adhere to – filtration systems, appropriate air flow, amount of light entering the building, and other such features.

OPPORTUNITIES FOR EXPANSION

A business will need to consider what might happen in the future and some might need to think about the possibilities for future expansion. Is there sufficient land to be able to expand in the future, what are the local planning regulations like, does the building itself provide the flexibility for future development? All these things might need to be considered by a start-up business; it may not be immediately relevant but a forward-thinking business will have to consider future development constraints.

COMPETITION

A start-up will need to consider the competition and where they are based in relation to the potential location identified. If there are lots of other businesses offering the same type of product in the same area then it may not be the best place to locate. On the other hand, it does provide the means by which consumers can identify those who are competitive quickly and easily, so there may be good reasons to locate near to rivals.

EXTERNAL ECONOMIES OF SCALE

External economies of scale are the advantages that can be gained as a result of the concentration of industry in a particular area. Such advantages might reduce costs for a new business. Such advantages include things like a supply of skilled labour, the availability of training courses at local colleges, the availability of specialist services or facilities (such as a dedicated fire service at a location where chemical firms are concentrated), the availability of specialist suppliers or component manufacturers, and so on.

Further material and resources relating to this section can be found at **www.collins.bized.co.uk**. Keep checking for updates.

Locating the business: Summary

- The decision about where to locate a business depends on a number of factors.
- The type of business will determine the relative importance of the factors affecting location.
- Key factors will affect the initial start-up costs but qualitative factors also need to be considered.
- The ideal location may not always be available to a new business start-up.

Summary questions

1   Explain why a potential manufacturing business might have different location requirements from a retail business.

2   What is the most important (ideal) reason that a start-up business would look for in choosing a location for its operations?

3   Identify two variable and two fixed costs that are included in the list of possible location costs.

4   Explain why bulk reducing and bulk increasing businesses might lead to different location factors being important.

5   Identify two different types of business for which high quality infrastructure would be an important factor in location decisions. Specify the type of infrastructure in each case.

6   Explain why it is important for a business such as an estate agent to be as near to its market as possible.

7   What are qualitative factors influencing location decisions for a start-up business?

8   Why might ease of access be an important consideration in the location decision of a start-up manufacturing business?

9   Explain why locating close to competition could be (a) a good thing; (b) a bad thing.

10   Using examples, explain the meaning of the term 'external economies of scale'.

Points for discussion

Identify five different types of small business in your area. Produce a map showing where they are located. Prepare a short presentation to your class explaining possible factors that might have influenced their location and some advantages and disadvantages of their location.

Exam practice

After a number of years working in a betting shop, Angela decided she was going to try and set up on her own as an independent bookmaker. She knew that the competition from the big players in the market would be fierce, but she had many years of experience and plenty of contacts in the industry. She also believed she knew what customers wanted. It was not just the chance to bet on a variety of sports and other activities, but it was the atmosphere and the ambience inside the shop itself.

She had developed a business plan outlining the basic idea, but to cement the cost and revenue projections she needed to find a suitable location for her business. She drew up a shortlist of ideal locations and then set about searching to try and match as many of these ideals against the available premises that she could find.

1 Identify and explain some of the key factors that Angela would have to look for in locating her bookmaking business. (8 marks)

2 What qualitative factors do you think Angela should consider in her decision of where to locate? (8 marks)

3 Angela has the choice of two possible locations. One is in the town centre and the other is on the main shopping street serving a large housing estate. Using your knowledge of business, prepare a report advising Angela on the factors that might influence her decision and recommend which she should choose. Explain your recommendation. (14 marks)

Total: 30 marks

Chapter 10   Employing people

In this chapter you will learn about the different classifications of people employed in a business. You will learn about the role of consultants and advisors for small businesses.

Types of employees used in small businesses

Most businesses will employ some people in its operations. However, there is a wide range of different types of employment that a business might use when hiring staff. For a small new business, it is important to be aware of the different types of employment and also the advantages and disadvantages associated with each.

Temporary employment

Temporary employment tends to be where an employee is hired on a non-fixed term basis. The pay for a temporary worker is usually based on an hourly or daily rate. Workers employed on a temporary basis are able to leave or be released without notice. Such a form of employment might be used by a business in a variety of circumstances and provides a flexible means of employing individuals. There are many agencies that will supply temporary workers. Their job is to put businesses that require temporary workers in touch with those who have the skills necessary for that job.

Temporary workers may be used for the following:

- To cover for staff who are on maternity leave or for other unforeseen or unexpected absences. A temporary worker might be recruited if a business knows someone is going to be absent for a time – if they have to go into hospital, for example.
- For seasonal reasons – there are many examples where workers are employed on a temporary basis during busy times of the year, especially with picking fruit, in the run-up to Christmas, during holiday periods, and so on.
- A business might want to employ someone on a temporary basis to assess their performance and suitability for a permanent post.
- The business might have specific projects that it is working on where it requires particular skills which can be supplied by a temporary worker.

Permanent employment

Staff employed on a permanent basis must have a contract of employment. Full-time workers are generally considered to be such if they work over 30 hours per week. This is the definition given by the Office for National Statistics (ONS) Labour Force Survey. Full-time workers have a number of rights as laid down by European Union (EU) law. This includes the right to paid holidays, a limit in the number of hours worked, rights over dismissal and redundancy, maternity rights and rights over discipline and grievance.

Given the range of employment laws for full-time workers, businesses need to make sure that they have appropriate policies in place to take account of the responsibilities they have to their workers. This includes organising income tax and National Insurance payments, pension rights and other possible benefits such as health insurance, life assurance, employee discounts, and so on. This is also likely to involve the business in higher costs and the possibility that it might lose flexibility. However, to balance this out, securing a worker on a permanent basis means that the skills and abilities that the worker brings to the business can be captured. It can bring certainty and continuity to the business and can aid planning.

It is important to realise that employing a permanent worker will cost more than the wage the business agrees to pay. This is because the employer will have to make contributions to National Insurance payments and possibly pension contributions if such a scheme operates in the business. For a small or new business, this, along with the associated administration, can be a financial burden and must be considered in advance.

Permanent employment can be split into two groups: full-time and part-time workers.

PART-TIME WORKERS

Part-time workers are generally those who are employed to work fewer than 30 hours per week. Many part-time workers enjoy this sort of employment contract because it provides them with a great deal of flexibility. Equally, for the business it can be very useful in providing flexibility and cover across different time periods.

Part-time staff have the same statutory rights as full-time staff, but it is likely that many of the benefits available to full-time staff will be provided to part-time staff on a pro-rata basis. If, for example, a business offers 25 days paid annual leave to its full-time staff where full time is defined as working 40 hours a week, then a part-time employee working 30 hours per week would be entitled to three-quarters of the paid leave of full-time staff – 18.75 days. This might be rounded up to 19 days or rounded down to 18.5 days.

FULL-TIME WORKERS

Full-time workers are generally those regarded as working in excess of 30 hours per week. However, it is important to remember that there are no hard and fast rules about what constitutes a full-time rather than a part-time worker. Full-time workers have all the rights and responsibilities outlined above.

Using consultants and advisors

Many businesses will make use of advisors and consultants both at start-up and during the lifetime of the business. Both of these can bring in expertise to the business, as well as an objective eye which can cast a different perspective on things and provide the business with a different viewpoint. It is often difficult to see problems and issues when you are heavily involved in an activity. Consultants and advisors are able to be impartial and objective in their advice. There is a considerable degree of overlap between the two, but in general, there are particular characteristics associated with each.

Consultants

A consultant is generally involved with larger firms. They are employed to both identify and diagnose potential problems or issues as well as provide solutions. When recruiting a consultant, there are a number of steps that a business might take to ensure they get the maximum benefit from the consultant.

- Make sure the objectives are clear – what do you want the consultant to do, what do you want the outcome to be, what timescale and budget do you want to allocate to the project?
- Clarify the relationship with the consultant – a one-off job focusing on a specific problem or a more regular 'drop-in' session to deal with a range of issues?
- Identify and get quotes from a small number of consultants who are qualified to carry out the work you want done – if the problem is perceived to be a human relations issue, then get an HR specialist, if it is operations management, an OM specialist, and so on.
- Consultants will normally expect to have to provide details about themselves and their experience, their understanding of the problems that the business might have and their experience in providing effective solutions. The consultant will also have to outline their fees, expenses and the arrangements for payment, time-frames involved, and so on.
- When a consultant is chosen, the business would normally meet with them and provide a full brief about the work they are to carry out. At this stage it is important that the relationship between the business and the consultant is clear – if the two do not get on, then problems will arise and the objectives may not be achieved. A contract is likely to be drawn up detailing the work and the agreement between the two parties. This can be expensive and so might only be appropriate for larger businesses.
- Once the consultancy begins, the business should make sure that it keeps regular contact with the consultant with meetings and feedback on progress. It may be necessary to provide the consultant with a space to work in and this has to be taken into consideration.
- Once the consultant's recommendations have been made, it is often seen as important to work with the consultant in implementing them to get the most out of the consultancy. At most stages in the process it is important to involve all the staff in what is happening to avoid the problems that can arise when change has to be implemented. The more the staff know and understand about what is happening, the less fear and uncertainty there is in the business.

Advisors

Advisors are normally employed in smaller businesses and at start-up. There are many independent professional business advisors who might be in a position to offer advice on a range of issues. These might include:

- cash flow problems
- advertising and promotion
- customer service
- debt management
- equality and diversity
- business strategy and planning
- marketing
- dealing with the media
- project management
- quality control
- sales
- training
- product development.

Most of the features outlined for working with a consultant apply to a business advisor. It is equally important to make sure that the advisor has competence and understanding in the area where the business needs help. For a small business it might be a legal requirement to use a business advisor. In this case the advisor might be an accountant who is required to audit the company accounts. Other advisors might work on particular issues or act as mentors guiding the business through start-up or an aspect of growth and development. They might act as a sounding board on which to bounce ideas and get feedback.

The government have set up a body called Business Link which provides online help for businesses. Allied to this are a series of local offices where advisors can be contacted and their expertise used. The Business Link portal is extensive, and contains a wide range of information and advice along with case studies to help people who are either planning on starting a business, in the process of setting up a business or who have just started and are in their first years of trading.

Further material and resources relating to this section can be found at **www.collins.bized.co.uk**. Keep checking for updates.

Employing people: Summary

- Businesses employ people on different terms depending on their requirements.
- Temporary workers can be used to cover a range of employment needs.
- Permanent workers require a contract of employment and have specific rights and responsibilities.
- Part-time workers are usually regarded as those working fewer than 30 hours per week.
- Full-time workers are usually regarded as those working in excess of 30 hours per week.
- Business advisors and consultants can be hired to bring particular expertise into a business.

Summary questions

1 Identify three possible reasons why a business might seek to hire temporary workers.

2 Explain one advantage and one disadvantage of hiring temporary workers.

3 Identify three responsibilities that a business has when hiring permanent staff.

4 Why is the cost of hiring a worker not simply the wages or salary that the job commands?

5 What is the difference between a part-time and a full-time worker?

6 What is meant by the term 'pro-rata benefits'?

7 Identify two advantages and two disadvantages of employing permanent staff.

8 What is the main difference between a consultant and an advisor?

9 Identify four things that a business should consider in hiring a consultant.

10 Identify five possible areas in which a business advisor might be used in a small business or a business start-up.

Points for discussion

Go to the Business Link website (http://www.businesslink.gov.uk/). Find the case study that is entitled 'Here's how Business Link helped my business' (http://www.businesslink.gov.uk/Promotions_files/businesslinkgovuk_businesslinkhelp.pdf). Next find the case study entitled 'Here's how my business overcame the pitfalls of employing family members'. Explain the role of a business advisor in such a situation.

Up-to-date links to these websites can be found at **www.collins.bized.co.uk**.

Exam practice

On October 1st 2006 a new law came into force – the Employment Equality (AGE) Regulations (2006) Act. In the same way that legislation attempted to outlaw discrimination on the grounds of race, sex, disability, sexual orientation and religion, now employers will not be able to specify a preference for 'young enthusiastic individual' or 'would suit retired person' in job adverts.

If an individual believes that they have been discriminated against on the grounds of age they can take their case to an employment tribunal. If an organisation is found guilty of breaching the new laws they can face unlimited fines. The new laws are meant to be of benefit not only to the elderly but also to the young who are sometimes discriminated against and given low paid jobs on account of their 'lack of experience'.

The laws will affect different businesses in different ways. Some will find that their costs will rise as they have to adjust to new pension rules and the possibility that they could be offering fringe benefits like private health insurance or life assurance to staff that choose to work beyond 60. Others might find themselves in difficult situations in recruitment. There would be nothing stopping a firm from having to employ a 60 year old to work in a young persons fashion store or equally a very young person from working in an organisation that deals with the elderly. A business associated with the young, such as advertising, public relations (PR) and IT, might now find that it has to think more carefully about the way it words its adverts and the grounds on which it recruits and deals with its employees.

Source: Adapted from Biz/ed In the News: http://www.bized.co.uk/cgi-bin/chron/chron.pl?id=2686

At the beginning of October 2006, the Work and Families Act came into force in the UK. Part of the Act is designed to help female employees in the workforce who wish to take a career break to start a family. There are pressures on women who want to do this because employers are concerned about filling their posts either on a temporary or permanent basis. For the women employees, many wish to continue their career after they have started a family and would like to return to their old jobs after having a baby.

There is a clear tension between the two – it is easy to see the perspective of the female employee. Why should they be penalised because of a biological function that is different from men? At the same time, businesses have to run and when key employees are absent for several months this can cause significant disruption, especially for small businesses.

The new Act changes the rights of women who want to have a family. Paid maternity leave is to be extended from the current six months to nine months. In addition, women will be entitled to paid maternity leave at the start of a period of employment whereas at the moment women have to have worked for at least nine months to be eligible. The new Act means that maternity leave will be a right when they start working although they still have to work nine months to qualify for Statutory Maternity Pay.

There is provision in the new Act for small businesses to get some help in coping with the administrative costs of dealing with a member of staff on maternity leave. The government picks up the cost of Statutory Maternity Pay but many small businesses are expecting that the new legislation will make their job of competing more difficult.

Source: adapted from Biz/ed In the News: http://www.bized.co.uk/cgi-bin/chron/chron.pl?id=2677

1 Using examples, explain the difference between temporary and permanent employment. (6 marks)

2 Explain two reasons why a small business might hire a mixture of part-time and full-time workers. (6 marks)

3 What is meant by the term 'statutory responsibilities' in relation to employment? (4 marks)

4 How do the two articles demonstrate some of the problems facing small businesses in employing people? (10 marks)

5 Evaluate the contribution an advisor or a consultant might make to a business seeking help in interpreting and adhering to new employment laws, such as those highlighted in the articles. (14 marks)

Total: 40 marks

UNIT 1
SECTION B

Planning and Financing a Business: Financial Planning

Section overview

This section details the main financial concepts and models used in decision-making that are key to the planning process for small businesses. It is important in any new business venture that the owner knows what their product costs, how much to sell it for and how many they need to sell to make a profit. Alongside this, new businesses need to plan and manage their finance to improve their chances of survival and performance by reducing the risks inherent in any business start-up.

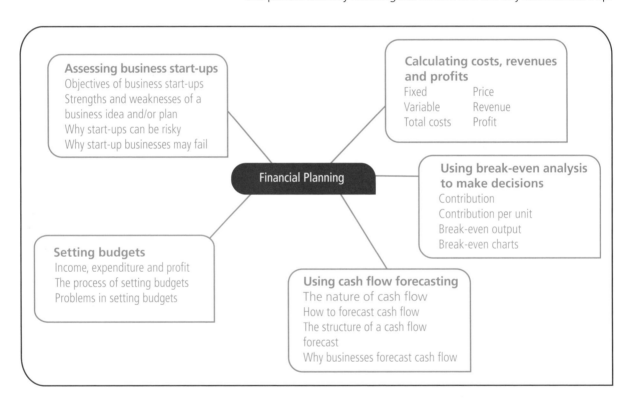

Assessing business start-ups
Objectives of business start-ups
Strengths and weaknesses of a business idea and/or plan
Why start-ups can be risky
Why start-up businesses may fail

Calculating costs, revenues and profits
Fixed   Price
Variable   Revenue
Total costs   Profit

Financial Planning

Using break-even analysis to make decisions
Contribution
Contribution per unit
Break-even output
Break-even charts

Setting budgets
Income, expenditure and profit
The process of setting budgets
Problems in setting budgets

Using cash flow forecasting
The nature of cash flow
How to forecast cash flow
The structure of a cash flow forecast
Why businesses forecast cash flow

Key concept

Financial planning

It doesn't matter how good or innovative an entrepreneur's business proposal is, or how well they have conducted any research and planned their business idea, if they don't have the finances in place to make their idea a success. For example, you could plan a really good marketing campaign for a new business or product launch but if you don't have the money to make the idea a reality then the plan itself will never happen.

Starting a business means not only raising finance to get the business off the ground in the first place, but also having funding in place to ensure that the business survives long enough to start generating clients, sales and profits. This involves making sure that:

- Costs are covered until revenue starts to be earned.
- Products are sold at a price sufficient to attract customers and make an acceptable profit.
- Finances are monitored and used wisely so the business does not overspend and run out of cash.
- The entrepreneur has planned the use of their finances to make sure sufficient funding is available to meet the business's objectives.

New businesses can fail for many reasons but with good financial planning several causes of business failure – such as running out of cash – should hopefully be avoided.

Activity

Ideally in pairs or small groups, consider starting a simple form of business like a takeaway sandwich shop, for example. Assume the shop will have one full-time employee (40 hours per week) and two part – time employees (15 hours per week each).

- First make a list of all the items you would need to buy before you could open the shop and research how much these items cost. (Assume the shop is to be rented.)
- Next make a list of all the costs the shop would face each month and research how much these items would cost.
- Now imagine it would take at least four months before the sandwich shop became well known enough to start making any profits. Estimate the minimum amount money you think you would need to raise to start this business.
- Finally compare your answers.

Discuss how easy it was to plan the finances for this business; were there large variations in people's estimates and why you think financial planning is an important aspect of success?

Chapter 11 Calculating costs, revenues and profits

The aim of this chapter is to provide an understanding of the different types of costs a business faces in its day to day activities, and how these costs and the price the business charges affect the business's ability to generate **revenue** and make **profits**.

Key terms

Business activity Looking at the level of goods and services the business is providing. Businesses can operate through a range of activities from supplying no goods at all up to their maximum capacity.

Fixed costs Costs that do not change with the level of business activity. A fixed cost would still exist, and must be paid, even if the business produced and sold nothing.

Variable costs Costs that change in direct relation to the level of business activity undertaken. The more the business does, the higher the variable costs become.

Loss A loss is made when the business's total costs are greater than the amount of revenue it made from selling its products.

Profit A profit will be made by a business if it is able to earn more revenue from selling its goods or services than the total costs generated at that level of business activity.

Revenue The amount of income a business makes from selling its goods or services to customers. This is sometimes called sales revenue or total revenue as well.

Total costs All the costs (fixed and variable) the business has to meet added together at any particular level of activity.

Fixed, variable and total costs

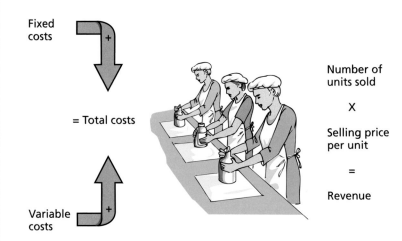

Figure 11.1 Business costs and revenue

If a business does not know how much it costs to produce a product, how does it know how much to sell it for? For any business organisation that has the aim of making a profit, it must be able to calculate how much any level of **business activity** would cost and what revenue it could potentially make from sales. If the business cannot sell its goods or services for an amount greater than the total cost of providing them, then the business will incur a **loss**.

It is vitally important that any business is able to control and manage its costs to try and prevent a loss from happening. To do this effectively, many businesses divide their costs into different categories: **fixed costs** and **variable costs**.

As fixed and variable costs behave differently in relation to the amount of output production or activity the business is engaged in, dividing costs into separate types enables managers to measure the impact of the different costs more easily.

This in turn makes it simpler to assess what level of profit, if any, is likely to be made at different levels of activity.

Fixed costs

Costs that do not vary in the short term in relation to the level of output or business activity are called fixed costs. This does not mean that these costs never change, but rather that if the business increases or decreases its volume of production or sales, these costs will not be affected.

Consider a small business like a sandwich shop. An example of a fixed cost might be the rent or mortgage payments on the business's premises. The same amount of rent or mortgage payment has to be paid each month, no matter how many customers the shop has or how many sandwiches are made. In the short term the business faces a fixed cost – a cost that has to be paid no matter what the level of business activity is.

Figure 11.1 shows that it does not matter if the business produces and sells 400 sandwiches, 200 or none at all; it must pay the same £300 at each and every level of output.

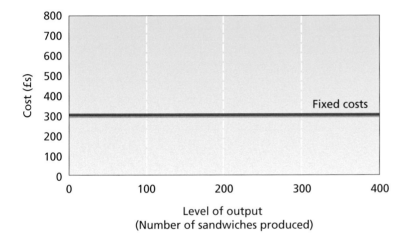

Figure 11.2   Fixed costs diagram

Other fixed costs that a business might have to pay could include business rates, insurance costs or the monthly salaries of managers. It is important to note that fixed costs only remain fixed for the short-term; in the longer term a business may well need to expand its premises or managers will want a pay rise which would lead to increases in the level of fixed costs.

Variable costs

Variable costs are the total opposite of fixed costs. This type of cost does vary in direct relation to the level of output or activity. So if, in our example, the sandwich shop started to produce and sell more sandwiches every day, these costs would increase as the number of sandwiches made increased.

Variable costs include items such as raw materials or the wages paid to staff. So in the production of a sandwich, the variable costs would include the cost of the ingredients for that sandwich and the employee's time taken to make it. Obviously, the more sandwiches that are made, the more ingredients and labour time that are required in order to make them, and thus the variable costs rise as the output of sandwiches also rises.

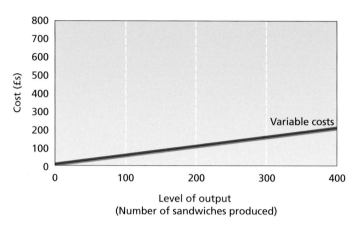

Figure 11.3 Variable costs diagram

The variable costs diagram (see Figure 11.3) demonstrates that if the sandwich shop produced and sold no sandwiches at all, the corresponding variable costs are also nothing, but as the output of sandwiches increases, so do the variable costs. The diagram shows that each additional sandwich made has a variable cost of 50p (40p for ingredients and 10p for labour), so the variable cost for 200 sandwiches = £100, for example.

The total variable costs at any level of output can be found using the following formula.

Total variable costs $=$ $\dfrac{\text{Variable costs per unit}}{\times}$ The number of units produced.

So in the sandwich shop, for example, the total variable costs for making 400 sandwiches would be:

50p × 400 = £200.

Total costs

The **total costs** for any level of output can be calculated by simply adding the variable costs at that level of output to the fixed costs.

Total costs = Total variable costs + Total fixed costs

The total cost of production is an important piece of information. Owners and managers need to know the value of total costs at different levels of output so they can take decisions on how many to produce and the resources required to do so.

Figure 11.4 demonstrates how total costs for the sandwich shop are found by adding fixed and variable costs together.

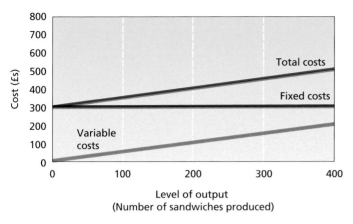

Figure 11.4 Total costs diagram

They can also use the total costs figure to calculate the total costs per unit, in other words, how much each individual product cost to make. This is done using the formula:

$$\text{Total costs per unit} = \frac{\text{Total costs}}{\text{Number of units produced}}$$

Activity

Activon manufacture quality recordable DVDs from their factory in Bristol that they then sell to computer retail outlets. The table below lays out their monthly production and cost schedule for different levels of output.

Monthly production of DVDs	Monthly fixed costs	Monthly variable costs	Total costs
0	£20,000	0	£20,000
20,000	£20,000	£1,600	
40,000	£20,000	£3,200	
60,000	£20,000	£4,800	
80,000	£20,000	£6,400	
100,000	£20,000		
120,000			
140,000			
160,000	£20,000	£12,800	£32,800
180,000			
200,000	£20,000	£16,000	£36,000

1　Complete the costs data for Activon's monthly production schedule.
2　Calculate the variable costs of producing one DVD.
3　Calculate the total costs per unit (total costs of manufacturing *one* DVD) at 20,000, 140,000 and 200,000 units of output.

Price, total revenue and profit

Price

The selling price of the product is an important issue in any business. Businesses will examine many factors when deciding what price to sell their products for. (Pricing strategies and tactics are covered in detail in Chapter 32 or by visiting the bized website).

In normal circumstances if a business reduces its selling price it can expect demand to increase and to sell more of its product. Similarly, a rise in price can be expected to reduce sales. The size of the rise or fall in sales will depend upon many factors, influencing the demand for that product including:

- the loyalty of customers
- competitors' prices
- the quality of the product in question.

The big issue that businesses face, however, is how the price they choose to sell their product at affects their total revenue.

Total revenue

A business's total revenue is its income or earnings over a period of time. You may also come across the terms sales revenue or turnover which have the same meaning. Businesses calculate their revenue from the sales of their products using the formula:

Total (sales) revenue = selling price per unit* × quantity sold

*Where a business sells a range of different products at varying prices, average selling price per unit is used.

Total revenue therefore also rises in relation to the number of products made and sold. Figure 11.5 demonstrates this for the sandwich shop. Assuming an average selling price per sandwich of £2.00, it can be seen that should the shop make and sell zero amount of sandwiches, then correspondingly the total revenue gained is also zero and that this rises proportionally as each additional sandwich is sold.

Thus for the sandwich shop:

- At 100 sandwiches total revenue (TR) would equal £200.
- At 200 sandwiches total revenue (TR) would equal £400.
- At 400 sandwiches total revenue (TR) would equal £800.

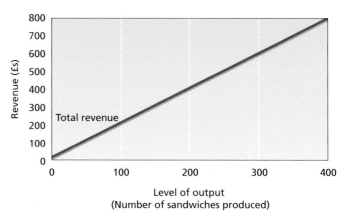

Figure 11.5 Total revenue diagram

Average selling price per sandwich	Number of sandwiches sold per day	Total revenue earned per day
£1.00	650	£650
£2.00	400	£800
£3.00	190	£570

Figure 11.6 Impact of price changes on revenue

Continuing the example of the sandwich shop, Figure 11.6 shows how the selling price of a product can affect the quantity of sandwiches sold and the knock-on effect to the total revenue earned.

If the average price of a sandwich increases from £2.00 to £3.00, the level of sales decreases significantly. This shows that demand for sandwiches is sensitive to price, perhaps because the sandwich shop faces a lot of competition from alternative outlets or products. In this case, increasing the price does not lead to the company making more revenue overall as it loses too many customers in the process.

Similarly if the shop reduces its price from £2.00 for each sandwich to only £1.00, the fall in price does not attract enough new customers into the shop to compensate for the amount of revenue lost from each sale at the lower price. This may be because either the real or perceived quality of the sandwiches provided also decreases.

Some businesses attempt to maximise their revenue by setting a low price and then trying to sell as much as possible. This makes sense in markets where consumers are trying to find the lowest possible price and are not loyal to any particular products or brands. For example, the market for basic foodstuffs is very price-competitive and many supermarkets have adopted a price-cutting approach in recent years to increase their sales and revenues.

On the other hand, some businesses sell products which are unique, currently in fashion or regarded as highly desirable. Some designer clothes producers such as Dior or D&G (right) can charge high prices and generate higher revenues than they might achieve with lower prices. Even though by charging very high prices some sales may be lost, not enough customers are deterred from buying overall as they seek the exclusivity, prestige or status of owning such products.

However, even if a business makes higher total revenue, this does not mean that increased profits are bound to follow.

Profit

Profit is one of the most important business objectives. It is the profit motive that drives many people towards starting their own business in the first place.

Business owners and managers want to know how successful they have been or how successful their business idea might be. The degree of profit (or loss) made is one of the main ways in which this can be determined. Profit is measured by:

Profit = total revenue – total costs

So the key to making a profit is how much the business manages to produce (and at what cost), compared to how much the business manages to sell (and at what price).

COMPARING THE FIGURES

By being able to classify their costs into fixed, variable and total costs, and measure these against the revenues generated at different levels of selling price and quantity, businesses are able to discover some very valuable information. For example:

- How much should they charge?
- How many do they have to sell to cover their costs and avoid losing money?
- How many do they need to sell to make an acceptable level of profit?
- At the forecast level of potential demand, is this sufficient to enable a new business to make a profit at all?
- If things change, how much can they afford to drop the selling price by, or let costs rise, before they start losing money?

Consider the information so far on our sandwich shop as shown in Figure 11.7.

Number of sandwiches sold per day	Average selling price per sandwich	Total revenue earned per day	Total costs (fixed+variable)	Profit/ (Loss)
650	£1.00	£650	£300 + (650 x 50p) = £625	£25
400	£2.00	£800	£300 + (400 x 50p) = £500	£300
190	£3.00	£570	£300 + (190 x 50p) = £395	£175

Figure 11.7   Comparison of costs, revenue and profit

Producing a table or chart such as Figure 11.7 allows owners or managers to see the relationship between costs, revenues and profits at different levels of output and selling price, and so make informed decisions on how to run their business, or even in some cases, if it was worth setting one up in the first place.

For example, using Figure 11.7, the owner of our sandwich shop would be able to see that even though the total revenue gained from selling sandwiches at £1.00 is greater than that generated when the sandwiches are sold for £3.00 overall, at a selling price of £1.00 each the business would only make £25. Thus they would be able to know even before they started that they potentially need to sell their sandwiches at around the £2.00 level and can now assess their probable level of custom at this price.

Further material and resources relating to this section can be found at **www.collins.bized.co.uk**. Keep checking for updates.

Calculating costs, revenues and profits: Summary

- Fixed costs are those such as rent, which remain unchanged when the level of business activity (output) alters. Variable costs, by contrast, alter in direct relation to changes in the level of activity.
- Revenue is determined by the price charged by the business for its product and the level of sales generated at that price.
- Profits are calculated by deducting total costs (fixed costs + variable costs) from the total revenue.

Summary questions

1   Explain the difference between a fixed and a variable cost with the aid of examples.

2   Calculate the total cost of manufacturing 70,000 units of output when fixed costs = £43,000 and variable costs = £2 per unit for labour and £1.25 per unit for materials.

3   Calculate the cost per unit when:
   - fixed costs are £3,000
   - variable costs per unit are £10
   - current output and sales equal 500 units.

4   Calculate total revenue when 2,500 units are sold for £6 each. Show the formula and your workings.

5   Explain why raising the selling price of a product does not always mean more revenue will be made overall.

6   (a) A business sells 20,000 MP3 players per year at an average selling price of £45. Its variable costs are £25 per unit and its annual fixed costs are £24,000. What is the total cost of producing the 20,000 units and what profit would it make if it sold all the units produced?

   (b) Calculate the effect on profits if the business raised its selling price to £50 per MP3, but the amount made and sold fell to 16,000 units.

Points for discussion

- Discuss the reasons why raising prices might not result in higher revenue or profits for a business.
- Examine if owners/managers have more control over fixed costs or variable costs.

Exam practice

Mary and Jack Tweddle own and run the Cotswold Hotel in Bourton-on-the-Water, Gloucestershire. They rely on the summer tourist trade to generate most of their profit. Their fixed costs are £12,000 per month. Their variable costs amount to £10 per customer per night. They currently charge £40 per customer per night. They can accommodate 20 customers at a time, totalling a maximum of 600 customers during a month. From June through to August, the hotel is completely full. On average, the hotel is only half full for the rest of the year. Mary and Jack are keen to find ways to increase the profitability of their business and are considering a range of options:

- increasing their charge to £55 per customer per night
- seeking to reduce the variable cost per customer per night to £8
- building additional rooms to increase the hotel's capacity to 800 customers per month
- raising the hotel's profile with an extensive marketing campaign.

Bourton-on-the-Water

1 Define the terms:
   - fixed costs
   - variable costs. (5 marks)

2 Calculate the current level of yearly profit made by the Cotswold Hotel. (10 marks)

3 Analyse the possible effect a change in price to £55 per customer per night might have on the level of total revenue generated by the Cotswold Hotel. (10 marks)

4 Evaluate the possible courses of action available to Mary and Jack for increasing the profitability of their business. (15 marks)

Total: 40 marks

Chapter 12   Using break-even analysis to make decisions

This chapter will help you to apply methods used by a business to analyse the impact of different costs and prices on profit. You will examine how costs, revenue and profit information is then used to inform business decisions, such as whether or not to launch a new business or product.

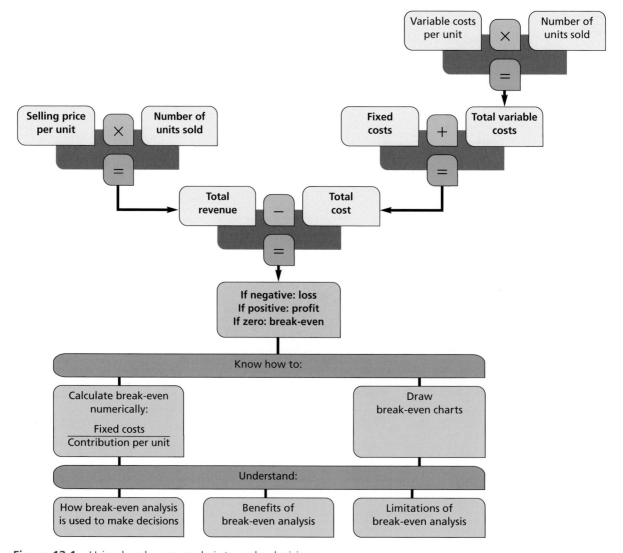

Figure 12.1   Using break-even analysis to make decisions

Why worry about profit?

Why should individuals and companies commit time and resources to a business? For many, it is because businesses have the potential to make a profit. After all, it is the profit motive that drives many entrepreneurs towards starting out in business in the first place.

However, before starting out in a new venture and risking their time and resources, it is useful to be able to assess what the likelihood of that business making a profit will be and by how much.

Many business ideas could be profitable but not at a high enough return to actually make them worthwhile. In the worst case scenario, a new business idea or product may sound good, but in reality it will never make any profit at all if not enough customers can be found to buy the product at a high enough price to cover all the costs.

Why use break-even?

A business can only make a profit when its total revenue is greater than its total costs. If costs are greater than revenue then the business will make a loss. **Break-even** is the point at which total revenue and total costs are equal. At this point the business will not make any losses *or* any profits.

Imagine you are an entrepreneur setting up a business or launching a product. It is important you know how much your product costs to manufacture or provide. This information will help you to decide:

- what your selling price needs to be
- how many products you have to sell to cover costs and avoid making a loss
- the minimum amount that need to be sold to make an acceptable profit
- if things change, by how much prices could drop, or costs increase, before the product became unprofitable.

Break-even analysis is a simple and valuable forecasting technique. Businesses can use break-even analysis to:

- estimate the levels of output they need to produce and sell to make an acceptable return on the time, money and resources they have risked
- assess the impact of price changes on profit and sales
- assess how changes in costs impact on profits
- determine their **margin of safety** and what changes in levels of demand they can survive.

Contribution and contribution per unit

Contribution is an important part of break-even analysis and is used in calculating how many items need to be sold to cover all the costs (fixed and variable). First a product needs to be sold for more than its own variable cost of production.

Consider if a sandwich's variable costs were:

- 10p – labour for making it
- 40p – cost of ingredients.

You wouldn't sell that sandwich for less than 50p or you would be losing money on every individual sandwich sold. So you need to set a selling price higher than the total variable cost of making it.

Key terms

Break-even The point at which a business sells the exact number of products so that its total revenue equals its total costs. In other words, at break-even the business makes no profit but also incurs no loss.

Contribution The amount of money a single item makes over and above its own variable cost of production. It represents the income generated by each sale that first goes towards paying the business's fixed costs and then towards making a profit.

Margin of safety The amount by which the current amount made and sold by the business (the SOP – see below) exceeds the amount necessary to break even.

Selected operating point (SOP) The actual level of output and sales at which the business is currently operating or, in the case of a new business, the forecast level of output and sales they anticipate.

The key terms **revenue**, **fixed costs**, **variable costs** and **total costs** are covered in Chapter 11.

However, even if you sold each sandwich at £2, you are still not yet making a profit. This is because although the selling price is enough to cover the variable costs, the business still has its fixed costs to pay. So, the excess money made from the sale of each sandwich (£1.50) is now used to pay the fixed costs.

This is called contribution or contribution per unit. Each individual sandwich the shop sells contributes £1.50 towards paying the fixed costs. So:

Contribution = the selling price per unit minus the variable cost per unit

£1.50 = £2.00 – 50p

If, in our example, the sandwich shop had fixed costs such as rent, insurance and some utility bills totalling £300 per day, then the shop needs to sell 200 sandwiches each day generating a £1.50 contribution before all the fixed costs were paid, that is, 200 × £1.50 = £300.

So, if the business sold fewer than 200 sandwiches per day, insufficient contributions would be made, the fixed costs would never be covered and the business would make a loss.

If, however, the business sells more than 200 sandwiches, each additional sandwich still makes a contribution of £1.50 but there are no more fixed costs to pay. This excess now becomes profit.

So, if the business made and sold 300 sandwiches per day, then 200 would be contributing to paying the fixed costs and 100 would be generating profit.

Calculating break-even

A business will find it useful to estimate the number of units it needs to sell to break even. This can be done numerically or by plotting a break-even chart.

To calculate the break-even point numerically, a business needs to know:

- the level of fixed costs
- the selling price per unit
- the variable costs per unit
- contribution per unit = selling price (per unit) minus variable cost (per unit).

For the sandwich shop discussed earlier, the contribution per sandwich is: £2.00 – £0.50 = £1.50.

It is now only a short step to calculating the break-even point. If fixed costs are £300 per day, how many sandwiches – generating £1.50 contribution each – must be sold to cover these fixed costs? The answer can be calculated using the formula:

$$\frac{\text{Fixed costs}}{\text{Contribution per unit}} = \text{Break-even output}$$

In this example, the answer is:

$$\frac{£300 \text{ fixed costs per day}}{£1.50 \text{ contribution per sandwich}} = 200 \text{ sandwiches per day need to be sold to break-even}$$

The 200th sandwich to be sold will generate the final £1.50 contribution needed to cover all the fixed costs. The 201st sandwich sold will generate a £1.50 contribution and this time it will be profit. Here we have calculated the break-even output per day; however, this could be done weekly, monthly or yearly as well.

There is a simple relationship between break-even and profit.

- If total output and sales are greater than break-even, then revenue is greater than cost: the business makes a profit.
- If total output and sales are equal to break-even, then revenue equals total costs: the business breaks even.
- If total output and sales are less than break-even, then revenue is less than total cost: the business makes a loss.

Activity

Read the case study below.

1   Calculate how many times George needs an average ride to run per year to break even.

2   Using the answer from question 1, calculate how many rides this is per day to break even, if the Whirlwind can operate for 250 days of the year.

3   Do you think George should go ahead with his idea?

For example...

Fares Fair

As a child, George Mooney was always fascinated by fairgrounds, rides and rollercoasters. His ambition in life was to become the managing director of one of the UK's major theme parks. However, when one day he happened to spot in his local paper an advert for the sale of a second-hand Whirlwind ride, he couldn't resist and immediately started to talk to his wife about quitting his job and remortgaging their house to buy the equipment.

His wife, Amy, suggested taking a more sensible and studied approach, and advised George to back his idea up with some facts and figures before she would even consider the idea. So, having spoken to the seller, George came back two days later with the following information:

- Fixed costs for running the ride each year included insurance, health and safety checks, maintenance, storage over winter and the cost of the equipment itself, which totalled £320,000 per year.
- The variable costs for running each ride included labour and power, and equalled £8 per ride.

Each ride can take a maximum of 25 passengers, but an average ride runs with 16 passengers on board each paying £1.50.

Break-even charts

The break-even point can also be represented by a chart. A break-even chart (see Figure 12.2) is a visual representation of a business's revenues and costs at different levels of output. This is useful, as diagrammatic representation makes it easier for non-mathematical people to understand what is going on. It enables the business to identify:

* how many units need to be sold to break even
* what level of profit or loss will be made at any output
* what effect a change in costs or selling price might have on the break-even point and the level of profit or loss.

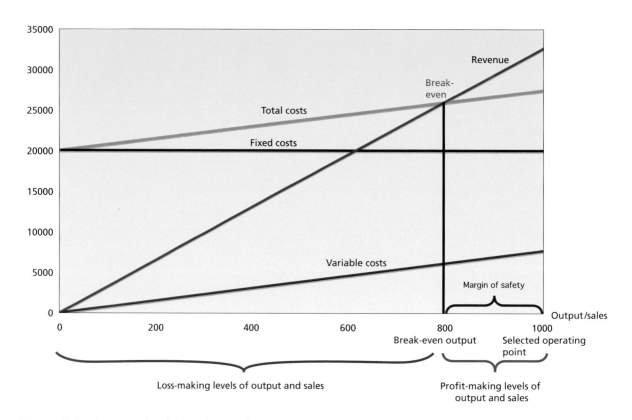

Figure 12.2   An example of a break-even chart

Constructing break-even charts

A break-even chart is compiled from plotting costs and revenue information on a graph. The horizontal axis shows the output scale (the number of units per period of time). The vertical axis displays the possible values of costs and revenues in pounds (£s). For the sandwich shop, the scales need to show an output of up to 400 sandwiches per day. If every sandwich were sold, revenue would be £800, and so this is the maximum value that needs to go on the vertical axis.

There are four stages to constructing a break-even chart, as shown in Figure 12.3.

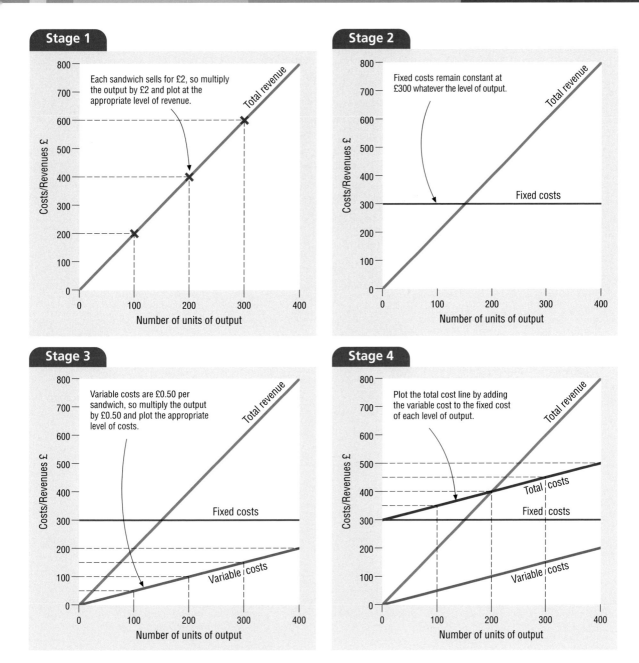

Figure 12.3 Constructing a break-even chart

STAGE 1: PLOT TOTAL REVENUE LINE

If no sandwiches are produced or sold, there will be £0 revenue, and so the total revenue line begins at the origin. Each sandwich is sold for £2. Multiplying any level of output by £2 will give the appropriate level of revenue on the vertical axis. The easiest way to plot the total revenue line is to calculate revenue for the maximum level of output, so for 400 sandwiches, the total revenue would be £800; plot this point and then draw the line from this point back to zero at the origin.

STAGE 2: PLOT FIXED COSTS LINE

Even if there is no output, fixed costs must be paid. As an increase in output has no effect on fixed costs, the fixed costs line will be horizontal. For the sandwich shop, the fixed costs are at £300 per day.

STAGE 3: PLOT VARIABLE COSTS LINE

If no sandwiches are produced, variable costs will be £0, and so this line begins at the origin. Each sandwich produced costs an additional £0.50. Multiplying any level of output by £0.50 will give the appropriate level of cost on the vertical axis. As with total revenue, the easiest way to plot the variable cost line is to calculate the variable costs for the maximum level of output, so for 400 sandwiches, variable costs would equal £200; plot this point and draw the line from this point back to zero at the origin.

STAGE 4: PLOT TOTAL COSTS LINE

To plot the total costs line, add the variable costs at each level of output to the fixed costs line. The total costs line will begin at £300 for zero output, rising to £500 at an output of 400 sandwiches as £300 fixed costs + £200 variable costs.

Analysing break-even charts

Once the break-even chart has been drawn, it can be interpreted to show the following (see Figure 12.4):

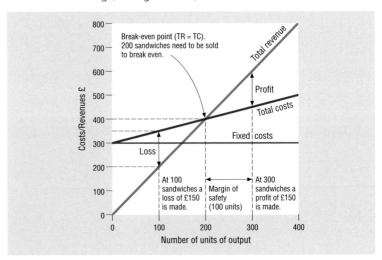

Figure 12.4   Analysing a break-even chart

BREAK-EVEN LEVEL OF OUTPUT

The point at which the total costs line crosses the total revenue line is the break-even point. Reading down from this point it can be seen that, to break even, 200 sandwiches must be sold each day. Or alternatively, £400 must be taken in revenue.

LEVEL OF PROFIT OR LOSS AT EACH LEVEL OF OUTPUT

At levels of output below 200, total costs are greater than total revenue, so the business is making a loss. The level of loss is represented by the vertical distance between the two lines. The amount of loss can be read off the vertical scale. The level of profit can be found at levels of output above 200 sandwiches per day.

MARGIN OF SAFETY

The number of units currently being produced above the break-even level is called the margin of safety. For example, if the sandwich shop were to produce 300 sandwiches per day, the margin of safety would be:

Current output	–	Break-even output	=	Margin of safety
300 units	–	200 units	=	100 units

The higher the margin of safety is, the more profitable the business will be and the less likely that a fall in demand will lead to making a loss.

BREAK-EVEN ANALYSIS: PROS AND CONS

Benefits	Limitations
• Break-even charts provide a clear, visual demonstration of some vital financial information. They show at a glance break-even output and levels of profit or loss. This knowledge allows a business to predict its likely profit from a certain output and to plan how many units it needs to make and sell in order to reach a profit target.	• To keep break-even analysis simple, a number of assumptions are made that are unrealistic. For example, it is assumed that: – all the output is also sold. Break-even analysis cannot cope with items that are made but not sold. – the total revenue and variable costs lines are linear (that is, they increase at a constant rate). In reality, both selling price and the variable costs per unit will change as output increases. Economies of scale, such as bulk-buying discounts, are likely to mean that variable costs per unit will fall at higher levels of output.
• Break-even analysis is not a complex, expensive or time-consuming process, and so could prove particularly useful to those starting up or running a small business. • Break-even charts can be used to show the likely financial impact of changes in costs or selling price (see Figures 12.5 and 12.6). • Break-even can be used to model whether or not a new business or product would be worthwhile before committing any resources into the venture. • Break-even charts can be used to model 'what if' situations before any real resources are committed to a business, project or product.	• The analysis is intended to help predict the effects of changes, such as selling price. It says nothing about the effect that such a change may have on customer demand and hence on actual level of profit or loss. This will depend on the price elasticity of demand, which is not considered in the break-even chart. • The constantly changing nature of costs and prices in the real world means that a break-even chart is unlikely to remain valid for very long. • Finally, it is worth noting that any information gained from break-even charts or calculations is only as accurate as the information it was based upon. Collecting accurate information is expensive and time-consuming, and often difficult for inexperienced entrepreneurs.

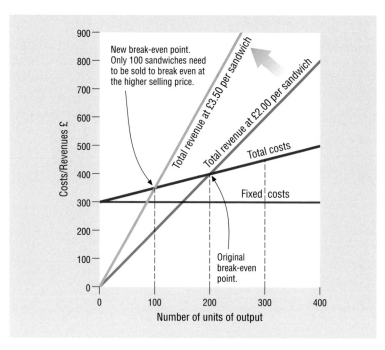

Figure 12.5   Impact of raising the price on break-even output

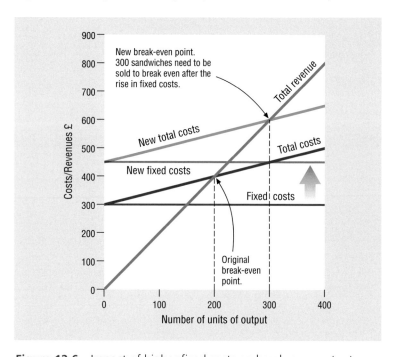

Figure 12.6   Impact of higher fixed costs on break-even output

The effects of changing costs and revenues on break-even output

Few business situations remain constant. Changes in the economy, markets, tastes and fashions affect costs and revenues. The break-even point will change if a business's costs or prices change. Figure 12.6 summarises the effect that some price and cost changes will have on a company's break-even position.

Change	Impact on break-even
Fixed or variable costs rise	Total costs also rise, so more units have to be sold to cover costs. The number of units needed to break even increases (see Figure 12.6).
Fixed or variable costs fall	Total costs also fall, so fewer units have to be sold to cover costs. The number of units needed to break even falls.
Sales price rises	Each unit produces more revenue, so costs are covered more quickly. The break-even number of units decreases (see Figure 12.5).
Sales price falls	Each unit sold earns less revenue, so it takes more units to cover costs. The break-even output point increases.

Figure 12.7 Factors affecting break-even

THE EFFECT OF RAISING SELLING PRICE

Figure 12.5 shows the impact of a higher price. The total revenue line becomes steeper as revenue rises at each level of output. An increase in the price per sandwich to £3.50 would cause the break-even output to fall to just 100 sandwiches.

THE EFFECT OF CHANGING COSTS

Figure 12.6 shows the impact on the business of higher fixed costs – such as an increase in rent. The fixed cost line shifts upwards from £300 to £450, and so the total cost line shifts upwards by the same amount. The impact is to raise the break-even level of output from 200 to 300 sandwiches per day.

Further material and resources relating to this section can be found at **www.collins.bized.co.uk**. Keep checking for updates.

Using break-even analysis to make decisions: Summary

- Break-even is an easy way to measure the impact on profits (or losses) as levels of business activity change.

- If you are considering starting a business or launching a new product, break-even analysis allows you to estimate the level of sales needed to make a profit.

- Break-even can be used to examine 'what if' situations – it allows a business to analyse the effect on break-even and profits if certain situations occur.

- Increases in costs make it more difficult to break even; falling costs mean fewer sales are needed to break even.

- Break-even is a quick, easy and simple decision-making technique. However, costs rise and fall frequently, so charts or calculations need to be regularly updated.

Summary questions

1 Explain the term 'break-even'. Why is the determination of the break-even point important?

2 Explain two ways in which break-even charts can help managers to make decisions.

3 If a business sells its products for £12 each and its variable costs are £3.20 for materials and components, plus £1.35 for labour and £0.86 for packaging, calculate:

- the contribution per unit
- the total contribution if 750 units are made and sold.

4 Clearly showing the contribution per unit in your workings, calculate the break-even level of output when:

- fixed costs are £490
- variable costs are £0.40 per unit
- selling price is £1.80.

5 Using the following information, draw a fully labelled break-even chart for Nautilus Enterprises – a new business set up to manufacture children's bath toys:

- fixed costs are £70,000 per year.
- variable costs are £1.50 per unit.
- selling price is £5.00.
- nautilus have a maximum capacity of 30,000 units of output but currently make and sell 25,000 units per year.

6 Explain what is meant by the term 'margin of safety'.

7 Calculate the profit or loss made by a business when:

- fixed costs are £10,000
- variable costs per unit are £100
- selling price per unit is £200
- the selected operating point (see Key terms on page 103) is 150 units.

Points for discussion

- Why might calculating break-even be more useful than drawing break-even charts? Conversely, when might drawing a chart prove helpful?
- Is break-even analysis equally useful to all types of business?

Exam practice

New Delhi Palace

The New Delhi Palace is a business idea by Sital and Roshni Mistry, to be set up in Reedham Ferry, Norfolk, following a holiday they had on the Norfolk Broads. They decided that the takeaway shops in the local area were poor in comparison to versions they had grown up with in their home town of Stalybridge. Although their idea is for an establishment slightly more expensive than many competitors, Sital and Roshni hope to generate a reputation for quality and generous portions to help them to establish a successful business. Figure 12.8 has data on the New Delhi Palace's predicted average costs and prices for its first financial year.

Annual sales /output of takeaway meals	Total variable costs (at £4.00 per meal)	Annual fixed costs (£s)	Total costs (£s)	Total revenue (selling price of £7.00 per meal
0	0	90,000		0
16,000	64,000			112,000
32,000	128,000			
48,000				
64,000				
80,000				

Figure 12.8 New Delhi Palace's costs and prices

1   Complete Figure 12.8 by calculating total costs and sales revenue at each level of production. (5 marks)

2   Using your findings, construct a break-even chart and calculate the profit or loss made at 30,000, 50,000 and 70,000 units of output. (10 marks)

3   Sital and Roshni expect their variable costs to rise by 10% per year and their rent to go up by £1,000 per month. Sital is unconcerned; she says a simple solution is to just raise prices by 10%. Analyse their new break-even point for their second year of trading should these changes take place, and advise Sital and Roshni of any other factors they should take into account while considering a price rise. (10 marks)

4   To what extent is break-even analysis a useful decision-making tool for the prospective owners of the New Delhi Palace? (15 marks)

Total: 40 marks

Chapter 13   Using cash flow forecasting

By the end of this chapter you should be able to complete and amend a **cash flow forecast** and understand the significance of cash flow forecasting to businesses.

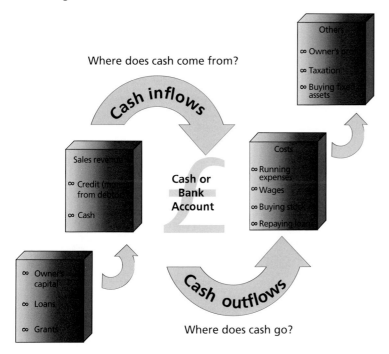

Where does cash come from?

Cash inflows

Sales revenue
∞ Credit (money from debtors)
∞ Cash

Cash or Bank Account
£

Costs
∞ Running expenses
∞ Wages
∞ Buying stock
∞ Repaying loans

Others
∞ Owner's profit
∞ Taxation
∞ Buying fixed assets

∞ Owner's capital
∞ Loans
∞ Grants

Cash outflows

Where does cash go?

Figure 13.1   An example of a cash flow chart for a new business start-up

The nature of cash flow

Every business needs direction; even a brand new start-up needs to consider what its objective is. Once an aim, objective or target of a business has been determined and agreed, a business needs to ensure that it actually has the finances in place to execute its plans. All new businesses face large **cash outflows** before any **cash inflows** can be forthcoming from customers.

Failure to have cash available to pay for costs, suppliers, contractors, licences or advertising/marketing of their product, may easily cause loss of customers and put any business behind competitors, or at worst lead to an inability to continue trading at all.

Consider any new business venture; it faces an immediate problem in that it has to have the finance to pay for all the items needed to start the business, such as:

- premises
- vehicles
- machinery
- stock
- equipment
- furniture.

This is not to mention stationery like letterheads and business cards, and any initial marketing costs to promote the new firm. Alongside this it is unlikely that huge amounts of custom will be generated immediately, so the business also needs sufficient cash to ensure it can keep running and pay all the bills, wages and expenses until the business has started to attract enough clients. It could take weeks, months or even longer for funds to start flowing in regularly from customers, depending on the start-up in question. Figure 13.2 demonstrates an example of this for a new business. Even though the business starts with £20,000, this is insufficient and it is not until at least month seven that the business starts to generate a positive cash flow.

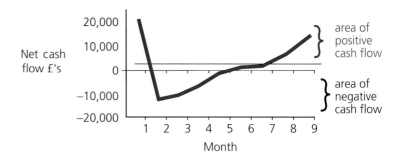

Figure 13.2   Example cash flow chart for a new business

Cash thus passes in and out of a business in a continuous cycle; if the supply of cash into a business is less than the amount flowing out, the business's bank account will become under pressure and eventually become overdrawn. If this situation persists or deepens the business can run out of cash as the banks refuse to lend any more and the business becomes bankrupt or liquidates as it cannot meet its financial commitments.

Preparing cash flow forecasts

Drawing up a cash flow forecast helps a business to maintain its position so that sufficient funds are available to finance its day to day operations. More small businesses in the UK fail as a result of poor cash flow than any other reason including lack of profits.

Preparing cash flow forecasts is a form of proactive management. All businesses are aware that the delay between the outlay on materials, stock and wages and the receipt of sales income can cause difficulties. So, rather than waiting for cash flow problems to arise and then trying desperately to solve them (reactive management), a skilled manager can anticipate the need to maintain a good cash position and actively plan in advance using cash flow forecasting.

A cash flow forecast is a detailed examination of a company's expected future cash inflows and outflows over a future period (such as one year ahead). They are usually calculated on a monthly basis and, by keeping a running total of the business's anticipated bank balance, managers can highlight times when cash difficulties may arise.

How to forecast cash flow

Banks encourage their business account holders to draw up cash flow forecasts. Banks produce a range of information and material to help their customers with forecasting; some, for example, provide templates that allow firms to compile cash flow forecasts online.

Cash flow forecasts are constructed using historical information (past company data or researched data for new ventures) and the forecasts contained in their budgets or business plan. The cash flow forecast is then constructed based on the predicted information of how, when and in what form money will come into and out of the business. This is done by estimating the amount and timing of cash inflows and cash outflows.

For new business start-ups most of their information must come from research, such as using market research to establish the likely number of customers and how much they would be willing to pay to forecast sales. Research can also be done in advance into the cost of premises, assets and likely running expenses. And potential suppliers of stock can be contacted to provide brochures, price lists or quotes. Researching a business carefully can massively reduce the risk of inaccurate cash flow forecasting.

CASH INFLOWS

Cash inflows are the monies received by a business. Cash inflows can come from a variety of sources, such as the examples below.

Sales revenue

These are payments from customers for goods bought. An important distinction is cash and credit sales. For cash sales, payment is received at once and hence the company can use it immediately. Whereas, with credit sales the customer is given a set amount of time to pay – the **credit term**. This could be anything from 30 days to deals like 'buy now, pay in 12 months' used by furniture retailers, for example, Northern Upholstery or Courts. In these instances, although the company has sold the goods, they need to be aware that they will not receive the cash for their own use perhaps for a considerable period of time and so the cash flow forecast needs to reflect when the company will actually receive the money as an inflow into its account.

> ## Guru's views
>
> 'Happiness is a positive cash flow'
>
> *–Fred Adler,* venture capitalist

Loans

Although they have to be paid back, the initial taking of a loan results in a cash inflow into the businesses account. Businesses can predict when they need to take loans, how much and what the purpose of the loan is, and so again this can be built into any forecast cash flow. However, in many cases the loan will have been taken for a specific purpose, such as purchasing new machinery, and so this money may become a cash outflow fairly rapidly as well.

Grants

Inflows of cash can be received from local, national or European government. These are often awarded to help companies create jobs or promote environmental protection. Unlike loans, grants do not have to be repaid at a later date.

Capital

This is money paid into a business by its owners, for example, the money initially invested by the owners to start the business or the funds received by a limited company when it sells more shares.

CASH OUTFLOWS

This is money paid out by the business, that is, leaving the business's account, and can occur due to payments for:

- purchases of stock or raw materials
- heat, light and water bills
- rent and rates on premises
- distribution expenses
- research and development
- telephone bills
- wages and salaries
- buying fixed assets
- interest on loans
- administration expenses
- advertising
- taxation.

Many of the above costs, such as wages and salaries, heat, light and water, are regular payments and as such are easy to forecast even if they are expected to increase; for example, employees may expect a wage rise in June. One-off or large payments such as purchasing a fixed asset should have been well planned and researched before happening and again can be easily included.

Other categories of expenditure exist, such as cleaning, stationery or repair costs. The actual categories for each business will vary depending on the type of industry. Also consider that businesses will often purchase items on credit terms as well as sell them.

The structure of a cash flow forecast

Because cash is so important to the survival of a business, businesses must constantly and carefully monitor their cash flow position. To do this, many businesses produce cash flow forecasts for the months or year ahead. They are made up of three sections:

- cash inflows
- cash outflows
- the running balance.

The cash flow forecast displays a calculation of the net effect of the cash inflows and outflows on the business's bank balance usually on a monthly basis, that is, it shows how much money the company anticipates it has (or has not) got in its bank account at the end of each month.

For example...

A cash flow forecast like Figure 13.3 would be compiled by taking information and forecasts from budgets and by using historical data. The calculations are made in the lines numbered 1–5. Lines 1 and 2 are simply the respective totals of the cash inflows and outflows. Lines 3–5 are the calculation of the running balance: the business's closing bank balance at the end of each month is forecast by adding the net cash flow (which might be a negative number, of course) to its starting bank balance.

Figure 13.3 demonstrates, for example, that in May the business's cash inflows (£136,700) were greatly exceeded by the cash outflows (£161,704), mainly due to the purchase of a new fixed asset, such as new machinery. This causes the business to actually go overdrawn by £1,980, and the business would have needed to arrange this in advance with their bank or one of their payments may not have been honoured. It can be seen, though, that by the end of the following month a positive cash flow is re-established.

	April	May	June	July
Cash inflows				
Sales	126,300	126,700	127,300	117,200
Loans	30,000	nil	nil	nil
Capital introduced	nil	10,000	nil	nil
(1) Total cash inflow	156,300	136,700	127,300	117,200
Cash outflows				
Purchases	20,136	20,144	20,176	20,700
Wages and salaries	42,080	42,720	43,680	43,520
Heat and light	800	800	800	800
Water	500	500	500	500
Telephone	1,120	1,120	1,120	1,120
Advertising	28,700	10,000	3,000	3,000
Administration expenses	19,240	19,870	20,100	20,000
Distribution expenses	6,400	6,550	6,720	6,680
Purchase of fixed asset	nil	60,000	nil	16,200
(2) Total cash outflow	118,976	161,704	96,096	112,520
Running balance				
(3) Opening bank balance	(14,300)	23,024	(1,980)	29,224
(4) Net cash flow (1 – 2)	37,324	(25,004)	31,204	4,680
(5) Closing bank balance (3 + 4)	23,024	(1,980)	29,224	33,904

Figure 13.3 An example of a cash flow forecast

Activity

Complete this cash flow forecast, by calculating the missing figures indicated by question marks. You can find a copy to download or print at **www.collins.bized.co.uk**

	May	June	July
Cash inflows			
Start-up capital	5,000		
Sales revenue		1,000	?
Total receipts	?	1,000	**1,200**
Cash outflows			
Payments			
Insurance	100	100	100
Stock purchases	0	650	780
Miscellaneous	50	50	50
Rent	1,000	1,000	?
Electricity			100
Telephone			75
Marketing costs		20	24
Shop fittings	?		
Water			150
Total payments	**3,150**	?	**2,279**
Total receipts	5,000	1,000	1,200
Total payments	3,150	?	2,279
Net cash flow	?	?	?
Opening balance		1,850	1,030
Closing balance	**1,850**	?	?

Why businesses forecast cash flow

A major benefit of cash flow forecasting is that it enables managers to anticipate periods when cash flows may be high or low, thereby indicating periods when cash might be available for spending and investment or, more importantly, periods when cash is likely to be tight.

Cash flow forecasting is not just a defensive activity. It brings a number of positive benefits for a business, including:

- ensuring liquid assets are available to meet payments and maintain working capital
- identifying periods of cash shortfall so remedial action like overdrafts can be arranged
- identifying periods of cash surplus so high-cost items can be purchased at little risk
- highlighting periods when large expenditure is not possible, so businesses may have to consider spreading payments for fixed assets over monthly instalments
- limiting the amount of borrowing and minimising interest payments, as a cash flow forecast should enable a business to borrow only the sum that it needs

- highlighting cash surpluses that can be more profitably invested elsewhere
- supporting applications to lenders by demonstrating that funds would be available to meet interest and capital repayments on loans.

By completing a cash flow forecast using a spreadsheet, the business can also model 'what if' situations. For example, the spreadsheet can automatically calculate the cash implications of offering consumers longer credit periods.

LIMITATIONS OF CASH FLOW FORECASTING

- Cash flow forecasts are only estimates. Sales may be lower than forecast or costs may be higher. A wide range of factors will affect the accuracy of the forecast.
- It is impossible to forecast every item of expenditure 100% accurately.
- The cash flow statement may reveal a cash problem, but may give little indication of the underlying causes (although, at least, management will be aware of the problem).
- Management must use cash flow forecasts as a working tool. Once a cash flow forecast has been prepared, it should be monitored regularly and updated to take into account changing economic circumstances, such as rising interest rates.

Further material and resources relating to this section can be found at **www.collins.bized.co.uk**. Keep checking for updates.

Using cash-flow forecasting: Summary

- Cash flow forecasts provide a prediction of how much money the company will have available for use at the end and start of each month.
- Cash flow forecasts provide the method whereby managers can anticipate periods of cash shortages or surpluses.
- There is often a considerable delay between companies having to expend money (cash outflows) and receiving payments from customers (cash inflows).
- By being proactive a business can aim to avoid problems associated with a poor cash flow position and consequently benefit from increased business stability and performance.

Summary questions

1 Why do banks encourage businesses to use cash flow forecasts?
2 Give two examples of cash inflows and two examples of cash outflows.
3 Explain the difference between cash and credit payments.
4 What is the significance of the running balance at the end of each month on a cash flow forecast?
5 State and explain two reasons why it is important for a new business start-up to draw up a cash flow forecast.
6 How might an overdraft facility be used by a business to aid short-term cash flow problems?

Points for discussion

- Why do the majority of new small business start-ups that fail do so for reasons of lack of cash?
- Discuss what options a company has to try and reduce any problems caused by time lags in the cash flow process.

Exam practice

Dylan O'Connell runs his own fresh fish wholesale business out of a small factory outlet in Tinsley, Sheffield. Business has been expanding lately and he has decided to approach the bank for a loan to help him purchase a new delivery vehicle. However, whilst Dylan's small business manager at the bank is satisfied that Dylan's company has been successful so far (making satisfactory profits for the last two years), he is not convinced the business can afford to spend the £22,000 Dylan wants on a new van with integral refrigerated units. Dylan is determined this is what his business needs to be able to provide a reliable and high-quality service to his restaurant clients.

Although the emphasis (and recent expansion) of Dylan's business is based on the quality of fish that he provides, he is convinced that by being able to deliver the product in perfect condition he will attract bigger clients and contracts, such as pub chains like Wetherspoons. Dylan has decided to produce a cash flow forecast for the next six months to help persuade the bank to finance his plan. The following estimates are available:

	Sales	Purchases
January	6,000	1,600
February	6,000	1,600
March	9,000	2,400
April	9,000	2,400
May	9,000	2,400
June	10,000	2,800

- Dylan intends to purchase the van in March by borrowing £22,000. He intends for the funds to enter his account during the first week of March and purchase the van in the following week.
- In order to help boost his sales immediately, Dylan is going to start advertising in a national trade magazine. This will cost him £700 in January and February, but will decrease to £500 per month for the rest of the period. He will also start to offer 30-day credit terms. He anticipates that from March, £2,000 of sales each month will be on credit.
- Dylan has a business mortgage on his outlet which costs £1,450 per month, but he is able to off-set part of this by renting out the flat above to students for £580 per month.
- Currently Dylan pays himself £1,750 per month and has one employee at a further £800 per month, though this is predicted to rise in March to £1,600 as Dylan expects he will need an extra employee to meet the increased demand.
- Utility costs to cover all the business bills are currently £850 per month and Dylan expects these to stay the same for the period.
- Running costs for the new van are difficult to estimate, but Dylan reckons that insurance and fuel will only amount to £360 per month.
- Other business costs, miscellaneous and sundry items usually come to about £150 each month.
- However, the bank would only lend him the £22,000 he needs over a period of three years and with interest at 8%, this would mean monthly repayments of £780 per month.
- Dylan currently has an opening bank balance of £640.

1   Compile the finished cash flow from the information given. (5 marks)

2   Analyse the strengths and weaknesses of Dylan's predicted cash flow position. (10 marks)

3   'Cash flows are impossible to predict accurately so they are of limited use to most businesses.' Discuss to what extent you think this statement is true.   (15 marks)

Total: 30 marks

Chapter 14   Setting budgets

After completing this chapter you should understand why businesses set **budgets**, and how to complete and amend budget information. You should also be aware of the difficulties or problems businesses face when undertaking a budgetary process

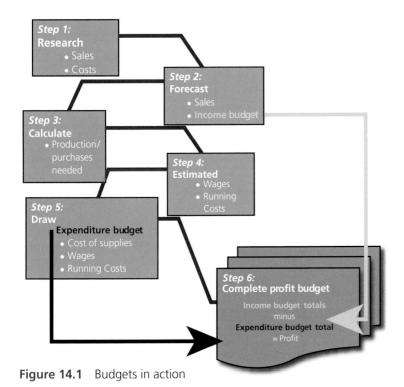

Figure 14.1   Budgets in action

The reasons for budgets and forecasts

Most business start-ups have an aim or mission statement. The mission statement is used to underpin a business's goals, objectives and targets. A new business needs to ensure that it has the available resources and finances needed to achieve its planned objectives. Alongside this, objectives and targets must be coordinated so that the whole company is working in the same direction at the same time to achieve its overall aim. This is where businesses use budgets because they:

- provide a plan of future activity and tasks
- ensure the finances are available to fund that activity
- prevent overspending and control costs
- set targets to be achieved such as sales, for example
- help employees to stay focused on achieving the company's objectives.

The financial proposals and targets contained within budgets are often challenging. Given unlimited funds, most people could organise a successful marketing campaign to raise sales – therefore, target achieved. However, can they do the same within a specified budget and time period?

Think of the launch of a new console like the *PlayStation 3*: the marketing and advertising budget has to be sufficient to raise awareness of the product with potential consumers, and stimulate them to make a purchase, but small enough that the company still makes a profit. Advertising, production and distribution must all be coordinated and financed. Budgets are essential in this planning process.

The process of setting budgets

Before any business can start to write its budgets for the forthcoming time period, usually one year, it is necessary to carry out some research. Budgets are detailed financial plans of the anticipated earnings and expenditure of the business. So in order to set realistic budgets, businesses must research:

- the likely level of consumer demand and trends in sales and prices
- running costs of the business, such as utility bills, rent, rates and insurances
- the amount, grade and pay levels of different types of labour
- the cost of supplies and materials.

Once all the required information has been collected, the business can start to plan its budgets. This starts with the sales or **income budget**, as once the firm has calculated its expected level of sales, it knows how much activity is going to be taking place within the business. From this it can then plan how much of any resource it needs and forecast the cost of providing those resources. Once expected income and costs are known, the business can then calculate its predicted profits.

Income, expenditure and profit budgets

As budgets are so valuable, they can actually be drawn up for any individual person, project or department. However, the main budgets and forecasts focus on key areas of business activity such as sales and expenditure. The budgetary process usually starts with forecasting sales.

Income budgets

Income budgets are often known as sales budgets. This is the key budget, as the amount a business sells determines the amount it needs to produce or supply, which in turn has implications for the number and type of staff that are employed and therefore how much activity will be taking place throughout major parts of the organisation. Sales are also the main area of generating cash inflows, so it is also a key indicator of how much money a business expects to receive.

FORECASTING SALES

Sales budgets are difficult to forecast as the amount a business will sell in future is affected by consumer tastes and fashions as well by the actions of competitors. Most new businesses must therefore use combinations of the following to try and forecast sales:

- historical data (secondary research)
- trend analysis
- market research (primary)
- their own experience and knowledge of the market and their customers.

One problem for businesses intending to sell more than one product is that the forecast sales may be different for each product, so they may have to draw up a separate forecast and budget for each product they sell.

Figure 14.2 shows an example of a sales budget; most new businesses will try to forecast up to at least their first year, but for simplicity we will only consider three months throughout this chapter.

Forecast sales (income budget)

	April	May	June
Sales value (£s)	15,540	15,860	15,340

Figure 14.2   An example of a three-month sales budget

Expenditure budgets

Once it has decided how much it is likely to sell, a business then calculates how much it needs to supply. Consider Figure 14.3. This shows the sales budget from Figure 14.2 but it has been expanded to show forecasted sales in value and in units; this is so there is an estimate both of how much income will be received from sales, and how many units the company needs to supply to satisfy the planned level demand.

Forecast sales (income budget)

	April	May	June
Sales value (£s)	15,540	15,860	15,340
At £20 each	Production/Purchases budget (units)		
= Units	777	793	767

Figure 14.3   An example of a three-month production or purchases budget

For a manufacturing business, a production budget would set out how many units need to be made, whereas a retail outlet would calculate the amount of stock it needed to buy.

This is an important budget for a new business, as if too little stock is available, a company could lose customers, sales and profits. If it has too much stock, then it risks either possessing goods that cannot be sold – especially a problem for perishable items like food products – or incurring potentially high storage costs. This budget is key as invariably the amount the company needs to supply is the major determinant of how much they need to spend on other areas of the business.

Now that the company knows how many stock items it needs in units, it can calculate the expenditure needed to provide this stock, that is, its cost in terms of purchasing materials. Assume in our example that each unit cost £10 to supply; this is demonstrated in Figure 14.4.

Production/Purchases budget (units)			
	April	May	June
= Units	777	793	767
Cost at £10 each	Production/Purchases budget (cost in £s)		
Supply cost (£s)	7,770	7,930	7,670

Figure 14.4   Production/Purchases budget

Next, managers need to plan how many, and what type of, employees they need. Managers need to know if they currently have too many employees or, more importantly, too few. This aspect of planning is crucial so that a business can make sure it has sufficient employees, but not so many that some stand around idle.

If a company gets this aspect of budgeting right, it will be optimising potential profits by not losing sales (by not having products or staff available) or wasting money on unproductive staff.

Finally, the company will then forecast any other areas of regular and expected costs in line with their expected level of activity. This would include items such as those below, but can include any item of expenditure the business considers necessary:

- rent and rates
- utility bills
- distribution costs
- administration
- repairs
- miscellaneous items.

An example of an **expenditure budget** is given is Figure 14.5. Expenditure budgets are useful for businesses as it makes them focus on cost areas and what their money is being spent on.

Forecast expenditure (£s)			
	April	May	June
Purchases	7,770	7,930	7,670
Wages	2,850	2,850	2,300
Rates	400	400	400
Utilities	300	300	300
Distribution	600	750	580
Administration	1,000	1,200	1,000
Repairs	800	800	800
Miscellaneous	240	240	240
Total	**13,960**	**14,470**	**13,290**

Figure 14.5   An example of an expenditure budget

Profit budgets/master budgets

Businesses often then create a **profit budget**, sometimes called a master budget (a forecasted profit and loss account) compiled from the individual budgets. This allows owners and managers to get an idea of how the cumulative affect of the budget decisions is likely to impact on profitability. Figure 14.6 demonstrates this for our example so far.

An example of a profit budget (£s)

	April	May	June	Total
Budgeted sales revenue	15,540	15,860	15,340	46,740
Budgeted expenditure	13,960	14,470	13,290	41,720
Budgeted profit	1,580	1,390	2,050	5,020

Figure 14.6   An example of a profit budget

The problems in setting budgets

As budgets rely on businesses being able to forecast information accurately, there can be some difficulties for many businesses in setting them, for example:

- A lack of effective research.
- Changes in consumer taste and fashion (these can occur rapidly in some markets, especially in technology or fashion goods).
- Unforeseen changes in the costs of supply (for example, price rises due to raw material shortages).
- Changes in the rate of interest effecting business costs, consumer incomes and hence the number of likely sales.
- Rapid changes in price caused by inflation.

As budgets are used to provide targets and give direction, further problems can arise if the budgets do prove to be inaccurate:

- Inaccurate or unrealistic budget setting will not give potential lenders or investors confidence in an entrepreneur's ability to set up and run a successful business.
- If targets are set too high, they may demotivate staff as they regard them as being impossible to achieve.
- Similarly, budget targets that are too easy to achieve will also not motivate, nor will they move the business towards its goals very effectively.
- For budgetary systems to work they need to be constantly monitored, or else they may be ignored; in this case the business will not be successfully controlling its costs and expenditure.

Further material and resources relating to this section can be found at **www.collins.bized.co.uk**. Keep checking for updates.

Setting budgets: Summary

- Budget forecasts provide a method by which owners can plan and coordinate business activities. They make owners/managers think about how to achieve goals.
- Budget forecasts provide managers and employees with targets. They allow performance to be monitored against the plan, and thereby identify possible areas of strength and weakness.
- Through planning, a business can ensure it has the right resources in place at the right time. The aim is to prevent the waste of resources without missing out on potential sales.
- To be successful, budgets need to be set accurately with realistic targets and regularly monitored.

Summary questions

1   Define what is meant by the term 'budget'.
2   Explain two reasons why a new business may choose to use a system of budgets in their planning process.
3   Give four examples of areas a business should research in order to help it set realistic budgets.
4   Why is it so important for a new business to accurately predict future sales levels?
5   List five items that might appear on the expenditure budget for a sandwich shop and five items that might appear on the expenditure budget for a clothing retail outlet such as Next. Identify if there are any similarities or differences between the two lists.
6   Forecasts and budgets are an important method of financial planning. How might the drawing up of budgets also act as a motivational tool?
7   Explain three reasons a new business start-up may find budgeting difficult.

Points for discussion

- It is likely that at some point a company's employees will want a pay rise. How will the calculation and drawing up of budgets help managers to make decisions on pay? In particular, how would the compilation of a profit budget help to inform the level of any pay rise offered? Use the basis of this argument to consider what other decisions budgets could help managers to make.
- 'Budgeting is too time-consuming, costly and difficult to be of any realistic use to a small business'. Discuss to what extent you think this statement is true.

Exam practice

As a kitchen assistant in a local high school in Mansfield, Margaret Tubshaw noticed a serious decline in the number of children having school dinners and a corresponding increase in those bringing packed lunches. A popular and approachable member of staff, Margaret took time out to speak with parents and discovered that recent television programmes and healthy-eating campaigns featuring celebrity chefs had influenced parents into changing what they provided their child with for lunch.

Faced with a declining demand for their services, the private company that actually ran the school meals' provision across the area introduced a series of compulsory redundancies and Margaret was one of those selected. However, armed with a reasonable lump sum, Margaret decided that now was the time to launch her own business, so she started to research into her potential idea she named 'Greenfeed'.

Margaret knew from her own experience that parents wanted to supply their children with items like fresh fruit and salad for their lunchboxes. From various consumer programmes and her own knowledge, she also knew that shopping patterns had changed and few families now shopped in local stores like greengrocers, and more and more shopped less regularly.

The idea of 'Greenfeed' was that for a fee of £10 per week, Margaret would deliver a box of guaranteed good-quality, fresh and organic fruit, vegetables and salad items straight to customers' doors.

Margaret discussed her idea with friends and family, and on the whole received a very positive response. She had several ideas of where she could get supplies from, so she set up a business account with her money, bought a van, some boxes for deliveries, had some flyers made up and started her business. Only after several weeks trading did her bank manager suggest she should draw up a profit budget for the next four months.

Margaret currently has 60 customers per week, mostly from contacts from her old school, but she anticipates that this will increase by 25% per month. Although customers' requirements vary, an average box of items costs Margaret £4.50 to supply. Margaret has no employees but pays herself a wage of £250 per week. Her insurance costs for the van are £65 per month and Margaret estimates her weekly fuel bill to be £110. As from the start of the next month, September, Margaret is going to place an advert in her local paper at a cost £80 per month. At the moment she works from home, but as the business expands, Margaret is aware she will need to get proper premises. She is currently investigating renting a small empty shop outlet at a cost of £200 per week from the start of October. In addition to paying rent, she will need to pay business rates for services like water, sewerage and waste collection; on the size of premises she is interested in these are currently £500 per quarter and her first payment would be due in December. Margaret also sets aside £50 per month for expenditure on miscellaneous items like postage, stationery and telephone costs.

1 Explain the process necessary to complete a profit budget. (5 marks)

2 Assuming all months are four weeks' long and all changes happen as Margaret predicts, complete her four-month profit budget for the four months September to December. (10 marks)

3 Analyse the strengths and weaknesses of Margaret's approach to starting her own business. (10 marks)

4 To what extent could Margaret have benefited by drawing a profit budget before her business started? (15 marks)

Total: 40 marks

Chapter 15   Assessing business start-ups

By the end of this chapter you should come to understand and appreciate how a new business can determine its level of success after its initial start-up and how and why many new businesses fail to succeed.

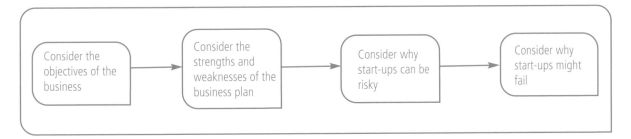

Figure 15.1   Assessing business start-ups

Objectives of business start-ups

In most respects the purpose of any new business start-up is to be successful. Success, however, can be measured in many different ways, which are dependent upon the type of business. A good start for any business is to set down **objectives** for its activities that act as guidelines and a standard against which it can measure itself. This will allow the business to assess and identify any shortfall in performance and seek solutions in the future.

Many businesses therefore start by outlining their aims and objectives in their **business plan** (see Chapter 4 for a detailed description of business plans) which becomes a formal statement of what they would like to achieve. The key to assessing a business's level of success then depends on measuring to what extent the business has been successful in meeting its objectives.

However, businesses do not exist in isolation; the environment in which they operate is constantly changing. Therefore, any business must also be flexible in its approach and as such must review its objectives at regular periods. Objectives that a new business may set can broadly be split into two main areas: financial objectives and market objectives, but we will also consider some others.

Financial objectives for start-up businesses

It is easy to think that the obvious financial objective is to make a profit and this is true in many ways. However, what profit? Is it sufficient to make any level of profit? There is a difference between making a profit and making an *acceptable* level of profit. Even the objective of making a profit needs to be defined. Some of the major financial objectives are listed below.

Key terms

Business plan A report to show the plans of the business, providing information about the market opportunity the business plans to target, how it will do so and what resources it requires.

Consumer inertia A consumer's unwillingness to move from a product that they are familiar with to trying or buying something new.

Objectives The targets that are set by the business that it wants to achieve in the foreseeable future.

BREAKING EVEN

This objective is often a short-term objective for a new business, that is, making sufficient sales revenue to cover its costs. All new businesses will start from a loss-making position and so must achieve break-even (see chapter 12) before any profits can be made. Even if not a complete success, at least if the business breaks even the owners and investors will not have lost any money.

MAXIMISING PROFITS

This occurs when a business tries to achieve the largest possible difference between how much their good or service costs to provide and what they can sell it for. This is difficult for a new business to achieve as in order to do so, the business must know as much about its consumers as possible, where to obtain the cheapest supplies, the most economical way of producing and delivering the product and the maximum price the consumer would be prepared to pay.

PROVIDING A STEADY INCOME

This is different from profit maximisation as in this case the business is saying that it would rather attempt to attain realistic sufficient profit goals than overstretch itself. This may be a more cautious approach but it is therefore also more achievable. Being able to meet steady and consistent sales targets, deliver goods on time and maintain quality standards may mean the difference between survival and failure.

PROVIDING A RETURN FOR INVESTORS

This objective aims to provide a steady and acceptable level of profits for shareholders and other investors. This does not mean that the business is seeking to make as much profit as possible, but instead to make the return on money invested worthwhile.

Marketing objectives for start-up businesses

RAISING CONSUMER AWARENESS

One of the first goals any new business must achieve is actually getting potential customers to know:

- they exist
- what their product/service is
- how to find/contact them
- how to make a purchase.

MAXIMISING SALES

At first many students might think this means the same as making profits but this is not the case. A new business may choose to sacrifice profitability in the short term by selling at a low price in order to establish a foothold in the market and generate a customer base. The more customers a business has, the less risk it is under, as losing one customer out of one thousand is not as potentially devastating as losing one customer out of ten.

ACHIEVING GROWTH

Many new businesses see growth as being the key to long-term success. A larger company is more likely to be financially stable and attract more investors. Therefore this objective concentrates on expanding the business's customers, outlets, product range, and so on. However, a too rapid growth brings the risk of overtrading (see page 160).

Other objectives

New businesses may well also set themselves other objectives or targets to achieve. In reality, a new business can set itself any objectives it wants in any area. But more commonly it might consider:

- Customer service targets such as efficiency and responsiveness, or after-sales service
- Environmental targets such as minimising pollution arising from the business or being carbon neutral
- Achieving industry standards such ISO 9000 or awards such as Investors in People.

Strengths and weaknesses of a business idea and/or plan

Many entrepreneurs don't think their business ideas through enough before facing the Dragons

A business plan consists of a detailed report that considers the key areas required in setting up a business. The exact details of business plans can vary, but should broadly cover four main areas:

- the form of the business and description of its activities
- the objectives of the business
- the market research and marketing plan for the new company
- a financial analysis covering cash flow forecast (see chapter 13) and projected profit and loss account.

The idea of a business plan is to make an entrepreneur think through his or her idea in detail before they or any investors risk time and resources in the business.

Strengths of business plans

Compiling a business plan can provide several key strengths to the potential success of any business idea.

- Targets – the setting of targets provides a basis for assessing the success of the start-up and provides a motivational aid for the entrepreneur and employees.
- Coordination – by planning activities that need to take place, the operations of the business should run more smoothly and effort should not be wasted or duplicated.
- Proactive – planning makes all those in the business think in advance about decisions and actions and therefore allows the business to consider how to prevent problems occurring rather than how to solve problems that have already happened.
- Contingency plan – in the process of drawing up plans to prevent problems the business can also consider 'what if' scenarios, for example, 'What if we start to develop cash flow difficulties?' This enables the business to contingency plan, that is, prepare what to do in advance so that if a problem does occur, the business does not need to panic as it already has plans in place to cope.
- Obtaining funds – one of the main strengths of a business plan is as a method of convincing lenders or investors to commit money into the idea. The business plan can show that the idea is well thought out, has the potential to succeed and, furthermore, demonstrates the entrepreneur's business intellect.

A strong business idea and plan should also demonstrate how the business idea is innovative, inventive or new in some way. This could range from an entirely original product concept to a novel or more modern way of providing an existing product or service.

Weaknesses of business plans

One of the major problems with business start-ups is that any entrepreneur starting their own business automatically feels that their business idea is a good one; otherwise they would not be doing it. This unfortunately leads to many business plans been over-optimistic on the level of sales they will attain and how quickly this will be accomplished. This can then lead on to two key weaknesses in that:

- start-up capital is underestimated
- cash inflows are overestimated.

If this happens, the business can quite quickly find itself in financial trouble, such as cash flow problems.

The drawing up of business plans involves the business setting budgets and targets. These can cause the business to focus solely on the plans and targets they have set and thus become inflexible to, or unaware of, changes in its marketplace.

A further weakness can be producing too detailed and in-depth a plan. Researching data and hiring experts for their input can be a costly undertaking and a problem can arise if the cost of producing the plan exceeds the usefulness of the information it provides.

Alongside these, whilst a business plan can provide for contingencies it is impossible for it to cover every eventuality and, in particular, accurately predict the responses of competitors to the new business. No business plan is going to be 100% accurate and so it should always be considered that they are best used as a guide to aid the business start-up to achieve success.

Why start-ups can be risky

Historically more business start-ups fail than succeed. The reasons why this occurs can be very varied: from lack of expertise and knowledge on the part of the owner to actually just having a bad product. Starting a business involves the owner being able to assess situations correctly, plan accurately and make suitably-informed decisions over a wide range of business functions. In this section we shall look at some of the main reasons why business start-ups can be risky.

Personal characteristics

To start a new business requires more than just having a good idea; to be a successful entrepreneur requires a person to possess a range of qualities. An individual may well have experience of working in a particular market sector before starting out on their own, or they may well be a very talented designer or engineer. However, this does not mean that they have the skills set necessary to run a business. A business enterprise covers a diverse range of areas and skills including:

- sales
- purchasing
- finance
- marketing
- administration
- human resource management
- distribution
- legislation
- production and IT in many cases.

It is unlikely any individual will be an expert in all these areas, and it is also unlikely that a new business could afford to hire experts in all these areas. An entrepreneur needs to be able to address all these factors to get their business running and to do so they need to possess certain personal characteristics, such as:

- problem-solving abilities
- communication and negotiation skills
- being ambitious, highly motivated to succeed and hard-working
- being enthusiastic, innovative and creative.

A lack of skills, knowledge or ability in any particular area can lead to a business taking larger risks than necessary, for example, buying stock in bulk to get a discount that then leads to a cash flow crisis.

Finance

Many new businesses face a problem in raising sufficient finance to start up and establish themselves; they also face a problem in estimating how much they will actually need to finance the start-up successfully. A new business not only needs sufficient money to purchase all the machinery, equipment and stock it needs, but also to pay for initial marketing to raise consumer awareness and then fund all the day to day running costs. The starting finance required needs to be able to do all this until the business is established enough that it is generating a satisfactory number of customers on a regular enough basis to ensure the business's ongoing survival.

This brings several problems:

- Many inexperienced entrepreneurs do not have the knowledge to forecast this accurately and so underestimate the amount of start-up capital they need. Thus they misjudge the amount they need to invest or borrow before they start and they then start the business with insufficient funding to survive long enough to grow.
- Raising all the required capital to start a new venture can be difficult for individuals without borrowing from banks or building societies. However, a new business has no track record of success, so to potential lenders any new business is a very high risk. As a result of this, lenders will charge new businesses very high interest rates. This further increases the costs of the business, by increasing cash outflows repaying loans and this reduces profits.
- Cash flow problems can occur easily. New businesses will often have a lot of their funds tied up in stock that needs to be sold before cash inflows from sales start to happen; however, before sufficient sales occur, the business has to pay ongoing costs like employees' wages, bills and marketing. This makes it easy for cash flow problems to occur.

Marketing

Marketing is a very important aspect to any new business, but is also an area that is very easy to get wrong.

First, insufficient or inaccurate research can provide misleading information. This information is then used as a basis for the financial figures in the business plan. If the market research is incorrect then so are all the forecasts. Conducting accurate market research is expensive and time-consuming.

Second, many new businesses are started by people who have built up experience in a market sector and who now decide to go it alone and set up their own company; this frequently happens as a result of redundancy. These entrepreneurs feel they have the knowledge and contacts necessary to build a successful business, but does not necessarily mean there is a gap in the market for them. **Consumer inertia** means that customers do not like change and will need definite reasons for switching from their established supplier to a new one, such as discounted prices. This reduces the new business's profitability and raises risk.

Finally, any new business must be marketed to its target market and again consumer inertia is a problem. Even for a new, exciting, innovative idea customers must be convinced to try it and then switch from their usual product. New business start-ups often have small marketing budgets (compared to established competitors) and less knowledge of which forms of marketing are most effective in that marketplace. One-off purchases by consumers are rarely enough to ensure a business's success; most require customers making regular repeat purchases to ensure steady cash inflows and profits.

Location

William Thomas Dillard was the founder of the Dillard's department store chain. With 330 stores in 29 states across America, Dillard's department store is the third largest department store chain in the United States and it is he that coined the phrase 'Location, location, location', stressing that location is the key to a successful retail business.

New business start-ups can be risky because of their location. For a new business, location can prove a problematic decision:

- good or best locations may already be taken by competitors
- if available, good locations are likely to prove expensive
- poor locations are likely to be cheaper but attract fewer customers.

Thus many new businesses face a conundrum in that acquiring good locations will increase their fixed costs; this in turn will raise their break-even point and make the business more risky. However, a good location should attract more custom. Alongside this, obtaining a good location may mean increased borrowing which again would increase costs and risk. However, a cheaper location would bring lower costs and risks, but also potentially lower sales.

Some businesses must also choose their location due to their resources and infrastructure requirements. For example:

- Does the business need to be close to suppliers?
- Does the business need to have good motorway, ferry or airport links?
- Does the business need good access for delivery lorries?
- What parking facilities are required for customers?
- Does the business need a workforce with a particular skills base?
- Does it need access to particular technology (high-speed Internet, for example)?

One factor that might influence a business's location decision is the level of financial support available from local and national government and the EU. These include the creation of local enterprise zones that encourage businesses to locate in depressed areas in return for which they may receive grants and subsidies from European Regional Development Funds that provide financial and other help to businesses.

Suppliers

A final consideration why new businesses can be a risky venture is that any new business is unlikely to receive the best deals from their suppliers. Due to their lack of a successful track record, or amount of

Guru's views

'Location is the key to most businesses, and the entrepreneurs typically build their reputation at a particular spot.'

– Phyllis Schlafly

Further material and resources relating to this section can be found at **www.collins.bized.co.uk**. Keep checking for updates.

A Dillard's store in a Florida mall

Activity

Research the various forms of government support available to new business start-ups. Then use the information you collect to produce a hand-out for potential new businesses detailing how government support could help to reduce the risks involved in starting their company.

finance they have available or level of customers and sales, new businesses are unlikely to receive:

- as favourable credit terms as an established successful business
- as high a discount as established regular repeat customers (the new business's competitors) get from the supplier
- preferential terms for delivery
- discounts for bulk purchases.

Alongside this a new business may not possess the knowledge of who is the best supplier, who is the cheapest, who is the most reliable or who produces the best/worst quality.

This all increases the risk that potentially they could choose the wrong supplier right from the start, especially if they just choose the one with the lowest prices.

Victims of their own success

One of the reasons why a new business can be a risky venture is that if the business proves to be successful and profitable, then this will attract other entrepreneurs who want a slice of that potential profit. This would increase competition in the marketplace and potentially put the new business at risk from larger rivals.

A new or innovative idea or product can be copied by competitors (unless protected under patent, see page 17) who could have the potential to manufacture more cheaply, distribute more widely or have a better reputation and brand name.

Very successful start-ups may find themselves under pressure of takeover or merger as larger companies seek to acquire the rights to any new products or protect their own interests and market share.

Why start-up businesses may fail

Start-up businesses can fail for any of the above reasons – the ones that make them risky propositions to begin with. On top of those factors that put them in jeopardy of failure, a number of other issues can occur that can cause even the most well-planned and well-executed business idea to ultimately fail.

Unexpected changes in demand

Social trends, technology and changes in lifestyle may affect many business's activities. In particular, a change in fashion or what's acceptable in society can leave some businesses with few or no consumers. When this happens, the market is said to have become obsolete. For example, how many people now want to buy electric typewriters or even VHS recorders?

Another example of this is changes in shopping habits or patterns. Many successful town centre businesses that may well have been trading for years have been forced to close due to the development of large out-of-town shopping malls. Music stores are suffering as many customers now choose to download songs and albums instead.

In some cases increases in demand can lead to business failure as the business extends its resources and finance to try to keep up with consumers. In this case the business can fall prey to the trap of overtrading and end up closing due to lack of working capital and cash flow difficulties.

Changes in government legislation can also impact on the demand for a business. In some cases the government could outlaw a product completely or rule it unsafe for sale without major costly changes to its design. Changes to costs can also play a part in a business's failure to succeed.

The Wii is the latest in a long line of different consoles that Nintendo has produced to keep up with technological change. Not all video game companies are as sucessful at confronting these changes, or customers' expectations

Unexpected changes in costs

If the costs of a business rise then this can have severe knock-on effects to the business's chances of survival. Increased costs mean:

- a higher break-even point, decreasing the margin of safety and profits and increasing risk
- increased cash outflows, thus increasing the risk of a cash flow problem occurring
- less funding available for other areas, for example, if costs of stock rise, to pay this increase means the new start-up may have to sacrifice some funds from its marketing budget
- increases in costs may lead the business to increase its selling price – this makes the new business less competitive and demand will fall.

If costs rise unexpectedly then any budgets such as cash flow will be wrong and the business can find itself in financial difficulties despite the amount of effort that went into the business plan. Costs can change unexpectedly for various reasons. The table below details some of the main causes.

Rises in interest rates	This causes the cost of borrowing and paying back interest on overdrafts, loans or mortgages to increase. This can make a profitable business into a loss-making business. Increased repayment rates can also lead to cash flow problems and alongside consumers have lower disposable incomes and so cut back on their own spending and demand for a business's products or services fall.
Changes in exchange rates	If the exchange rate falls then any materials that are imported become more expensive to buy. Or, if the business exports then a rise in exchange rates will make their products more expensive to foreign consumers.
Inflation	This is the term given to the general trend of prices to rise. This again increases costs for a business and employees will want regular pay rises to protect their own income levels and buying power.
Changes in levels of supply	If the supply of a raw material or component is reduced then its price increases; this increases costs for any business purchasing it.

Figure 15.1 Causes of changes in costs

Unavailability of supplies

A business idea is only going to be successful if the business is able to supply its customers with a product or service that satisfies the consumer's wants and needs. Failure to supply the product quite literally means that the business will have no sales and thus no cash inflows or profit, and if a customer is let down then they will usually go elsewhere (to a competitor) and buy their product instead. Once a customer is lost it is very difficult to win them back again. Supplies may become unavailable for several reasons.

SHORTAGES IN SUPPLY

A shortage in a raw material may occur for the simple reason that many supplier markets are seasonal, for example, buying strawberries in summer compared to trying to buy strawberries in winter. Strawberries in winter may well be available (imported from abroad) but at a prohibitive level of cost.

Crop or raw material failures can occur as well, which means that certain supplies are not available at all. In 2007 there was a worldwide shortage of wheat causing the cost and prices of all wheat-based products to rise. Similarly BSE, foot and mouth and Asian bird flu have all had impacts on the availability and cost of goods ranging from meat-based products to leather goods.

Competitor power can mean that in attempt to force a new business out of a market a competitor buys up all the supplies currently available. Alternatively, they use their buying power to instruct suppliers not to supply the new enterprise on the threat of losing their established custom. This can then make supplies impossible and very expensive for the new business to obtain.

More simple reasons for the unavailability of supplies can occur, for example, breakdowns in the supplier's factory or a lack of skilled staff to produce the amount of goods required. In these cases, established businesses are more likely to see their orders satisfied before any new business.

Delays

A new business can experience delays in getting its product to the customer for various reasons. First, there are problems with supply as discussed above. Second, there can be problems with deliveries and distribution. Third, administration problems for a new business can mean that orders become muddled or lost. The key point being that any form of delay is unlikely to please customers who are then unlikely to repeat purchase. Word of mouth can be negative as well as positive and a new business that is experiencing teething problems can quickly develop a bad reputation for poor quality service.

Delay can also occur in obtaining payments from debtors. Many customers do not pay within or on the credit terms that they are given. Not receiving payments from debtors on time means that expected cash inflows do not occur as predicted and thus cash flow problems can arise. Large businesses often delay payments to smaller suppliers as they know that the smaller suppliers cannot afford to risk losing their custom and so will try and keep funds within their own bank accounts for as long as possible.

Delays in receiving payments from customers can have a knock-on effect to then delaying payments from the new business to its suppliers. This again does not help the new business to build a good reputation or relations with its suppliers. This can lead to difficulty in obtaining credit terms (if they are seen as unreliable in paying their accounts) and/or discounts, and in extreme cases suppliers refusing to supply.

Assessing business start-ups: Summary

- The objectives of a business provide a guide and set of targets for the business to aim towards. They then also provide a basis by which success can be measured.
- A business plan helps to outline the objectives, coordinate the activities of the business and can help the business in obtaining funds from lenders or investors.
- Business plans, though, can be over-optimistic, too detailed and make the business become inflexible as it strives to meet its pre-set objectives.
- Starting a new business can be a risky venture. New businesses can suffer from lack of knowledge or skills, insufficient funding, poor market research and marketing techniques.
- New businesses are also risky as they frequently will not get the best location or deals from their suppliers.
- Very successful new businesses will be seen as a potential threat by competitors who may then seek to eliminate them.
- Despite a strong idea and good planning, new start-ups may still fail due to unexpected changes in demand and costs, problems with supply or delays in receiving and making payments.

Summary questions

1 What is meant by the term 'objective'?

2 Explain two financial objectives a new business start-up may have.

3 Outline how a business plan can help a new business to achieve success.

4 Explain two reasons why a business plan might not guarantee that the business is successful.

5 Give two reasons why an individual may not make a successful entrepreneur, even if they have industry experience.

6 Explain three problems that may occur as a result of starting a business with insufficient funding.

7 Explain what is meant by 'consumer inertia'.

8 How might problems with suppliers and supplies effect a new business's level of competitiveness?

9 List four reasons why costs may change unexpectedly.

10 Explain why increasing levels of cost increase the risk factor of a new business.

Points for discussion

- As most business start-ups are set up with the objective of making a profit, why isn't profit maximisation the only objective? (Consider what the consumer's viewpoint would be of a profit-maximising company.)
- Given the fact that business plans are unable to predict events that could cause the potential failure of the business, is there any point in compiling them at all?

Exam practice

Nigel Jones qualified with a degree in geography from Wolverhampton University and subsequently went on to secure a position with Robinson's as a National Accounts Manager selling the successful range of soft drinks to large supermarket chains like Asda, Tesco and Sainsbury's. After a successful career in the industry, Nigel decided it was time to relax from the fast-paced market and pressure he was used to and spend more time with his family. Nigel had acquired some money in a bequest from his grandfather and so he opened 'The Sandwich Cellar', his own sandwich shop in Sheffield.

Nigel did a little research into initial costs to ensure he could afford to support the business for at least six months whilst he built up a customer base. However, he failed to do any market research as he felt that it was unnecessary for the type of business he was opening, especially as Nigel has secured a prime location opposite a local college and conveniently placed near to several large offices and a range of smaller businesses.

At first things went well and Nigel swiftly built up a good trade with a mixture of students and office workers patronising his shop. Nigel's objective had always been to supply a good product for a fair price and build up his sales and profits on that basis. However, four months in and Nigel's business is starting to suffer. A new sandwich delivery service has set up and is now catering to some of his office clients by delivering straight to their desks and supplying not just sandwiches but also a range of options such as tortilla wraps and ciabattas with a range of luxury fillings. The college canteen has recently dropped its prices to try and gain students back from Nigel and on top of that the worldwide shortage of wheat has forced up wheat prices and Nigel's bread suppliers have correspondingly increased the prices of all their products. Nigel has decided at least he can take action to find a new supplier.

1 Explain two problems Nigel may encounter when sourcing a new supplier for his business. (5 marks)

2 Analyse the advantages and disadvantages to Nigel's business of conducting market research prior to starting his business. (10 marks)

3 Consider the potential problems that the rise in the price of wheat could cause to businesses like 'The Sandwich Cellar'. (15 marks)

4 Given Nigel's current problems, to what extent would drawing up a business plan have guaranteed his success? (10 marks)

Total: 40 marks

UNIT 2
SECTION A

Managing a Business:
Finance

Section overview

Managing a Business:
Finance

This section looks at the importance of managing a business's finances. It starts by examining the benefits and drawbacks of using budgets, and how to assess if the finances are well managed. It then looks at how businesses can try to prevent cash flow problems from occurring and how to solve them if they do. In addition, any business owner wants to know how well their business has performed, so the final part of this section considers how to measure profitability and ways in which profitability might be improved.

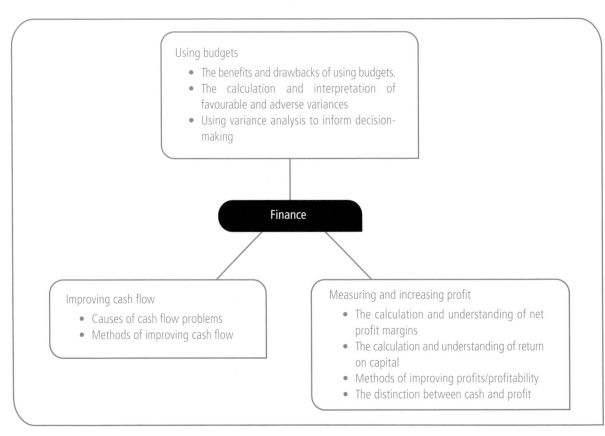

Using budgets
- The benefits and drawbacks of using budgets.
- The calculation and interpretation of favourable and adverse variances
- Using variance analysis to inform decision-making

Finance

Improving cash flow
- Causes of cash flow problems
- Methods of improving cash flow

Measuring and increasing profit
- The calculation and understanding of net profit margins
- The calculation and understanding of return on capital
- Methods of improving profits/profitability
- The distinction between cash and profit

Key concept

Finance

Once a business has survived its start-up period and achieved any initial objectives, then the owner's direction and financial focus needs to change from having sufficient finance to get started and surviving long enough to make a profit to improving the business's position and making it stronger.

Managing a business's finance involves planning and setting financial targets, and then assessing how good the business has been at achieving them. Financial results are one of the key areas in determining how well a business has performed; in particular it involves looking at what the business has achieved, identifying any areas of strength and weakness and using this information to improve the business's financial position for the future.

By undertaking a continual review of financial targets, achievement and performance, business owners should be able to make their business more financially stable and raise profitability, thus helping to ensure success into the future.

Chapter 16   Using budgets

The aim of this chapter is for you to understand how **budgets** can be used in practice to improve the financial performance of a business. This involves being able to calculate and interpret variances, and then using the information gained to help make decisions.

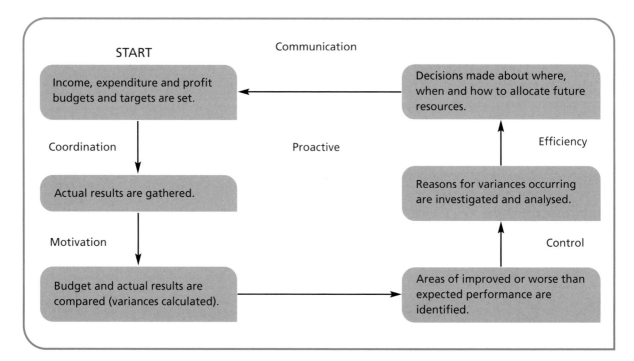

Figure 16.1   The budgetary process and benefits

From Chapter 14 you should be familiar with the concept of setting income, expenditure and profit budgets as financial plans for a future period. Businesses draw up budgets for a number of reasons, the main ones being to help the business plan to:

- achieve its objectives
- set targets
- control costs.

However, the setting of the budget is only the first stage of the process of **budgetary control**. A system of budgetary control then involves using the budgets that were set to monitor the performance of the business and how well it did in achieving the targets that were set.

That means as well as a being vitally important in business planning, budgets also provide a range of other benefits. But, like many things in business, they also have a number of associated drawbacks. These are examined in detail below.

The benefits and drawbacks of budgeting

Benefits of using budgets

The process of setting budgets and targets can help to:

- Aid communication throughout a business – managers have to communicate with each other and employees. This helps to improve both horizontal and vertical communication within the business.
- Aid coordination of activities. This occurs in three ways:
  - ensuring all parts of the business are working towards common goals
  - making sure the right resources (money, people and equipment) are in the right place at the right time
  - avoiding duplication of tasks by individuals or departments.
- Make managers consider expenditure decisions in advance (proactivity). This improves cost efficiency as resources are less likely to be wasted.
- Provide a system against which performance can be judged by giving measurable targets to aim for.
- Motivate staff (through communication and target-setting) and establishing a sense of achievement when budgets are met.
- Persuade potential lenders or investors of the security of the business.

One of the main benefits to be gained from budgetary exercises is in the monitoring of business performance, that is:

- Did the business perform as expected?
- Did some areas perform better or worse than planned?
- Were costs/revenues higher or lower than anticipated?
- And most importantly, why did any variations in what was planned occur?

This monitoring activity is done using a process termed **variance analysis**.

DELEGATED BUDGETS

Delegated budgets occur when a business passes the responsibility and authority for the budgetary process down the hierarchy. In other words, the control of the budgets is taken out of managers' hands and given to individuals or teams at all levels of the business. This has several benefits associated with it:

- Potentially the number of managers needed can be reduced, which in turn lowers the cost of wages for the company.
- Employees are motivated by being given trust, responsibility, and more diverse and interesting jobs.
- Employees take ownership of the budget (as it is made up of their own ideas rather than ones passed down from above) and are thus more committed to achieving the targets set.

Be careful: not all businesses use delegated budgets. To be used effectively, managers must be prepared to hand control of some

Key terms

Adverse variance This occurs when the business's actual results are worse than those anticipated and planned for in the budget. These have the result of reducing final profits in the short term.

Budget A financial plan drawn up to outline the future operations of the business. Budgets are used to set targets, monitor performance and control operations.

Budgetary control A system of monitoring the performance of a business by comparing the actual performance to the targets that were set, and then seeking to find out why any differences occurred. This is often done using variance analysis.

Favourable variance This occurs when the actual results are better than those anticipated and planned for in the budget. These have the effect of raising profit in the short term.

Variance analysis This is one way of examining how well a business did compared to what it expected to do, that is, it is the comparison of what actually happened with what the business budgeted (planned to happen).

financial decision-making over to employees. This means the manager must first be willing to do so and, second, have employees they feel they can trust. For many new businesses the owners may well be unwilling to relinquish such control in the early years.

Drawbacks of using budgets

As a business grows, the budgetary process will become more complex. The time required in consultation and communication to prepare the budgets will also increase, as will the time needed to monitor outcomes. This has several impacts:

- The cost of the process also rises.
- The burdens placed on managers or employees increase, creating excessive stress.
- The cost of training staff (especially with delegated budgets) expands.

Similarly, the process of regularly setting and using budgets can bring problems to the business as well, such as:

- Budgets can become a source of conflict between managers and staff. Allocating funds fairly between departments, projects, teams or individuals can be difficult and can often be influenced by an individual's skill at negotiating rather than a genuine need.
- Businesses may become inflexible, with the necessity to achieve pre-agreed budgeted targets; other opportunities that present themselves may be ignored or overlooked.
- Budgets are only short-term plans (usually a maximum of one year), but they may become viewed by managers or employees as the only important targets and, as such, the focus on longer-term issues or goals can be lost. For example, cutting back on staff training to stay within this year's budget could lead to an inadequate or inefficient workforce for years into the future.
- Finally, if staff feel that their budget targets are unrealistic, unfair, inaccurate or have been imposed without proper consultation, then they may become demotivated, or even ignore the process entirely.

Further information and resources on different methods of setting budgets (historical, zero based or flexible) can be found at **www.collins.bized.co.uk**. Keep checking for updates.

The calculation and interpretation of favourable and adverse variances

Setting the budgets for a business is only the first stage in the budgetary process. The next stage is to actually monitor what has happened. This fulfils several functions:

- Were targets met?
- Were the budgets (financial plans) accurate?
- What areas does the business need to focus on in future?

Variance analysis compares actual performance with the forecast performance, that is, what did happen compared to what the business planned to happen. A variance occurs when what actually happened was different from what the business had planned. For example, the business planned sales revenue of £140,000 over three months but only received £125,000. The purpose of this exercise is to pinpoint and highlight areas of good and poor performance.

Calculation of variances

In simple terms, all variance analysis involves is placing the budgeted figures side by side with the actual figures incurred and then working out the difference between the two (budgeted and actual). This would be done for the income, expenditure and profit budgets, as is shown in Figure 16.2.

	Budgeted amount	Actual amount	Variance
Income	£62,000	£67,000	£5,000 favourable
Expenditure	£37,000	£40,800	£3,800 adverse
Profit	£25,000	£26,200	£1,200 favourable

Figure 16.2 An example of variance analysis

A business can choose to be as detailed in its analysis of variances as it wants to be. For example, many businesses would investigate the difference between each individual category of expenditure or the sales of each product in their range. The divergence between the actual and budgeted figure is called a variance and these can be either favourable or adverse.

A **favourable variance** occurs when the actual performance produces more profit for the business than budgeted for, either because:

- actual sales revenue was higher than budgeted for
- actual costs (expenditure) were lower than planned.

An **adverse variance** occurs when actual results are less profitable than had been budgeted, either because:

- actual costs were higher than planned
- actual sales revenue was lower than budgeted.

Don't assume an adverse variance is necessarily bad or a favourable variance is good. In the example in Figure 16.2, expenditure is higher than expected and thus adverse but even an adverse variance does not mean things have gone wrong; a business may get an adverse variance for the cost of labour, but this may mean it hired more skilled employees who did a better-quality job and hence the business was able to attract more sales or sell its products for a higher price.

Similarly, a positive variance may occur because the business used cheaper and lower-quality materials. Short-term this will produce a positive variance, but long-term may result in a loss of customer loyalty and future profits.

Further examples of possible adverse or favourable variances and their remedies can be found at **www.collins.bized.co.uk**. Keep checking for updates.

Activity

A juicy business

Nature's Bounty Ltd manufactures a range of organic fruit juices for sale in supermarkets and health food stores. It has set sales and expenditure budgets for each of the different fruit juices it makes. Information for the last year of trading has been collated in the table below to show the budgeted and actual performance of each type of fruit juice.

Fruit juice	Sales variances (£'000)			Expenditure variances (£'000)		
	Budget	Actual	Variance	Budget	Actual	Variance
Sunshine Orange	450	400	50 adverse	200	180	
Orchard Apple	350	380		180		30 adverse
Tangy Tropical	400	480			240	40 adverse
Morning Grapefruit		120	30 adverse	100	120	

1 Complete the missing information in the table.
2 Calculate the total profit variance for Nature's Bounty Ltd.
3 Of what value is the information in the table to Nature's Bounty Ltd?

Variance analysis and decision-making

Having found any difference (variance), managers then try to determine why the variance occurred. This is done by:

- determining any areas that performed below expectations
- identifying why this poor performance occurred
- taking steps to prevent the same factors causing poor performance in future.

Similarly, managers could identify aspects of the company that achieved better results than forecast and:

- identify *why* this increase in performance occurred
- try to repeat this in future and thus build on areas of strength and increase performance.

This helps managers to decide which aspects of the business need more time, effort and resources and which need less, and so also forms the basis for setting targets in the future.

Carrying out variance analysis regularly can also highlight if financial plans are inaccurate. Business is a dynamic subject, that is, circumstances change (tastes, technology, fashions and prices); variance analysis will draw managers' attention to where changes are occurring. This prevents budgets from becoming out of date and irrelevant. It also keeps managers aware of changing market circumstances so the business does not miss out on any opportunities or fail to spot upcoming threats to their success.

In the long-term the consistent use of the budgetary process – setting budgets, examination of variances, monitoring and control – should allow the business to become more accurate at financial planning, more efficient at allocating and using its resources, and subsequently more profitable in future periods.

Further material and resources relating to this section can be found at **www.collins.bized.co.uk**. Keep checking for updates.

Using budgets: **Summary**

- The budgetary process can bring many benefits to businesses, such as increased communication, coordination and motivation, as well providing a system for measuring performance.
- The time and resources needed to undertake a full budgetary system can be costly and could be wasteful should the budget prove inaccurate.
- Variance analysis allows an assessment of budget accuracy and identification of problem areas.
- Variance analysis allows managers to make informed decisions where to allocate their time and resources to improve the business's future performance.

Summary questions

1 Explain what is meant by the term 'budgetary control'.

2 Explain two benefits and two drawbacks of using budgets.

3 What is meant by the term 'delegated budgets'?

4 Explain what is meant by the terms 'favourable' and 'adverse' variances.

5 Why doesn't the term 'favourable' necessarily mean a good result occurred?

6 Elmwood Ltd makes traditional hardwood kitchen units. The production manager has identified an adverse variance for the amount of time it took his workforce to produce a set of custom-built units. Explain to the production manager why this adverse variance may not necessarily be a bad result.

7 Give two reasons how a positive variance could occur.

8 Explain three ways in which using a system of budgetary control can aid business managers in decision-making.

Points for discussion

Although all businesses can benefit from the budgetary process, do you think it is as important for a small local business like your local takeaway outlet to draw up budgets as it is for a multinational public limited company like Cadbury? Would each type of business receive the same level of benefit from budgetary activities?

What problems could result from poor or inaccurate budget-setting for businesses acting in fast-moving markets?

Exam practice

Between the sheets

Coulthers is a well-established manufacturer of quality bed linen, supplying many major department stores. In the late 1990s, Coulthers experienced a slump in sales and, for the first time in its history, made a loss. A new finance director, James Melwood, was brought in to identify ways in which the financial health of the company could be improved.

Melwood focused initially on the company's budgeting process. Expenditure seemed to have grown each year, with few attempts to improve cost efficiency. The budgeted expenditure had been based on that of the previous year, with a percentage increase added for inflation. Even when sales and output had fallen, expenditure had continued to grow. Managers within the firm were defensive; each claiming that their own area needed the financial resources it was being given. There was also considerable confusion as to where the problems lay within the business. No one seemed to know which of the company's products were profitable and which were not.

Melwood's proposals were for a complete reform of the budgeting process. Each product type – duvet covers, sheets and pillowcases – would be made into a separate profit area. Each would have its own revenue and expenditure budgets set. Variances from budgeted figures would be carefully scrutinised to identify and solve potential problems. The new system produced some interesting results:

Product type	Revenue £'000		Expenditure £'000		Profit/Loss £'000	
	Budget	Actual	Budget	Actual	Budget	Actual
Duvet covers	850	750	650	600		
Sheets	500	450	400	400		
Pillowcases	350	200	300	270		

1 Complete the table and calculate the total profit variance for Coulthers. (10 marks)

2 With reference to the case study, explain two reasons why a favourable variance may not always imply a positive result. (5 marks)

3 Analyse the advantages and disadvantages of using a budgetary system to a business like Coulthers. (10 marks)

4 'Budgets are only useful for planning and achieving short-term goals.' To what extent do you agree with this statement? (15 marks)

Total: 40 marks

Chapter 17   Improving cash flow

After completing this topic you should have an appreciation of how and why a business can find itself short of **cash** (a cash flow crisis) and what steps it could possibly take to resolve the situation.

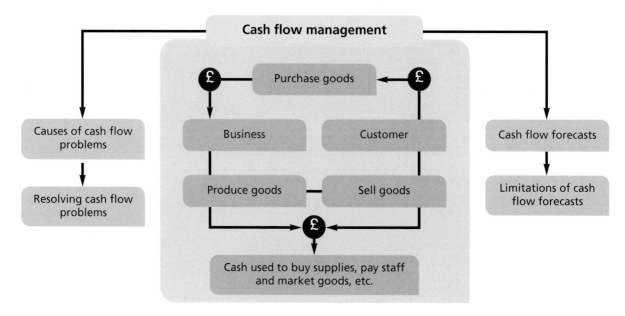

Examining cash flow forecasts

Drawing up cash flow forecasts, as in Chapter 13, is only the first step; the next process is to examine what they mean. Cash flow forecasts can be used to pinpoint periods when the business is cash rich; in other words, it has large amounts of cash available. This is the ideal time to make expensive purchases, undertake training programmes or start investments and research, as this can be done without putting the company at risk. Alternatively the forecasts can be used to identify:

- if there are any cash flow problems that are going to occur
- when they are going to occur
- how bad are they going to be
- what the business can do about it.

This can be done in two ways: a simple analysis can be undertaken by examining the closing balances at the end of each month to determine whether or not any cash flow problems are likely (that is, a low or negative cash balance); however, a more in-depth examination would involve not only looking at what the cash flow forecast predicted, but also determining:

- the accuracy or realism of the forecast (for example, when applying for loans, many business applicants tend to be overly optimistic, for instance, assuming that extra expenditure on advertising will automatically lead to greater sales);

- *why* the cash flow problem has happened: is it a temporary one-off problem or several cumulative underlying difficulties (see Causes of cash flow problems below);
- whether any period where a shortage of cash is identified is likely to deepen or improve over time, that is, whether it is a short-term or long-term problem.

The key is that no matter what the cause of the cash flow shortage, it has to be solved, because if it continues or gets worse the business will find itself unable to pay:

- creditors (suppliers of stock) who will then stop supplying goods
- employees' wages, who may then strike or leave the business
- bills such as electricity, telephone or water, the suppliers of which may well cut off their services
- loans, mortgages or other liabilities.

This is why cash flow problems can often lead to what is termed a shortage of **working capital**, as quite literally the business has no money with which it can work and finance its day to day operations. Identifying the reason why the cash flow problem has arisen can in many cases go a long way to providing the answer how to remedy it.

Causes of cash flow problems

Cash shortages happen for all sorts of reasons; many businesses simply suffer from the fact that money has to be spent out on premises, stock, marketing and other running costs before any cash starts to flow in from customers. Consider that every single retail outlet, even your local corner shop, has to stock all of its shelves and continuously keep re-stocking them to attract customers initially and keep on attracting them.

Alternatively, for many new businesses setting up has been a struggle and as soon as the owner sees their business making profits they start to pay themselves too high a wage. Or they fail to reduce the amount they pay themselves in times of decreased sales as they have personal financial commitments to meet, such as mortgages and household bills.

Other common causes of cash flow problems or working capital shortages are outlined below.

EXCESSIVE BORROWING

To be competitive in many markets requires expensive equipment, marketing or a prime location, and many businesses take loans and mortgages to achieve this. However, these need repaying, with interest. But having the right resources and location does not automatically mean quality products, good customer service and high sales. Businesses must also be well managed.

INVESTING TOO MUCH IN ASSETS

Unnecessary or incorrectly timed spending on expensive machinery or vehicles, for example, which could be hired or leased rather than bought, can tie up too much money in non-liquid **assets** and leave the business with little cash available.

Key terms

Assets The items that a business owns, for example, buildings, vehicles and its stock of goods.

Cash Any money actually held by a business at any particular point in time. This can be real physical notes and coins, and any money currently in the business's bank account.

Overtrading This occurs when a firm expands too rapidly, without having the cash resources in place to finance the expansion adequately and meet its day to day commitments as well.

Trade credit An arrangement in which suppliers allow customers a period of time (usually one or two months) to pay their bills; the offering of goods for sale and purchase on payment terms.

Working capital This represents exactly what its title suggests: it is the money that the business has available to work with to fund its day-to-day activities.

EXCESSIVE TRADE CREDIT

In order to attract more customers many businesses will offer 30, 60 or 90 days credit payment terms. Some companies even advertise 'buy now, pay next year'. The objective of this is to increase sales; however, this may often mean that cash inflows from a sale will not be realised quickly enough to meet outflows, that is, they will be faced with bills, wages and suppliers to pay before they themselves have received the cash in from customers.

EXCESSIVE STOCKS

Buying in bulk is cheaper per unit than buying the same amount in several small orders, thereby helping to reduce costs and raise profit. However, bulk, bought goods still need to be paid for and hence there is an associated large outflow of cash as opposed to several staggered smaller payments. Stocks then need to be stored, causing more cash outflows on storage costs with no cash inflows until the stock is sold.

Stock costs money to store

OVERTRADING

Overtrading results when a business tries to expand too quickly for the funds it has available. This is the case when expansion and growth – such as opening new outlets or buying a bigger factory – cause the business to encounter substantial financial outflow before generating a compensating inflow from sales. At the same time, the business already has payment commitments from existing areas of the business, such as wages and bills, and these can become difficult to meet due to the money being used to fund any expansion. As working capital becomes overextended, a profitable, successful business can face serious financial difficulty, including bankruptcy or liquidation.

SEASONAL FLUCTUATIONS

Seasonal businesses like theme parks, seaside hotels, sales of sun cream, open air swimming pools can find cash flow management difficult. Income can vary considerably between peak and off-peak periods, but some outgoings such as loans, mortgage or other fixed costs remain relatively constant every month. The effect of this is to place a large pressure on cash and working capital during out-of-season periods.

EXTERNAL FACTORS

These are more difficult to anticipate and correspondingly remedy, as in many cases they are out of the control of the business itself, and may include:

- actions of competitors, like a special offer or promotional campaign, that causes your business to lose sales
- interest rate increases causing increased loan payments
- increases in the strength of the pound against other currencies leading to increased competition from cheaper imports and fewer export sales
- innovation leading to product obsolescence (how many people now own a typewriter or a record player?)
- changes in legislation, for example, tougher pollution laws or an increase in the minimum wage, meaning increased business expenditure.

POOR PLANNING

This is a frequent cause of cash flow difficulty. Many businesses do not forecast cash flow at all. Others do so, but forget to include or anticipate all areas of expenditure, for example, tax payments. Many are simply over-optimistic when forecasting, for example, that sales receipts will increase massively due to any expenditure on marketing at all. Or they fail to recognise and foresee the full impact of seasonal or cyclical factors that can cause cash inflows to slow dramatically. For example, every four years there are events like the football or rugby World Cups and every time the rugby World Cup comes round, sales of national team replica football shirts fall.

Methods of improving cash flow

The clear reason, therefore, for drawing up a cash flow forecast is to prevent a business from running out of cash and not being able to meet its day to day running costs. In general, cash flow problems can be avoided by regular monitoring and careful management. Yet the problems outlined above can and do occur, especially the unforeseen ones. This raises the obvious question of how businesses can improve their situation when they do face or anticipate facing cash flow difficulties.

OVERDRAFTS

One commonly used solution is to arrange an overdraft in advance as soon as any problems are foreseen; though this may not address the underlying reasons why any cash flow shortage occurred, it does provide a safety net. An overdraft is essentially a short-term bank loan, allowing a business to draw more money from the bank than they actually have in their account. This causes the bank account to go into a negative balance, and although an overdraft may improve the short-term cash position, it will require making regular high-interest payments, so it does have implications for future cash outflows and reduces profits. Overdrafts are a form of flexible loan; as soon as the business has enough money, it can pay the overdraft back and stop paying interest. Thus an overdraft is very useful if a business only anticipates it may need extra funds for a short space of time.

SHORT-TERM LOANS

Arranging a short-term loan with a bank is relatively easy; this allows the business to receive a sum of money which it can deposit in its account, thus giving it more cash immediately available to meet its commitments and avoiding any possibilities of cash shortages. The business then repays it over an agreed period of time, making regular monthly payments. Although carrying interest charges, loans often have a lower rate of interest charged than overdrafts. However, they are not as flexible as overdrafts and the business will be committed to making payments for the whole term of the loan agreed; again this has implications for future cash outflows and for lowering profits.

FACTORING

Factoring debts is a service offered by banks or specialist factoring companies. Factoring debts involves selling debts owed by credit customers (debtors) to a factoring service who will give the business selling the debt an immediate cash advance, usually approximately 80% of the amount of money owed by the debtor. The factor collects the whole debt from the customer as it falls due for payment, and pays the business a further 10% or 15% of the debts' value taking the percentage difference left over as commission for their services. This method does provide a cash solution, but has a detrimental effect on profits as the business only receives 90–95% of the value of the debt owed.

SALE OF ASSETS

Selling assets, such as machinery and vehicles, is another way to gain a cash injection, although this then implies that the company no longer has the productive use of those assets. This is a good method so long as those assets sold were not needed or used by the business. However, it must be remembered that some forms of specialist machinery may be very difficult or impossible to sell, and sales of other assets such as premises or land usually take months to complete, so whilst it is possible to raise cash in this way it is only really helpful if the cash flow shortage has been anticipated in advance and the business has planned sales of assets to meet the predicted shortfall. Vehicles, however, can be sold relatively easily and quickly.

Businesses may hold substantial stocks which could possibly also be sold. However, this does depend on what form these stocks are in. Raw materials or partly-made products (work in progress) again may not be easy to sell, or sell and get a fair value. Even to be able to sell totally finished goods quickly to raise cash, businesses often have to reduce the price substantially.

SALE AND LEASEBACK OF ASSETS

An asset such as premises, machinery or vehicles is sold and then leased back from its new owner. Doing this means that the business gets an injection of cash from selling the asset, but still gets to be able to use the asset as they lease it back; however, they have to pay the new owner of the asset (the leaser) long-term monthly payments. So whilst improving cash flow short term, this method has further implications for increased outflows long term; it also reduces profits.

For example...

Once the UK's biggest construction and engineering company, Jarvis has suffered a catalogue of

problems since a train derailment on a track it maintained killed seven passengers in 2002. It also overstretched itself by bidding for a large amount of Private Finance Initiative (PFI) contracts. In a bid to get back on track, Jarvis sold assets to focus on its new core businesses. In December 2004 it disposed of its stake in the Tube Lines consortium, which was its most valuable asset, for £146.8m.

Adapted from BBC article http://news.bbc.co.uk/1/hi/business/4746431.stm

Preventing cash flow problems

If you compare the solutions above, a common theme is that in order to solve a cash flow problem *now*, the business must either lose something it values or commit itself to a longer-term payment process and/or interest payments as well. However, in many cases these actions do ensure the business's survival. Outlined below are a series of actions a business could take to try and avoid or minimise any possible future cash crises.

- Buying and holding fewer stocks, perhaps adopting a just-in-time approach, thus tying up less cash.
- Improving credit control, by allowing less time for customers to settle their bills (though this may have an impact on the number of customers the company has).
- Rescheduling payments so that large outgoings are spread over a period of several smaller payments, or so that large outflows take place only at times of cash surpluses, for example, paying the rent monthly rather than quarterly, or purchasing new fixed assets only at times when the company is cash rich.
- Extending trade credit from suppliers. Negotiating longer payment terms with suppliers will allow the company more time to generate cash inflows, making outflows easier. Ideally, a company should negotiate a longer payment period with suppliers than it offers to customers.

Alternatively, the company can try improving inflows by stimulating sales, although most forms of promotion will involve an initial cash outflow that potentially makes any cash flow problem worse.

Activity

Consider the following:

- Starbucks has undergone a rapid expansion in their number of outlets in recent years. How would Starbucks try to encourage custom and stimulate sales for a new store? What implications would this have on its cash flow before its sees the sales benefit from any increase in customers?

- Yaoh manufacture sun cream and skin care products suitable for vegans. This type of niche business may suffer from seasonal fluctuations in sales that might cause cash flow problems. What steps could Yaoh take to try and prevent cash flow problems from occurring?
- Although large companies like Woolworths, for example, do not sell goods to customers on credit, it is still possible for them to suffer cash flow problems. Think of two reasons why this situation could occur.
- All the ideas for improving a business's cash position have potential drawbacks. Consider the reaction of (potential) customers of electrical goods retailers like Comet and Currys if credit terms are restricted or removed entirely.

Further material and resources relating to this section can be found at **www.collins.bized.co.uk**. Keep checking for updates.

Improving cash flow: **Summary**

- Analysing cash flow involves more than just noticing whether or not a company goes into a negative situation. It also involves identifying periods when a business may be cash rich.
- It is important for businesses to determine not only that a cash flow problem could occur, but how deep it could be, how long it could last and why it occurred in the first place.
- Cash flow problems are encountered by many businesses during their lifetimes; identification of the cause of the cash flow problem will often provide pointers towards its solution.
- Methods of solving cash flow shortages often involve a trade-off between receiving cash now and higher future outflows.
- Methods of boosting cash inflows from sales through promotion will actually involve increased cash outflows. These solutions are therefore often not appropriate or feasible for some businesses to adopt.
- Prevention is better than treatment. Being proactive, anticipating problems and implementing effective cash flow planning and management is much better than reacting to cash flow problems once they have happened.

Summary questions

1 Define the term 'working capital'.

2 Give three reasons for analysing a business's cash flow statement.

3 Explain two consequences a business might face if it has insufficient cash available to meet its commitments.

4 Describe how a period of growth and expansion could cause a business to experience a cash flow shortage.

5 Explain two changes to external factors that could cause a business to face cash flow problems.

6 Outline the advantages and disadvantages of three actions a business could take to tackle short-term cash flow problems.

7 Explain two methods a business could use to try and prevent cash flow problems from occurring.

Exam practice

Webb Designs

Lee Webb runs a website design company specialising in producing websites for sports products, sports therapy and online fitness programmes. Until recently he had another designer working for him and two trainees. The problem appears to be that although Lee's company is receiving more and more orders, he doesn't ever seem to have the cash resources to be able to pay his workforce on time. This is despite the fact he took out a loan in May to help him meet his commitments and buy new equipment and software applications. This has lead to the resignation of his designer and one trainee, and consequently a loss in the amount of business the company is able to complete now he is left with only one trainee.

Figure 17.2 shows data from Lee's actual cash flow for the last four months.

	April	May	June	July
Cash inflows				
Sales	15,300	11,700	9,600	9,500
Loans received		10,000		
(1) Total cash inflow		21,700		
Cash outflows				
Wages and salaries	11,000	6,140	4,700	3,890
Office expenses	1,200	1,200	1,400	1,400
Heat and light	90	90	90	90
Water	110	110	110	110
Office rent	3,000	nil	nil	3,000
Rates (for the year)	n/a	4,200	n/a	n/a
Telephone/broadband	1,200	1,230	1,190	1,185
Advertising	150	150	150	150
Loan payments	nil	nil	345	345
Business insurance	300	300	300	300
Motor expenses	570	480	390	410
Capital expenditure (new equipment)		8,000		
(2) Total cash outflow				
(3) Opening bank balance/ (overdraft)	(400)			
(4) Net cash flow (1 – 2)				
(5) Closing bank balance (3 + 4)				

Figure 17.2   Webb Design's cash flow

1   Complete the cash flow forecast. (7 marks)

2   Undertake an analysis of your completed cash flow statement. What difficulties has Lee encountered over the last few months? (8 marks)

3   Using the information given, and any ideas of your own, analyse the possible options Lee could employ to solve and improve his situation. (10 marks)

4   To what extent are the factors that influence their cash flow under the control of Webb Design? Discuss. (15 marks)

Total: 40 marks

Chapter 18 Measuring and increasing profit

The objective of this chapter is for you to learn how businesses measure and assess how good their performance has been, by looking at their profits, and then considering how these profits might be improved.

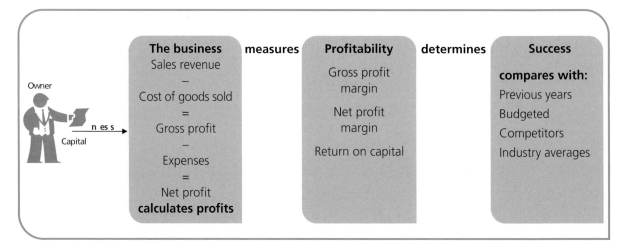

Figure 18.1 Measuring profit

The purpose of financial information is to provide data on how a business has performed over a period of time. Analysing profit results represents one way business performance can be assessed and is used for three main purposes:

- financial control
- planning
- accountability.

The analysis of profitability can help in interpreting financial information and assist owners and managers in achieving their objectives.

However, the results gained using these techniques mean absolutely nothing unless the organisation's objectives are also considered. Different businesses have different objectives. For example, for a sole trader like a family butchers shop to make an overall net profit of £200,000 could be regarded as being quite a healthy return. However, if we contrast this with the objectives of a major plc such as BP, who made a net profit of $22.5 billion dollars in 2006, a similar result of £200,000 at any time would be regarded as disastrous. Interpreting profit results is therefore largely dependent on the type of business it is and its objectives, which then have an influence on whether or not we consider particular results to be acceptable or unacceptable. For example, is making a profit of 1p acceptable?

- No, if every other business in our industry made thousands and we had invested our life savings into the business.
- Yes, if everybody else in our industry made a loss due to adverse economic conditions, at 1p we have outperformed every other business.

Measuring profitability

For most private business enterprises one of their main objectives is to make a profit. However, it is not sufficient just to measure the amount of profit made. Look at figure 18.2. Companies A and B both trade in the same market and at the end of the year they report profits as follows:

Company A		Company B	
Profit	£200,000	Profit	£2 million

Figure 18.2

In your judgement which is the better company? It would be reasonable to argue that Company B looks the better option. However, if we now consider some additional information:

Company A		Company B	
Profit	£200,000	Profit	£2 million
Capital invested	£400,000	Capital invested	£10 million
% return on investment	50%	% return on investment	20%

Figure 18.3

In figure 18.3 we can see that Company A has actually made a much higher return to the owners on the amount of **capital** tied up in the business compared to Company B.

So, as you can see it is not only the quantity of profit that matters, but also the amount of investment needed to generate this profit.

Because profit is so important and such a significant measure of performance, we actually measure different types: **gross profits** and **net profits**. This helps owners and managers to pinpoint areas of good and bad performance and so inform their decision-making for the future.

Profit performance is measured using three main formulas called:

- **the gross profit margin**
- **the net profit margin**
- **the return on capital.**

All these convert profit figures into percentage performance results. The reason for this is that it makes the results and comparison of the results easier to understand.

The calculation and understanding of gross profit margins

The gross profit margin examines the level of profit made from sales after the cost of the goods sold has been taken off. It shows the proportion of money generated through sales that the company has left.

Key terms

Capital The amount of money the owners have or an owner has invested in the business.

Gross profit This represents the amount of profit a company has made on its buying and selling activities only. It measures the amount of revenue generated from selling goods against how much those goods cost.

Gross profit margin This represents how good the business is at buying and selling. It shows the percentage profit left from the selling price after the cost of the goods which have been sold is taken off.

$$= \frac{\text{Gross profit}}{\text{Turnover (sales)}} \times 100$$
= expressed as a %

Net profit This represents the overall level of profit made by the business at the end of the period. It takes into account gross profit and then also takes off all the running expenses of the business. Net profit = gross profit − running costs (expenses).

Net profit margin This represents how well a business is being run. This shows what percentage of profit is left after all the day-to-day running costs have been deducted.

$$= \frac{\text{Net profit}}{\text{Turnover (sales)}} \times 100$$
= expressed as a %

Return on capital This is calculated to show the owner what percentage return they are receiving on the money they have invested into their business.

$$= \frac{\text{Net profit}}{\text{Capital invested}} \times 100$$
= expressed as a %

Gross profit = sales revenue – the cost of the goods sold.

For example:

> If we sell ten products for £100 each, then sales revenue = £1,000.
> But if each product cost £40 to purchase/manufacture then the cost of the goods we just sold = £400.

This would mean that the business has made £600 profit (£1,000 – £400) on buying and selling these goods. This is the gross profit.

The **gross profit margin** then represents the relationship between the profits made on buying and selling activities as a percentage. This is done so that our results can be more easily compared and understood.

$$\text{Gross profit margin} = \frac{\text{gross profit}}{\text{sales}} \times 100 = ?\%$$

So from our example:

$$\text{Gross profit margin} = \frac{600}{1,000} \times 100 = 60\%$$

Understanding the gross profit margin result

For the gross profit margin, the higher the percentage result the better, as this means that proportionally more of the selling price is left as profit. However, the level of gross profit margin made will vary considerably between different markets and products.

For example, the amount of gross profit percentage (sometimes called mark-up) put on clothes (especially fashion items) is far higher than that put on food. Some industries will try and sell a low volume of items but at very high prices and margins, whereas others will use very small margins and lower prices but attempt to maximise the volume of sales made. So any result gained must be looked at in the context of the industry in which the firm operates.

Alongside industry comparisons, the business should also make comparisons with its own figures from previous years to establish whether or not their trading position has become more or less profitable.

Improving the gross profit margin

The gross profit margin can be improved by:

- raising sales revenue whilst keeping the cost of sales static, that is, increasing price
- reducing the cost of the goods sold whilst maintaining the same level of sales revenue, that is, purchasing or manufacturing the goods for less
- a combination of the two.

The calculation and understanding of net profit margins

As opposed to gross profit margin, this ratio measures the relationship between the net profit (profit made after all other expenses have been deducted) and the level of sales made.

Net profit = gross profit – all the business expenses (day to day running costs)

or

Net profit = sales revenue – total costs

So, if we imagine that in our example above where we sold ten products for £100 each, on top of the cost of the goods that we are selling (10 × £40 each = £400), we also had to pay various expenses such as wages, fuel costs, administration or marketing totalling a further £500 then:

Net profit = gross profit – all the business expenses (day to day running costs)

= £600 – £500

= **£100**

Whereas gross profit margin measured the proportion of profit made on buying and selling, the net profit margin measures the percentage amount of profit left after all the running costs of the business are accounted for; in essence this is showing how efficiently a business is being run.

$$\text{Net profit margin} = \frac{\text{net profit}}{\text{sales}} \times 100 = ?\%$$

So from our example:

$$\text{Net profit margin} = \frac{100}{1{,}000} \times 100 = 10\%$$

Understanding the net profit margin result

The net profit margin is used to determine how good the firm has been in controlling its day to day running costs, for example, expenses. So, as with gross profit, a higher percentage result is preferred, as the higher the result, the less profit is being taken up by costs and so the more efficiently the business is being run and managed.

Again, any result should be compared with previous years' results and with other businesses in the same industry to judge relative efficiency, that is, a rising net profit margin would suggest that the company is becoming more efficient year on year.

The net profit margin should also be compared with the gross profit margin; if the gross profit margin has improved but the net profit margin declined, this shows that profits made on trading are becoming better, however the expenses incurred in the running of the business are also increasing and at a faster rate than profits. Thus efficiency is declining.

This can be investigated further by measuring each category of expenses in comparison to sales to determine where the problems are occurring. If any category of expenses has risen disproportionately compared with previous years, this may be a good indicator of the cause of the problem.

Improving the net profit margin

The net profit margin can be improved by the following:

- Improvements in the gross profit margin, for example, increasing the level of sales whilst keeping the same level of running costs; since

    Net profit = gross profit – expenses

    so any improvements in gross profit will have a knock-on effect to net profit margin results
- Reducing expenses whilst maintaining the same level of sales revenue, that is, increasing efficiency; for example, if we can spend less on marketing or reduce wages but still generate the same level of sales, we would have more profit left at the end and thus the net profit margin would improve.

The calculation and understanding of return on capital

The return on capital is often considered to be one of the most important measures of how successful a business is and how well it has performed. It measures what percentage return the owners have received from the money they have invested in the business. For example, if you placed your money in a savings account, you might earn 8% interest; this is the percentage return you are receiving from the bank on your money in that account. If, on the other hand, you chose to invest your money in a business, you do not earn interest, but instead get a share of the profits, so you would want to know what percentage return you were getting on the money you had invested. This is found by using the return on capital formula.

Return on capital is given by:

$$\text{Return on capital} = \frac{\text{net profit}}{\text{capital invested}} \times 100 = ?\%$$

For each business the idea is to determine how much profit has been made compared to the total amount of money invested in that business. For example, to make £100,000 profit when you have a £1 million to invest (a 10% return on your money) is somewhat easier than making the same £100,000 profit when you have only got £500,000 of capital in your business (that is, trying to make a 20% return on your money).

Understanding the return on capital result

As with the other profitability ratios examined so far, the higher the value of the ratio, the better. A higher percentage shows owners are getting a greater return on the money they have invested.

Inevitably again, this figure needs to be compared with previous years and other businesses to determine whether this year's result is satisfactory or not. It also needs to be considered alongside the businesses objectives; businesses frequently sacrifice short-term profits to achieve longer-term growth and expansion. Consider, for instance, that investing more money in a business to upgrade machinery may well not see immediate results, as employees take time to be trained to use it and to learn to use it efficiently and effectively; during this period of adjustment return on capital will fall.

As a final consideration this result needs to be compared with the percentage return offered by interest-bearing accounts at banks and building societies. For example, what is the point of a sole trader investing all his or her money in their business, working very hard all year and making a return on capital of 7%, if they could actually get a higher return placing their money in a savings account earning 10%? However, there are non-financial benefits resulting from being your own boss. Ideally, the return on capital should be higher than any return that could be gained from interest-earning accounts.

Improving the return on capital result

Ways for improving the return on capital are given below.

- Increasing the level of net profit generated without investing any more capital. This can be done by either:
  - improving the gross profit margin, that is, selling goods for more or buying them cheaper
  - improving the efficiency of the business, that is, reducing the day to day running costs so more profit is left.
- Keeping the same level of profits but decreasing the amount of capital it takes to generate them. In other words, investing less money into the business, but making it work harder so profit levels are maintained. This could be done by selling any assets the business owns that are not being used and the owners withdrawing the money from the company.

Methods of improving profits/profitability

With profit being such an important measure of business success, it is obvious that businesses will want to seek out and concentrate on ways in which their profitability can be improved. There are many ways in which this can be achieved, but like many other aspects of Business Studies, they frequently involve a potential trade-off with negative side effects. It must also be taken into account in each case whether the gain in profitability and implications are short- or long-term in nature. If improving profitability was that easy, then businesses would simply get better and better all the time. However, here we will consider some of the options available.

Raising prices

From examination of the gross profit margin it can be seen that simply raising the price of goods sold would increase the amount of margin on each product and hence improve profitability. But would it actually lead to higher profits overall? Potentially this is possible, but only if the business does not lose too many customers because of the increase in price. The exact effect of raising a product's price on the amount of revenue a company generates is dependant on how sensitive consumers in that market are to changes in price. This is measured by the product's price elasticity of demand. In other words, what will consumers do if the price is changed? This depends very much on the type of product on offer. There are two situations to consider:

Elastic products and inelastic products

An elastic product is one whereby any change in price causes a larger change in the amount of people who will buy it. In this instance, if the company raises its price then it would find that a proportionally large amount of its customers will stop purchasing it. So, for example, a 10% price increase causes a 20% fall in demand. An elastic product is one where consumers can easily switch from one product to another and they don't particularly mind which one they buy (they have little brand loyalty) for example cans of Fizzy drinks or chocolate bars. Raising the price of Fanta to be higher than the price of Coca-cola, Pepsi or other canned drinks, for example, would result in most consumers switching their demand to buying one of the cheaper alternatives available.

On the other hand, with an inelastic product if the company raises its product's price then it will only put off proportionally fewer customers from buying it – it will lose some customers, demand will fall, but the increase in price more than makes up for this. For example, a 20% rise in price only causes 8% of consumers to stop buying that specific product. This can occur for several reasons:

* The product in question is a necessity and people must buy it no matter what its price as they have fewer or no alternatives that they could buy instead. Good examples of this situation include products like petrol, milk, bread or products with addictive substances, like cigarettes.
* The product has brand loyalty and consumers will buy that brand as they believe that – despite the price increase – it is the best on the market, the one they want or must have (fashion), or the one that provides them with the most satisfaction. For example, some of Heinz tomato ketchup's consumers would not consider purchasing an alternative product.
* The product has a USP (Unique Selling Point). Although alternatives are available, none of them are quite able to offer exactly the same features as the original.
* The price of the product is not the key issue why consumers buy it. For example, if you put the price of a Ferrari up you only make it more exclusive and potentially desirable. It doesn't matter to most Ferrari customers if their new car costs £250,000 or £260,000.

For inelastic products the amount of consumers who stop buying the product is proportionally less than the amount of extra revenue the company will generate by raising the price. So companies with inelastic products can gain more revenue if they put they price up. This is why businesses spend large amounts of money developing USP's and brand names to make their products more inelastic.

In some cases a business with elastic products can raise its price and find itself in the situation where it does increase profits short term but loses out in the longer term, as it takes time for customers to eventually find and switch to cheaper alternatives.

Further material and resources relating to this section can be found at **www.collins.bized.co.uk**. Keep checking for updates.

Alternatively, a business with inelastic products which is able to raise its prices and lose relatively few customers will soon find itself attracting new competitors into its own market as they too want to benefit from the potential high profits to be made, and so again any benefits may be short-lived, whilst increased competition remains for the longer term.

Cutting costs

Again by looking at the gross and net profit margins it can be determined that if either the cost of the products or the running costs of the business are reduced, profitability will increase. But which costs? And how to reduce them?

Some suggestions for ways a business could cut costs are listed below.

- It could find a cheaper supplier. But will this also mean a drop in quality? Or are they less reliable? How would customers react to lower quality goods at the same price as before, or what would they do if they want a product now but your business has none in stock?
- It could bulk buy to reduce unit costs. But then the business has to store and protect the goods from theft, damage and wastage whilst they wait to be sold.
- It could cut staff wages or reduce training. This will improve short-term profits. But what happens to staff motivation, employee skill levels, labour turnover or quality of new staff attracted, and correspondingly, therefore, what happens to long-term productivity, efficiency and profits?

A business could cut back in all sorts of areas: marketing, market research, research and development and investment in machinery, for example. All of these have the positive effect of boosting short-term profits but also carry farther-reaching negative implications for the long-term.

Other alternatives

Businesses could switch their point of focus around and concentrate on improving profits and profitability in the long term. This could be done by investing in:

- training – higher-skilled employees are more competent and less wasteful
- motivation programmes – motivated employees are more productive
- new machinery or equipment – better, faster machinery also improves efficiency
- accurate market research – this makes advertising more focused and effective
- new systems – up to date IT systems can help cut costs of stock ordering, stock control and waste, or help reduce design costs or the time it takes for administration processes
- research and development – to develop USPs (Unique Selling Points) that have the potential to be priced more highly.

However, all the above possibilities imply higher initial costs and lower short-term profits, and all require the key word 'investing'. If owners invest more capital, this then (in the short term) will reduce their return on capital result. If they borrow the money to finance investment, then corresponding interest payments will also reduce profitability and also negatively affect cash flow.

It also needs to be understood that no matter what your business does, making increased profits is not guaranteed, as businesses cannot control:

- competitor actions
- changes in consumer trends, tastes, fashions
- changes to legislation
- economic conditions.

The distinction between cash and profit

The distinction between cash and profit is fairly straightforward; to start with, cash is real; it physically exists in notes and coins or in deposits in the business's bank account. Profit, on the other hand does not physically exist; it is simply a measure of the excess of revenue over costs. In other words, although businesses count profit at the end of a financial period, this is just a summation of all the revenue they have received from sales throughout that time minus all the costs they have had to pay.

For example...

Adam's specialist bike shop

In January this year Adam Loughman decided to give up his job as an accountant and follow his lifelong passion to become a professional mountain biker. To help support himself he also set up his own business, selling specialist mountain bikes to other enthusiasts.

Adam rents a shop for £1,000 per month, with the first payment due after one month from opening. He buys 10 bikes on one month's credit; each bike costs £1,000 and Adam sells them for £1,300. Adam sells all the bikes within two weeks of opening, generating £13,000 of income (and an initial profit of £3,000).

Cash = £13,000 sales
Profit = 10 × 300 = £3,000
Stock = £0

Adam then uses the £3,000 profit to buy three more bikes, but he has used up his best contacts already, so no more sales take place for the month.

Cash = £10,000
Profit = 10 × 300 = £3,000
Stock = £3,000

At the end of the month, Adam is now faced with paying his bills. He has to pay his supplier £10,000 and his landlord £1,000 for rent. However, Adam does not currently have enough money to pay both. He has to approach the bank for a £1,000 overdraft to enable him to pay his rent.

Cash now = £–1,000
Profit now = £3,000 – £1,000 = £2,000
Stock = £3,000

Adam still has on paper £2,000 profit and still possesses three bikes in stock. However, unless Adam can find new buyers he will soon have a cash flow crisis on his hands.

The figures above show that Adam's cash balance at the end of the month (£–1,000) equals his cash in (£13,000) minus his cash out (£10,000 purchases + £1,000 rent + £3,000 purchases). However, his profit (£2,000) at the end of the month is equal to his revenue generated (13,000 sales) minus his costs (£10,000 purchases + £1,000 rent).

So:

Profit = revenue – costs
Cash = cash in – cash out

Adam could solve his cash flow problem by introducing some capital into the business. This would improve his cash position but not his profits. Similarly, imagine the scenario if Adam was approached by a customer who wanted to buy all three of the bikes he had in stock at £1,300 each, Adam would receive £3,900 in payment but only raise an additional £900 in profit. So profit is only a method of measuring how well a business has done, not the amount of money it physically has. This is why it is absolutely possible that on occasion, profit-making businesses can run out of cash and face cash flow problems.

Activity

1 Plot the movement of cash and profit for Adam's bike shop as two separate lines on a chart.

2 Given that at the end of the month Adam's sales = £13,000; gross profit = £3,000; net profit = £2,000; calculate his:
   - gross profit margin
   - net profit margin.

3 Assume Adam has started his business with £7,000 of his own capital:
   - calculate his cash balance at the end of the month
   - calculate his net profit at the end of the month.

Measuring and increasing profit: **Summary**

- Measuring profits allows owners and managers to determine how successful their business has been and to identify areas for improvement.
- The gross profit margin shows how good the business has performed in terms of trading activities, buying and selling.
- The net profit margin shows how efficient the business is overall. It shows the percentage return left from sales revenue after all the business's costs have been accounted for.
- The return on capital demonstrates the percentage return an owner is making on their investment.
- The results of any analysis undertaken must be compared to previous years' budgeted results, competitors' or industry averages to determine the true level of any success.
- There are many ways in which a business can raise profits, but often these involve a trade-off between short-term and long-term goals and/or cash flow considerations.
- Profit does not physically exist in notes and coins in a business's bank account. It is simply a measure of the excess of revenues over costs.

Summary questions

1 Define what is meant by the term 'capital'.

2 State the formula for gross profit margin and give two ways in which any result could be improved.

3 State the formula for net profit margin and give two ways in which any result could be improved.

4 State the formula for return on capital and give two ways in which any result could be improved.

5 Explain two methods a business can use to analyse and compare its results.

6 Explain why cutting costs may not always lead to increased profits in the longer term.

7 Distinguish between cash and profit.

Points for discussion

- Although the analyses of financial results like the gross and net profit margins are important, what else would you need to know about a business and its environment before fully deciding on its degree of success?
- 'In order to boost profitability, a business must increase its sales revenue.' To what extent is this statement true?

Exam practice

In your capacity as a financial advisor you have been approached by one of your clients asking you to assess two possible investment opportunities. Study the following financial statements and then answer the questions that follow. Note: Companies A and B are in two different types of market.

	Company A £	Company B £
Net profit	10,000	20,000
Capital invested	50,000	100,000
Sales	500,000	200,000
Cost of sales	110,000	45,000

1 Calculate the following for each company:

(a) The gross profit.

(b) The net profit margin.

(c) The gross profit margin.

(d) The return on capital. (8 marks)

2 Using your results from question 1, comment on the strengths and weaknesses you can identify in each company. (8 marks)

3 Company A has decided that in order to improve its results it needs to undertake an extensive marketing campaign to boost sales and profits. Analyse the likely success of this approach on Company A's results. (9 marks)

4 'A profitable company is a successful and secure company.' To what extent do you agree with this statement? (15 marks)

Total: 40 marks

UNIT 2
SECTION B

Finance:

People in business

Section overview

This section details the main ways a business focuses on the way it organises its workforce, measures their effectiveness and tries to improve its employees' efficiency, productivity and profitability over time. A business's workforce is key to the success of any business, and this section seeks to explore the issues faced by managers and human resource management when making decisions regarding their organisational structure, employees, job roles, and job design and reward systems.

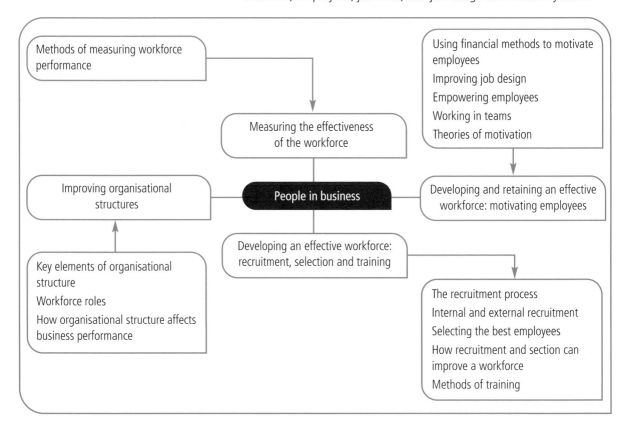

Key concept

People in business

It is often said that the people are the most important asset of a business, and in many ways this is true. The employees of a business are the ones who actually produce the goods or services and interact with customers on a regular basis, and it is through the employees' levels of commitment, training and motivation that the image of a company will be formed.

From the managers who are making the strategic decisions to the shop floor employees, it is the people involved in an organisation who influence the quality of the good or service provided and the level of service and satisfaction that customers receive. Businesses therefore want a workforce that is competent, productive and efficient. To achieve this, a business must recruit, retain and train their workforce to gain the necessary skills they require to operate effectively, and simultaneously motivate employees to be productive and efficient. An unsuitable, idle or unproductive employee can cost a business much more than just their wages.

These factors in turn will influence costs, the level of sales, repeat customers, and ultimately the profitability and success of the business.

For example...

The irresistible lure of the duvet and the tantalising prospect of a day filled with tea and daytime TV resulted in 21m 'suspect sickies' last year that cost the UK economy £1.6bn, a survey has revealed.

A poll conducted by the CBI and insurers AXA revealed that employees took an average of seven days off sick in 2006, and lost 175m working days. This compares with an average of 6.6 days in 2005, and 164m days lost. Long-term absence of 20 days or more accounted for 43% of all working time lost, costing £5.8bn. The total cost of workplace absence last year was £13bn.

Source: http://www.guardian.co.uk/business/2007/apr/10/ukeconomy.workandcareers

Activity

Consider your timetable (including free periods) for a week at your school or college.

- Total up the number of hours you are present on the premises and then work out the amount of time you are actually engaged in productive activities to do with your educational or skills development. This includes looking at what proportion of your lesson time you actually spend engaged on tasks and activities set, as opposed to socialising, talking with friends, e-mailing, surfing the net or just daydreaming. Try to do this is accurately as possible. If you have a job and would prefer to base this activity on your working hours, please do so.
- Work out what percentage of your total time is been spent productively.
- If possible, gather the results from three other class members.
- If this was your business, how would you feel if your employees – whom you are paying – did not apply themselves to their job 100% of the time?
- What steps would you take to try and make your employees more productive?

Chapter 19   Improving organisational structures

By the end of this chapter you should appreciate the different ways in which businesses can be organised and the impact different types of organisation have on business performance.

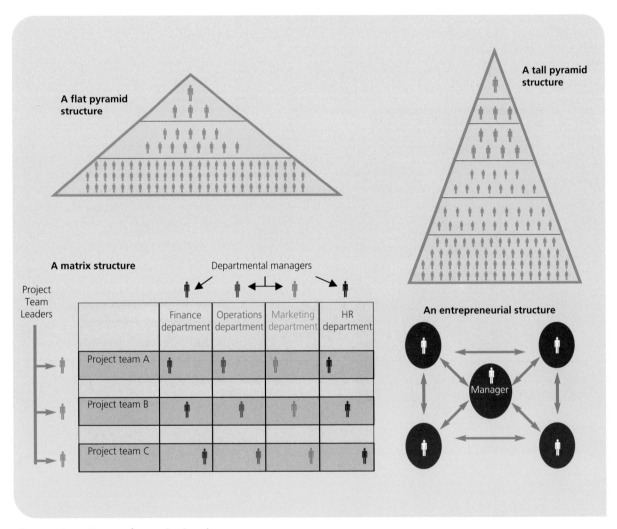

Figure 19.1   Types of organisational structure

Key elements of organisational structure

The organisational structure of a business represents the particular way that business has been arranged in order to help it carry out its business activity. The organisational structure shows a number of important aspects about a business.

- First, it shows the structure of authority within the business. Who is in charge of and responsible for whom.
- Second, it shows the roles and titles of individuals within the business, that is, who is responsible for different areas.
- Third, it shows the staff to whom individual employees are accountable.
- Finally it shows the routes by which communication passes through and around the business.

Types of organisational structure

Figure 19.1 details the main types of organisational structure in use by businesses today.

Hierarchical or pyramid structures

The most traditional form of business is the hierarchical/pyramid structure because of its shape. This structure separates employees into different layers depending on their seniority in the business. Pyramid structures can be regarded as being tall or flat depending on the number of layers of employees. In this type of organisation the business is often divided into departments with clearly defined job roles within departmental areas. This type of structure is often formal and bureaucratic.

Matrix structures

A matrix structure is more commonly adopted by businesses that have a project or task-based approach to work. In a matrix structure business departments still exist but individual employees from those departments also work within project or task teams. In figure 19.1 you can see that an individual belongs not only to a specific department but also to a specified project. This type of structure puts together teams of people with a range of skills from different areas that are needed to get a certain task or project completed. Matrix structures are less formal than pyramid structures and employees are placed within projects based on their ability to contribute to its success, not their formal status in the hierarchy.

Entrepreneurial structures

This form of structure is often adopted by small businesses or organisations where speed of decision making and communications are vital to success. An entrepreneurial structure is characterised by being dominated by one central figure (usually the owner or entrepreneur). The organisation has little formality or hierarchy as this structure relies on the central figure issuing power and instructions to a few key employees. The key support workers must possess good skills and be very flexible in their approach to make this structure successful.

Levels of hierarchy

The number of layers of staff within an organisation determines the **levels of hierarchy** present.

Each layer shown within the business organisational structure represents a level of authority, and the higher up the layers you go, the more authority the individuals possess. Equally, therefore, the lower down the structure you go, the less authority the employees have. Typically a structure like this would show managing directors at the top,

Key terms

Delegation This occurs when a manager passes down the authority for completing a task to a subordinate employee.

Levels of hierarchy The number of different layers of staff there are in an organisation.

Organisational charts A way of representing the way a business is organised and its lines of communication in a pictorial form.

Span of control The number of subordinate employees a manager is directly responsible for.

TALL/HIERARCHICAL STRUCTURES

Advantages	Disadvantages
• Clearlines of formal authority and responsibility.	• Slow communications and decision-making.
• Narrow spans of control.	• Large number of managers/supervisors required.
• Promotion opportunities.	• Slow communications.

FLAT/HIERARCHICAL STRUCTURES

Advantages	Disadvantages
• Fast communications and decision-making.	• Lines of authority and responsibility can become blurred.
• Low number of managers/supervisors required.	• Wide spans of control.
• Workforce is given wider scope and responsibility.	• Lack of promotion opportunities.

MATRIX STRUCTURES

Advantages	Disadvantages
• Allows fast decision-making.	• Slow communications and decision-making.
• Allows for improved communications.	• Large number of managers/supervisors required.
• Promotion opportunities (departmental and project-based).	• Lines of authority become crossed.

ENTREPRENEURIAL STRUCTURES

Advantages	Disadvantages
• Relatively flat.	• Lack of promotion opportunities.
• Good communication channels.	• Potential information overload for manager.
• Speed of decision-making.	• Wide spans of control are common in this form of structure.

passing down through managers, assistant managers, supervisors, and so on, down to junior members of staff at the bottom.

The number of levels present within an organisation is an important factor to consider. For example, the more levels there are, the longer it will take for any messages or instructions to flow from the top of the organisation to the bottom, and the longer it will take for any questions/queries to flow from the bottom to the top. The hierarchy or number of levels present represents what is known as the 'chain of command'. Any instruction or communication is passed through the organisation, up or down, via the chain of command. The taller the structure, the longer the chain of command becomes. A tall structure is regarded as being any organisation that has more than three levels in the hierarchy and a flat structure has three levels or less.

Spans of control

A span of control is the number of people reporting directly to one person who has authority over them, for example, the number of employees an individual manager is responsible for in his or her area. Spans of control can be considered to be wide or narrow, that is, a manager has the responsibility for a large number of subordinate staff (wide span of control) or only has responsibility for a few (narrow span of control).

The narrower a manager's span of control is, the fewer the number of employees they have to look after. This means that the managers are able to devote more time per employee and keep a close control over their activities. The wider the span of control, the more individuals that the manager is responsible for, and so the less time they have for each. Each individual is not as closely controlled, but there is a need for fewer managers overall as each manager controls more staff.

It is normal for spans of control to become narrower the further up the business hierarchy you travel. This is because the more senior the member of staff, the more complex their own duties become and so the harder it becomes to manage each individual effectively. There is therefore an obvious relationship between spans of control and levels of hierarchy present; the taller the organisational structure, the more levels there are and the narrower the span of control, that is, the more levels present, the fewer people on each level and so the narrower the span. Again looking at Figure 19.1, the middle managers in the flat structure have a much wider span of employees beneath them than any corresponding level from the tall structure.

NARROW SPAN OF CONTROL

Advantages	Disadvantages
• Managers control fewer employees and so can spend more time with each.	• More managers are needed so business costs increase.
• Less stress for each individual as job roles and responsibilities are clearly defined.	• Close supervision of employees and narrow job roles can cause demotivation.
• The narrower span means more layers in the hierarchy and thus more opportunities for more frequent promotion.	

WIDE SPAN OF CONTROL

Advantages	Disadvantages
• Each employee has a broader job role allowing them to use and develop more skills. • Needs fewer managers to be employed thus saving cost on management wages. • Less close supervision and more independence for employees can promote feelings of trust, responsibility and motivation in the workforce.	• The manager has less time for each individual employee. • Fewer layers and managers mean fewer promotion opportunities for subordinates.

Workloads and job allocation

According to business theorists the 'ideal' span of control for any manager ranges from five to eight, but the correct span of control for any manager depends on the size, type and culture of the business and the type of employees they have, alongside the nature of the task the employees are performing. For example, it would not be uncommon for a manager whose subordinates are fairly unskilled and who are involved in fairly simple, similar and repetitive tasks to have a span of control of ten to fifteen employees.

The key factor here is that both managers and employees have the time necessary to be able to perform their tasks, and time available to be able to communicate with each other as necessary. Managers and employees have to communicate in various ways to:

- pass and receive instructions
- provide feedback on progress and information
- agree targets and deadlines
- discuss problems and action plans.

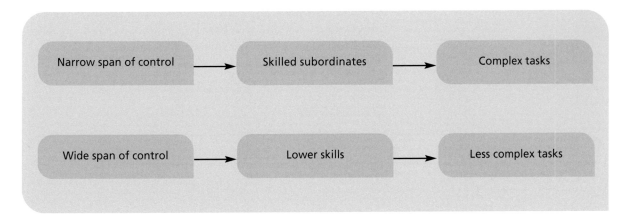

Figure 19.2 The relationship between span of control and employees' abilities

The general rule is that the more skilled the employee, the more complex the tasks they can be allocated to undertake, and the more responsibility and authority they can be allowed in making decisions for themselves. However, alongside this, therefore, is the corresponding factor that the more complex their tasks, the more help and direction they may need at times and the more skills and more time any manager must have to deal with these areas effectively, so the narrower their span of control should be. This is shown in Figure 19.2.

Problems thus arise with workloads and job allocation when managers are given too wide a span to control for the complexity of the tasks their subordinates are undertaking. Alternatively, if a manager has too narrow a span of relatively low-skilled staff, in this case the manager may have too much time and may over-supervise employees, or become inefficient and demotivated from having too much idle time.

Delegation

One way for managers to be able to deal with wider spans of authority with higher-skilled staff performing more complex tasks is to use **delegation**. Delegation occurs when a manager passes down the authority to complete a certain task to a more junior member of staff. This means giving the subordinate the power to make and enforce decisions on the manager's behalf.

The subordinate now becomes responsible for the staff who have been allocated to the task along with all materials, resources and budget relating to the job. As the task proceeds, the subordinate has to account to the manager on progress, as it is still the manager's ultimate responsibility that the task is completed. It is therefore now the manager's job to see that targets are being met, but the subordinate's responsibility as to how they are met. If any tasks or targets are not completed satisfactorily it is still the manager who will be held accountable as they are still responsible for the performance of their staff.

The table below outlines the key advantages and disadvantages of delegation.

The key to good delegation in practice is to have mutual trust between managers and subordinates – trust that delegated tasks will be carried out efficiently and effectively, and trust that tasks delegated are worthwhile and a true recognition of that employee's skills and development. This process relies heavily on good communication.

DELEGATION

Advantages	Disadvantages
• Frees up manager's time, thus allowing a wider span to be managed.	• Delegating authority can be risky if staff are untrained or lack skills.
• Motivates subordinates.	• Managers may only delegate dull or impossible tasks.
• Allows subordinates to develop higher skills.	• Some staff may not want extra authority or responsibility and so be demotivated.

Communication flows

Small businesses with few employees may have very short and direct lines of communication; everyone knows who everyone else is and what job role they do. Thus decision-makers can quickly be informed of important issues and the business can react quickly to any changes or developments. Any actions that need to be taken can then, in return, be quickly communicated throughout the organisation and put into effect.

As a business grows, so does the difficulty in ensuring effective communications. The more employees a business has, the more difficult it becomes communicating to each individual. The taller the structure and the more levels of hierarchy any communication has to pass through, the longer any message will take and the more likely that a barrier to communication could arise, such as the message getting lost or being delivered to the wrong person. To combat this, organisational structures are designed to show the way in which communication should flow in an organisation. For example, if a particular instruction or message is for a particular level of employee, then the **organisational chart** should show all employees on that level, such as assistant managers, who they are and what area they work in. Or the message may be for a particular area, again the chart should then show to which manager the communication should be given, to pass on to that area, division or project, for example.

Key problems arise in the flow of communications in that the taller the structure, the longer the chain of command and thus the slower any form of communication from top to bottom will be (vertical communication). However, the flatter the structure (fewer levels), the faster the speed of vertical communications, but often the less clear the specific lines of authority within particular areas. Tall structures often face difficulties with horizontal communications as well (communications between areas on the same level), as functional lines of authority and responsibility (chains of command) flow vertically up and down throughout the organisation and not from side to side.

To combat the problems of slow speed of communications (vertically and horizontally) or unclear channels, many business adopt the model of a matrix structure (see Figure 19.1) which involves a combination of departmental and team-based structures. This has the effect of reducing apparent layers in the communication process and should make the speed of communications faster and thus improve the decision-making and responsiveness of the business.

Workforce roles

For a business to operate effectively it needs to have a range of job roles and skills. These range from the people running the business and making the strategic decisions to the employees carrying out the day to day tasks and functions. The key job roles in most organisations are directors, managers, supervisors and team leaders. These are examined individually below.

Directors

Directors are essentially members of the board who control an organisation. Directors are appointed by the shareholders of a business to control and manage the activities and affairs of the business on their behalf. In practice, directors themselves are often shareholders as well. The role of directors is largely strategic, that is, to determine the aims and direction of the business. It is their role to determine the culture of the organisation and what it is trying to achieve. The directors generate a corporate or strategic plan for the whole organisation and then use this to set corporate objectives which are then passed down the hierarchy as targets for specific areas, divisions, functions, projects or departments to achieve. The board of directors usually appoints one of its members to act as chairperson or managing director. It is the managing director's responsibility to see that the policies decided on by the board are implemented into the business.

Managers

Below the level of directors there can be several layers of managers: senior managers, departmental managers, project managers or assistant managers, for example. It is the duty of managers to undertake tasks and activities as given to them by directors, and to see to the implementation of company policy. Managers' activities can be grouped into four main functions: planning, organising, leadership and controlling (see the table below). In effect, it is managers who take the responsibility for the day to day decision-making within the business.

THE FUNCTIONS OF MANAGERS

Planning	Organising	Leadership	Controlling
This involves setting out long-, medium- and short-term detailed schemes for attaining the business's objectives. Examples include setting budgets or planning a marketing campaign.	To implement plans and achieve objectives managers must effectively organise their staff and resources to ensure that each area has what it needs at the right place and at the right time.	Managers need to employ their skills to ensure employees are working towards the business's objectives. This includes gaining the trust, commitment and cooperation of employees, and providing direction for their activities.	Finally, managers have a responsibility to monitor the effectiveness of their operations and evaluate their own and their employees' performance. This requires setting and measuring standards and then generating action plans.

Supervisors/team leaders

A supervisor or team leader provides a link between the management levels and the normal operatives and support staff of the business. They fit in the hierarchical level just below management and in essence are responsible for very specific projects, activities or functions. Supervisors and team leaders tend only to deal with the day to day tasks of their area and only direct individuals under their specific control in the performance of that task; they tend not to have wider management responsibilities. The responsibilities of a supervisor or team leader include:

- decision-making in respect of issues that occur on a day to day basis
- monitoring short-term work targets
- controlling the day to day allocation of work tasks
- notifying managers of operational problems as they occur
- implementing corrective actions.

A distinction can be made between the terms 'supervisor' and 'team leader', though in reality many businesses use the two terms as meaning the same. In many organisations a supervisor allocates and controls day to day activities but does not actually get hands on with the work themselves. A team leader on the other hand would be supposed to allocate and control activities in much the same way, but also then be a part of the team working on the completion of those tasks as well.

It is worth noting that many supervisors or team leaders may well have more involved management functions as well if extra responsibilities have been delegated into their control.

How organisational structure affects business performance

A variety of factors can influence the way in which a business chooses to be structured. These include the following:

- **Management style** Some managers will prefer to retain direct control over their organisation whereas others may be more willing to delegate.
- **The size of the business** The larger a business is, the more likely it will need formal control systems and formal, systematic lines of communication. Larger businesses tend towards taller/hierarchical or matrix structures.
- **The market in which it operates** This can influence a business's design. In a market where change is frequent and speed of response is paramount, such as technological, fashion or highly-competitive industries, the business will need a structure that promotes speed of communications, quick decisions and flexibility. This type of business may well choose to deliberately employ a flatter organisational design.

A business must take all these factors and more into account when considering how it should be organised. However, each type of structure has some definite advantages and disadvantages in performance, such as the speed at which decisions can be made or how communications flow around the business.

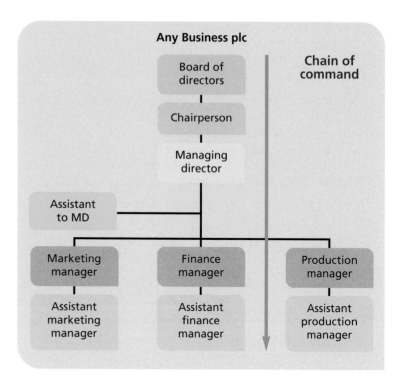

Figure 19.2 Chain of command

Further material and resources relating to this section can be found at **www.collins.bized.co.uk**. Keep checking for updates.

Activity

Look at the diagram in Figure 19.2 and then answer the following questions.

1 What is the managing director's span of control?
2 List the chain of command from the managing director to the assistant finance manager.
3 How many levels of hierarchy are shown?
4 Identify what type of organisational structure this is.
5 Explain two advantages and two disadvantages of this type of structure.

6 From the following information draw an organisational structure chart for Croft Ltd:

• The business has four levels of hierarchy.
• The managing director has a span of control of four.
• There are four functional managers: Finance, Marketing, Operation and Human Resources.
• Each functional manager has two supervisors.
• Each pair of supervisors is jointly responsible for ten operations staff.

Improving organisational structures: Summary

- Levels of hierarchy refer to the number of layers within an organisation. A tall structure has more than three layers and a flat structure has three or fewer layers.
- The span of control measures the number of subordinates a manager has direct control of.
- Workloads and job allocations have to be matched to the level of skills employees possess and the type of tasks undertaken.
- Delegation occurs when a manager hands authority for completing a task to a subordinate but retains responsibility for its completion.
- Different types of organisational structure affect the speed and ease with which communications flow vertically and horizontally within a business.
- The main workforce roles in most businesses include directors, managers, supervisors and team leaders.
- The way in which a business is organised can have a direct effect on performance by influencing levels of hierarchy, spans of control, speed of communications, speed of decision-making and employee promotion opportunities.

Summary questions

1 State two uses of an organisational chart.

2 Distinguish between a flat and a tall structure.

3 Explain what is meant by the term 'span of control'.

4 What are the disadvantages for a business of having spans of control that are too wide?

5 What are the main advantages for managers of delegating authority?

6 What is the main role of a director in a business?

7 Describe the four main functions of managers.

8 Describe two ways in which organisational design could affect a business's performance.

Points for discussion

- Despite the evident drawbacks, tall hierarchical structures are still the most common form of business structure. Discuss why this might be the case.
- In order to improve the speed of their responsiveness to market changes, many organisations have attempted to flatten their structures, at the same time accepting wider spans of control. Discuss the factors for and against this type of approach.

Exam practice

Canon, which produces automotive, aerospace and cinematography products, is renowned for giving its engineering teams as much autonomy (independence) as possible. 'Someone once said that in a bureaucracy the boss is your only customer,' says Harry Gilfillan, the business development manager. 'Management teams and long chains of command often stifle creativity because they put people in boxes. We don't operate in a hierarchy and there are no management teams.'

This approach leaves staff free to apply their skills and creativity, streamlines product development and keeps lead times short. Purchasing is delegated to shop-floor personnel, who have budgetary responsibility and deal directly with salespeople. Matrix style teams are set up to work on particular projects. The structure of the company is based on the customer, not on a formal hierarchy.

1 Define the term 'hierarchy'. (5 marks)

2 Examine the advantages and disadvantages of employing a system of delegation. (10 marks)

3 Analyse the benefits and drawbacks of matrix-style structures. (10 marks)

4 Discuss how Canon could measure the effectiveness of its approach to organisational design. (15 marks)

Total: 40 marks

Chapter 20   Measuring the effectiveness of the workforce

This chapter is concerned with how businesses can see if their workforce is happy and productive, and whether they are becoming more or less efficient over time. By the end of this chapter you should be able to calculate three key workforce performance indicators and interpret what they mean about the state of that business's employees.

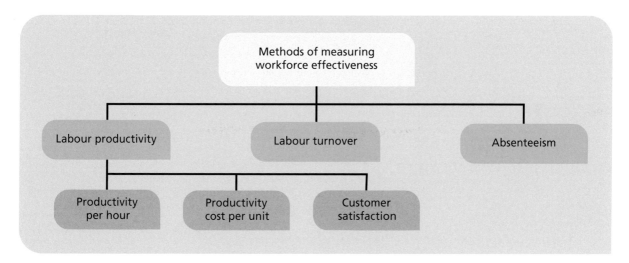

Figure 20.1   Methods of measuring workforce effectiveness

Methods of measuring workforce performance

Recognition that the employees are a business's most valuable asset has lead to the emergence of HRM (human resource management) as a key function in business. HRM focuses on managing and developing people to help achieve the business's overall aims. The success of human resource management can be assessed in relation to a range of specific targets and measures. These are: **labour productivity, labour turnover** and **absenteeism**.

Labour productivity

Labour productivity is a measure of the average output per worker over a period of time. Higher productivity means that each worker is producing more units of output, on average, in the same amount of time as before. The more productive an employee is, the more production costs can be cut, and this will mean the business is more cost-competitive, and hence an increase in profit margins. Increased labour productivity is a measure of the success of HRM policies because it is likely to reflect the skills, attitudes and motivation of the workforce – aspects that it would otherwise be difficult to measure.

Key terms

Absenteeism The percentage rate of staff who have taken days off work over a set time period.

Labour productivity How effective employees are at producing goods and how many units an employee produces over a set period of time.

Labour turnover How good a company is at keeping its staff and the percentage number of staff who have left the business over a set period of time.

Labour productivity can be measured in two ways.

Output per worker over time

$$\text{Labour productivity per hour} = \frac{\text{Output}}{\text{Number of labour hours}}$$

For example, if 4,000 units of a product were made in one week by 20 employees who each worked four shifts during the week and each shift was eight hours long, then:

$$\text{Labour productivity per hour} = \frac{4,000}{(20 \times 4 \times 8)} = 6.25 \text{ units per hour}$$

Labour cost per unit

$$\text{Labour productivity cost per unit} = \frac{\text{Output}}{\text{Total wages}}$$

Following the same example, if each employee was paid £12.50 per hour they worked, then:

$$\text{Labour productivity cost per unit} = \frac{4,000}{(20 \times 4 \times 8 \times £12.50)}$$

$$= £0.50 \text{ or } 50\text{p per unit}$$

It is often necessary to use both calculations to get an accurate measure of labour productivity. This is because higher-skilled workers should be more productive, but would also cost more, so a comparison between results needs to be made.

IMPROVING PRODUCTIVITY

Labour productivity can be increased if employees are able to make more units in the time period allowed or if they can make the same amount but for a cheaper cost. The main ways this can be achieved are:

- increasing employee skill levels through training and development
- increasing investment in production machinery used by employees, that is, buy better, up-to-date, faster and more efficient equipment for them to use
- increasing workforce motivation, so employees spend more of their time at work in a productive fashion and less time in non-productive pursuits, for example, surfing the net for private reasons.

However, although all of the above will increase the productivity of employees, each comes with its own associated cost, training and investment, so is not free after all and hence any productivity gains must exceed any money spent to make the increase worthwhile.

QUALITY

It is also worth making a point here about product quality. A business's employees can quite easily raise their labour productivity per hour by simply making more products in that time than they normally do on average. However, in most industries there is little point in them doing so if, in reality, it just means they are rushing their work and turning out products of a poor quality.

Poor quality products can lead to loss of customer satisfaction and demand, and thus a fall in future sales. Increased costs to the business can also occur, as poor quality products may be faulty or defective, and need to be reworked or simply thrown away.

So, businesses must ensure that any increases in productivity do not come at the expense of a reduction in the level of quality, particularly if quality is a key factor in why consumers choose their product.

SERVICE INDUSTRIES

For businesses that do not manufacture a product, measuring workforce effectiveness can be a more difficult task as there is no physical quantifiable output that can be counted. However, these types of business will still want to know how well their workforce is operating. Service sector industries will thus use a variety of different methods to measure their workforce. These could include:

- measuring the number of customer complaints received in a time period
- measuring the average length of time it takes for a customer to be served or for their call to be answered
- customer satisfaction surveys which require customers to complete a questionnaire regarding the level of service they received.

Guru's views

'Ultimately, whatever the form of economic activity, it is people that count the most.'

– *Lord Sieff*

Labour turnover

Labour turnover is a measure of the rate of change of personnel within a company's workforce. It is calculated as:

$$\text{Labour turnover \%} = \frac{\text{Number of staff leaving per time period}}{\text{Average number of staff employed per time period.}} \times 100$$

So if, during one year, five members of staff left out of a workforce of 50 people, the rate of labour turnover would be:

$$\text{Labour turnover} = \frac{5}{50} \times 100 = 10\%$$

Reducing labour turnover is a target for most businesses, because high labour turnover brings with it a number of costs:

- disruption and lost output or sales when an employee leaves
- costs of recruiting, selecting and training a replacement employee
- unsettling impact on remaining employees, which could harm morale
- loss of experience, skills and knowledge.

Tackling high labour turnover will depend on its causes. Possible causes can include:

- uncompetitive wage rates
- poor morale among the workforce
- low job satisfaction
- poor working conditions

- failure of recruitment and selection processes to find the appropriate person for a job
- failure to develop skills and talents of the workforce.

The HRM function will need to identify the specific causes for any high level of labour turnover and plan how to remedy this effectively.

However, a successful HRM policy will not necessarily mean a 0% labour turnover, which represents no changeover of staff over a period of time. This is because:

- there will always be some staff wanting to leave for personal reasons (retirement age, and so on)
- new staff can add fresh ideas and enthusiasm to a business
- a business may need new skills in its workforce that are best gained through new recruitment rather than retraining existing staff.

Effective HRM will seek to balance the benefits against the costs of labour turnover to achieve a low, but healthy rate of turnover.

Absenteeism

Absenteeism refers to the number of staff who take days off work compared to the overall size of the workforce. It is measured as:

Rate of absenteeism %

$$= \frac{\text{Number of staff absent per time period}}{\text{Average number of staff employed per time period}} \times 100$$

So, if over the period of one month 25 employees had time off due to illness or medical appointments, for example, and on average that business employed 275 full-time staff per month then:

$$\text{Rate of absenteeism \%} = \frac{25}{275} \times 100 = 9.09\%$$

This means that on average in our example, 9.09% of staff are absent from work at some point during that month.

Businesses seek to reduce absenteeism, because high rates of absenteeism:

- reduce productivity – since output is lost when staff miss work
- increase employment costs – because additional workers need to be employed to cover absences, or overtime needs to be paid to existing workers
- harm the morale and motivation of the whole workforce, as some employees start to feel they are been asked to do more than their fair share or cannot complete tasks due to other staff absences.

Further material and resources relating to this section can be found at **www.collins.bized.co.uk**. Keep checking for updates.

Solutions to high rates of absenteeism depend largely on the reasons why the absences are occurring to begin with. In other words, the remedy is specific to the cause. Potential causes of staff absences and their possible remedies are shown in the table on the next page.

POSSIBLE CAUSES OF ABSENTEEISM	APPROPRIATE SOLUTIONS
• Failure to ensure health and safety in the workplace, causing accidents or illness to members of staff.	• Improve working conditions to remove hazards and create a more pleasant working environment.
• Stress caused by poor relationships with managers or colleagues, for example, by bullying.	• Strong action against bullying or harassment, as well as efforts to encourage teamwork and to create a positive social atmosphere.
• Boring, stressful and unrewarding jobs.	• Job redesign to include enrichment and opportunities for staff development.
• Lack of financial incentive, for example, no loss of pay through absence.	• Financial incentives to link pay to productivity and attendance, for example, piece rates/ performance-related pay or attendance bonuses.

Measuring the effectiveness of the workforce: Summary

- Labour productivity is a way of measuring how efficient a workforce is at producing finished products.
- Labour productivity can be measured by calculating either the output per employee or the labour cost per unit.
- Labour productivity can be increased but sometimes at a cost to the quality of the products being produced. Increased productivity must go hand in hand with maintaining quality standards.
- Service companies can measure their workforce's effectiveness by measuring standards such as customer complaint levels, customer waiting times or customer satisfaction surveys.
- Higher rates of labour productivity indicate an increasingly efficient workforce and corresponding lower production costs. This in turn leads to increased profit margins.
- Happy employees will stay with their current employer; unhappy employees will seek employment elsewhere. Labour turnover measures the amount of employees leaving the business.
- High rates of labour turnover raise the business's costs as staff who leave need to be replaced, increasing the frequency and costs of recruitment.
- A certain level of labour turnover is healthy for a business as new staff will bring in fresh ideas.
- High rates of staff absence will adversely effect labour productivity; absent staff are not productive and hence cost per product will increase.

Summary questions

1 Explain two methods of measuring labour productivity.

2 Explain why is it necessary to have two ways of measuring labour productivity.

3 Explain how a service sector business like a restaurant could measure the effectiveness of its staff.

4 Why might a certain level of labour turnover be seen as being good for a business?

5 Give three reasons how high rates of absenteeism can adversely affect a business's performance.

Point for discussion

Some industries, like fast food outlets, are well known for their high rates of labour turnover but seem to make little effort to address this issue. Discuss the reasons (for and against) why businesses in these areas might take this approach.

Exam practice

Margrave Engineering Ltd produces high-quality electrical cable for use in top-end hi-fi and computer equipment. Whilst their market is fairly specialised, Margrave does not retail to the general public, selling only to large electronic manufacturers. It is becoming increasingly competitive as more and more companies switch from their traditional engineering base into the growing and profitable technological markets.

Kay and Richard Margrave believe that in order to stay competitive they must constantly seek ways to improve their productivity and stay ahead of their competition in the level of service and customer satisfaction that they offer. Richard says quite frequently that 'for any business to ensure its long-term success it must continually focus on improving its productivity levels'.

Richard has recently researched the possibility of purchasing a new wire spindling machine, a new type of technology only just available which allows electrical core wires to be twisted much more densely than traditional methods. The advantage of this is that in general terms the denser the wire, the better its conductivity and the better the performance of the product. Richard has also been assured that once employees have been trained to use the new technology their higher skill levels will increase Margrave Engineering's labour productivity. Kay hopes that this sort of investment might also help to improve the business's labour turnover and absenteeism figures.

1 Explain two ways any increase or decrease in labour productivity could be measured. (5 marks)

2 Analyse two factors other than increases in productivity that could have an influence on whether or not Margrave Engineering should buy the new technology. (10 marks)

3 Discuss the factors why Kay Margrave might hope that 'this sort of investment might also help to improve the business's labour turnover and absenteeism figures'. (10 marks)

4 To what extent do you agree with the statement that 'to ensure its long-term success a business must continually focus on improving its productivity levels'? (15 marks)

Total: 40 marks

Chapter 21 Developing an effective workforce: recruitment, selection, training

The aim of this chapter is for you to understand how companies attract, recruit and train their employees to be the best they can, and the impact that doing this correctly can have on improving a business's workforce.

A careers fair

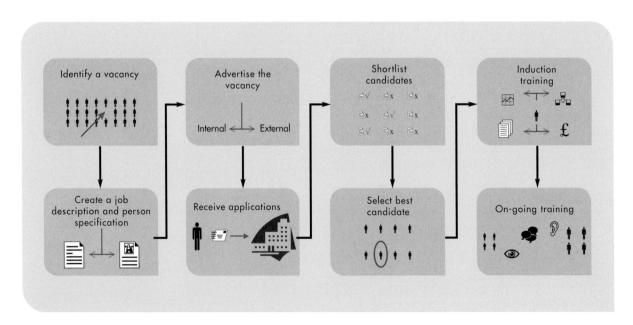

Figure 21.1 Recruitment, selection and training

The recruitment process

The idea of the **recruitment** process is to try to ensure that the right person is chosen for the job that is currently available. As you will see through this chapter, the recruitment process can be an expensive and time-consuming exercise, so getting recruitment right represents a worthwhile investment. The aim is to:

- recruit high quality staff, with the necessary skills and experience
- ensure that the process is efficient and cost-effective.

Failing to recruit the right staff can have a massive, negative impact on the business's performance. Figure 21.1 details the stages of the recruitment process a business must complete to attract applications from potential candidates.

Identifying a vacancy

There could be several reasons a business needs to recruit more employees. Vacancies (job openings) may occur within a business for many reasons. These include:

- a member of staff promoted within the business
- a member of staff resigning
- a member of staff retiring, or a death in service
- new posts being created or new job roles being introduced
- business expansion and/or diversity into new markets
- increase in demand for their products.

However, businesses also have to look closely at other factors that may affect their demand for staff in the future. There are many areas which might increase (or decrease) the need for staff within a business. For example, development of new technology may mean that the same output can be achieved with fewer staff or changes in legislation may restrict the hours that individual employees can work.

Job descriptions and person specifications

Having identified that a vacancy exists, the business must now ensure that it attracts and appoints the right person to the job. By attracting the correct and best employees for any particular job role, businesses can gain increases in efficiency and productivity and thus have a competitive advantage over rivals. Therefore, before advertising the post the business must make very careful decisions about what the job available is, what the successful candidate must be able to do, what skills they must possess and what personal characteristics would be suitable.

JOB DESCRIPTION

A **job description** involves putting together a detailed description of the tasks, responsibilities and working conditions of the post available. A job description should be created for every job role within the business and is composed of five main areas:

1 Job title – a descriptive title that should convey what the main purpose of the job is, for example, Telesales Representative or Logistics Manager.

Key terms

External recruitment When the business advertises for suitably qualified applicants who do not currently work for the business.

Induction A period of initial training given when a new employee joins a company.

Internal recruitment When a business fills a vacancy from within its existing workforce.

Job description A detailed list of the roles and responsibilities involved in a particular job.

Off-the-job training Methods of training that involve the employee stopping their normal work while training takes place.

On-the-job training Methods of training that take place while the employee is still engaged in his or her work tasks.

Person specifications The skills and personal characteristics necessary in the person required to fill a job.

Recruitment The process the business goes through to find the best staff for the business.

Selection The procedure the business follows to choose the best staff from those who apply.

2 Purpose – a short summary of the principle function of the role. For example, for the Logistics Manager above the purpose might be described as follows: 'A logistics manager is responsible for managing processes involved in a supply chain and liaises with a variety of parties, including suppliers of raw materials, manufacturers, retailers and, increasingly, consumers'.

3 Key tasks – a list of the specific activities the post holder is required to carry out. So again for a Logistics Manager, these may include:

- monitoring the quality, cost and efficiency of the movement and storage of goods
- coordinating and controlling the order cycle and associated information systems
- analysing data to monitor performance and plan improvements
- allocating and managing staff resources according to changing needs
- liaising and negotiating with customers and suppliers
- developing business by gaining new contracts, analysing logistical problems and producing new solutions
- implementing health and safety procedures
- managing staff training issues
- motivating other members of the team
- project management
- setting objectives.

4 Scope of the role – this outlines the range of the job's responsibilities, including who the post holder is responsible to and who they are responsible for (their span of control).

5 Special requirements – this section details any specific other requirements that the business offering the vacancy needs. For example, this may include a specific level of qualification, or the need to be able to work shifts or travel away from home.

The job description should be able to give anyone reading it a clear picture of the main activities and responsibilities anybody appointed would be expected to be able to perform.

PERSON SPECIFICATION

The **person specification** is based more on the personal characteristics required than job responsibilities. It sets out the desired qualities the ideal candidate should possess. The person specification identifies the skills and abilities required to perform the job successfully. It allows selectors to make accurate comparisons between applicants and usually involves a checklist against which to judge the desirability of each candidate. A person specification usually consists of three key areas:

- Essential requirements – personal characteristics that the candidate must possess to be considered for the post.
- Desirable requirements – qualities and attributes that would be advantageous but not essential to starting the job. For example, it might be good for a candidate to have a particular qualification or experience, but if they did not yet have it they could start the job and then be trained.

- Contraindicators – a list of criteria or characteristics that would make any candidate immediately unsuitable for the job role offered, for example, any unspent criminal convictions.

Examples of matching job adverts, job descriptions and person specifications can be found at **www.collins.bized.co.uk**. Keep checking for updates.

Advertising the post

All job adverts should use the job description and person specification to form the basis of trying to attract the right applicant. Job adverts should be worded to appeal to potential applicants that possess the required skills and attributes, but should also deter people without the correct qualifications. They should also be well written and presented to provide a positive image of the business that is advertising.

The advert then needs to be placed in the correct place so that it will attract suitably qualified individuals to apply. However, advertising can be expensive so the positioning and cost of the advert needs to reflect the level and experience of staff required. Advertising job vacancies can take place through a number of mediums that vary quite considerably in terms of cost and audience, such as:

- newspapers – local and national
- specialist trade/industry magazines
- job centres
- Internet recruitment sites
- company's own website
- recruitment agencies
- direct contact with schools, colleges or universities.

The job advert also needs to detail the process any interested party needs to complete in order to apply for the post.

Methods of application

The application process can vary from company to company, but usually takes the form of providing one or all of the following:

- Submitting a CV – (Curriculum Vitae) this is a document that outlines a candidate's education, professional qualifications, employment history and experience to date.
- Completing an application form – this is a generic form sent out by the company to each interested applicant which they then need to fill out and return. This has several advantages over submitting CVs as the business can direct applicants to key questions that are particularly relevant to the job and all applicants will supply their information in the same format, which makes comparison of individuals much easier. Many companies now have their application forms available online for candidates to download, or via e-mail.
- Letters of application – these are letters sent by potential candidates to the business that outline their reasons why they think they are suitable for the post being offered and what their relevant experience is. This can give businesses a good idea of candidates' abilities, knowledge and skills but make it very difficult for accurate comparison as the structure and information in each letter will have wide variations.

Whichever method is chosen, candidates must then submit their completed applications to the business. The business also needs to decide on whether or not the job is also open to internal candidates to apply.

Internal and external recruitment

When a vacancy arises the business must decide whether or not it wishes to recruit from existing employees or attract new experience into the business. Internal recruits have the advantage that they will be familiar with the business, its processes, routines and methods of operation, whereas external candidates have the advantage that they can bring new ideas, methods or knowledge to the company.

Internal recruitment

Internal recruitment can take place by promoting an existing employee from their current post into the vacancy that is now available; alternatively a business can redeploy an individual from their current job role into a new one. Internal recruitment has a number of benefits for the business:

- It is cheaper for the business as there is no expensive external advertising.
- Internal recruitment policies enable existing employees access to chances for promotion in future. This can act as a motivator for them to perform better in their current roles.
- Selecting the best candidate for the post can be easier as the potential candidates are already well known to the business.
- Candidates have experience of the business's culture and operations and do not need **induction** training and settling-in periods.

The drawback with internal recruitment is that the business only has a limited number of employees from which it can make its **selection**; it might be the case that existing employees do not have the skills or experience that the business really needs.

In some circumstances the business may just reorganise and in this case instead of appointing an existing employee to the vacancy, it simply shares out the workload amongst its existing employees, giving each one more responsibility.

External recruitment

Owners and managers often want to have a wider choice of candidates for the selection process, so they may choose to advertise any vacancy externally. **External recruitment** attracts new employees into the business, and selecting from a larger potential pool of candidates gives the business the opportunity to attract applications from more highly-qualified, skilled or experienced applicants.

However, advertising externally is a more expensive process and the candidates are not previously known to the business. This makes selecting the best candidate more difficult and therefore there also needs to be a rigorous selection process in place. This again makes external recruitment a more costly and time-consuming exercise for the business than internal.

Figure 21.2 summarises the internal and external methods of recruitment available.

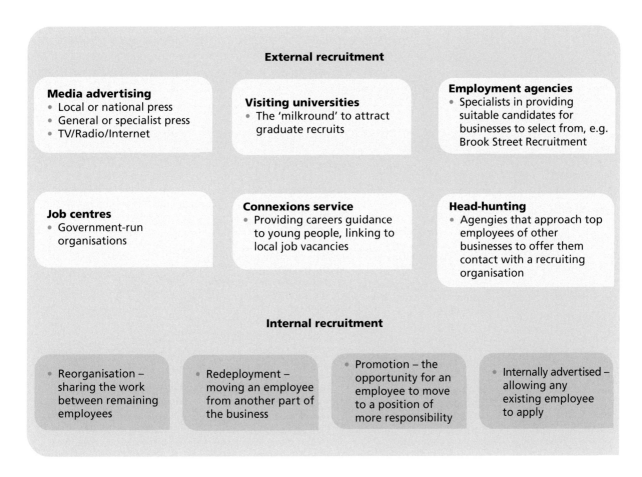

Figure 21.2 Methods of recruitment

Selecting the best employees

The selection process is about choosing the right candidate for the job. The first stage in this is to draw up a shortlist of candidates from the applications received, that is, in many cases it would be impossible for a business to interview all the applicants for a job, so it must reduce this number down to a more manageable level; this is called shortlisting. Shortlisting is usually done by comparing the candidates' applications with the criteria listed on the job description and person specification. Candidates who pass the shortlisting stage are then invited to go through to the final stages of the selection process.

The table below lists the selection methods in widespread use by many businesses, and highlights their benefits and drawbacks. In most businesses, the most widely-used selection process is the interview and obtaining references from previous employers, however, as the table below shows, this is not the only method available.

Benefits and drawbacks of different selection methods

However, as has been discussed, recruitment and selection can be an expensive and time-consuming process, so businesses must think about the methods of selection they use compared to the vacancy they have available. For instance, evidence shows assessment centres are an effective method for selecting employees for managerial or executive positions, but would be far too expensive, time-consuming and therefore inappropriate a method to use if recruiting a Sales Assistant, for example.

Selection method	Description	Benefits	Drawbacks
Application forms/Curriculum vitae (CV)	• How 97% of UK businesses collect information about candidates – through use of their own application form or a curriculum vitae (CV) prepared by the candidate. • Summary of a candidate's qualifications, skills and experience.	• Enable key data to be compared with the person specification, so that unsuitable candidates are sifted out; provide a good basis for interview questions for the rest. • Advantage of a standard format offered by application forms – easier to sort – and the opportunity to ask carefully chosen questions.	• Leave important questions unanswered – cannot alone provide for effective selection. • The information desired by the business perhaps not provided by CV.
Interviews	• Face-to-face meetings to question short-listed candidates and find out more about their suitability for the job. • Should be conducted in a structured and objective way that allows candidates to be compared fairly.	• Provide an opportunity to discuss the written details submitted by the candidate as well as wider issues about the job and the candidate's qualities and ambitions. • Enable the business to evaluate whether the candidate would fit in, and relate well to colleagues. • Allow the business to sell itself to candidates and thereby encourage the best one to accept a job offer.	• Impressions formed on the basis of candidate's appearance or interview technique, due to subjective nature of interviews. • Interviews unreliable indicators of a candidate's ability to succeed in a job, according to research findings.
References	• Contact details, provided by candidates, of previous employers or other individuals that will confirm a candidate's qualities or experience.	• Provide important evidence that the skills and experiences claimed by a candidate are genuine.	• Far from objective and not necessarily reliable – candidates choose referees that are likely to commend them for the job.

Testing	• Ability tests – testing a specific skill relevant to the job, e.g. numeracy. • Personality tests – also known as psychometric testing – seeking to measure aspects of the candidate's attitudes and characteristics, e.g. risk-taking or risk-avoiding; increasingly common in the UK for executive recruitment.	• A cost-effective and easy-to-use method, providing further evidence of a candidate's suitability. • Can directly simulate the challenges and requirements of the job to see whether a candidate, if appointed, could cope.	• Not necessarily objective or fair – may be biased in choice or wording of questions. • Some candidates becoming skilled in giving the 'right' answers in personality tests. • Notion of 'ideal' personality type perhaps leading to an organisation full of personality 'clones'.
Assessment centres	• Short-listed candidates invited to an assessment centre to undergo a range of assessment techniques – interviews, testing, group exercises, simulations – that reflect the demands of the job. • Performances of each individual observed and rated by trained assessors.	• A reliable and valid selection technique using a wide range of methods relevant to the job role. • Objectivity to the selection process brought by qualified assessors, while line managers involved in observation and decision-making.	• A time-consuming and expensive method of selection which is therefore only appropriate for large firms and executive positions.

How recruitment and selection can improve a workforce

The costs of the recruitment and selection process in time and money can be considerable, but the costs of selecting and appointing the wrong person for a job can be even greater. If we choose the wrong person for a position then the business could suffer problems associated with:

- low productivity
- poor quality production
- poor customer service and relations
- increased labour turnover and further costs of recruitment and selection replacing other employees who have left.

Selecting the right employee for the right post can help to bring about improvements in all the above areas. As well as this, do not forget the key benefits, such as bringing in fresh ideas and working practices, or acting as a motivator for existing staff.

A significant way in which the recruitment and selection process can improve the overall workforce performance is that a good process should reduce the labour turnover of the business. If you select the right staff then they are likely to be happy and content to stay with the business – this will reduce recruitment and selection costs in the medium- to long-term.

Methods of training

Developing an effective workforce, though, is not just about recruiting the right employees. Business is a dynamic operation, and markets, tastes, fashions, laws and technology change constantly. This means that unless a business wants its workforce to fall behind and give its competitors an advantage, it needs to correspondingly update and develop its workforce's abilities and competence. This is done through training which is the process of teaching employees new skills or developing qualities and characteristics they already possess.

Training should be an ongoing process throughout an employee's career, to reflect the changing needs of the business and the market in which it operates. The first stage of training any employee should receive is induction training, and this should then be built upon with continuous development through **on-the-job** or **off-the-job** training techniques.

Benefits

Whatever the type of training undertaken, the business should benefit in a range of ways. These include:

- Low labour turnover – employees will wish to stay with a company that is improving their skills and experience.
- Improved productivity – higher-skilled employees are able to work more quickly and with fewer mistakes over a wider range of tasks.
- Increased motivation and staff moral – employees who are receiving training feel valued by the business they work for and feel that training increases their own value, and this can prove to be a motivational factor for many.
- Lower rates of absenteeism – increased motivation and the desire to achieve new skills and qualifications can lead to employees taking less time off work.
- Improved quality of goods, service, and health and safety records.

Training the workforce of a business can thus in turn help to reduce costs through increasing efficiency and productivity, to increase revenues through improved image and service levels and therefore raise profitability. It can also help to improve the company's competitive advantage, as a well-trained workforce is likely to be more flexible, more innovative and more willing to suggest and implement new ideas.

Drawbacks

However, although training a workforce comes with many benefits, there are also some drawbacks to consider. The most obvious one is cost, including:

- Paying for the training provider, materials and/or venue.
- Disruption and lost productivity whilst employees undertake training.
- Expenses payments, for example, travel costs of employees training away from the workplace.
- Extra management and administration to identify, organise, implement, record and monitor training programmes.

One of the main problems businesses encounter when training their employees is that they often don't always get to receive the full benefits of that training. Because other businesses may not have invested time or money paying for training programmes, they can use this saved expenditure to offer higher wages instead. This enables businesses who don't train their staff to poach readily trained employees. The new business then receives the benefits of that employee's higher skill. The cost of training and the potential of poaching leads many businesses to under-provide training for their staff.

Induction training

Most businesses now have a formal programme of induction training for any new employee. The idea of induction training is to train a new employee quickly in the broad responsibilities of their job, and introduce them to the systems, policies and structure of the business they are now working for.

Induction training allows a new employee to settle into their new role and become more productive more quickly. New employees should be able to function in their job role and know from the outset what they are meant to be doing, how they are meant to do it and who they need to approach if they have a problem. This prevents new employees from making costly mistakes or remaining idle due to lack of direction or instruction. It also helps to introduce the new employee to their colleagues and hopefully helps them to feel more welcome or prevent feelings of isolation from occurring. This in turn will again help to reduce labour turnover (that is, leaving the job very quickly) and helps to prevent further costs of recruitment and selection.

On-the-job training

This type of training takes place whilst the employee is in the workplace and undertaking their normal working role. This is not specifically for new employees who have just joined, but a method of training for both new and old employees alike. On-the-job training is designed to help raise employees' skills and abilities but with no loss of their time and productivity from their day to day tasks.

On-the-job training can take several forms. These are:

- **Coaching** – where a supervisor or more experienced employee guides a trainee through the stages involved in a job, or teaches the employee how to improve the quality of their work as they progress through a task.
- **Mentoring** – where a lowered-skilled employee is assigned a more experienced colleague who they can approach for help/advice on how they can best carry out a particular task or solve a problem.
- **Job rotation** – instead of employees sticking to a given task or tasks, they are moved round the business to work on different tasks and in different areas. This broadens their skills and also their knowledge of how the company operates, allowing different departments and areas greater understanding of each others' requirements. This also makes the employees' work more varied and hopefully, therefore, more stimulating and motivating.

- **Job shadowing** – in this instance a less experienced employee follows and observes the work of a more experienced colleague. This allows the less-skilled employee to see for themselves how more-skilled employees handle different situations and tasks, and learn from observing their actions.
- **Sitting with Nellie** – this is a similar approach to job shadowing above, but combines an element of coaching as well. In this method the junior employee observes the senior employee performing a task (as in work shadowing) but then has a go at performing the task themselves with the senior employee offering help and guidance where and when required (coaching). This technique is employed until the inexperienced employee feels happy, confident and practised enough to be able to carry out the task in future on their own.

Off-the-job training

This type of training method involves the employee stopping their normal tasks and undertaking a training course away from their routine activities. Off-the-job training can still take place in the workplace but frequently involves studying off-site at a college, university or specialist training agency. Off-the-job training methods include:

- **In-house courses/qualifications** – these are training courses provided by the employer themselves, often using more experienced employees to deliver the material to more junior staff. For example, a member of the finance department may provide training for all departmental managers on budgeting, or a member of the production team may provide training to office staff on health and safety in the factory.
- **Bought-in training** – in many cases businesses may not have the in-house experience or staff to deliver the training they need, for example, if legislation has changed and the business needs to comply with new procedures. In this situation the business may well hire an outside training company to come in and deliver the training it needs.
- **External courses** – this type of training occurs when an employee is sent off-site to receive training from another agency. This may include a range of activities from one-day events to regular release from the workplace to study a formal qualification at a college or university. This type of training has several advantages:

  - the employee can gain a nationally recognised qualification
  - the course may be better quality than could be delivered in-house
  - it may be cheaper for the company for an employee to join an existing course than providing one themselves.

- **Computer-based training** – many training courses are now available online or via PC-based resource packages. The advantage of this form of training is that it can be accessed and undertaken by the employee at any time, even from home, and the same package can be used to deliver the same training to different employees at different times. Thus employees can develop their skills at their own pace and each piece of training is relevant to them at that stage.

Further material and resources relating to this section can be found at **www.collins.bized.co.uk**. Keep checking for updates.

Comparing types of training

Both on and off-the-job training are valuable techniques for raising employee skills. However, each type has some distinct advantages and disadvantages, examined in Figure 21.3.

	On-the-job training	Off-the-job training
Advantages	• Job and company specific. • Comparatively inexpensive. • Easy to organise and monitor.	• Delivered by specialists. • Trainee can concentrate on the course, no work place distractions. • Training can be nationally accredited and provide employees with recognised qualifications.
Disadvantages	• Trainers may not have specialist training skills. • Can be disruptive to the work environment as **trainers** are taken away from their normal working role. • Employees may not receive recognised qualifications and so may question the value of the training.	• Training may be more general and not be job or company specific. • Off-the-job training is comparatively more expensive • Can be disruptive to the work environment as **trainees** are away from their normal working role.

Figure 21.3 Advantages and disadvantages of on-the-job and off-the-job training

For example...

Of course!

Training has become the Holy Grail to some organisations – evidence of how much management truly cares about the workforce. No wonder so many employers see it as an asset. Ideally, not only do staff acquire skills that will help them to work more efficiently, they also get a moral boost – it's gratifying to think you are perceived as worthwhile to invest in.

Unfortunately, it doesn't always work out that way. Even with carefully identified training needs and full management support, the most effective training is not always the result. Many off-the-job business courses are too long or try to cram too much into one day. It is often more efficient (though more hassle) to spread courses over several half-days. And, since – apparently – we forget 70 per cent of everything we have learned on a course within three days, some managers think twice before sending employees on expensive training courses.

Activity

1 What is meant by off-the-job training?

2 State two advantages to an organisation of having well-trained employees.

3 State and explain two problems that might be associated with having a poorly trained workforce.

4 Consider whether 'ineffective' training might be better than no training at all.

Developing an effective workforce: recruitment, selection, training: **Summary**

- The objective of the recruitment and selection process is to try and ensure that the best person available is chosen to fill any existing vacancy.
- Every vacancy should have a corresponding job description and person specification that detail the tasks, working conditions and responsibilities of the post alongside the essential or desirable characteristics the ideal candidate should possess.
- Jobs can be advertised in a variety of ways but they need to be placed so they attract the right calibre/grade of employee and portray the business as one they would like to work for.
- Employees can apply for a post in three main ways, by submitting: a CV, an application form, a letter of application or any combination of these, for example, an application form and a covering letter.
- Internal recruitment is cheaper and easier to undertake, and the potential for promotion can prove motivating for existing employees.
- External recruitment is a more expensive process but can bring fresh ideas, methods and knowledge to the business.
- By getting recruitment and selection right the business can hope to achieve increased efficiency, productivity and profits.
- To remain competitive in the short- and long-term, businesses should continually train and develop their employees. This can take the form of induction, off-the-job or on-the-job methods of training.

Summary questions

1　Give three reasons why a vacancy can occur in a business.

2　Distinguish between a job description and a person specification.

3　Explain the importance of a job description and person specification in the recruitment and selection process.

4　Outline three advantages of advertising and recruiting a vacancy internally.

5　Explain two disadvantages of external recruitment.

6　Suggest two reasons why a business may prefer applicants to complete a standard application form rather than submit their CVs.

7　Outline two methods of selection that might be appropriate for selecting a new senior member of staff such as a department manager.

8　Outline three objectives of an induction training programme.

9　Distinguish between off-the-job and on-the-job training and give one advantage and one disadvantage of each.

10　Explain two reasons why training is important to a business.

Points for discussion

'Training is time-consuming and expensive for businesses and many feel it is a waste of time, as well-trained employees are poached by other companies who can afford to pay higher wages as they don't invest in training for their employees.'

- Given this viewpoint, discuss whether or not training of employees is essential to a business's long-term success.

'The customer is the most important factor in any business's success.'

- Discuss to what extent training can help a business to satisfy their customers' wants and needs.

Exam practice

'Are you a high flyer?'

KLMJ Commercial Investments is a highly successful venture capitalist company based throughout the European Union. The KLMJ graduate recruitment and promotion scheme was designed with the specific intention of attracting and retaining some of the world's very best university graduates. Candidates must be prickly, focused, intolerant of failure and proven achievers.

The company seeks to externally recruit only exceptionally talented staff with between one and three years' experience in banking, investment or commercial developments, who also possess an established track record of excellence. KLMJ look for over-achievers who feel that their current position is not offering them the opportunities for development and reward that they demand.

The application process for KLMJ is very rigorous. KLMJ do not advertise vacancies; they expect potential candidates to come to them. Candidates must submit a twenty-page application and a CV. Then they must take part in numerous interviews, a psychometric test, a four-day event at an assessment centre and finally, for the successful few, a two-day residential interview with Kurt Miechelson, one of the founding directors of KLMJ.

Induction training is short and tough, successful candidates are expected to hit the ground running and to make an immediate impact. Those appointed are often expected to take on a senior role within one of the company's enterprises and produce targeted improvements in performance from the outset.

The rewards though are substantial. Salaries start at £60,000 to £80,000 per year, with healthy bonuses and fringe benefits like a company car and private health schemes. KLMJ Commercial Investments has to date created over twenty millionaires. If candidates get through the recruitment and selection process and then survive induction they could really be flying high.

1 What is meant by the term 'induction training'? (5 marks)

2 Explain the advantages to KLMJ of using an assessment centre as part of its selection process. (10 marks)

3 Analyse the strengths and weakness of KLMJ's external recruitment policy. (10 marks)

4 Given that successful recruitment is never certain, discuss the advantages and disadvantages of KLMJ Commercial Investment's approach to recruitment. (15 marks)

Total: 40 marks

Chapter 22 Developing and retaining an effective workforce: motivating employees

Motivated employees perform better, benefiting not only the individuals concerned but the company as a whole. By the end of this chapter you should understand the different approaches businesses adopt to try and motivate their staff.

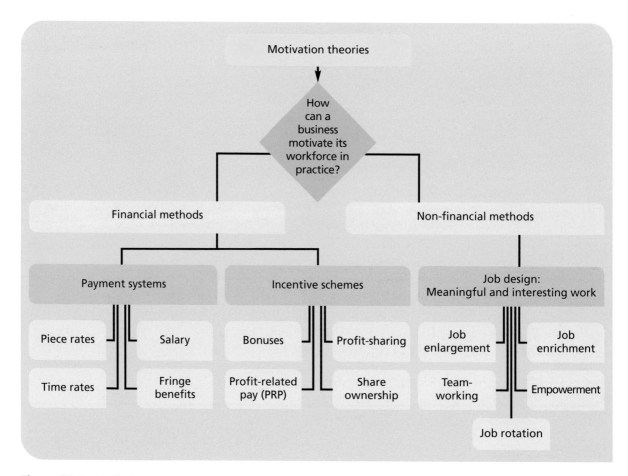

Figure 22.1 Motivating employees

Why motivate employees?

Businesses need to ensure that their employees are motivated or they can potentially suffer from poor performance and high staff turnover rates. Poor performance can lose business through poor quality goods or service, for example, and staff replacement is extremely costly.

If employees are unhappy in their work they are unlikely to perform as well as they might, and they are more likely to want to leave. The goal for businesses is to find ways of motivating their staff to stay in the business – **staff retention** – and to perform to the best of their ability. Employees' **motivation** can be affected by many different factors, from pay levels to the way they are managed and the environment they work in.

It is therefore important to offer the right pay, incentives and working conditions package to the right level of employee; employees at different levels within a business's hierarchy will want and desire different things. For example, a £1,000 pay rise to a junior employee may prove quite an effective incentive, but for the Finance Director such an increase may not provide any extra incentive.

A motivated workforce is important because it can help a business to boost its profitability, through both increased revenues and reduced costs.

- Increased effort results in higher productivity.
- Pride in the work leads to improved quality.
- Loyalty to the business reduces labour turnover.
- Commitment to the business reduces absenteeism and the likelihood of industrial conflict.
- Personal development can allow the business to get the very best from its workers' skills.

Businesses use a variety of financial and non-financial motivators to create a reward package suitable for their employees. But the 'package' of rewards offered to employees must achieve certain objectives:

- a motivated and productive workforce
- a workforce that is flexible in meeting the organisation's needs
- the recruitment and retention of the best workers
- value for money in ensuring the reward is cost-effective in what it achieves.

To start with we will examine the variety of financial motivators businesses can offer, instead of just a basic pay.

Using financial methods to motivate employees

No theory of motivation ignores the relevance of money. Some theorists see it as a factor of primary importance; others, see money as important in preventing employee dissatisfaction but not a motivator in itself.

Financial rewards can be divided into two types:

- payment systems – methods of calculating and providing the basic pay for a job
- incentive schemes – rewards to recruit, retain and motivate workers.

Key terms

Commission Employees (usually salespeople) are paid a percentage of the value of what they have sold by way of reward.

Delegation Giving authority to lower levels of management so they have the power to use the business's resources to produce and deliver goods and services.

Empowerment Giving employees greater control by providing them with decision-making powers that have an effect on their working lives.

Fringe benefits Payments to workers in a non-monetary form, such as company cars or private health care.

Job enlargement Giving workers more tasks to do in the same production process, so they can see a product from start to finish.

Job enrichment The system of making an employee's tasks more interesting, challenging and varied across a wider range of activities.

Motivation The desire, interest or drive to want to work.

Performance-related pay An incentive scheme that is used to motivate employees by linking their pay to the achievement of pre-agreed performance targets.

Piece rate A method of paying employees for each unit of output they produce.

Profit-sharing A scheme which involves distributing a share of the profits made by the company to its workforce.

Share ownership This is similar to a profit-share scheme except that employees gain shares in the company and then receive a share of profits via dividend distribution.

Staff retention This measures a business's ability to keep its employees.

Time rates Employees are paid a set rate for a specific length of time, for example, per hour or per shift.

Payment systems

PIECE RATES

A **piece rate** system pays workers for each unit of output that they produce. The main problem with this method is that there is no guaranteed level of basic pay, and no sickness or holiday pay. Piece rates are most commonly used in manufacturing industries, such as clothing. Piece rates are thought to motivate employees because they directly reward those who work harder, that is, the more an individual produces, the more they themselves get paid. The theory is then that this should encourage employees to work as hard as they can as they will directly benefit from it. However, piece rates have been criticised for:

- producing low pay and insecurity, even for those who work hard
- encouraging workers to sacrifice quality in the search for a greater quantity of output
- making the workforce resistant to change, for fear that it will harm their rate of earnings.

TIME RATES

With **time rates**, employees are paid for the length of time that they work. This may be an hourly rate, common in the retail sector, or a weekly wage for completing a set number of hours or shifts. Overtime, possibly at a higher rate, may be paid for working longer than the agreed number of hours. Time rates encourage workers to produce a higher quality of work than do piece rates, as there is no focus on the quantity produced. Time rates are also commonly used in the service sector where there is no measurable unit of output.

However, their power to motivate is questionable, in that:

- there is no reward for those who work the hardest or achieve the most within the time
- there is still little security of income, leaving pay a potential source of anxiety and dissatisfaction
- workers on a weekly wage have no encouragement to be flexible in how or when they work, leaving businesses overstaffed at times and understaffed at others.

SALARY

Employees on a salary system are paid an agreed sum for a year's work. This is beneficial for the business in that there is much greater flexibility in terms of when and how long an employee may work in a day, week or month. A fixed salary encourages workers to be flexible and open to change, knowing that their financial rewards will be unaffected.

However, a salary system provides no incentive to work hard, as employees know that their financial reward will be the same regardless of effort.

FRINGE BENEFITS

In addition to money payments, many organisations offer other forms of reward as part of a worker's basic pay. These are called **fringe benefits** and can include:

- company cars
- private medical insurance
- discounts on company products
- leisure and social facilities.

Fringe benefits have become increasingly important as part of the total payment package given to employees – particularly for management and executive positions. They offer employees a feeling of status that can prove to be a motivating factor, but fringe benefits can swiftly become an expected 'right' and thus lose any motivational effect. They could equally become a cause of status envy and dissatisfaction between employees.

Incentive schemes

Businesses have available a number of other ways to improve an employee's pay package. These usually try to motivate employees to work harder by offering them a chance at increased personal rewards in return for meeting specific objectives or targets. The most common of these is the idea of offering an employee a bonus.

BONUSES

A bonus is the general term for an additional financial reward given to a worker in recognition of the contribution that he or she has made. Examples include:

- piece-rate bonus – an additional payment to workers for each unit of output that they produce above a stated target
- **commission** – a percentage of the sales price of a product that is paid to the salesperson as a reward for making the sale
- one-off payment – a lump sum paid to an individual, team or whole workforce as a reward for their efforts. It may be a seasonal bonus, such as a Christmas bonus, or a reward for attendance, quality or service.

Bonuses, such as commission, can act as an incentive because they offer the prospect of additional reward for increased effort or for achieving a certain target. On the other hand, bonuses may come to be expected as part of the overall payment package, breaking the link between effort and reward. In addition, bonuses can cause conflict due to jealousy between workers. In this instance employees may actively work against each other trying to ensure that they are the employee or branch, for example, that earns the bonus.

PERFORMANCE-RELATED PAY (PRP)

Another type of bonus scheme is **performance-related pay (PRP)**. This provides a financial reward to an employee for meeting agreed, individual targets. Employees will agree performance targets with a line manager and then their individual performance is measured against the targets set. The size of the reward payment they then receive will reflect their degree of achievement.

PRP is now commonly used for executives in both the private and the public sectors. It represents a management equivalent to piece rate, in the sense that it provides a financial reward for the 'output' of managers. However, some companies have become sceptical of its benefits, because:

- the potential exists for conflict between employees and their line managers over the targets that are set, achievement and the level of reward they should receive;
- PRP is individual and so fails to promote teamwork and a spirit of unity;
- the business needs to keep financial rewards to an affordable level, so frequently PRP payments are too small to make any great motivational impact.

PROFIT-SHARING

Under this system employees are offered a share of the annual profits made by the business. In contrast to the individual approach of PRP, **profit-sharing** encourages employees to work collectively to the benefit of the whole organisation. How far this is a motivator to employees depends on the proportion of the organisation's profit that will be shared out to them, and whether worker commitment is sufficient to make that business sufficient profit to begin with.

SHARE OWNERSHIP

Incentive schemes that provide company shares to employees as the reward produce similar benefits to profit-sharing schemes. As shareowners, employees will benefit financially from the success of the business through the issuing of dividends and growth in the business's share price.

At the heart of most **share ownership** schemes is the concept of a share option. A share option is the right to buy a share at an agreed price at a given future date. The agreed price is likely to be the share's market price at the beginning of the scheme, or even a discounted rate below this. If the share price rises over the period of the scheme, the employee will gain significantly. On the agreed date, the employee will be able to 'exercise' the option and then sell the shares at a much higher price.

Share ownership schemes are, typically, of two types:

- savings-related schemes, which allow staff to save a set amount from their pay each month over a period of time and then exchange these savings for share options
- incentives for executives, which often link the number of share options offered to status or performance.

Share options should encourage employees to work towards achieving the business's objectives as they will directly benefit from any increases in profits or the company's value.

Improving job design

According to some motivational theorists, financial rewards by themselves are not enough to motivate workers. Employees have other needs that must also be met. These focus not on the monetary reward for work, but on the personal reward an employee gains from doing a job.

The 'design' of the job is therefore crucial to motivation and above all, a job must be meaningful and interesting. To achieve this end, each worker's job role should provide:

- variety – avoiding repetitive and dull tasks that become boring and lose the employee's interest or desire to do well
- closure – the opportunity to see a job or product through to completion, using '**job enlargement**'
- challenge – work that develops skills and offers advancement, achieved through '**job enrichment**'
- control – over key decisions related to the job role, a process known as '**empowerment**'
- cooperation – the opportunity to work and interact with others, achieved by promoting 'team-working'.

Enrichment

Job enrichment means trying out different ways to make an employee's job more challenging or rewarding. The theory here is that employees will be motivated because they enjoy their work; it is more varied and interesting and they feel that it is allowing them to grow and develop as an individual. Methods of enriching an employee's job include:

- providing an increased range of roles and activities within the job
- allowing workers the opportunity to use and develop different skills
- offering opportunities to demonstrate an individual's capabilities
- enabling workers to take responsibility for their actions and working environment
- training workers to enable them to advance their own skills.

Job enrichment, however, is not easy to achieve for all job roles. Unskilled, manual labour rarely lends itself to the right opportunities for enrichment, and some workers may not want more responsibility. The changes required in the way a business is organised and structured to enable job enrichment to take place could also prove expensive and disruptive.

For example...

Google

All Google engineers are encouraged to spend 20% of their work time (one day per week) on projects that interest them. Some of Google's newer services, such as Gmail, Google News, Orkut, and AdSense originated from these independent activities. In a talk at Stanford University, Marissa Mayer, Google's Vice President of Search Products and User Experience, stated that her analysis showed that half of the new product launches originated from the 20% time.

The 'Googleplex' in Mountain View, California

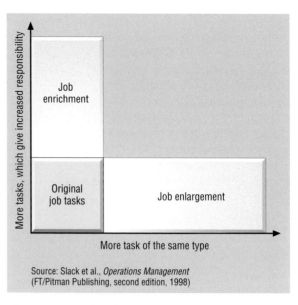

Source: Slack et al., *Operations Management*
(FT/Pitman Publishing, second edition, 1998)

Figure 22.2 Job enlargement versus job enrichment

Enlargement

Job enlargement involves allowing a worker to perform more tasks in a production process so that they are then able to work on a product from start to finish and see the completed product at the end. This is known as job enlargement, because it involves giving workers more tasks to do of the same type and in the same process. The idea is that employees will gain greater job satisfaction by performing more varied tasks and then seeing the end result of their efforts.

Job enlargement is not, however, a solution on its own. Giving workers more work to do can cause resentment if they feel they are being asked to work harder without extra financial reward. Increasing the 'horizontal loading' of a job – doing more of the same – may not in itself make a job more interesting.

Empowering employees

Giving employees the power to make the decisions that affect their working lives is known as empowerment. This could include the right to make decisions over how and when work is done, and taking responsibility for those decisions.

To empower workers is to go a stage further than to delegate. Delegation involves being given the authority by a manager to make decisions in a specific area, such as quality control. Empowered workers, however, would be given a far more wide-ranging power to implement their own ideas in any aspect of their jobs, such as changing the layout of the factory floor and the flow of work.

Empowerment therefore gives employees responsibility, which in turn provides opportunities for advancement and making the work itself more interesting. Not only can empowerment motivate, but it can get the best out of the workforce by making use of their talents and ideas. If decisions are taken by those who know most about the issues involved, they might be better decisions.

However, in practice, empowerment may cause a number of problems:

- The reality may fall far short of the theory, with little power really being given by managers who do not trust the workforce.
- Empowerment may be used as an excuse to cut costs by removing levels of middle management and increasing the workload of the remaining employees.
- Genuine empowerment poses the danger that effective control and coordination may be lost, leading to expensive mistakes or a lack of strategic direction.

Working in teams

Many motivational theorists emphasise the importance of teamwork in motivation. Teamwork helps to meet workers' social needs for interaction and friendship in the workplace. Team working involves:

- organising employees into small groups (teams)
- setting objectives for the team to achieve
- giving the team responsibility and rewards for achieving targets, such as improved quality
- training workers to be able to carry out any role within the team.

Many organisations, such as General Motors, Levi Strauss and Jaguar, have reported benefits from team working. These include:

- increased job satisfaction
- higher productivity
- improved product quality
- reduced labour turnover and absenteeism
- enhanced employee flexibility.

Where team working fails it is often because:

- teams were not given clear objectives or the authority to achieve them
- individuals refuse to cooperate with the team approach
- teams are cut off from management or from the rest of the organisation
- an individual approach may be better in some situations.

Theories of motivation

F W Taylor

The work of Frederick Winslow Taylor (1856–1917) shaped the views of managers on motivation for most of the twentieth century and remains influential today.

Taylor studied the movements and working practices of workers in the USA at the turn of the 20th century – most famously, those involved in pig-iron production at the Bethlehem Steel Works in Bethlehem, Pennsylvania. These 'time and motion studies' found that workers took their own decisions about the methods and speed required to do a job, and that many of their ways of working were inefficient.

Activity

1 Working in groups, compare and contrast your own experiences of how businesses attempt to motivate their workers. If you have a part-time job, what motivational policies are used at your workplace? If not, what strategies are used by your school or college to motivate students?

2 Next consider the following:
- Do the motivational strategies work?
- Do they work for all employees or just some?
- Do they cause any resentment among staff?
- Could they be improved?
- What other strategies might be better?

Guru's views

'When a naturally energetic man works for a few days beside a lazy one, the logic of the situation is unanswerable: "Why should I work hard when that lazy fellow gets the same pay that I do and does only half as much work?"'

– F W Taylor

F W Taylor, the father of 'scientific management'

THEORY OF SCIENTIFIC MANAGEMENT

Taylor's ideas to improve efficiency became known as scientific management. He believed managers could find the 'best way' to complete a job through a scientific procedure of observation, experiment and calculations. Based on these ideas, he set out a number of recommendations:

- Managers should study the tasks being carried out by workers and identify the quickest way of doing each one. Any unnecessary movement or tasks should be eliminated.
- The skills of each employee should be matched to the tasks that need to be carried out, and each given specific instructions on what to do and how to do it.
- All workers should be supervised and controlled, and those who do not work efficiently should be punished – the 'stick'.
- Workers should be rewarded financially for being efficient, and pay schemes designed to pay more to those who produce more – the 'carrot'. Taylor believed that money motivates – 'a fair day's pay for a fair day's work'. Workers seek to maximise their pay, he said, and want managers to design a system that will allow them to do this.

THEORY INTO PRACTICE

Taylor's ideas formed the basis for the mass production assembly lines that dominated manufacturing in the twentieth century. To put 'scientific management' into practice involves:

- eliminating wasted time and resources in production
- closely supervising workers, controlling their methods and speed of work, possibly through the use of a conveyor-belt system, which dictates the speed they must work at
- introducing either a piece rate system of payment – where workers are paid so much for each unit ('piece') of output they produce – or a financial incentive system based on meeting output targets.

PROBLEMS

A number of objections have been raised to Taylor's theory:

- The theory assumes there is a scientific 'best way' to organise production, but this ignores differences between workers, which may affect the success of any one method.
- The approach treats workers as machines to be used and controlled, creating an atmosphere of conflict between workers and managers.
- Money is not the only motivator, nor is it the most important one for some people. Taylor's ideas ignore the personal and social needs of individuals at work.

Elton Mayo

Elton Mayo lectured on psychology in Australia in the early 20th century and from 1922 in the USA. Following F W Taylor's work-study research, Mayo studied the impact of rest breaks on workers' productivity. Just as Taylor had found that the right type of work methods and payment systems could improve productivity, Mayo was investigating

Elton Mayo, believer in teamwork and rest breaks

whether there was a similarly ideal length or frequency of rest break. Initial experiments suggested regular breaks boosted productivity, and led Mayo to call for the more humane treatment of employees at work.

Mayo's most famous studies took his ideas a stage further. Experiments between 1927 and 1932 at the Hawthorne Plant of the Western Electric Company in Chicago became the foundation for the 'human relations school' of management theory. The Hawthorne studies involved varying working conditions, such as lighting, heating and hours of work, and measuring the impact on the productivity of small groups of workers. A change in conditions was made every 12 weeks, but beforehand researchers would discuss the change fully with the workers. The results surprised everyone.

Every change that was introduced brought higher productivity. Productivity went up even when no changes were made. The final change was to go back to the original working conditions – with the effect of achieving the highest productivity of all.

THEORY OF HUMAN RELATIONS

Mayo drew two different but equally important conclusions from the surprising results of his workplace experiments:

1 The importance of teamwork. The experiments had led to groups of individuals becoming a team, whose members worked closely in cooperation with each other. A sense of team spirit, and doing what the group expected, motivated employees to work harder.

2 The need for managers to take an interest in their workers. Workers responded well to being observed and to the feeling of importance that this produced. The morale-boosting effect of the experiments suggested that managers who communicated closely with workers and showed an interest in them would be rewarded with an increase in productivity – the so-called Hawthorne effect.

THEORY INTO PRACTICE

Mayo's findings led to a number of practical conclusions for motivating workers:

- Getting the physical conditions of work and the financial rewards right are less important than getting right the social conditions – teamwork and good communication are essential.

The benefits of working together

Guru's views

'British management doesn't seem to understand the importance of the human factor.'

– *Prince Charles*

- Giving workers the opportunity to be involved in making decisions and to be creative is more likely to motivate them than Taylor's assembly-line approach.
- Personnel departments that focus on the wellbeing of workers are central to business success.

PROBLEMS

Mayo's theory has been criticised on at least two grounds:

- The experiments themselves were far from scientific – only small groups of workers were observed, and subsequent experiments have failed to confirm the findings.
- Workers will not always share the goals of managers, despite their best efforts. Trade unions may see these efforts as management attempts to fool workers into boosting productivity when there is little gain for workers in doing so.

Abraham Maslow

In 1954 the American psychologist Abraham Maslow put forward his theory of what motivates human beings. His ideas did not apply solely to the workplace but nevertheless had an important message for business.

THEORY OF THE HIERARCHY OF NEEDS

Maslow suggested that all human beings have the same types of needs and that these could be organised as a hierarchy of needs. The five levels of needs he referred to are shown in Figure 22.3.

At the base of the hierarchy lie 'physiological needs' – the essentials for human survival, such as food and rest. Maslow placed this type of need at the bottom of the hierarchy because such needs are the most

Abraham Maslow put forward the theory of the hierarchy of needs

Guru's views

'It is quite true that humans live by bread alone – when there is no bread. But what happens to their desires when there is bread?'

– *Abraham Maslow*

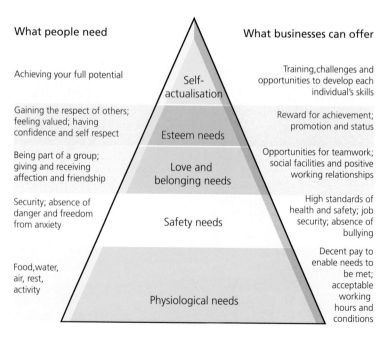

Figure 22.3 Maslow's hierarchy of needs

fundamental set of needs for any human being. They will always be the first type of need that must be satisfied.

Once this level of needs is met, it no longer remains a focus or a motivation. Instead, it is the next level of needs in the hierarchy that an individual seeks to satisfy. So, once their physiological needs have been met, people seek the 'safety' needs of security and freedom from anxiety. Motivation stems from each individual's desire to have their next level of needs met. The final level of needs, 'self-actualisation', refers to the need to fulfil one's potential. Once all other levels of need are met, it is this need that can continue to motivate.

THEORY INTO PRACTICE

Maslow's theory has important practical implications for businesses:

- To motivate a workforce requires an approach that will identify the level of need of each individual.
- Each worker will first need sufficient pay to provide for his or her basic physiological needs, then will seek job security and a safe working environment. Figure 22.3 shows how businesses might seek to meet each level of needs in the hierarchy.
- Financial rewards alone will not motivate. Boosting workers' esteem and developing their talents will be crucial. But, without decent pay and job security, these are worthless.

PROBLEMS

Opponents of Maslow have found his theory unconvincing on several grounds:

- Any generalisation about 'levels' of human needs is bound to have exceptions – businesses may find they have workers who place little value on gaining praise or developing their potential. Some workers – such as artists or musicians – may even seek creativity needs before financial reward.
- Even if Maslow's theory holds good, workers may not seek all levels of need within the workplace. They may be satisfied with pay alone from their job, meeting other needs through their leisure time.
- Matching rewards to needs for each and every worker is a well-nigh impossible task in practice.

Frederick Herzberg

Frederick Herzberg, an American psychologist, conducted research in the 1950s that directly addressed the question of motivation. He asked 200 engineers and accountants which factors in their work created job satisfaction and which caused dissatisfaction. His results are presented in a simplified form in Figure 22.4.

The results showed that six factors, including achievement and recognition, were frequently mentioned as causing satisfaction at work. On the other hand, ten factors, such as company policy and working conditions, were often mentioned as causes of dissatisfaction, but rarely as a source of pleasure!

Guru's views

'How do I motivate someone to play the piano? First, I teach them how to play it.'

– *Frederick Herzberg*

Frederick Herzberg proposed the 'two-factor theory'

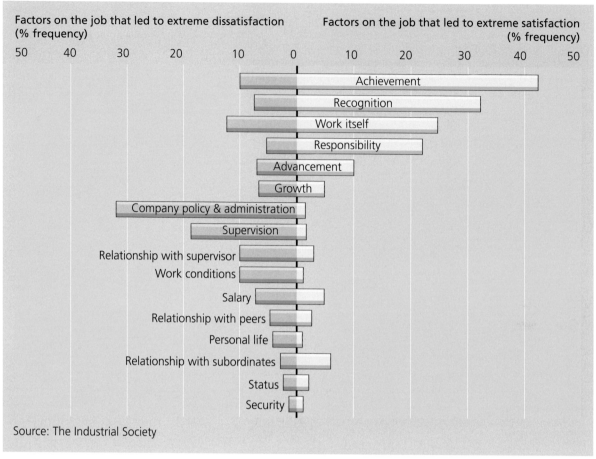

Figure 22.4 Factors leading to job satisfaction and dissatisfaction

'TWO-FACTOR THEORY'

Herzberg used this research to develop his 'two-factor theory' of motivation. This states that there are two sets of factors – motivators and hygiene factors – that are both important in motivating workers, but for very different reasons.

1 Motivators

The factors that have the potential to motivate workers by providing job satisfaction include:

- a sense of achievement
- recognition of effort
- interesting work
- responsibility
- opportunities for promotion
- opportunities for self-improvement.

These factors help to meet the human need to grow psychologically. If a job can provide these motivators, workers will want to work and will enjoy their work. If the motivators are absent from the job, this does not by itself create dissatisfaction – only a lack of motivation.

2 Hygiene factors

Just as poor hygiene can cause illness, the factors that can cause dissatisfaction in the workplace are all related to the working environment. They include:

- company policy
- relationships with supervisors or colleagues
- working conditions
- pay and status
- security.

Herzberg believed that our 'animal' nature leads us to seek the avoidance of pain. If a job can avoid problems in all of the areas listed, it will stop us feeling that work is a painful experience. It will prevent dissatisfaction. However, no matter how good these factors are in a job, they will not, by themselves, motivate someone – that is down to the motivators. Good hygiene can stop you getting ill, but it cannot make you happy.

THEORY INTO PRACTICE

Several practical conclusions can be drawn from the two-factor theory:

- To motivate a workforce, a business must first make sure that all of the hygiene factors are being met – a decent salary, fair rules and policies and pleasant working conditions.
- The motivators must be there – ensuring that the job itself is meaningful and interesting, that workers are trained to do their jobs well and that they have the opportunity to develop their skills.

Specifically, Herzberg advocated 'job enrichment' – building a variety of tasks, skills and responsibilities into each job.

PROBLEMS

Herzberg's theory has encountered major criticisms.

- Subsequent research around the world has failed to confirm that Herzberg's theory can generally be applied to workers in every business.
- Some jobs, especially low-skilled ones, cannot be easily 'enriched', and many workers may not seek responsibility or advancement.

Further material and resources relating to this section can be found at **www.collins.bized.co.uk**. Keep checking for updates.

Developing and retaining an effective workforce: motivating employees: **Summary**

- Motivated employees are happier employees. They should therefore be more productive, give better quality and wish to stay with the business.
- There are many different types of financial motivators available to businesses but different 'packages' need to be applied to different types of employee.
- The effect of financial motivators can be short-lived. To motivate employees in practice involves addressing their personal and social needs, as well as financial ones.
- Improving an employee's job design involves giving them more varied, interesting and challenging tasks to perform. This can be done using the theories of job enrichment or job enlargement.
- Empowering employees provides for their personal development needs by giving them increased responsibility and decision-making powers over their own area of work.
- Working in teams should help to motivate employees as their social needs in the workplace are provided for. This in turn helps to reduce labour turnover and increases an employee's job satisfaction.
- There are several key motivational theorists who all propose different approaches to motivating employees. Applying motivational strategies in practice is very much dependent on the type of employee and their position in the business's hierarchy.

Summary questions

1   Give three reasons why a business might want to motivate its employees.
2   Although the financial incentives offered to employees can vary from piece rates to profit shares, they are all designed to achieve the same results from employees. List three objectives that pay systems are designed to achieve.
3   Give two advantages and two disadvantages of using a time rate system of pay.
4   How are fringe benefits used to motivate? Use examples to support your answer.
5   Explain the benefits and problems of PRP.
6   Distinguish between profit sharing and share ownership schemes.
7   List the five characteristics of a meaningful and interesting job.
8   Distinguish between job enlargement and job enrichment.
9   Why does job enrichment not always succeed in motivating a workforce?
10   Explain the difference between empowerment and delegation.
11   What are the potential benefits of team working? Why might they not be achieved?

Points for discussion

'Motivating workers is expensive for businesses and often fails in practice.'

- Given this viewpoint, discuss whether or not motivated employees are essential to a business's long-term success.
- According to some motivational theorists, pay either does not motivate at all or only works as a motivator in the short term. Discuss whether or not you believe all employees are equally motivated by financial rewards.

Exam practice

Plasmouldings Ltd have been in business for 23 years manufacturing disposable plastic cutlery for use in canteens and takeaways across the UK. As a product that is frequently given away free by the customers, price is a key component in Plasmouldings' success.

Gavin Croft, the managing director and major shareholder in Plasmouldings Ltd, is always keen to listen to cost-saving or productivity-enhancing ideas from his employees, and currently runs a bonus system whereby any employee's suggestion that is actually put into practice in the factory receives a £250 bonus.

Gavin's head of Human Resources, Shakir Khan, has recently approached him with what he believes would be a good way to save cost and raise productivity simultaneously. Currently all staff on the production line are paid via a piece rate system, that is, they receive a set payment for each set of cutlery that they detach from their moulds. Each set is then passed on to the next stage where quality checkers make sure there are no defects and suitable products then progress to the packaging department.

Shakir is aware that a constant cost to the company is recruiting new production line staff. Employees see the production line work as being boring and poorly paid and so staff retention in this area is poor. Shakir's idea is to introduce a new pay system of a basic time rate and then bonuses for meeting production targets. He also wants employees to work in teams and introduce job enlargement by having employees vary their jobs taking turns in each of the three departments. However, Gavin is not convinced; Shakir's pay proposals would raise the monthly wage cost to the company and Gavin believes any changes to pay systems as a financial motivator would only have a short-term motivational effect. Gavin also knows that for employees to be able to work at speed in different areas of the business will require training and that this too would increase the company's costs. Gavin feels that if any changes were to be made to current factory working practices, more would be gained by adopting an approach of job enrichment throughout the company.

1 What is meant by the term 'staff retention'? (2 marks)

2 Explain the potential disadvantages of introducing a system of bonus payments for production line employees. (5 marks)

3 Analyse the advantages and disadvantages of a piece rate system of pay to a business like Plasmouldings Ltd. (10 marks)

4 Outline the reasons why Gavin might believe that job enrichment would bring more benefits than job enlargement to his business. (8 marks)

5 To what extent do you agree with Gavin's statement that any financial motivators would only have a short-term effect? (15 marks)

Total: 40 marks

UNIT 2
SECTION C

Managing a Business:
Operations management

Section overview

Managing a Business:
Operations management

This section looks at how a business manages its day to day operations. This is called operations management (OM). Businesses will have to look at all the resources they use in production and find ways in which they can organise these resources to meet certain targets they have set themselves. You will learn about how technology is used in business and how decision-making can affect quality, customer service, and how the relationships with suppliers can influence day to day operations.

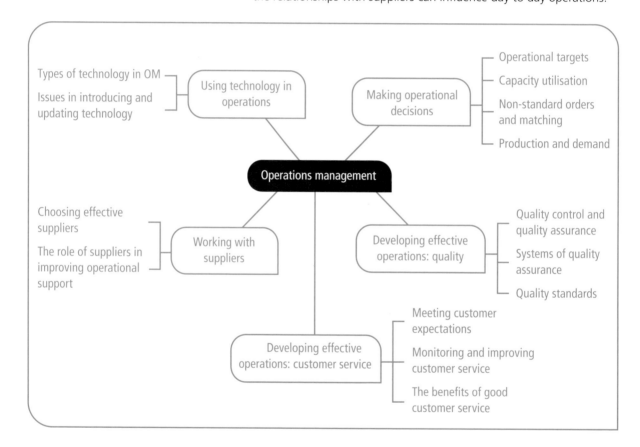

Key concept

Efficiency

Efficiency can mean different things in different contexts. Whatever definition is used, however, any business organisation – and that includes those in the public sector – will be mindful of efficiency. Efficiency can be summarised as 'getting more from less'. It is about making the most of the resources you have either by maximising the output or minimising the inputs. In business we can measure efficiency in different ways.

- Productivity

  Efficiency might be associated with ways of reorganising the business to produce the same amount of products or level of service (output) but with fewer resources (inputs), such as raw materials, labour, or capital. Or it could even be producing more products or a better level of service with fewer resources. Improvements in labour productivity can be measured by looking at output against the total number of employees over a particular time period.

- Cost

  Efficiency might be associated with finding ways of producing more products or a better level of service (output), but at a lower overall cost (investment). Improvements in cost can be measured by looking at output against investment.

- Unit cost

  Efficiency might be associated with finding ways of reducing the cost per unit (the average cost of a particular product). Improvements (reductions) in average costs can be measured by looking at dividing the total cost of production by the number of units produced.

Improvements in efficiency might be seen as being a good thing but we have to remember that improving efficiency might benefit some stakeholders but have negative effects on other stakeholders. A re-organisation of a businesses operation might lead to greater output at lower cost but it might involve the sacrifice of a number of jobs that are deemed redundant. When looking at efficiency, therefore, we have to be mindful of the opportunity costs involved in decision making.

Many businesses these days will look at efficiency from a social or environmental angle. Social efficiency incorporates some consideration of the costs and the benefits to society as a whole of a businesses operation. If the decision to change operations not only reduces costs but also leads to a reduced impact on society in the form of pollution or energy use then this might be an important consideration in a business's decision.

Underpinning all of the discussions about operations management, therefore, has to be a consideration of efficiency; but we must be careful to clarify what definition of this concept we are using. A decision to invest in new technology to generate energy for a plant might be inefficient in terms of the cost per unit produced compared to traditional methods but might be far more socially efficient and a business might believe that its social responsibilities outweigh its concern with costs. (You may view such a decision with some cynicism but businesses do think about the balance of costs and benefits in this way!).

Chapter 23 Making operational decisions

This chapter will look in more detail at the way in which businesses manage their day to day operations. This is referred to as operations management. Whether it is McDonalds working out how best to get a *Big Mac* to its customers, a chip manufacturer producing highly sensitive, minute pieces of technology, or a franchise milk delivery operation, they all have to think about the best way of combining the factors of production to improve efficiency. As technology continues to develop at pace, it plays an increasing role in operations management.

Operational targets

Operations management is the organisation of resources to produce goods and services. Every product you buy and every service you use is the outcome of a production process – the transforming (changing) of inputs (the factors of production) into outputs (goods and services). Operations management is associated with **efficiency**. Efficiency is about achieving the maximum output from a given set of inputs at the lowest possible cost. Factor inputs can be organised in different ways to produce a given output. The role of operations management is to constantly review the way factor inputs are organised to see if efficiencies can be gained.

Operational targets relate to the following three areas:

- unit costs
- quality
- **capacity utilisation**.

Unit costs

In producing any given output a business will incur costs. Land, labour and capital all have to be purchased and an entrepreneur will be looking to make a profit. The price of acquiring land is called 'rent'; the price for acquiring labour is called 'wages' and the price of capital is 'interest'. The reward to enterprise is profit. Together these so-called factor rewards comprise the costs of production.

Costs of production are classified as **fixed costs** and **variable costs**.

- Fixed costs are those that occur which are not dependent on or determined by the amount produced – rent, rates, insurance, administration costs, and so on. Note that fixed costs can change – rent, rates, insurance costs, and so on, can all rise and fall, but the point is that they do not change with the level of output or trade carried out.
- Variable costs are those that vary directly with the amount produced. Raw materials, some types of labour costs,

Key terms

Capacity The maximum possible output that can be produced over a period of time.

Capacity management The process of planning and controlling the capacity of an organisation to meet the demands of its customers.

Capacity utilisation The proportion of capacity that is actually used over a period of time.

Efficiency This is about making the most of the resources you have, either by maximising the output or minimising the inputs. To maximise output, the business must produce as much as possible from a given set of inputs, such as labour, equipment and raw materials. To minimise inputs, it must ensure that no resources are wasted in the production process.

Fixed costs The costs that are not dependent on the level of output or trade.

Price sensitivity How customers respond to price changes. Will demand change by a great deal or hardly at all if prices change? This is also known as **price elasticity of demand.**

component parts and energy used directly in production are examples.

Together these costs make up the **total cost** of production. We can use the following formula to summarise this relationship:

TC = FC + VC

The total cost for producing any product or service tends to rise as the amount produced rises. However, because fixed costs tend to be stable in relation to output, the cost per unit can fall as output rises. The cost per unit refers to the cost of producing one unit of output. This is also called average cost.

Unit cost is found by dividing the total cost of production by the amount produced:

Unit cost = total cost / output

If a business produced 50,000 units of a good and the total cost of doing so was £100,000, then the unit or average costs would be:

100,000 / 50,000 = £2.00 per unit

Note that this is the average cost of producing a given amount of output. As output rises, fixed costs stay stable whereas the variable costs rise directly with output. It is possible, therefore, that the rate at which total costs rise is slower than that which output rises. This leads to a fall in unit costs.

If total costs rose faster than the rate of growth of output, then unit costs would rise. When this occurs the firm is becoming less efficient. Finding ways to organise production differently can help to reduce unit costs and increase efficiency.

Key terms

Rationalisation The process of reorganising a business to reduce capacity and increase efficiency.

Stock Any type of stored materials within a business, but typically raw material and components, work in progress or finished goods waiting to be sold.

Subcontracting Using the resources of another organisation to help fulfil customer demand.

Total cost The sum of the variable and fixed costs of production.

Underutilisation The use of well below 100% of an organisation's maximum potential output.

Unit or average costs The cost of producing one unit of output found by dividing total costs by the amount produced.

Variable costs The costs of production that are determined directly by the amount produced or the level of trade.

For example...

Sonja has a business that manufactures men's ties for export across the world. The fixed costs of the business are £75,000 a month and the variable costs per tie are £3.00. Each month, on average,

Sonja's business produces 15,000 ties. The total variable costs per month, therefore, are £45,000. The fixed costs are £75,000 so total costs are £120,000. The unit cost of each tie works out at £120,000 / 15,000 = £8 per tie.

Sonja wins a contract to supply a major retail store in the United States and as a result, the output per month rises to 20,000. The variable costs are now £60,000. The order has meant that Sonja has had to invest in some new equipment, and the administration in processing the new contract has also risen. Fixed costs per month as a result have risen to £80,000. The total cost per month is now £140,000. The unit cost per tie is now £140,000 / 20,000 = £7.

In the example above it was assumed that Sonja had to buy new equipment. It might be that Sonja could have reorganised the production process to manage the additional orders she had won. In so doing she might have been able to increase production without buying any additional machinery. She might have reorganised the staff working times to increase production over a longer period of time – through shift work, for example. In such a case it might have been that the fixed costs would not have risen as much, but maybe the variable costs would have increased slightly.

If fixed costs rose from £75,000 to £78,000 and variable costs rose by 5p per unit, then her new total costs would have been £139,000. This would make her unit costs fall to £6.95.

In many cases firms might find that there is equipment available that can increase the speed or efficiency with which a process can be carried out. A new cutting machine for the cloth that Sonja uses in tie production might be able to cut out twice as many ties per hour. Providing the cost of buying the machine was not twice as much, then Sonja would have seen her unit costs fall.

These simple examples show how there is not one way of producing a good or service. Different amounts of labour can be used, different types of machinery could be used, more or less land might be needed and the business might find ways to access raw materials or components cheaper.

The way a business organises its factors of production impacts on its costs and its output, and this in turn affects total costs and therefore unit costs. We can identify three important relationships between inputs and unit costs:

- If output rises by a greater proportion than the cost of factor inputs, unit costs will fall.
- If output rises by the same proportion as the cost of factor inputs, then unit costs will stay the same.
- If output rises by a smaller proportion than the cost of factor inputs, then unit costs will rise.

One important target for those involved with operations management, therefore, is to find ways in which the business can be made more efficient. In so doing, this can help to reduce unit costs. This, in turn, can give the business competitive advantage and also enable the business to be able to be more competitive on price or to increase its margins.

Quality

Operational targets relating to quality centre on having a clear definition of quality. The following factors may be important in defining quality:

- fit for purpose – does the product or service do what it is intended to do?
- excellence – in its function, appearance or overall image
- free of faults or errors
- durable – long-lasting, without the need for repair or replacement
- value for money – a reasonable price for the standard of the product.

Quality does not have to mean 'top of the range', but any definition of quality must include the idea of satisfying the needs and expectations of different customers. For example, a watch that is technically excellent but not very attractive may not be considered a quality product if what customers value most is appearance. The challenge to business is to understand the expectations of customers and then meet differing needs from different types of customer.

Operations management has an important role to play in ensuring that quality standards are maintained in line with the expectations of customers. We will deal with quality in more detail in Chapter 24.

Capacity utilisation

Capacity refers to how much a business is capable of producing over a given period of time with the resources it has at its disposal. In other words, it is the maximum possible output from an organisation determined by the resources available, such as buildings, equipment and people. This physical capacity determines the largest output that could be achieved each day, month or year if resources are used to their maximum.

For example, the capacity of a cinema is limited to 1,000 seats, because there are five screens – each with 200 seats available. However, if each screen is able to run five performances a day, the capacity of the cinema is 5,000 customers per day. If the number of screenings was increased to seven per day then capacity would rise to 7,000.

The key targets in capacity **management** are:

- What maximum capacity level should the business settle on over the long term?
- What proportion of this maximum capacity should the business be using at any one time (its capacity utilisation)? 100%? 90%? Or less?
- Should the business ignore short-term changes in demand and keep capacity constant? Should it attempt to vary its capacity to match fluctuations in demand? Or should it attempt to change demand to fit the capacity available?

We will look in more detail at capacity utilisation in the next section.

Calculating and managing capacity utilisation

Capacity

A police force must decide how many officers should be on duty without knowing in advance what the level of crime or disturbance will be at any given time. Manufacturers of suntan cream must plan how much to produce without knowing whether a hot summer is in store. An airline must decide how many flights and seats to offer without knowing how many passengers wish to fly. A travel agent will have to book hotel accommodation at resorts without knowing whether there will be enough customers to fill all the places.

Any organisation has to try and find a way in which it can calculate how many resources (factors of production) it needs and what output levels it needs to produce. It has to do this in the face of uncertain demand. This is the task facing a business in managing capacity.

THE OBJECTIVES OF CAPACITY MANAGEMENT

In making capacity management decisions, an organisation must seek to balance three key objectives as described below.

Efficiency

Costs need to be kept down and waste avoided. If the maximum capacity is not being fully utilised (used) there is an element of waste that will raise unit costs. This might be a machine that is capable of producing 4,000 units per day but which is currently only being used to produce 3,000 units per day. In a hairdressing salon, an empty chair also represents waste. It may be that there is a member of staff waiting around to attend to a customer – the worker may still have to be paid even though there is no client to work on. Waste does not only raise costs but it also means that potential revenue which could be generated is lost. On the other hand, over-producing when there is a lack of demand will lead to a build-up of stock causing wasted space, time and money.

Quality

The business must ensure that quality is maximised and not suffering because capacity is being overstretched. Attempts to increase output might cause difficulties in securing sufficient resources and possibly even the skilled labour that might be required. If the business tries to meet the increased output with sub-standard resources or with labour that does not have the right skills, then quality could be compromised.

Customer service

The flexibility to respond to unexpected changes in demand is vital. Businesses can experience sudden increases in demand for a product and equally face sudden decreases. The operations management system has to be flexible enough to be able to cope with such changes. If customers cannot buy the products they want at the time they want them it can damage a business's reputation and also lead to lost future sales and a lack of confidence in the business. Sainsbury's, the supermarket giant, spent £1.8 billion on improving its distribution and ordering functions with a new IT system in 2000. Unfortunately, the system did not work properly and stores were left with bare shelves. Customers went to other supermarkets and Sainsbury's lost market share and in 2004 had to announce its first ever loss.

CAPACITY UTILISATION

The term 'capacity utilisation' refers to the proportion of the maximum capacity that is actually used during a period of time. It is measured as:

$$\text{Percentage capacity utilisation} = \frac{\text{Actual output (per period of time)}}{\text{Maximum possible output (per period of time)}} \times 100$$

For example, Aston Villa Football Club play their home matches at Villa Park in Birmingham. The ground capacity is currently 42,500. Over the 2006–2007 season, the average gate was 35,000. The percentage capacity utilisation therefore was:

$$\frac{35,000}{42,500} \times 100 = 82.3\%$$

Capacity utilisation is called different things in different industries. In a factory environment it may be called 'uptime'. The proportion of seats occupied on an aircraft is called its 'load factor'. Hotels measure their capacity utilisation by looking at 'room occupancy levels'.

To be utilising its capacity fully, a business must make use of all its available productive resources. Operating at, or near, full capacity is often taken as a sign of a successful business. It suggests that demand is high and that no potential output is being lost. The result should be that the business is maximising its sales. However, full capacity is not always ideal for reasons that will be explored later.

UNDERUTILISATION

When actual production is well below the maximum capacity, it is known as **underutilisation**. This can occur for a number of reasons:

- Demand may have fallen due to changing consumer tastes, changes in economic activity, bad publicity, quality problems or seasonal fluctuations. A new competitor may be stealing market share and reducing the business's sales.
- Capacity has been increased to too high a level. The business may have expanded its assets or the workforce to a level well above that which is needed to meet demand. This may have been caused by inaccurate sales forecasts or excessive optimism in predicting demand.
- There is inefficiency in the production process, caused by 'bottlenecks' in the system, poor working practices or shortages of raw materials. Processes that rely on several machines to carry out production might operate at different capacity levels. When this occurs a slow machine can cause a bottleneck and slow output. The other machines are therefore underutilised. Large firms can overcome this by buying multiples of each machine to maximise capacity, but smaller firms may not be able to afford to do this.

Underutilisation cannot always be put down to problems or inefficiencies on the 'shop floor' – the cause could lie elsewhere in the business or outside in its market. Underutilisation brings a number of problems.

- Costs will rise. Businesses pay their overheads, known as fixed costs, for resources such as premises or equipment. When capacity is fully utilised, overheads are spread across the maximum possible number of units of output. The fixed costs per unit (the average fixed costs – AFC) are therefore at a minimum. However, when less output is produced, fixed costs do not fall and each unit of output must bear a higher share of the fixed costs. For example:

– A factory spends £10,000 a week on paying its fixed costs.
– At full capacity, it can produce 5,000 units per week.
– As well as variable costs (cost of producing each unit), each unit must bear £2 of the fixed costs (£10,000 for 5,000 units).
– If the factory only produces 2,500 units in a particular week, its capacity utilisation is 50%. Each of the 2,500 units must now cover £4 of the fixed costs. Fixed costs per unit have doubled.

- Profits will fall. If unit costs rise and selling price remains the same, then profit margins will fall. In addition, potential output has not been produced and this translates to a loss of potential sales revenue. It may be that a lack of demand is the cause of underutilisation, in which case the sales opportunities were never there. Nevertheless, the profitability of the business will suffer.
- Prices may have to rise. To cover the higher fixed costs per unit and to boost revenue, prices may have to be increased. Increasing price can be a problem because the business might expect demand to fall. What is important is *how much* the demand will fall as a result of the rise in price. This is called **price sensitivity** or **price elasticity of demand**. The price elasticity of demand can have important effects on the level of revenue earned following a price change.
- Employees may feel insecure. When a business utilises only a proportion of its capacity, employees may fear for their own prospects. The workforce may be cut in order to reduce capacity and costs. Part-time and temporary staff, who may have previously been brought in to raise capacity, may be the first to go; but all employees may fear for the prospects of the business.

Operational issues dealing with non-standard orders and matching production and demand

The difficulties firms face in predicting demand and the inherent instability of demand present the operations management team with significant challenges. Ideally the business would want to match its orders or its sales with its output. In reality this is rarely the case so a business has to work to try and minimise the mismatch between orders/sales and capacity. This means keeping under- and over-capacity utilisation to a minimum. Factor input use has to be constantly monitored and changes made to maintain efficiency as high as possible. There are a number of ways that a business might use to manage capacity utilisation.

Overtime

Assuming that a business has the capacity in its capital, it can utilise the flexibility of its staff to meet changing demand conditions. In particularly busy times a business can bring in overtime schedules. This is a means of giving staff the chance to work over their normal contracted hours of work. In such cases a business might offer incentives to take up the overtime. This may be in the form of time off in lieu at other (less busy) times, or additional payments. Typically a business might offer time and a half or double time as an incentive. If a worker normally earns £8 an hour for their contracted work, time and a half would pay them £12 an hour and double time, £16 per hour. In times when the level of demand falls off, the business can reduce overtime accordingly.

Overtime is a useful means of responding to changing demand because it is quick, easy and flexible. In addition, most employees recognise their role in the business when times are busy or slack and understand overtime. It does not involve the business in instituting long-term inflexible contractual arrangements.

Hiring temporary or part-time staff

Businesses might use the services of a temping agency to hire staff in times when demand is high. Hiring temporary workers can allow the business a great deal of flexibility. In addition, some businesses will hire part-time workers on temporary contracts for a specified period of time to help cover for periods of high demand. The Royal Mail use such temporary staff in the run-up to Christmas and many shops and stores will offer temporary Christmas jobs to help them cope with the level of demand in the few weeks leading up to Christmas and for the post-Christmas sales period. Similar situations exist for summer holiday work in resorts, or fruit-picking.

Rationalisation

This process of cutting back capacity when faced with excess capacity is known as **rationalisation**. Rationalisation means finding ways to reorganise production in order to reduce costs and become more efficient. It might involve closing down one or more plants. For example, a business might have two manufacturing centres – one in Scotland and one in the south of England. The one in Scotland is working at 60% capacity whilst the one in the south of England is operating at 35% capacity. The business might decide to close down the plant in the south of England and shift production to the plant in Scotland. The plant in Scotland can now run nearer to full capacity and the firm saves the costs of running the inefficient plant in the south of England. Closing plants like this, however, is not easy and there may be associated costs of exit – redundancy for staff, removal expenses for staff, and so on, not to mention the possible anger at such a move.

MG Rover supporters and employees stage a protest about the closure of the Longbridge plant in 2005.

Subcontracting

The business may consider undertaking work for other firms – **subcontracting**. This is common practice in some industries, such as maintenance or building work, where small companies can only meet the needs of a large job through the use of subcontractors. The solution is not ideal for either business. The company with a lack of capacity may not be able to guarantee the quality of subcontractors' work. The construction company Multiplex experienced huge problems when it subcontracted the construction of the steel arch for the redevelopment of Wembley Stadium. The two parties fell into dispute about who was liable for rising steel prices and the dispute led to delays in the completion of the project. Equally, the subcontractors are not building their own direct customer links.

However, many businesses build up strong relationships with subcontractors over a period of time, and in such cases working with subcontractors can be a very useful way of meeting demand and bringing in skills and expertise that the business does not have. In addition to this, the subcontractors might have access to specialist equipment and machinery that could be very expensive if just purchased for a specific part of a job.

Managing stocks effectively

Many businesses need **stocks** of some description. Stocks of component parts are needed to ensure production can be carried out and stock is needed to meet customer demand. However, holding stock means that cash has been spent on acquiring it in the first place and stock also has to be stored, managed and in some cases maintained. A business has to balance the importance of having sufficient stock to maintain production or satisfy customer demand with the cost of so doing. If stocks can be managed effectively then these two things can be balanced out. Holding too much stock can eat into cash flow and many manufacturing firms have recognised this. Many now try and operate systems that keep stocks to a minimum. This is called 'just-in-time' stock control (JIT). Such systems rely on excellent communication and distribution systems as well as relationships between suppliers and the business.

Further material and resources relating to this section can be found at **www.collins.bized.co.uk**. Keep checking for updates.

Making operational decisions: **Summary**

- Operations management is the organisation of resources to produce goods and services.
- Firms will have three main operational targets:
  - minimising unit costs
  - maintaining and improving quality
  - managing capacity utilisation effectively.
- Unit cost is the cost of producing one unit of output.
- Quality relates to five key areas:
  - fit for purpose
  - excellence
  - free of faults or errors
  - durable
  - value for money.
- Capacity refers to the maximum amount a business can produce given its available resources.
- Capacity utilisation refers to the proportion of maximum capacity that is actually used during a period of time.
- There are three main objectives of capacity utilisation:
  - efficiency
  - quality
  - customer service.
- Under- and over-capacity can present problems to a business.
- Businesses have to manage capacity to meet unpredictable demand patterns.
- Firms can match orders to demand more effectively by:
  - using overtime
  - hiring temporary and part-time workers
  - rationalisation
  - subcontracting
  - managing stock effectively.

Summary questions

1 Give a definition of the term 'operations management'.

2 Identify and briefly explain the three operational targets businesses will have.

3 If the total cost of production in a month was £60,000 and output during that time was 240,000, what would be the unit cost?

4 Why is the maintenance of quality considered an important operational target for a business?

5 What does the statement 'the firm is operating at 30% of capacity' mean?

6 State, and explain, three implications for a business of operating at 100% of capacity.

7 Why do businesses want to operate at the highest capacity utilisation possible?

8 What is meant by 'rationalisation'? What does it often involve?

9 Outline three ways that a firm might deal with over-capacity.

10 Outline three ways that a firm might deal with under-capacity.

Activity

Boil is a high quality kettle manufacturer providing kettles to five-star hotels for guest rooms. Due to favourable economic conditions, they anticipated increased demand and set about increasing capacity.

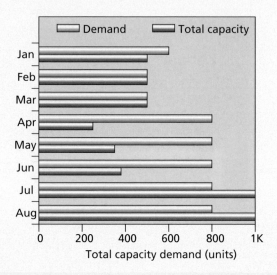

Figure 23.1 Capacity and demand analysis for Boil

1 Explain what might have caused the reduction in capacity in April? What might have been happening in May and June?

2 What might have been the effect on Boil of total capacity falling short of demand from April to June?

Exam practice

Budget airline Ryanair reported a 23% rise in pre-tax profits for the six months to the end of September 2007. The positive figures came despite oil prices reaching nearly $100 a barrel during the summer and autumn of 2007. Rising oil prices put pressure on airlines given the proportion of operating costs taken up by fuel. Some reports put the figure as high as 35–40% of costs. Ryanair seems to have managed to improve profit; question is, therefore, how has it done this?

The airline is very good at managing its capacity. Many of the flights leave full and capacity utilisation is high. The company face unpredictable demand levels. It knows that demand for flights to holiday destinations will rise during the summer and holiday periods but it is more difficult to predict exactly what the level of demand might be. It can vary with such factors as the weather in the UK! Demand for business travel is more stable throughout the year but the company does face peaks and troughs in demand at different times.

Ryanair has also focused on where it could extract more revenue. Ryanair has called these additional revenue streams 'ancillary revenues' in its report. It includes things such as the sale of goods and food and drink on board, insurance and car hire. In addition to this it introduced a charge for every bag stored in the aircraft hold – £2.50. The introduction was met with some controversy but it seems to have been a success for the company.

Source: adapted from Biz/ed 'In the News': http://www.bized.co.uk/cgi-bin/chron/chron.pl?id=2961

1 Explain, using an example, how Ryanair would calculate the unit cost of a flight between (say) Bristol and Edinburgh. Show your workings. (6 marks)

2 If Ryanair has a capacity utilisation of 93%, what does this mean? Explain your answer. (4 marks)

3 If oil prices are rising and the price of aircraft fuel is rising, explain what is likely to happen to unit costs and profit margins. (6 marks)

4 Identify and explain THREE factors that might cause underutilisation for a budget airline like Ryanair. (6 marks)

5 Explain how Ryanair's 'ancillary revenues' might affect the perception of quality and customer service of the airline. (8 marks)

6 Evaluate TWO methods that Ryanair might use to cope with a sudden and significant rise in demand for flights. (10 marks)

Total: 40 marks

Chapter 24   Developing effective operations: quality

In this chapter you will learn about the meaning and importance of quality in business. You will learn about the difference between **quality control** and **quality assurance**, and about the different systems that businesses use to monitor and improve quality.

Key terms

Benchmarking A way of improving quality by comparing one aspect of the business against the best practice of competitors, leading companies from other industries or other parts within the organisation.

Quality assurance (QA) Ensuring that quality is guaranteed throughout an organisation and that both the final product and service will meet customer expectations.

Quality chains A feature of TQM (see below) that views each link in the production process as a link between supplier and customer, so that it is the responsibility of each worker to ensure that customers' requirements are met.

Quality control The inspection of products to check they meet the necessary standards.

Statistical process control A sophisticated quality control technique that monitors production to ensure any variation in key quality standards is kept to a minimum.

Total quality management (TQM) An approach to business that emphasises the involvement of everyone in an organisation in getting the product and service right first time.

Zero defects A goal of TQM, to make no errors in production so that product quality is achieved first time around.

The meaning of quality

Quality is a subjective term. What I might regard as quality, you might not. Quality in business is not just about producing a product that uses expensive components or raw materials, and neither is a quality service one that has offices with plush sofas and gold fittings! Quality is all about meeting the expectations and needs of consumers.

Many young people do not wish to buy an item of clothing that is going to last them for ten years; a pair of trousers might be bought with a particular event in mind. Once that event is over the trousers might not be worn again. Quality in this instance might relate to the functionality of the trousers in doing their job at the event – making the person look and feel good. Contrast this with an older person who might be choosing a jacket. The individual might define quality as relating to the cloth that is used, the tailoring and the durability of the garment. A quality item in this case might be one that does indeed last for ten years.

Quality relates to being fit for purpose. The purpose is that defined by the consumer. In the example above the purpose of the two garments for the two different types of consumer were quite different; they had different needs and thus different perspectives as to what constituted 'quality'. If the business can anticipate and meet those needs and perceptions, then it can provide 'quality'.

We saw in the last chapter how quality can be defined and it is worth reminding ourselves of the key factors that define quality in business:

- Fit for purpose – the product does what it intends to do and meets the needs and perceptions of the consumer. For example, a quality drill will be able to tackle all the challenges that are put against it.
- Excellence – this might relate to its function, appearance or overall image. For example, a laptop might be considered excellent if it has a very large memory, is fast, and has an appealing design and large screen.
- Free of faults or errors – this can be relevant for a complex piece of technical equipment built for the military, through to aircraft, right down to a humble screw – you do not expect the thread to be damaged!
- Durable – long-lasting, without the need for repair or replacement. For example, consumers may be prepared to pay more for white goods like fridges, washing machines and

dishwashers if they are reliable and will last a long time without the need for repair.

- Value for money – a reasonable price for the standard of the product. What constitutes a reasonable price will be dependent to a large extent on the perception of the consumer of their needs in relation to the amount of money they have to give up to acquire the good or service.

By satisfying customer needs, a business can gain a competitive edge. To maintain customer loyalty, quality needs to be consistent. Individual incidents – such as the recall of a faulty product – may destroy a reputation for quality that has taken many years to build.

In recent decades, consumers have become increasingly well informed about product quality. Information from groups such as the Consumers Association, from the Internet and from labelling – now required by law – have given consumers more choice and enable consumers to make comparisons of quality more easily. Consumers have also become more familiar and confident about feeding back quality issues to businesses and, where quality does not meet expectations or business claims, seeking compensation. All these factors have brought the importance of quality to a business sharply into focus.

The importance of quality

By satisfying customer needs a business can gain a competitive edge. To maintain customer loyalty and ensure repeat purchase, quality needs to be consistent. If quality standards fall a business can suffer as it's reputation, which often takes many years to develop, can be destroyed in a relatively short space of time.

Reaching a high standard of quality and then maintaining and improving those quality standards over time can bring a number of advantages:

INCREASE IN SALES AND HIGHER REVENUE

Businesses with a reputation for quality can capture greater market share and improve sales as a result. In addition, customers are often prepared to pay more for a quality product and this gives the firm more flexibility on pricing. Increasing the price of a quality product might not result in any perceptible fall in demand for the product or service, with the result that the revenue will rise. High quality products, therefore, might be associated with a more price inelastic demand.

THE IMPACT ON COSTS

Quality does not just mean the quality of the end product to the consumer; many businesses will be concerned to maintain quality throughout their operations. This can help to reduce the number of faulty products, identify problems in production at an early stage, reduce waste, reduce the rime needed to deal with customer complaints and result in fewer claims under warranties and guarantees. All of these things would impact in costs so if they can be kept to a minimum then the firm's costs can be kept under a greater degree of control helping to make them more competitive.

QUALITY AS A UNIQUE SELLING POINT (USP)

Many products will deliberately market themselves as high quality and use this quality as their USP. The lager, Stella Artois, for example, marketed itself as being 'reassuringly expensive' – a reference to the quality it believes customers are prepared to pay for.

The distinction between quality control and quality assurance

Quality control is an approach to business that looks to improve the quality of products as they leave the factory. This involves the inspection of products to check they meet the necessary standards. The quality control process follows the stages shown in Figure 24.1. Checks on product quality can be made at the start, during or at the end of the production process.

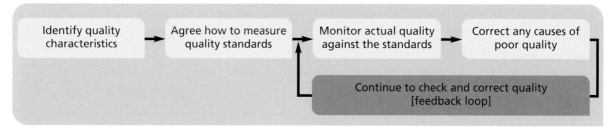

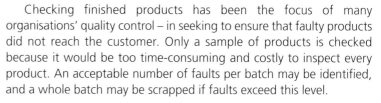

Figure 24.1   The stages of quality control

Checking finished products has been the focus of many organisations' quality control – in seeking to ensure that faulty products did not reach the customer. Only a sample of products is checked because it would be too time-consuming and costly to inspect every product. An acceptable number of faults per batch may be identified, and a whole batch may be scrapped if faults exceed this level.

However, relying on this method to ensure quality is risky; faulty products may slip through untested. It assumes that there is an acceptable level of faults and, even though this may be low, it may still have a negative impact on the business. This method also creates an impression that ensuring quality is the job of quality inspectors and not of the production workers themselves.

A philosophy started to develop that saw any level of fault or defect as being unacceptable and damaging to the business. This led to the development of quality assurance.

Quality assurance (QA) is an altogether different approach to quality. It emphasises quality throughout the organisation; it is the responsibility of everyone in the organisation to maintain quality. This philosophy gives empowerment to any individual to raise quality concerns. We can summarise the main differences between quality control and quality assurance as follows:

- QA emphasises customer needs rather than just meeting technical standards.
- QA ensures that quality is built into a product rather than faults being inspected out. This means that processes are

designed to reduce potential quality issues to a minimum. The business does not wait for a problem to occur; it tries to anticipate the problem before it arises and designs the production process to eliminate it.

- QA develops systems to ensure quality in all aspects of the business, not just production. This means that every individual has a responsibility. The receptionist who greets clients on the phone or in person is as much a part of the quality process as the design engineer on the production line.
- QA shifts away from checking by inspectors and towards self-checking, with workers taking responsibility for checking the quality of their own work.

As with any system in a business, there are costs involved in introducing and maintaining QA systems:

- There will need to be investment into equipment for quality monitoring during the production process. This equipment might also need to be supplemented by computer programmes which also require expensive software development and maintenance.
- It will be difficult for the business to understand and meet customer needs and expectations without market research. QA will therefore involve market research costs to identify customer expectations about a product.
- There might be considerable costs in training all staff to achieve quality outputs. This might include training and recruitment of staff to monitor QA systems and to be well versed in the software used in computer-based QA systems.
- The introduction of QA systems will create disruption and will involve time to implement. This invariably not only increases cost but also means revenue streams might be disrupted as there is reorganisation of business procedures.

However, the potential gains from effective QA systems are considerable in comparison to more limited forms of quality control. These benefits can be summarised as follows:

- Faults can be eliminated or minimised. Repairing or replacing faulty items is expensive and time-consuming so reducing these to a minimum helps to control costs.
- It reduces the chance of faulty products reaching the customer. The business is not relying on sampling and inspection to prevent this. Customer satisfaction should increase. If it does so then brand loyalty can also be increased and this increases the chance of repeat purchases and also generates word-of-mouth promotion.
- All aspects of customer expectations are considered, including service, and in the long term this will produce customer loyalty and increased sales.
- Many businesses will need to have some form of customer support team. These teams focus on dealing with customers. If customers have cause for complaint then it increases their workload. Reducing the number of complaints means that businesses can focus on other, value-added, methods of providing customer support.

Systems of quality assurance

A quality assurance system is a means by which a business can set standards, apply those standards across the business's activities and have systems in place to ensure that these standards are maintained and improved wherever possible. Some businesses will set up their own internal systems for establishing and monitoring quality. However, to ensure that the quality standards are accepted industry-wide, businesses may well look to match these systems to external standards and regulation. There are a number of such external systems.

ISO 9000

ISO stands for International Standardisation Organisation. There are many different ISO ratings. ISO 9000 is an international standard for quality assurance. Most countries have their own national standards (such as BS5750 in the UK), but the purpose of ISO 9000 is to have a quality assurance system recognised throughout the world. On achieving the standard a business can advertise that it is ISO rated. If the business can get this recognition it is able to immediately communicate to all its stakeholders the message that it operates at the highest levels of quality in all its processes. Once achieved, the business has to have systems in place to constantly monitor its quality to ensure it continues to meet the standards. The ISO 9000 standard, therefore, ensures that a business maintains quality at a consistent level.

To achieve ISO 9000 an organisation must:

- design and document the procedures for controlling and supporting quality
- choose an independent organisation, such as the British Standards Institution (BSI), to inspect and confirm that the standards have been met
- act on any problems identified and be reinspected twice a year.

Registering for accreditation with ISO can bring a number of benefits:

- ISO 9000 guidelines, and support from an external organisation such as the BSI, can help to improve existing procedures.
- ISO 9000 provides an incentive to stick to the procedures because of the external, independent check.
- The causes of quality problems can be identified and the costs of poor quality reduced.
- Businesses can base their activities (products and services offered) on requirements that are accepted widely across the globe.
- As these standards have a worldwide acceptance, consumers are served with an increasingly wide choice of products and services.
- Technology becomes compatible across most business organisations.
- Customers can see the organisation takes quality seriously and has quality assurance systems in place at all stages of production.

- Some customers (notably business-to-business (B2B)) may insist on ISO 9000 certification – particularly when they are buying components for their own production process. This can help to secure contracts and orders.
- Sales, image and reputation can all be improved as a result of the recognition.

Not all organisations choose to register for ISO 9000 certification, however, believing it will make little improvement to existing procedures. It could also cause a number of problems, such as the following:

- A focus on systems and paperwork may make the business too bureaucratic and inward-looking.
- Meeting the standards can be costly and time-consuming, with the costs of changing systems, training, writing documents and paying for ISO 9000 registration.
- Alternative approaches to achieving quality such as continuous improvement, which may be more suitable for some organisations, are not included in the ISO 9000.

British Standards Institution (BSI)

The Kite mark and the CE mark are both important standards of quality. The CE mark confirms the product meets EU directives.

Trade associations

Trade associations draw up codes of practice for their members to adhere to – membership of such an association is an indication of quality, for example, Corgi gas suppliers, British Soft Drinks Association, National Federation of Builders, and so on.

Warranties and guarantees

Warranties and guarantees are methods by which a business is able to communicate trust with its consumers. The offer of such things tells the consumer that the business and its products can be trusted. A guarantee will be offered free of charge but having done so is subject to legal regulations covered by the Sale and Supply of Goods to Consumers Regulations Act, 2002. Under this law a guarantee provides 'an agreement to provide some benefit for a set period of time in the event of the goods or services being defective'. For example, if someone buys a kettle, it is likely to come with a year-long guarantee. If the product fails within the period of the guarantee, then the business would either replace it or repair it. Guarantees do not usually include damage or failure caused by misuse. A guarantee does not mean that the business relinquishes its responsibilities under UK consumer law, so if the product breaches any of these laws then the consumer still has a right to action under the law.

Warranties are similar to but different from guarantees. A warranty is a legally-binding assurance that any material defects or failures in the product covering a set period will be put right by the business. As with guarantees they do not invalidate the business's legal responsibilities under consumer law.

These methods are important in quality assurance because if they were not offered, consumers might think twice about buying the products. Why would a business not offer such things – because they were worried that the products would fail?

Best practice benchmarking

Benchmarking is a way of improving quality by comparing an aspect of the business against best practice of competitors, leading firms from other industries or even within other parts of the organisation. The aims of benchmarking are to:

- find out how well one aspect of your own business is performing in comparison to other organisations
- set a standard for your own business to match or exceed the best of the rest
- find new ideas and ways of doing things that can be put into practice in your own business.

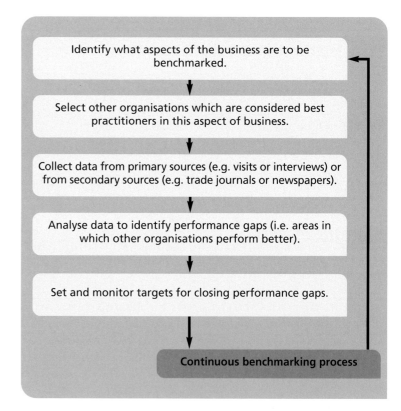

Figure 24.2   Stages in the benchmarking process

Benchmarking can bring a number of benefits:

- By identifying areas for improvement and observing how other organisations work, a business can learn a great deal about improving their own quality or efficiency.
- It can save time and money compared to working in isolation and only learning by trial and error.
- The focus of benchmarking is on how to be the best in each area examined. It helps to set clear targets that drive a business forward rather than just making do with current performance.

Some limitations of benchmarking need to be considered:

- Rivals may not allow access to crucial information, and organisations from other industries may not prove similar enough to be a useful comparison.
- If benchmarking means that an organisation merely copies what others are already doing rather than striving to lead, it will never be better than its rivals – or the first to innovate.
- Benchmarking could become no more than a paperwork exercise, identifying relevant information but not doing anything with it. Unless turned into a strategy for improvement, benchmarking is pointless.

Six Sigma methodology

The term 'Six Sigma' was first coined by Motorola engineer, Bill Smith. It is a method of operating that takes information and data generated by the business and uses statistical analysis of this data to drive improvement. The methodology focuses on identifying and reducing defects in all processes to anticipate and exceed customer expectations and needs. To achieve Six Sigma (the term relates to standard deviations from the mean and specification limits for a process), a business has to reduce defects to fewer than 3.4 per million possibilities.

Six Sigma is now a major influence on production methods and quality assurance, and is used by a wide range of businesses. General Electric (GE) is one business that has implemented the methodology. They report that they have gained benefits to the tune of $10 billion in the first five years of implementation. As with other quality systems, implementation of this process does necessitate organisational change, training and planning which can be costly and time-consuming.

Total quality management (TQM)

Total quality management is an extension of the move from quality control to quality assurance. Its goals are:

- to create a culture of quality
- to involve all employees, whatever their role within the business
- to seek continuous improvement in quality
- to see quality from the customer's point of view.

The message of TQM emerged from the ideas of Dr W Edwards Deming and Joseph M Juran. From the 1950s onwards, many Japanese manufacturers put these ideas into practice – helping to establish Japan as leaders in the global market. Deming outlined 14 points for quality assurance. The following are some of the key ones:

- Don't rely on mass inspection to achieve quality. Cut inspection by building quality into the product in the first place. (Point 3)
- Get rid of work standards (quotas) on the factory floor; encourage leadership rather than management by numbers. (Point 11)
- Cut out slogans and targets asking for **zero defects** and higher productivity. These only cause bitterness, as most of the reasons for low quality and low productivity are to do with the system, not the fault of the workforce. (Point 10)

The key features of TQM are:

- A focus on the customer – understanding customer needs and using this to ensure the business meets their expectations. Market research is crucial in monitoring quality standards and seeking ways to improve.
- The involvement of all – workers at every level must be involved in the achievement of quality. The talents and ideas of each worker must be brought together. Teamwork is particularly useful in sharing ideas and motivating employees to improve quality. Quality circles are an example of this. Groups of employees meet on a regular basis to consider ways of improving procedures to benefit quality. They are then empowered by management to put their suggestions into practice.
- **Quality chains** – because many workers are remote from the final customer, each link in the production process is viewed as a link between supplier and customer. So the next stage in the production process is seen as an internal customer. It is the responsibility of each worker to ensure that this customer's requirements are met. In this way, quality is built in at every stage and problems are immediately identified.
- Getting it right first time – TQM aims to achieve zero defects by ensuring quality is built in at every stage of production, and in every other function of the business. All costs of poor quality should be eliminated and, in theory, there should be no need for quality inspection at the end of the production process.
- Leadership on quality from the top – a commitment to quality needs to be established through clear leadership and management.
- Monitoring quality – the use of sophisticated quality control techniques (known as **statistical process control**) to ensure any variation in key quality standards is kept to a minimum.
- Continuous improvement – a constant search for further ways to improve quality. This is called Kaizen and stems from the Toyota Motor Corporation in Japan. The word 'Kaizen' is Japanese for 'change for better' or 'improvement'.

TQM's total approach to quality has been the foundation for the success of many businesses, including Motorola and Hewlett-Packard. Many others who have tried to implement TQM, however, have experienced little benefit. The table below summarises the potential costs and benefits of TQM.

Whether TQM is successful for any one organisation depends on whether or not:

- there is clear leadership from the top
- the workforce is genuinely and fully involved
- training, time and support are provided to reinforce the policy
- quality is considered broadly enough to include all aspects of business performance
- procedures are adapted to meet the specific needs of an organisation.

Guru's views

'You do not have to do this; survival is not compulsory.'

– Deming

THE COSTS AND BENEFITS OF TOTAL QUALITY MANAGEMENT

Benefits	Costs
• All aspects of quality in the business considered.	• May become just another set of procedures to be followed, making the business slow and bureaucratic.
• Costs of poor quality eliminated by getting it right first time.	• May be seen as an end in itself with all the focus on processes not on the final product.
• Clear focus on customer needs helps to make the business more competitive.	• Too much responsibility may be given to workers, who could lack proper leadership.
• Provides a positive and motivating working environment.	• May place too much stress on workers in demanding constant improvement, which could be demotivating.
• Makes the best use of the talents of the workforce.	• The disruption of change and the costs of training could outweigh the benefits.

Quality standards

There are many different types of quality standards covering many different industries and processes. The ISO has developed around 16,500 standards and new ones are being added every year. They cover all aspects of business operation. The main ones cover such diverse industries as manufacturing, printing, forestry, agriculture, financial services, insurance, chemicals, bio-technology, software development, aviation, pest control, telecommunications, recycling, tourism and many more.

The main areas where a business will have to demonstrate standards cover the following main sections:

- management systems
- management responsibilities
- resource management
- product realisation
- measurement, analysis and improvement.

Further material and resources relating to this section can be found at **www.collins.bized.co.uk**. Keep checking for updates.

Developing effective operations:
quality: Summary

- Quality in business is about producing goods and services that are fit for purpose and which meet the needs and expectations of consumers.
- There is a distinction between quality control and quality assurance – quality control refers to inspections at various stages of the production process, whereas quality assurance is a philosophy that embraces quality at all levels of the organisation.
- Introducing quality control systems does bring benefits, but it also involves some costs.
- Businesses have to balance out the two – some businesses might not see any significant benefit from quality control systems but spend a great deal on them.
- Quality systems involve setting standards and finding ways to measure output and process against those standards, and maintain and improve the standards over time.
- Most firms will have internal QA systems but many also adhere to externally-set systems.
- The ISO has a large number of standards relating to all aspects of the business.
- Seeking some form of certification from an external body like the ISO does have costs.
- For businesses, for such systems to be successful, the benefits they gain from additional sales must outweigh the costs of gaining the accreditation and maintaining the standards.

Summary questions

1 What are the key features of a definition of quality?
2 Explain how achieving quality can increase revenues and help reduce costs.
3 Why are there costs in achieving quality?
4 How does quality assurance differ from quality control?
5 Identify and explain THREE costs and THREE benefits of using a quality assurance system.
6 What is ISO 9000 and how might a business benefit from it?
7 Explain the features of total quality management (TQM).
8 What are the benefits of TQM?
9 Why might TQM not prove successful?
10 What are the benefits and problems of using benchmarking?

Activity

- Choose three different businesses of varying sizes each producing a different product or service. They can be businesses that are well known nationally or internationally, or local ones with which you are familiar.
- Try to make a list of the ways in which each business might need to focus on quality.
- Identify and explain two benefits and two costs to each business of improving quality throughout the organisation.

Exam practice

Many businesses spend millions on quality control and quality assurance systems; how many times have you made a phone call to a business and been told that 'this call may be recorded for quality control purposes'? Business guru Peter Drucker had very firm views on the subject. He said:

> 'Quality in a product or service is not what the supplier puts in. It is what the customer gets out and is willing to pay for. A product is not quality because it is hard to make and cost a lot of money, as manufacturers typically believe. This is incompetence. Customers pay only for what is of use to them and gives them value. Nothing else constitutes value.' (*Source: Consumer Behaviour*, Ray Wright, Thomson Learning Publications)

If this is the case, how are we to interpret the problems facing Mattel, the toy maker, with their quality control issues? Mattel has outsourced manufacture of many of its toys to China and over a period in August 2007 had to recall millions of products because of 'quality' issues. Globally, the firm has recalled more than 18 million toys. The toys include many popular ranges including *Doggy Daycare*, *Polly Pocket*, *Batman*, *Barbie* and a model car from the Pixar film *Cars*. There is a range of problems associated with the toys but predominantly, they centre on the use of lead in paint and the use of magnets that could come loose and pose a choking hazard for children.

The recall came at a particularly difficult time for Mattel and for toy retailers. The end of August sparks the start of the Christmas sales season and having withdrawn so many products, Mattel had to find ways of replacing the stock quickly to take advantage of the 2007 Christmas market. The problems seem to have stemmed from the use of a sub contracted manufacturer in China who used paint sourced from an unauthorised supplier. In the case of the magnets, production control seems to have lapsed in some way.

The issue for Mattel, which has unreservedly apologised to customers for the problems, is how it maintains quality controls in the plants it uses. Like many other businesses, it is unlikely to own manufacturing plants in China, outsourcing to them instead. Making sure that the standards set are adhered to is a major problem. Referring back to Drucker's quote, is this a problem for Mattel or for the consumer?

Source: adapted from Biz/ed 'In the News' http://10.160.146.92/cgi-bin/chron/chron.pl?id=2909

1 Provide a definition of the term 'quality'. (4 marks)

2 Using examples, explain the difference between quality control and quality assurance. (6 marks)

3 Analyse the possible reasons why Mattel faced quality issues with its products. (6 marks)

4 Discuss some of the problems facing a business like Mattel in seeking to maintain quality standards when it outsources many of its operations. (10 marks)

5 To what extent would a quality assurance system such as ISO 9000 help reduce the quality problems that Mattel has faced? (14 marks)

Total: 40 marks

Chapter 25 Developing effective operations: customer service

In this chapter you will learn about the importance of developing good customer service systems in a business. You will learn how this helps a business to meet the needs of their customers before, during and after any transaction takes place, and about the benefits that can be gained from high levels of customer service.

Methods of meeting customer service expectations

Customer service can be seen as the ways in which a business seeks to enhance the level of customer satisfaction and experience in their relationship with the business and its products or services. In so doing, the customer believes that the business has met and exceeded their expectations.

The development of customer services is related to the development of market-orientated businesses where businesses put the needs of the customer first. Developing high levels of customer service can mean that a business can gain competitive advantage. The precise ways that a business provides these levels of service might be difficult for a rival to emulate.

Customer expectations may manifest themselves in several ways:

- The customer might expect the business to be honest in its dealings with all stakeholders – suppliers, employees, and so on.
- The customer might expect the business to meet national and international standards and regulations, and have high ethical and environmental standards.
- The customer might expect the product to be free from defects and to be safe and reliable.
- The customer might expect the price to be reflective of the principle of 'fit for purpose' and to reflect what the consumer considers to be value for money.
- The customer will expect the business to abide by the laws of the land – including European Union laws and directives.
- The customer will expect to be treated by staff of the business in an appropriate manner.
- The customer will expect deliveries to be made on time and for goods to arrive in good condition.

In order to meet high levels of customer service, a business will have to put in place a series of systems. This might range from having a dedicated call centre that deals with customer service issues through to a small business training its staff in customer service techniques. Whether the business is **B2B** or **B2C**, the principles are the same.

There are a number of methods of meeting customer expectations once these standards have been set. Some are of these are listed below.

Market research

Information from market research can help to build a profile of customers and help the business to understand its customers and their expectations. The source of this market research can be through traditional primary methods – surveys, focus groups, and so on but also utilising the information that can be gathered from within the business. Management can be a valuable source of information and no business can really afford to ignore the experience and the views of its employees, many of whom are most likely to be at the forefront of dealing with customers or involved in the production process itself. Market research can also come from people who are not currently customers. Valuable information can come from those who use rival products – why do they use those rival products and why do they not use yours? If customers have been lost they can be contacted and asked why they went elsewhere. Such information is valuable in building an understanding of customer needs and expectations.

Training

Businesses might need to spend a considerable amount of time and resources in training staff into the nature of the standards of customer service and the expectations of consumers. They will need to know how to handle a wide range of different situations, from aggressive and abusive customers to customers who have difficult and challenging complaints. This requires a considerable range of interpersonal skills. It is one thing for a business to say that it puts customer service very high in its priorities, and it might have a range of systems to ensure that this happens. If the customer experience, however, does not match those claims, then the business can quickly find itself losing competitive advantage.

Customers see that the claims are merely claims and that they have no substance. It is imperative, therefore, that the staff who work in any part of the organisation are properly trained and know what the standards are of customer service in the business. This training will have to be supplemented by refresher courses and updates on a regular basis to help remind staff of its importance and ensure staff understand any changes to the standards. Such changes are likely to be informed by the market research feedback that the firm carries out.

Quality assurance and quality control systems

We have seen in the previous section the role and importance of quality systems in a business. Such quality systems and standards can also relate to customer service and there are ISO standards on this aspect of business operations.

Quality standards

The first thing the business has to do is to define what standards they are going to operate to. The Institute of Customer Service identifies a number of considerations in setting these standards which include deciding on the number of standards a business should have, how they are to be used and how they are created in the first place.

Service standards might be expressed in three main ways:

- timeliness
- accuracy
- appropriateness.

Timeliness relates to the decisions the firm makes about how it communicates with its customers. For example, if a customer contacts a business – regardless of what the contact may be about, is there a time limit that the customer should experience before being responded to? This might be in the form of the number of rings of a telephone before it is answered, the number of days that a customer can expect a delivery to be made, and so on.

Accuracy refers to the information that is communicated to a customer. This might be through an advert, through a telephone conversation, in the description of the product or service, the labelling on the product, whether the number of items on a package is what the customer expects or is detailed in the instructions, and so on. If a business boasts of 100% accuracy then it has to ensure it meets those standards. It is not sufficient to state 100% accuracy but then to tell the customer that most of the orders are fulfilled accurately most of the time!

Appropriateness relates to the necessity of ensuring that customer expectations have been met. If a customer writes to a business with a complaint, for example, then the reply given by the business must ensure that it does deal with the specific complaint and not skirt round the main issue.

Monitoring and improving customer service

Once customer service standards have been set and implemented, the task shifts to monitoring and improving the level of customer service. In order to do this the business has to have established ways of checking to see that the standards that it has set up are being adhered to, and discovering where there might be further opportunities for improvement.

Monitoring customer service can be achieved in the following ways.

Mystery shoppers

Members of the business will go into shops, phone up the customer service helpline, and so on, posing as ordinary members of the public in an attempt to see how they are treated and whether the customer service standards are being maintained or even exceeded. The use of **mystery shoppers** helps the business to identify where there might be lapses in standards and where additional training may be required.

Recording customer/business exchanges

Many businesses will have a system whereby a selection of phone conversations between customers and the business will be recorded so that issues may be identified. Again these issues can be dealt with in on-going training of staff, or new standards put into place to deal with situations that arise that had not been considered. In some cases the business might also follow up selected customers and ask them to answer further questions about their experience.

Customer surveys

Businesses may often employ specialist market research companies to carry out surveys on their behalf and to collate and summarise the findings they receive. This is typical in the motor industry when a customer has had their car serviced or maintained in some way. A follow-up questionnaire arrives in the post a short time after asking customers to rate their experience against certain standards – time taken to do the work, the attitude and response of reception staff, value for money, whether the car was returned clean, whether a courtesy car was offered, and so on.

Metrics

Businesses will collect data on the levels of customer service offered against standards set, and circulate these around staff either in the form of a newsletter or in regular meetings (these are sometimes referred to as post-mortems!). Such **metrics** might include situations handled per period of time, the amount of time spent per enquiry as an average, the proportion of enquiries handled to the satisfaction of the customer and the business itself, average response times, average waiting times and more specific data referred to as 'dollar value'. This involves calculating the value of the products involved in any dispute or query and dividing it by the number of situations that arise.

The benefits of high levels of customer service

Businesses in all sectors need to be aware of the importance of customer service. Whether the business is B2B or B2C, it is the buyer of their product or service that keeps the company in business. A company like Rolls Royce needs to be aware of the needs and expectations of their clients – other very large firms like Boeing or Airbus who buy aircraft engines from Rolls Royce. A high-street butcher has to ensure that customer expectations of the quality of the meat they sell is maintained if they are to retain that custom; a train operator has to ensure that trains not only run on time as customers expect, but that they are clean, and that staff are courteous and knowledgeable. Being aware of the needs and expectations of customers is essential; the simple reason is that if these needs and expectations are met or exceeded, then the business has more chance of survival and growth.

We can classify the benefits as follows.

Increased sales

A reputation for high levels of customer service in its widest sense (that is, that products meet customer needs and expectations as well as the experience of customers with human interaction) can lead to increased sales. This might occur through word of mouth. Many smaller businesses will cite word of mouth as one of the most important reasons for increased sales. If a friend has had a good experience in their dealings with a business and tells their friends and colleagues, such a testimony is highly valued in comparison to other methods of promotion such as advertising; such views are trusted. With increased sales comes the prospect of increased revenue.

Pricing policies

Firms with high levels of customer service are in a position where they can offer greater flexibility on pricing policies. Dell computers, for example, were more expensive than other PC manufacturers and suppliers but they were able to justify the additional expense because of the reputation for quality (meeting the needs and expectations of consumers) and the level of customer service they offered.

Repeat purchases

Businesses that are involved in selling high volumes, in particular, rely on repeat purchases. Confectionery manufacturers and crisp manufacturers, for example, sell low-priced products that tend to have small margins associated with them. What they need in order to make appropriate profits is people coming back repeatedly to buy their product. If they provide the right sort of customer service then they are more likely to achieve this. This is also the case with small businesses especially in the early stages of growth. A hairdressing salon, a plumber, an electrician, a baker – all may rely on repeat purchases as a means of building up a customer base and then hoping that word of mouth helps to spread the message about the business.

Brand loyalty

It is not only high-volume sellers that rely on repeat purchase, however. High levels of customer service can also be of benefit to businesses that sell higher-priced, high-margin goods. Examples of these include dishwashers, washing machines, TVs, PCs, fridges, and so on. These goods tend to be purchased infrequently – possibly only once every eight to ten years. However, if the customer experience meets their needs and exceeds their expectations, then not only is it more likely that the customer will eventually replace their item with another from the same brand, but may also be more likely to buy other similar items from that company. If an individual has a good experience with a Hotpoint washing machine, they may also be more likely to think about buying a Hotpoint dishwasher or tumble dryer, and so on.

Competitive advantage

Competitive advantage refers to ways in which a business can develop advantages which rivals find hard to copy and which can lead to customers choosing their product or service rather than a rival's. Developing high levels of customer service is not something that is easy to do. In larger businesses, especially, the task of making sure that everyone in the organisation maintains or exceeds the standards set can be a significant challenge to business leaders. If a business is able to develop appropriate standards of customer service and consistently meets or exceeds them, then this can be a source of competitive advantage. If a consumer felt that customer service was higher in one business than another, then that may be the thing that persuades them to give their custom to that particular business. It may not be easy for a rival to develop similar or better standards of customer service quickly and this is where competitive advantage can be gained.

Difficulties in maintaining customer service standards

In theory, a business can set very high standards of customer service and tell customers that it has these high standards. Making sure that the customer does, in fact, experience these standards and more is the challenge facing most businesses. There are issues of motivation that are very closely linked to successful customer service levels in a business. Much of the direct customer service experience will fall on the employees in a business. If an employee does not feel ownership of those standards, if they feel alienated from the business, if they do not feel that they are supported in being able to meet standards that are set, then the systems that are put in place can fall apart and the customer experience can be very different from that which the company might be stating in its advertising.

Further material and resources relating to this section can be found at **www.collins.bized.co.uk**. Keep checking for updates.

Developing effective operations: customer service: Summary

- High levels of customer service are becoming an increasingly important part of business operations in an increasingly competitive marketplace.
- High levels of customer service start with the business setting minimum standards in relation to customer needs and expectation.
- Customer service standards can be set in terms of timeliness, accuracy and appropriateness.
- Methods of meeting customer service standards include market research, quality control and quality assurance systems and training.
- Having set standards, a business has to ensure that these are monitored and improved.
- Methods of monitoring include market research, mystery shoppers, monitoring telephone conversations and metrics.
- High levels of customer service can bring benefits which include increased sales, brand loyalty, competitive advantage, flexibility on pricing policies and repeat purchases.
- The challenge for business leaders is to ensure that everyone in the organisation – whether large or small – knows, understands, carries out and exceeds the levels of customer service that customers expect.

Summary questions

1. Explain the meaning of the term 'customer service'.

2. State five ways in which customer service may manifest itself.

3. Explain three methods of meeting customer service.

4. Explain, using examples, the meaning of the following in relation to customer service standards:

   - timeliness
   - accuracy
   - appropriateness.

5. Identify and explain three ways that a business might monitor standards of customer service – give your explanation using a different business context for each.

6. Explain, using an appropriate example, how a high level of customer service can provide a business with competitive advantage.

7. Why might high levels of customer service enable a business to have greater flexibility with its pricing policies?

8. Explain how good customer service can benefit a firm in building brand loyalty.

9. How might the use of metrics generated within a business inform and improve its customer service offering?

10. Discuss some of the difficulties facing a business in providing high levels of customer service.

Points for discussion

Look at the following website: http://www.tesco.com/
customerservices/custServAroundTheStore.htm
This gives some details about the levels of customer service at Tesco.

- Comment on how Tesco might have developed its customer
  service levels and how the business might monitor and
  improve the levels of customer service in their stores.

Exam practice

Music Zone was formed in 1984. Russ Grainger, the founder, started selling CDs from a market stall in Manchester. It grew to what might be considered a healthy size and had 104 stores around the country. Its mission statement made it very clear what the company aimed to do.

> 'Music Zone is owned and run by a team that firmly believes our customers will continue to shop with us if we consistently offer a full range of entertainment products at great value prices. We make our shops easy to use and fun and deliver the highest levels of customer service consistently across the whole business. We believe that if we continue to deliver our retail proposition and we keep expanding and reaching more people that we will become the first choice for music and DVDs on Britain's high streets. This is our aim.' (*Source:* Music Zone.)

The statement makes the company's ambition very clear but is also an interesting pointer about some key aspects of business. Stores such as Music Zone sell low value-added products. For a business selling these sorts of items, repeat purchase is important. Such businesses need customers to come into the store, buy an item, and then enjoy the experience or the value they feel they are getting so much that they are willing to go back there again and buy more items. To survive long term these sorts of businesses rely on people not just coming back once but again and again and again...

Music Zone may well have been a perfectly good shopping experience for the customer. Unfortunately, despite the expansion the firm has faced huge competitive pressures. These include the development of online retailing, the decision by supermarkets to not only stock chart CDs but also to use their size to exploit the tax advantages that could be gained by selling stock via Jersey and last, but by no means least, the developments in the way that people listen to music. The changes in technology mean that not only are CDs now rather 'bulky' items but also that many people do not need to buy CDs to listen to music – downloads have risen dramatically in the last few years.

As a result of all these competitive pressures, the firm has been forced to call in the administrators. Right until the end, the firm was hoping to be able to pull things round. In December 2006 it opened a new store in Glasgow! It had to cease trading with the loss of over 1000 jobs across the country.

Source: adapted from Biz/ed 'In the News' http://10.160.146.92/cgi-bin/chron/chron.pl?id=2909

1 Using an example, explain the meaning of the term 'customer service'. (4 marks)

2 Explain why repeat purchase is an important part of the business requirements of a company like Music Zone selling low-margin products. (6 marks)

3 (a) Describe the possible customer experience, needs and expectations of a customer using a store like Music Zone. (8 marks)

(b) To what extent do you think that the mission statement of Music Zone meets the customer needs and expectations outlined in your answer to (a) above? (10 marks)

4 To what extent is a high level of customer service a guarantee of success for a business? Illustrate your answer by referring to the case study. (12 marks)

Total: 40 marks

Chapter 26   Working with suppliers

In this chapter you will learn about the relationship a business has with its suppliers. This relationship is often crucial to the success of a business and depends on a variety of factors such as price, payment terms, quality, capacity, reliability and flexibility.

Choosing effective suppliers

Small businesses need supplies of raw materials and components, goods to sell, equipment to help provide the services they offer, and so on. In each case the business is heavily dependent on the relationship with (often) many suppliers. In very simple terms, if relationships with suppliers break down and **supply chains** break, then a business can face considerable difficulties.

For large firms the web of networks involved in moving goods from producer to consumer (whether B2B or B2C) can be incredibly complex. The web of organisations, activities and resources involved in getting a good from producer to consumer is called the supply chain. Because of the complexity of many supply chains the relationship that a business builds with its suppliers is critical. The potential for any of the many parts of the chain to break down or be subject to some form of problem is considerable. In fact, many large businesses spend large sums of money working out where there are vulnerabilities in their supply chains and putting in place plans and strategies to limit their exposure to such supply chain breakdowns.

To get some idea of the extent of the potential problem facing larger firms, take this example of the journey of a processor produced by Intel (see Figure 26.1). Intel's Pentium processors start their life in Japan. Toshiba produce silicon ingots that are then sliced into thin wafers by Toshiba and other producers. These are then transported across the Pacific Ocean to the United States where they go to plants in Arizona and Oregon. They have circuits etched into them before being flown back to Malaysia to Intel plants in that country. They have more work done on them before being packaged and transported back to Intel warehouses in Arizona. From there they are shipped to the factories of the PC manufacturer Dell. These factories are located in Ireland, Brazil, the US, Malaysia and China and will even go to some of Dell's sub contracted producers in Taiwan.

This incredible journey might sound unbelievable and possibly highly inefficient. However, we can be reasonably certain that Intel will have spent many hours and a considerable investment working out the cost effectiveness of such a supply chain. If there was a way of processing the products cheaper then Intel would probably do it! What the example does highlight is how complex supply chains can become. Making sure that the suppliers that are chosen to be partners in the business are right for the business is very important.

Key terms

Differentiation The means by which a business makes a product different from that of its rivals.

Homogenous goods Goods that are virtually indistinguishable from one another, for example, one pint of milk from one farmer is almost identical to that of another.

Productivity A measure of efficiency that looks at output per factor of production per time period.

Supply chain The various organisations, activities, businesses and resources involved in moving a product or service from one business to another business, or to the customer.

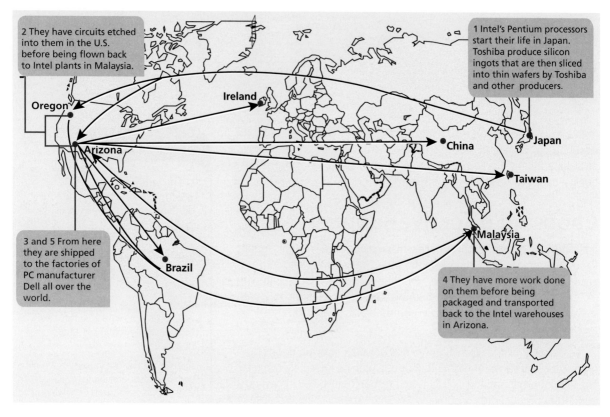

Text within figure:

2 They have circuits etched into them in the U.S. before being flown back to Intel plants in Malaysia.

1 Intel's Pentium processors start their life in Japan. Toshiba produce silicon ingots that are then sliced into thin wafers by Toshiba and other producers.

3 and 5 From here they are shipped to the factories of PC manufacturer Dell all over the world.

4 They have more work done on them before being packaged and transported back to the Intel warehouses in Arizona.

Map labels: Oregon, Ireland, Arizona, China, Japan, Taiwan, Brazil, Malaysia

Figure 26.1   Journey of an Intel processor

In the supply chain there will be many different types of business activity. Some businesses will be involved in supplying raw materials, some will be processing raw materials, others will be supplying services for each stage – banking, insurance and security services, for example, whilst others will be supplying transport and storage services. Firms like Intel will use many different businesses in the supply chain rather than do it all themselves because these firms will be specialists in their field. This specialisation helps to improve efficiency and is likely to mean it is more cost-effective for Intel to build relationships with these specialists and employ them to do the work on their behalf.

The role that suppliers play in improving operational performance

Operational performance for many businesses is measured in terms of increased sales, increased **productivity**, increases in quality, increases in revenue, reductions in cost, increases in repeat purchase, improvements in customer feedback or ratings, and so on. Ultimately, all these factors are ways in which a business might measure its success. In order to achieve any of these measures, the business will have to rely on people and processes in its own organisation, but also on the commitment and performance of its suppliers.

There is an argument that a business should limit its supplier relationships to as few as possible in order to build the relationship and reduce the potential for vulnerabilities for disruption. However, it is also pointed out that the reliance on one supplier can cause big problems if that supplier gets into difficulties. For example, in 2001, Land Rover failed to receive supplies of chassis from its sole supplier of that component, UPF Thompson. When Land Rover made enquiries as to why the shipment had not arrived they found that UPF Thompson were insolvent due to losses they had incurred on another business venture the company had undertaken which was nothing to do with Land Rover.

When this type of disruption occurs it can be very damaging both in the short-term and the long-term. Clearly, the role that a supplier plays in the performance of a business is important. The supplier can have an impact on costs and on quality, and the reliability of the relationship can mean that the business's relationship with its final customers can also be affected. These effects can be both positive and negative.

If the supplier consistently meets the needs of the business, then it is better able to reduce costs, increase sales and improve efficiency. Many businesses who are engaged in some form of manufacturing make use of production techniques that include JIT ('just-in-time') and lean production methods.

Lean production aims to eliminate waste within the production process. It brings together a variety of approaches to production that seek to produce more using less, while maximising quality of output. Many of its elements were inspired by the success of the Toyota Motor Company in becoming one of the world's leading car producers. The new techniques of Toyota contrasted with the more traditional mass-manufacturing techniques of US manufacturers, such as General Motors. While Toyota could produce a car in just 18 assembly hours, GM took 40.7; and while GM experienced defects at the rate of 130 per 100 cars, Toyota experienced just 45 per 100.

JIT production techniques aim to minimise stocks of raw materials, work in progress and finished products. JIT production requires the conventional approach to manufacturing to be turned on its head. Stocks are 'pulled' into the production process when they are needed – 'just-in-time' – rather than the traditional approach of being 'pushed' in 'just-in-case' they are needed.

To achieve these sorts of improvements, the relationships with suppliers have to be of the highest quality. These have to be based on trust as well as mutual respect and all of the practical things covered above such as flexibility and reliability. For many larger businesses, therefore, the role of suppliers is vital in achieving the business's targets.

The main factors that affect the choice of supplier

Price

In negotiating a relationship with a supplier, the price of the goods or services supplied will be central. There may be a very competitive marketplace in which the supplier is operating. In such a situation the price the supplier can offer might be the factor that enables them to win a contract. Of course price is not the only factor! The grocery industry in the UK is a good example of a highly competitive market place. Supermarkets like Tesco, Sainsbury's, Morrisons and Asda buy fruit and vegetables in large quantities. They are dominant buyers in the market.

However, producers of fruit and vegetables tend to be much smaller and have little control over prices or the market they operate in. As a result, a small farmer might come to rely almost completely on selling his/her produce to the big four. This can often mean that profit margins for farmers are very slim in an attempt to compete. They know that if their price is too high then the supermarket has the option of going to thousands of other similar producers to buy their supplies.

Price may be an important determinant of supplier choice in a market where the product is **homogenous**. In the strict definition of the term, homogenous means identical. The more difficult a product is to **differentiate** – to make different – the more likely that price will be the determining factor in supplier choice.

It might also be important for a business to consider price if the component or raw material plays a large part in the production process. The higher the proportion of total costs a part is, the more keenly will price be a factor in choosing a supplier. Firms such as Airbus and Boeing have to negotiate with companies like Rolls Royce to supply highly complex technical equipment like engines for aircraft. These are expensive to produce and may form an important cost component of production. Price therefore is important and must be weighed against the quality of the product supplied.

Payment terms

B2B supplier arrangements invariably come with a range of payment terms which specify the details about what type of payment is required (cash, cheque, bank draft, and so on), the timescale for the payment, specific details about what happens if payment terms are not adhered to and any early payment discounts that may be available.

The payment time period is a form of credit. The goods might be delivered on the 1st of the month and payment is not required until 28 days later. In this example, the business receiving the goods effectively has a 28-day interest-free loan. Setting and managing payment terms can be a useful means of short-term finance. In addition, the business who is the supplier has to manage its payment periods carefully to be able to manage its cash flow.

When initialising a new supplier relationship, a business should make sure that the terms and conditions of payment are made clear and understood before entering into any formal agreement. This can help to avoid potential misunderstandings at the outset. If the business does not agree with the terms and conditions then it can either look to renegotiate them or find an alternative supplier who they are more satisfied with.

As with price, larger firms negotiating with smaller suppliers can use their market power to extract more favourable terms and conditions, and even impose such terms and conditions as a prerequisite of securing a contract to supply. Some might extend the payment period – possibly three or six months in some cases. Smaller businesses may find such terms very difficult to meet.

Payment terms might also include the use of electronic means of making payments such as the Bacs system, which processes 5.5 billion payments a year, or the CHAPS system run by APACS, the trade association for payments and for institutions that deliver payment services. Such services can help businesses to ensure that payments are made quickly and that they are secure.

To check a supplier before entering into an agreement, a business can run a credit check to look at the credit history of the company they are dealing with. This can be done through specialist agencies such as Experian, looking at company accounts (those for a private limited company can be purchased from Companies House), and through bank references. Such a check might be very important if dealing with suppliers abroad or if entering into an agreement with a new supplier.

Quality

Chapter 24 looked in detail at quality issues facing business. Engaging a supplier that provides quality products or services in the widest sense of the term may be more important than price for some businesses, but will be important to most businesses. If raw materials or components are of poor quality (faulty, inconsistent, do not work, etc.) then it is likely to impact on the business's own drive for high quality and cause disruption to production schedules.

In selecting appropriate suppliers, a business can use the external forms of quality assurance standard outlined in Chapter 24 – ISO 9000 for example, as well as its own standards which can be communicated to the business concerned. Tesco, for example, have a contract with a food manufacturer based in the Midlands called Kettleby Foods. Tesco insist on a number of quality standards being met by Kettleby Foods, who in turn will also have their own quality standards. This includes being able to trace the origin and journey of the all the raw materials and ingredients used in production, checking weight tolerances of food products, checking for foreign objects in food, and so on.

Kettleby Foods know that Tesco can implement various penalties if quality standards are not maintained. This might include heavy fines or even the withdrawal of Tesco from the contract and them shifting their business elsewhere.

For Kettleby Foods, therefore, it is very much in their interests to maintain the high standards they set in order to maintain the very good relationship they have with Tesco. For Tesco, maintaining the relationship is also important to avoid potentially expensive disruption to supply. High quality, therefore, is in everyone's interest.

Capacity

It will be important for a business when seeking to enter into an agreement with a supplier, that the supplier is in a position to meet the needs of the business. This means it will have to check to make sure that the supplier is able to meet the demand from the business. In addition, it is important to ensure that there is some flexibility in the capacity of the supplier – that they can increase supply when demand increases and cope with sudden downturns in demand.

The focus on capacity will be particularly important for businesses that do experience sudden changes in demand and orders. One way of informing those in the supply chain of capacity changes is to try and forecast changes in demand accurately. However, even in businesses where the level of demand is fairly constant, there can be significant variations in demand throughout the supply chain.

This might be due to a phenomenon called the 'bull-whip effect'. The term was coined by pharmaceutical company Procter and Gamble. The company noticed wide variations in order patterns along the supply chain in the United States for its nappies. The use of nappies by babies is relatively constant and Procter and Gamble would have expected the chain to reflect the levels of orders being received by them from retailers like Wal-Mart, Carrefour and K-Mart. It appeared that there were greater and greater variations in stock levels and subsequent orders further up the supply chain. (Up the supply chain refers to the earliest stages of the production and distribution process for a product). Such an effect had an impact on the relative capacity requirements of organisations at different stages of the supply chain.

The effect is largely due to difficulties in coordination and communication between different businesses in the supply chain. Such an effect can have important implications for planning of capacity management and may be a factor that influences the decision by a business to either act as a supplier or for a business to take on a supplier.

Reliability

The reliability of a supplier has taken on an even more important role in selecting appropriate suppliers given the move to just-in-time (JIT) stock control methods and lean production. The business has to be confident that the supplier will be able to meet orders, maintain quality, be responsive to changes that may occur and be willing to enter into a long-term partnership for the benefit of all. Many service industries that have IT suppliers insist on service level agreements (SLAs) which specify the amount of downtime that systems experience during specified periods. These can be very rigorous but serve to remind all of the importance of the relationship with the customer. If SLAs are breached then financial penalties may be due by the supplier to the business.

Flexibility

As has already been hinted at, the necessity for a supplier to be able to be flexible to respond to change not only in order levels but also product design, specifications, service levels, productivity levels, and so on, is essential. Building in flexibility can be a big challenge to any supplier, however, if this is a requirement of the business, then ways have to be found to try and meet this need in the same way that any business tries to meet the needs of its customers.

 Further material and resources relating to this section can be found at **www.collins.bized.co.uk**. Keep checking for updates.

Working with suppliers: **Summary**

- Modern businesses have extensive supply chains that link many different organisations and resources to get the product from the producer to the consumer.
- The choice of supplier is an important decision for small and large businesses.
- The main factors influencing the choice of supplier will include:
  - price
  - payment term
  - quality
  - reliability
  - capacity
  - flexibility.
- Suppliers play an important role in helping businesses meet operational targets and improving performance.

Summary questions

1 Why do businesses need to make use of suppliers?

2 What do you understand by the term 'supply chain'?

3 In what type of market is price likely to be an important determinant of supplier?

4 Why is price likely to be important in choosing suppliers for a company such as Nokia when buying processor chips for mobile phones?

5 Why can appropriate payment terms be beneficial to a business?

6 How can electronic payment systems such as Bacs and CHAPs be a benefit to a business?

7 Outline two reasons why a business will expect reliability in its suppliers.

8 Explain why a business needs its suppliers to be flexible.

9 If a business has an operational target of increasing productivity, how can a supplier help it to achieve that target?

10 What role do suppliers play in modern production techniques using lean production and JIT?

Activity

Go to the following website: http://www.bized.co.uk/compfact/kettleby/ketindex.htm

This offers a profile of Kettleby Foods, a supplier of ready meals to the supermarket Tesco.

Using the information in this profile, answer the following questions:

- What sort of suppliers do you think Kettleby Foods need to engage?
- What factors might Kettleby Foods consider in choosing these suppliers?
- What qualities do you think Tesco expect from Kettleby Foods as supplier to the company?
- Identify and explain ONE advantage and ONE disadvantage to Kettleby Foods of supplying the vast majority of its products to just one company.

Exam practice

For many small businesses, getting payment from their customers is difficult. It is highly unlikely that payment is made on delivery. Most B2B activity will rely on the supplier generating an invoice. The invoice might allow the buyer a period of time to settle the invoice – 28 days is often regarded as standard. The skill for many smaller businesses is to manage the time differences between outgoings and the revenue streams that are generated from sales, and this is where difficulties arise.

Many small businesses complain that larger businesses are very slow in paying their debts. The market power lies with the bigger business. If they don't pay on time, what is the small business to do? Threaten legal action? Withdraw their supplies? Of course, they could try these things, but they are likely to be putting themselves into real difficulties if they did. So often they have to suffer; this is a regular cause of cash flow problems. If they do eventually go out of business, the larger firm normally manages to find another supplier willing to fill the gap.

Halfords, the motoring and leisure retailer, informed its suppliers in late 2005 that it was changing its trading terms at the end of January 2006. Halfords increased its payment terms to 120 days from 90 and announced that it would seek a 5% price reduction on all units. For many small businesses, they will have little choice but to accept the terms from this bigger buyer, which will put enormous pressure on their cash flow positions.

The Federation of Private Business (FPB) pointed out that Halfords made profits of £46 million, had revenues of £337.3 million, ran 402 stores and had rising sales and profit figures in recent years. It accused Halfords of using its dominant market position to squeeze its suppliers. The FPB point out that Halfords' success is due in part to the quality of the goods supplied to it and that it has a responsibility to pay its debts promptly.

Source: adapted from Biz/ed 'In the News' http://www.bized.co.uk/cgi-bin/chron/chron.pl?id=2499

1 Identify four types of businesses which are likely to be suppliers to Halfords. (4 marks)

2 Identify and explain TWO possible reasons why Halfords might have extended the payment terms to its suppliers. (6 marks)

3 Describe THREE factors that Halfords may have considered in selecting suppliers to its business. (6 marks)

4 Analyse the possible problems facing some of the suppliers to Halfords of the change in payment terms. (10 marks)

5 How far do you agree with the FPB's view that 'Halfords' success is due in part to the quality of the goods supplied to it and that it has a responsibility to pay its debts promptly'? (14 marks)

Total: 40 marks

Chapter 27   Using technology in operations

Technology plays an increasing role in life in general, and in operations management, this is no different. You will learn about the different types of technology used in operations management and the benefits of using this technology. You will also learn that there are implications to businesses of introducing technology, which they must be aware of.

Types of technology in operations management

Businesses have to combine factors of production in appropriate ways to create production. However, there are a number of different ways that these factors can be combined to generate output. In the early days of manufacturing, many factories used a higher proportion of labour in production. Such a business would be described as labour intensive. As technology has improved, many manufacturing businesses have become more **technology intensive**. In the 21st century, the sophistication of the technology used is providing greater opportunities for businesses to be able to improve **productivity** and to be more creative about the way they produce and communicate with their customers.

The main types of technology that have been used in operations management are described below.

Robotics

The use of robots in business operations is now routine. A robot is a device that is capable of being programmed to perform certain tasks. These tasks may be ones that are tedious and repetitive or which require a high degree of consistency and accuracy. One of the key benefits of robots is that many of them can perform multiple tasks either by reprogramming them or by changing the type of tool that they use to perform a task.

Robots have been extensively used in car manufacturing, for example, where they perform tasks such as welding. They are also used to carry parts around the factory following a predetermined route. Robots can also be designed to have incredible strength and as such are able to carry out tasks that are beyond humans. In the case of car manufacturing, the task of fitting exhaust systems is a heavy one. Workers carrying out these tasks can generally only work around 20 minutes in every hour simply because of the physical strain the task imposes. Robots can be designed to cope with such tasks for much longer and in so doing can help to increase productivity.

Other areas where robots can be employed include cutting, loading, packaging, order picking, assembly work, coating, painting, bonding, drilling, grinding, exploration and investigation (for example, moving through sewer or drainage pipes), trimming, cleaning and handling – particularly if the material being handled is dangerous.

Key terms

Automation A system or method of using a machine or electronic device to carry out a process, thus reducing human intervention to a minimum.

CAD/CAM Computer-aided design and computer-aided manufacture.

Kanban A card used in the production process that accompanies each item through the production process. It triggers the production of more parts to be delivered to the workstation.

Productivity The output of a business measured in relation to the factor inputs used and the time period. Productivity is output per factor input per time period. If a factory employs 100 workers and they produce 5,000 units per month, then labour productivity per month is 50 units per worker.

Stakeholders Any individuals, groups or organisations who have an interest in a business, for example, employees, shareholders, customers and suppliers.

Technology intensive A business that uses a high proportion of technology in the production process in relation to other factor inputs.

In the bottled water industry, the increased use of water coolers in businesses has presented the industry with new challenges. The average water container used for coolers is around 5kg. These containers, when full, can weigh up to 20kg. For those in the industry, filling, stacking and transporting these containers presents its own problems. Robots, however, can be used to stack these containers on racks and then load them for transport. No human could operate at speeds of loading up to 3,000 of these containers per hour, but that is what robots are capable of in this industry.

Robots also do not need to have breaks or go to the toilet; they do not go for cigarette breaks or need to go home to see their families and sleep. This means that robots can carry out tasks quicker and do more per hour than their human counterparts; if output per period of time increases, then productivity increases. When productivity is improved, the average cost per unit is reduced and this can give the firm greater flexibility over pricing policies. It might also give a firm a competitive advantage over their rivals.

Automation

The development of computer technology has allowed businesses to use them to automate processes and procedures. The term **automation** refers to a system or method of using a machine or electronic device to carry out a process, thus reducing human intervention to a minimum.

One of the key areas where automation is used in business is in stock control. 'Just-in-time' and **Kanban** stock control systems rely on automated processes to pull stock when it is needed. A Kanban is a card that accompanies components as they move through production. These cards act as a signalling system to trigger re-ordering of components and supplies and thus improve stock control, and helps keep costs under control. Even in traditional buffer stock control systems, computers can be used to alert operators when orders need to be placed when stocks reach the re-order level.

Automation is also used to regulate workflows, to organise files and data, in generating e-commerce solutions, sending out information to customers and employees, accounting procedures, preparing and disseminating reports on operational processes, payroll operations and customer relationship management (CRM). In this latter case, a business might use a registration system on its website. This records user details – e-mail address, occupation, area of interest, business, and so on. It can then organise the data so that a business can access accurate information about its users and help target appropriate markets with advertising or promotions.

Many businesses make use of automated systems to deal with customer service queries. This might include the ability of customers to call in meter readings for utility bills, get checks on their account details for credit cards, book tickets for events, travel and even for car parking, and get information about a range of services including travel, concert arrangements, and so on.

In the financial markets, automation has been employed for a number of years. On the world's stock exchanges, for example, share trading can be automated. If share prices fall or rise to a certain level the system can trigger an automatic sale of those shares.

Many businesses make use of automated payment systems to make transfers. The Bacs system (the term came from the acronym Bankers Automated Clearing System) processes over 5 billion payments every year with a value in excess of £3 trillion (3 million million or 3×10^{12}). It is owned by 13 of the biggest banks and building societies in Europe. Their services include payments to and from B2C and B2B organisations via direct debit and wage and salary payments.

There is currently a debate related to two aspects of automation. Business Process Automation (BPA) looks at ways in which technology can be used in business systems to control and reduce costs. Such systems focus on ways in which computer software can replace human activity throughout an organisation in order to improve efficiency. Business Process Management (BPM) is a wider activity of which BPA is a part. BPM proponents argue that before a system can be automated, a careful analysis has to be carried out of the business processes and systems running in an organisation. Having carried out such a detailed analysis, processes can then be redesigned to include automation if appropriate. Such a view would tend to suggest that automation is being looked at from a high level strategic perspective. However, critics point out that business changes so rapidly that BPM will almost, by definition, be analysing yesterday's processes. BPA, they argue, delivers greater benefits because it focuses on real time changes to business processes.

Communications

Technology has revolutionised business communications. This communication can be internal – to and between its employees, for example, or external – to its shareholders and customers. In many respects communication is now possible 365 days a year. The main uses of technology in communication are listed below.

TELEPHONE AND FAX

These are hardly new devices but are still very important in many businesses. The use of teleconferencing facilities has also grown. Such facilities allow employees in different locations to 'meet' and discuss issues. This can save on travel costs and can facilitate speedier decision-making.

E-MAIL

E-mail provides the opportunity to speed up communication within a business. It can get messages to employees quickly and efficiently, and has the added bonus of providing a record of such 'conversations'. E-mail can also be an effective means of communicating with external **stakeholders**. Many businesses will have a newsletter service that provides customers with updates on products, services and so on. Marketers have not been slow to see the possibilities presented by e-mail for marketing. Viral marketing techniques, where businesses use the Internet or e-mail to spread messages about a product or service quickly and cheaply, have become more popular. In 2006, for example, a South African wine company called Stormhoek included a 40% off voucher at certain off-licences intended for the use of suppliers and employees of the business through its website. However, the news spread very quickly and over 800,000 downloads of the vouchers were made in the first month! In this case the spread of the message may have caused the company problems, but it highlights how effective e-mail can be in spreading a message.

VIDEO CONFERENCING

Improvements in video conferencing technology have enabled businesses to set up meetings with suppliers, other plants, partners and other stakeholders, reducing the need to travel extensively. The technology does have a cost but it is invariably much cheaper than flying individuals across the globe and paying for their expenses and accommodation!

MOBILE PHONES AND TEXT MESSAGING

A number of businesses will provide employees with mobile phones for business use. The development of the BlackBerry® has also enabled workers to receive and send e-mails on the move. It is now possible to contact employees wherever they are, at any time of the day. The use of mobile phones is also helpful in improving customer service – staff can contact customers, for example, to advise them of a time of arrival if an appointment has been made to visit the customer.

LOYALTY CARDS

The use of loyalty cards such as Tesco's *Clubcard*, the *Nectar* card, the Holiday Inn *Priority Club* and many more, are ways in which a business can improve the communications between itself and its customers. When customers use these cards, the data are fed to computers which enable the business to analyse behaviour and sales patterns. This can then be used to target particular products or promotions at customers more effectively. The customer gets to see/hear information about products that they are interested in and the business saves money by not wasting advertising.

THE INTERNET

Many businesses can see the value of having a website. A website enables a business to be in touch with its customers all around the world at any time of day or night. It can be used to communicate with its customers as well as providing customers with access to information.

Design technology

The improvements in computer graphics and the sophistication with which computers can now handle data means that businesses involved in design can make extensive use of such technology in production.

This can range from fashion design, the design of books and magazines, computer-generated images for movies and adverts, using design packages in building, landscaping, horticulture and architecture, aircraft design, and so on. In addition to the facility to be able to view designs from different angles, in 3D etc., such design packages make testing of tolerances and stresses, forces and other key constraints much easier.

Many businesses now make use of **CAD/CAM** systems and software. This involves the use of computers in the design process and also in manufacturing. Designs for a range of products can be done using a computer. This has the advantage of enabling the designer to experiment with designs to improve the specification of products. Different tolerances, materials, aerodynamics, processes, and so on, can all be investigated.

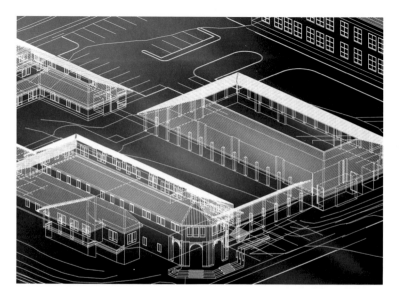

Architects, for example, can design and test buildings against extremes of weather, natural disasters like floods, drought, earthquakes and hurricanes and even resistance to attack by terrorists. Engineers working on the design of a new wing for an aircraft can not only design the wing with great accuracy, but also load in a variety of different parameters to test the rigidity and performance of the wing in different conditions. This can help in narrowing down potential problems when the prototype is eventually built, and again help to keep costs under control.

The system provides the designer with a range of feedback in relation to design specifications which can help them to meet consumer needs and legal and regulatory requirements better. Once the design process is complete, CAM systems can be used to control the machines and the overall manufacturing process.

Issues in introducing and updating technology

In the discussion above we have seen that there are a number of benefits to the use of technology in business. These benefits can be substantial but they have to be tempered with an appreciation of the limitations of the technology as well as the potential costs.

The benefits

The benefits of technology are summarised below.

REDUCING COSTS

Technology can help to control and reduce costs. Technology can have a monitoring function as well as a more practical production function. If technology can get a task or process done quicker than human or other factor input, then costs can be reduced. To balance this out one has to consider the cost of introducing and updating the technology. Some technology projects in the public sector have been hailed as a means of improving service and speeding up processes, but in practice have suffered varying degrees of problems in their implementation. The public sector accounts for over 50% of the total spending on IT in the UK. Projects ranging from the National Health Service (NHS) to the 2012 Olympics, the criminal justice system, homeland security and the police, are all in the process of being developed. The cost, however, comes in at around £14 billion a year! If the benefits are not valued in excess of £14 billion, questions have to be asked as to whether the systems are really worth it.

In addition to the expense of introducing systems, consideration has to be taken of the costs of maintaining it, updating the system and training people to work with and use the system. For businesses this represents an on-going cost which has to be factored into decision-making.

IMPROVING QUALITY

The use of technology in a business can help to improve all manner of quality aspects. Computers can check productivity levels, provide reports on resource use, problems and costs; software can be used that utilises the principles of statistical process control (SPC). SPC is a statistical device to monitor the variations in product quality and process in relation to its targets. Technology can also be used to replace humans and can be far more efficient in production thus increasing productivity as well as quality – machines can be programmed to not make mistakes! Robots can be more accurate and reliable in the production process. As a result, the increased sophistication in technology enables a business to improve quality in its widest sense throughout the business's operations.

REDUCING WASTE

Using technology can help a business to reduce waste. Components, ingredients, design processes, and so on, can all benefit from the use of technology in calculating efficient input–output ratios and as such help keep waste to a minimum. The use of JIT stock control models is a further benefit in reducing waste. Waste reduction further saves costs, can be useful in providing a business with 'green' credentials and improves quality.

INCREASING PRODUCTIVITY

We have already seen how technology can improve the speed and efficiency with which tasks and processes can be carried out. If the use of technology increases output in a shorter period of time or even in the same time that human input could have operated, then productivity will increase.

Other considerations

LIMITATIONS OF ROBOTS

We have seen that robots can provide many benefits to a business, but they do have limitations that must be considered. The design of the operations process is critical. Designing too complex a process and putting too many demands on robots can cause malfunctions and delays in the production cycle. The work of each robot in the process has to be coordinated so that they operate at similar speeds and capacities. There are important factors to consider in relation to the design of the process – health and safety considerations, workers have to be trained in the use and implications of using robots, etc. This involves not only training in the use of the robot, but also in the software that is used to program them.

Some tasks are appropriate for robots to undertake but others, even though they might involve the same task, are not. For example, many robots can accurately and efficiently carry out welding tasks: they can accurately carry out the same task over and over with a high degree of efficiency. If the welding task is what is called a 'repeat' task then each subsequent job might require a weld but not necessarily the same type of weld. The robot might be programmed to move in the same direction and hit the weld at the same spot, but programming it to recognise when a different weld is required at a different place and to use its judgement as to when such moves might be appropriate might present considerable programming challenges.

Many robotic applications are now becoming more affordable. However, businesses do need to consider carefully the return on their investment. They have to consider the cost of installing the machines, the cost of reorganising the production process, the costs in terms of worker motivation and morale (especially if workers' roles are being replaced), and the estimated benefits that can be gained over the lifetime of the machine.

THE EFFECTS OF AUTOMATION

Automation can bring a number of benefits to a business but, in a similar way that robotics has limitations, a business needs to consider the effects of automation. As with robotics, the introduction of automation brings with it changes to work flows, possible redundancies and the need for training. Training staff comes at a cost not only in financial terms in putting on training sessions, but also in lost output whilst training is being given. Automation may create a greater sense of alienation amongst workers, and for customers the use of automated systems in dealing with queries can bring frustration and anger. Some businesses are now reviewing some of the automated customer service processes they have following complaints that customers prefer to talk to a human being. NatWest, for example, make a big play in their advertising that customers can talk to real human beings and see this as a source of competitive advantage over their rivals.

When automated systems are introduced, businesses need to consider how they impact on their stakeholders – employees and suppliers. Employees can find change difficult to deal with and may feel that the technology is too challenging or demanding, even if they from offered training in its use. There might be benefits from automation, but this has to be balanced with the impact on the working environment of a business and the productivity of those working in the business.

COMMUNICATIONS PROBLEMS

Communications might have improved with the use of e-mail and the Internet and other means considered above, but it has also brought with it other problems and issues. There are complaints from some workers that e-mail and BlackBerry® facilities, for example, mean that a business almost expects its employees to be available at any time regardless of other commitments. It can increase the pressure on workers to feel that they have to be available and respond to communication, and can increase the stress that accompanies work.

The use of e-mail and technology in the workplace can be highly beneficial, but can also serve as a distraction. Staff can spend time surfing the Internet, exchanging non-work e-mails and also send out e-mails that might leak important information. The number of workers being sacked for abusing a company's e-mail policies is growing. In addition, there are increasing concerns over the time that employees spend surfing the Web and sending personal e-mails. One estimate is that at least one working day a week is lost to staff focusing on personal e-mailing and Web surfing. The growing popularity of social networking sites such as My Space, Facebook and Bebo are further complicating matters.

LEGAL AND SECURITY CONSIDERATIONS

There are also major considerations for businesses in the extent to which they have to put systems in place to protect workers from harassment and discrimination from e-mails. If a worker receives an abusive or insulting e-mail being circulated as a 'joke', what liabilities does the business have under law to protect its workers from receiving such messages?

In addition to this, there are numerous legal considerations that a business has to consider in setting up technology and in building and operating a website. Many of these obligations come under the Disability Discrimination Act (1995) and the Special Educational Needs and Disability Act (2001). Websites have to conform to these accessibility and disability requirements, and Web designers have to have the skills and knowledge to make sure that business websites conform to these requirements. If businesses ignore the law they put themselves at risk of being sued. Making sure they comply, however, can add to costs.

Gathering information about customers through communications techniques might benefit the marketing function but it also carries with it responsibilities. Systems have to be put in place to protect the details of people on such databases. How a business is able to use the data it has on living people is governed by the Data Protection Act (1998). Again, if breaches of the Act are made, a business can be sued. Breaches of such Acts also carry with it other side effects.

In April 2007, US retailer TJX, which owns TJ Maxx, revealed that hackers had broken into its databases over a period of months and gained information to over 45 million payments cards used by its customers dating back to 2002. Such breaches of security can badly damage the reputation of a business and cause it to lose customers. Once this happens, not only does the business have the cost of improving its security systems, but also in winning back the confidence and trust of its customers.

Further material and resources relating to this section can be found at **www.collins.bized.co.uk**. Keep checking for updates.

Using technology in operations: **Summary**

- Technology plays an increasing role in all aspects of a business's operations.
- There are four main types of technology used in business:
  - robotics
  - automation technology
  - communications technology
  - design technology.
- The use of technology can help to reduce costs, improve efficiency and productivity, improve quality and reduce waste.
- Consideration has to be given to the costs of introducing, maintaining and updating technology in relation to the benefits that technology brings.
- Technology has its downsides and firms need to be aware of these in developing their systems.

Summary questions

1 What would be meant by the term 'technology intensive business'?

2 Give a definition of the term 'robotics'.

3 Describe four different uses of a robot in business.

4 Outline two advantages and two disadvantages of the use of robots in manufacturing.

5 How can automation lead to improvements in customer service?

6 Explain the difference between BPA and BPM.

7 Outline three different types of communications technology commonly used in businesses.

8 Examine the costs and benefits of communications technologies in business organisations.

9 Describe the benefits of design technologies to relevant businesses.

10 To what extent is technology always a 'good' thing to introduce in a business?

Activity

- Take a trip around your local supermarket. Note down as many examples of technology that you can observe being used in the store.
  NB It is good practice to talk to a member of the staff before you begin taking notes in a store, to alert them and seek their permission to do your research. Most store managers are very supportive of this sort of research.
- What other types of technology do you think that the store might use that are not so obvious to consumers, but which help to improve the performance of the business?
- Create a short presentation outlining your findings and present this to your class. Consider the costs and benefits of the different technologies in your presentation.

Exam practice

In the United States, potato chip manufacturer (in the UK read 'crisp manufacturer') Frito-Lay, who are owned by PepsiCo, are planning a major investment in further technology at its plant in Casa Grande in Arizona. The project is called *nat zero*. The aim is to enable the factory to move away from taking power from the national grid and instead generating its power needs through natural means and through utilising its waste products.

The plant currently uses enough fuel in its production process to heat 13,000 homes during the winter. Its use of energy comes from the way the chips are made. 500,000 pounds of potatoes are delivered each day; they are washed (using precious water resources), sliced, fried and packaged to the tune of 212 million bags of snacks every year.

Its plan is to find ways of recovering the water it uses in the production process through a filtration system. The waste that is left from this filtration process will then be used to generate power through an anaerobic digester which will generate methane gas and which will power the boilers on the plant. In addition to this, vacuum hoses have been installed which recover moisture from potatoes and which then adds to the water recovery as well as reducing the heat needed to fry the chips. It also plans to build 50 acres of solar energy devices called solar concentrators. Arizona does have plenty of hot sun to exploit. The devices are parabolic mirrors that magnify the suns rays and focus the energy on water filled tubes. The water is heated and is used to power a steam generator.

The project is due to be completed by 2010 and is expected to cut Frito-Lay's greenhouse gas emissions by up to three quarters.

Source: Adapted from Biz/ed 'In the News' http://www.bized.co.uk/cgi-bin/chron/chron.pl?id=2969

1 Consider the role of robots and automation in the production of a product like potato chips (crisps). (6 marks)

2 How might Frito-Lay benefit from the introduction of automation into its business? (6 marks)

3 Discuss THREE possible costs to Frito-Lay of the increased use of technology in its business. (12 marks)

4 How might Frito-Lay define 'success' in its plans to invest in the *nat zero* project? (6 marks)

5 Assess the factors that a firm like Frito-Lay needs to consider when making a decision on a major investment as described in the article. (10 marks)

Total: 40 marks

UNIT 2
SECTION D

Managing a Business:
Marketing and the competitive environment

Section overview

UNIT 2
SECTION D

Managing a Business:
Marketing and the competitive environment

This section will help you to understand the importance of marketing in a business. Marketing is all about getting to know your customers, understanding their needs and trying to meet those needs, whilst at the same time making a profit.

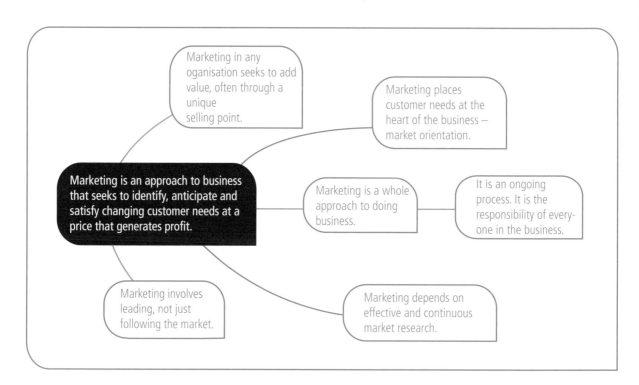

Marketing in any oganisation seeks to add value, often through a unique selling point.

Marketing places customer needs at the heart of the business – market orientation.

Marketing is an approach to business that seeks to identify, anticipate and satisfy changing customer needs at a price that generates profit.

Marketing is a whole approach to doing business.

It is an ongoing process. It is the responsibility of every-one in the business.

Marketing involves leading, not just following the market.

Marketing depends on effective and continuous market research.

Key concept

Marketing

A market is any place that brings together buyers and sellers with a view to agreeing a price. The buyer represents the demand for a product, and the supplier and the seller provide the supply. If any of these factors are missing, we do not have a market.

The term 'marketing' has lots of interpretations. We need to be clear at the outset that we understand these different interpretations, and that we can distinguish between them. We need to make one thing very clear at the outset: marketing is not just about advertising. We have to remember that the seller is aiming to try and sell a good or a service, but without a willing and able buyer, the business has no future.

Take the following examples where the term 'market' is used:

- 'Let's put it to the market.'
- 'We need to market this aggressively.'
- 'We need to carry out market research.'
- 'The market rose today.'
- 'We need to focus our attention on the market.'
- 'Market orientation rather than product orientation is the way forward.'
- 'Market forces will drive this product.'
- 'We need to adjust the elements of the marketing mix.'
- 'We need to test out the market.'
- 'The marketing department have identified factors that mean we need to change the way we operate.'

Each of these statements means something different, but all have one thing in common: the term 'market' requires an understanding that both the buyer and seller are involved. If you remember back to our original definition, then it starts to makes sense.

Activity

Look at each of the bullet points above and try to write a sentence that explains what each one means, bearing in mind what we have said about the definition of a market. We have done one for you below.

- 'We have to follow the lead given by the market.'

The business has to take notice of what its customers are saying when developing and offering its products/services for sale.

HMV (the 'seller') provides supply to meet the demand for CDs and DVDs (the 'product')

Chapter 28   Effective marketing

This chapter will help you to understand what we mean by marketing, and how businesses market their products and services. You will learn that marketing can take different forms: business to business (B2B) and business to consumer (B2C), and that effective marketing depends upon understanding customer needs – not only now but also in the future.

What is marketing?

To understand what effective marketing is we need to be clear about what the term 'marketing' means. Below you will find a series of definitions given about marketing.

> 'The management process that identifies, anticipates and satisfies customer requirement profitably.'
> (The Chartered Institute of Marketing)
>
> 'The whole business seen from the customer's point of view.'
> (Drucker)
>
> 'The right product, in the right place, at the right time, at the right price.'
> (Adcock et al.)
>
> 'Essentially about marshalling the resources of an organisation so that they meet the changing needs of the customer on whom the organisation depends.'
> (Palmer)

Notice that in each of the definitions above, the term 'advertising' does not feature at all. What is common to all these definitions is a reference to the consumer in some form or another. The definition from the Chartered Institute of Marketing (CIM) is one that captures the two elements of the market – the consumer and the supplier – the best.

The marketing process

Marketing needs to be seen as more than just a one-off action, such as an advertising campaign. It has to be seen as an ongoing process of researching, planning, implementing and reviewing strategies to meet customers' needs.

A process is a designed sequence or series of changes in a system – in this case, the system is that which gets a product or a service from the initial stages of its life through to the final consumer. However, that system does not stop there. The consumer has an important part to play in providing feedback to the organisation. That feedback might be verbal, requested or accessed in other formal ways or could be through

Key terms

Competitive advantage The ways in which a firm appeals to its consumers through adding value, making the firm unique in some way. This uniqueness can both be defended and is distinctive, and means that it is difficult for its rivals to be able to imitate or replicate these features.

Cost leadership Achieving competitive advantage through a lower cost base, allowing a firm to compete successfully on price (potentially offering the lowest prices in a market).

Differentiated Products are different from those offered by competitors; this may mean adding or altering features for the product to appeal to specific segments.

Market share The percentage of the total sales in a market achieved by any one firm.

Mass market A large market containing many customers buying similar products.

Niche market A small and clearly identifiable segment of a market; for example, the market for expensive home audio equipment.

consumers simply 'voting with their feet' – not buying the product or service!

Once that feedback is gained, then the business uses it to look again at what it is producing and amend its offering to make sure that it at least maintains and hopefully improves its business position. This constant striving to maintain the business's position involves all aspects of the business – not just the marketing department. We also have to remember that many small businesses do not have the facilities or the capacity to have a dedicated marketing department. This does not mean that 'marketing' is any less important; in fact, it could be that the marketing of a small business is even more important.

Marketing is about the focus of the whole business and, therefore, the responsibility of everyone in it. Drucker's definition of marketing emphasises the importance of the role of the customer – whoever that customer might be. It is not just you and me who are customers – other businesses, the government, international agencies and suppliers might all be possible customers of a business. If the business does not take note of what its customers want, then it is unlikely to have much of a future.

B2B and B2C marketing

If one business is selling goods or services to another business, then the marketing might be different from that which might be carried out when selling a good or service to a customer.

For example, when you go to a store and buy a CD or DVD, you are the customer. A store like HMV or Zavvi will be keen to know about the needs of someone like you. They might want to know your age, gender, interests and hobbies, how many times you buy a DVD or a CD in a month, what type of DVDs or CDs you buy, how much you spend at any one time, whether you buy CDs and DVDs from other stores or online, whether you download music more than buy it on disc, and so on. Armed with this type of information, the business can then spend time planning its products and the experience the customer has in the store to best meet the needs of their customers. This is called B2C marketing.

When you buy the DVD or CD you might not think too much about how it got to the store. Representatives of the different music companies – Universal, SonyBMG, EMI and so on – will be looking to get HMV to make sure that its products and artists are placed effectively to maximise the possible sales potential. They will talk to HMV about how their business is operating, what changes they are experiencing in the way the market operates, new artists they are trying to promote, how they can provide a better service to the store, and so on. This type of marketing is called B2B marketing.

A number of companies have taken marketing to new levels. Customers often do not need just a core product; they also need other things with which they can identify themselves and the product or service. In so doing, the business is able to exploit new markets, create **competitive advantage** and add value.

For example...

Disney

Disney came to realise that their business was more than just making and promoting films. It was about a whole concept of childhood imagination that provided opportunities in other markets. The development of merchandise and theme parks has become a total approach to meeting customer needs and fulfilling their mission, 'to make people happy'.

Caterpillar

Caterpillar has done something similar. The company are primarily known for producing heavy duty industrial and construction equipment. They have taken that theme and transferred it to a range of products that reflects their core business, but which taps into completely different markets. These products include caps, T-shirts, watches, belts, luggage, footwear, ties, sunglasses, gloves, jackets, mugs, flasks, umbrellas and more!

Nike

Nike began by selling training shoes. The company has now branched out into the production of a whole range of sporting and leisure wear that encompasses virtually every sport. Whether you are a football fan, a basketball nut, a rugby fanatic or a baseball bozo, Nike will be familiar to you.

However, the risk involved in the marketing process should not be taken lightly. There are plenty of examples of where businesses have tried to use their success in one market to branch out into another with disastrous results. Motorcycle firm Harley Davidson attempted to launch a range of perfumes without success; food manufacturer Heinz attempted to move into the household cleaning market with a natural cleaning vinegar with similar results; the BIC company, famous for producing ballpoint pens, attempted to move into the market for men and women's underwear – it too failed.

The purpose of marketing

The main purpose of marketing is to add value. What this means is that the consumer places a value on the good or service that is higher than the material costs. By focusing on customer needs, a business can make adjustments to the marketing mix in order to meet those needs more effectively. This, in turn, can also provide the business with competitive advantage.

Effective marketing: identifying customer needs

Above all else, marketing is about being customer driven. This is known as market orientation. A market-orientated business begins by asking what consumers want when they buy a product, and then seeks to develop products to meet these needs. Decisions about product design, pricing, promotion and distribution will be based on market analysis to ensure that what the business offers is what the consumer wants. Coca-Cola's development of new flavours, such as Cherry Coke or Lemon Diet Coke, is a response to the changing wants of different groups of consumers. These products would not have been developed without finding out from consumers whether it would be something that they would actually want.

Guru's views

'While great devices are invented in the laboratory, great products are invented in the marketing department.'

–William Davidor, Author

Effective marketing: anticipating customer needs

Changes in the market and the needs of customers can be anticipated, allowing the business to be the first to react and in so doing, gain some form of competitive advantage. Anticipating customer needs might come about through careful market research, but might also arise as a result of thinking within the business about current market trends, the state of technology and thinking about what consumers might want next year, the year after, in five year's time, ten year's time, and so on. It is this sort of 'futures thinking' that is part of the work of those in research and development (R&D) teams in businesses.

For small businesses, identifying, anticipating and meeting customer needs efficiently are equally important but are often a real challenge. Many small businesses will not have the benefit of being a household name like Coca-Cola or Nike, or of having large R&D teams, or access to large amounts of funds. If firms such as Nike or Coca-Cola produce a product that does not fully meet market needs and flops, they may be large enough to be able to withstand the financial shock. A small business invariably has no such comfort zone.

The vast majority of new small business enterprises may have some very good ideas. Many do fail, however, despite having a basically sound business model. One of the main reasons is likely to be a lack of care in researching the market. It is imperative for a small business to identify who their likely market is going to be and how big that market is.

Activity

- Sophie has become a skilled plumber and is very good at her job. On the basis of the information in the example box below, would you advise Sophie to set up on her own?
- What else might Sophie offer to meet the needs of her potential customers more effectively if she did decide to set up on her own?

For example...

The following is an example of how this might work.

Sophie is an eighteen-year-old school leaver. She read an article about the short-age of skilled plumbers in the country. She decided to leave school and train to be a plumber. After several years working for a plumbing firm and learning her trade, she decided to set up on her own. The cost of setting up and running the business was £350,000 a year. That means that to break even, Sophie needed to generate £350,000 in sales. Each job generates an average of £500 in revenue. This means that Sophie has to do 700 jobs a year – and that is just to break even. Sophie needed to find out whether there were 700 potential customers in the area where she lived. Sophie used UpMyStreet to find a profile of her area.

Sophie found out that there are 14,000 households in her area. These are all potential customers, but she knew that only a fraction of these will need plumbing services at any one time. Sophie has found out that she needs to get 5% of those households in her area each year using her services. She found out that the average number of plumbing incidents in an average home each year was 0.5; this narrowed down her potential market to 7,000. This meant that she would have to capture 10% of this market if she was to generate enough sales to break even.

Her local Yellow Pages show that there are over 50 plumbers advertising their services. If every household in her area called out a plumber just once a year and each plumber had an equal share of the business, then that would mean only 280 jobs a year.

This short scenario assumes lots of things, but remember that Sophie was only looking at figures to break even and not to make a profit. It could be that this initial research might tell Sophie that it was not going to be easy to survive. She might have to fight hard to win customers and it may be that she needs to find out what customers are looking for in a plumber and ensure that she meets those needs if she is to gain any competitive advantage.

Examples of niche marketing

Caterham sports car - premium-priced and small sales volumes

Golf clubs – golfing is a small, clearly identifiable segment of the sports market

Chanel fashion label - highly-differentiated products

The above example highlights a number of important points about marketing. To be successful, a business has to have customers who will buy their products or services in sufficient quantity to generate a profit. This means that the business has to consider the cost of production in relation to the price that customers are willing to pay for the product or service, and the number of people who would be able and willing to buy at that price. If the business gets to a stage where it is generating profit from its sales, it is important that it then analyses its market at all times to identify and anticipate possible changes in customer needs and what its competitors are doing in the marketplace. This means that marketing is an ongoing process.

Mass and niche markets

The approach to marketing can be dependent on the type of business. Some businesses sell very similar products to millions of customers throughout the world. Other companies might be involved in selling very specific and highly **differentiated** products or services to only a small number of customers. Philips, for example, produces microchips for mobile phones as part of their business. They might only have a handful of customers such as Nokia or Sony Ericsson, and produce a very specialised product that only caters for a small but clearly identifiable part of a market, but that does not mean they only sell a few. Philips actually sells millions of microchips to firms like Nokia for mobile phones. The key point is they are individually designed to suit the needs of Nokia – a B2B market and a tiny part of the overall market for microchips.

We need, therefore, to understand the difference between mass and niche marketing and to have some understanding of how a business will identify different parts of markets.

A **mass market** is a large market containing many customers buying similar products.

A **niche market** is a small and clearly identifiable segment of a market; for example, the market for expensive home audio equipment is a small part of the overall market for home entertainment equipment.

Niche marketing

Niche marketing (also known as focused marketing) involves selling goods to small, clearly identifiable segments of a market. Niche markets are usually characterised by some or all of the following:

- premium-priced products – good potential for profitability
- often, but not necessarily, small sales volumes
- highly-differentiated products, for example, weapons for the defence industry
- where people who work in the industry have specific skills and expertise referred to as a high-skills base – it is difficult for large competitors to easily replicate or hire these skills.

Examples of niche markets include the market for specialist sports cars, such as the Caterham Lotus Super 7, or the market for tailor-made clothing.

Choosing to pursue a niche marketing strategy has a significant effect on the type of marketing activities undertaken. Promotion will be very specific, the product needs to be clearly differentiated and the outlets it is sold in must reflect its image.

ADVANTAGES OF NICHE MARKETING

- Niche marketing can mean a firm can charge premium prices and reap generous profits as a result.
- Niche markets may allow small firms to be able to compete effectively even if the dominant market is large – for example, specialist furniture makers.

DISADVANTAGES OF NICHE MARKETING

- When the market is small, high fixed costs are not spread across large output volumes. This means that prices tend to be high which might put off potential customers.
- If costs of production are relatively high, niche markets may not be able to sustain a firm in business as the market may be too small.

Mass marketing

In contrast to niche marketing, mass marketing aims for high sales volume at the expense of low prices. Mass markets are characterised by:

- low margins on sales
- undifferentiated products
- a wide range of sales outlets and wide availability
- extensive promotion
- high sales volume.

Mass market products include items such as sugar, salt, fruit and vegetables. If a business sells a truly undifferentiated product, then it may pursue a strategy of **cost leadership**. This is where the business seeks to have the lowest costs in the market which then allows them to be competitive on price (supermarkets such as CostCo and Aldi are examples). The problem with this strategy is that if price wars do break out (where firms keep cutting prices to try and capture **market share**) some firms in the market may well not survive because they cannot force costs down any further. Prices may be forced so low that it is difficult to make a profit. (American farmers growing potatoes to sell to fast-food chains face this problem.)

ADVANTAGES OF MASS MARKETING

- Mass marketing can lead to economies of scale being gained. This lowers average costs and can mean cheaper prices for consumers or higher profit margins for businesses.
- Mass marketing accompanied by differentiation or appropriate branding can mean high profits.

DISADVANTAGES OF MASS MARKETING

- Mass marketing can mean a lack of variation in a market – standardised products may be boring and lack individuality.
- The opportunities for firms to enter mass markets mean that competition can drive down margins to almost zero.

Examples of mass marketing

Milk – undifferentiated products and wide availability

Baked beans – high sales volume

Ikea - extensive promotion and high sales volume

Effective marketing: **Summary**

- Effective marketing has to be recognised as an ongoing process.
- Effective marketing involves identifying consumer needs, anticipating future consumer needs, identifying changing consumer needs and finding ways to satisfy those needs at a price which will allow the firm to generate a profit.
- Effective marketing is something that involves everyone in a business.
- Mass markets refer to markets where large numbers of people buy very similar products.
- Niche markets refer to clearly identifiable, small parts of a market.

Summary questions

1 Of the definitions of marketing on page 292, which would you consider to be the best definition and why?

2 Using examples, distinguish between B2B and B2C marketing.

3 What is one of the main purposes of marketing?

4 What is meant by the phrase 'marketing is a process'?

5 What is the difference between identifying customer needs and anticipating customer needs?

6 Using examples, explain the difference between mass and niche markets.

7 Identify two advantages and two disadvantages of mass marketing.

8 Identify two advantages and two disadvantages of niche marketing.

9 'Figure out what is desirable and make that what you deliver; or figure out what you can deliver and make that desirable. But remember, the former is a lot easier than the latter' (Sergio Zyman, Coca-Cola's former Chief Marketing Officer). Explain the relevance of marketing to this quote.

10 Explain the meaning of the term 'cost leadership'.

Points for discussion

All over the place

Most, if not all of you, have heard of FCUK. Most major high streets now have a branch of French Connection, and the company's adverts can be seen on billboards across the country. This was not true just a few years ago. French Connection was a small retailer, with an exclusive image, very few outlets and premium prices – a classic example of niche marketing. The launch of the FCUK slogan was part of the company's aggressive strategy to move into the mass market – a strategy that has clearly worked.

Exam practice

Read the article below and then answer the questions which follow.

High street music retailer HMV announced that it was revising its business strategy after its profits were halved in 2006. HMV has seen sales of physical products like CDs falling and knows it has to do something to better meet customer needs and take on the growing competition that it faces. One of the problems facing HMV is that it has a number of stores across the country and these stores represent significant overheads. The company has to find some way of getting more people into these stores and spend money in them in order to help cover the cost of these overheads.

It has announced some outline plans for its new strategy which include selling digital downloads in its stores, placing a greater emphasis on its online business and making other related products available in its stores. Such products will include MP3 players, digital radios and mobile phones. It has signed an agreement with mobile phone service provider '3' to operate a concession in some of its high-street stores.

All these measures are designed to try and expand the range of products it sells, reduce its reliance on the sale of CDs and revive its business. How far this will help to reverse the decline in sales of the business is open to question. Are HMV reacting too slowly to the changing marketplace? Will these measures help to bring back customers to the stores? Would you rather go to an HMV store to buy music downloads or would you rather do this in the comfort of your home?

Source: adapted from Biz/ed 'In the News' article: http://www.bized.co.uk/cgi-bin/chron/chron.pl?id=2929

1 Using an example drawn from the evidence, explain the meaning of the term 'overheads'. (4 marks)

2 Analyse the role of marketing to a firm like HMV. (9 marks)

3 Discuss the factors that HMV might have considered in its marketing plans to try and meet its new strategy. (12 marks)

4 Discuss how identifying and anticipating customer needs could help HMV to improve its performance. (15 marks)

Total: 40 marks

Chapter 29   Designing an effective marketing mix

In this chapter you will learn about the **marketing mix** and how the combination of price, product, promotion and place is important in the success of marketing. You will learn that there are a number of factors that influence the degree of importance of each of these factors in the mix. Finally, you will understand how the success of marketing depends not only on integrating the four elements of the mix, but getting all functions of the business involved.

What is the marketing mix?

The marketing mix is commonly associated with the 4Ps – price, product, promotion and place. The 'mix' in the term refers to the way in which these four important aspects of marketing are brought together to anticipate, identify and satisfy consumer needs effectively. In some cases, the product might be a very significant factor in the mix, in other cases it might be price; in others, promotion might be vital whereas in still others, place might be the dominant factor. In reality, all are important but some might just be more important than others in some cases.

Price: the amount of money that a consumer has to part with to acquire a good or service.

Product: the good or service made available to the public by a business.

Promotion: the various means by which a business seeks to make the public aware of the product it has for sale.

Place: the means by which a business gets its product to the consumer.

You can think of the marketing mix a little bit like a cake. The final cake is a product of all the ingredients that go into it. For some types of cake, there might be a little more butter used; in others, eggs might be essential whereas in others the flour might be the vital ingredient. When they are all mixed together you end up with the cake, but exactly what type of cake might vary depending on the relative weight of the ingredients in the mixture. That is what the marketing mix is like.

Marketing objectives

The extent to which these factors will influence the mix will be dependent to a large extent on the marketing objectives that the firm has identified. These objectives will help a business to be able to get to a particular position that it has identified – its strategic aim. This strategic aim might be expressed in very simple terms. For example, Canon, the manufacturers of image reproduction technologies like cameras and photocopiers amongst many other things, had a simple slogan 'Kill Kodak'. Kodak was one of its main rivals in the market and

Key terms

Market challenger Often the focus of marketing strategy is on the challenge element, attempting to appeal to the desire to favour the underdog.

Market follower A business with a small market share that closely follows (and copies) the strategies of the market leaders.

Market leader The business with the greatest share of a market.

The marketing mix The combination of price, product, promotion and place that a firm can adapt to meet the needs of its customers more effectively.

its marketing objectives might have included some or all of the following to enable it to achieve this long term goal:

- to increase market share
- to increase product awareness or brand recognition
- to increase product usage
- to expand into new market segments
- to develop new products.

In truth, many businesses will have some or all of these objectives in mind in their marketing strategies; in some cases one of the objectives might be more important than others at different times in the marketing process. In some cases, large firms with a number of different products or services might have different objectives for each different product. Small firms will share these objectives but the scale of the measurement of 'success' in them might be different.

Factors influencing the marketing mix

The main factors affecting the marketing mix are:

- **The marketing objectives of the business**. If a business has the objective of increasing market share it might influence the price it decides to charge, if it has the objective of increasing the product usage then it might need to focus on changing the product itself and so on.
- **The access to finance**. Access to finance may be a constraint on the extent to which funds can be invested into developing the product or investing in distribution facilities. A business might want to hire the use of an advertising agency to run a promotional campaign for them but may have limited funds to do so.
- **Changes in technology**. Technology can advance rapidly but a business might not be in a position to utilise that technology because it does not have the finance to invest in it or the skills to implement it. Businesses like Tesco, for example, are able to invest heavily in technology that streamlines their distribution function. Smaller businesses may not be in a position to be able to do this and so have to modify their marketing mix accordingly.
- **The feedback from market research**. Market research can provide valuable information on pricing, the product itself, how people access the product or service and how they respond to promotion campaigns. This can inform future decision making on the elements of the mix.
- **Social factors**. Changing social habits and factors might necessitate the firm re-thinking aspects of the marketing mix. The concern over the environment, for example, might mean that a business has to adjust its product and distribution systems to reduce its carbon footprint. Promotional campaigns may have to include a greater emphasis on what the business is doing to reduce the impact its operations have on the environment.

Exactly what level of importance each element in the mix plays will be dependent on a variety of factors.

- When a new product or service is being developed, the business will have to think carefully about how each element will fit with their knowledge of the market and customer needs. Some markets have customers that are very sensitive to prices – if the price charged is too high, they will not buy it or will look to buy competitors' products.
- In other markets, the quality of the product might be more important to consumers than the price. For example, with hi-tech equipment like computers, mobile phones, hi-fi equipment and TVs, quality and reliability might be the things that consumers have uppermost in their mind. If they have to pay an extra £50 to get this, then they may be prepared to do so.

The mobile phone industry is characterised by heavy emphasis on promotion. Stores selling phones and service provider packages know that many of the actual handsets available are pretty much the same in most respects. What they can offer that is different is the wide range of promotional offers covering different packages – contract, pay as you go, offers of extra minutes, text messages, and so on.

Exactly what influences the mix will be a combination of the expertise of those involved in the business, the feedback they get from market research, intuition, risk and experience. Let us look at two examples of businesses to see how the different elements of the mix can change over time.

For example...

The iPod

The iPod has been an extremely successful product for Apple. It had all the ingredients of the marketing mix, but exactly what it was that contributed to its success may be difficult to pinpoint – set the price too high and it might not have sold as well; get the product wrong in some way and it might not have captured the public imagination; equally get the promotion wrong and customers might be turned off the product – however good it might be.

Apple CEO Steve Jobs introduces the Apple iPod Touch

It is sometimes difficult, therefore, to really attribute the success of any product to one particular element. This is why the integration of the mix is so important. When the iPod came out they were not exactly cheap but they still sold. Was it the product itself therefore that made the difference? In part the iPod was not that much different to other personal music players on the market. It had, initially, limited capacity and there were complaints about the battery life. What seemed to really catch the eye was the design – it could not really have been produced by any other firm than Apple; it had that iconic design which Apple has become known for.

The design may well have been the thing that Apple focused on when it was being promoted – they are hardly likely to have promoted it by telling people that the battery life was limited! Then there was place – the way in which the product is distributed and how it makes its way to the final consumer. In some respects, it was not easy to get hold of an iPod in the early stages of the product life cycle; retail outlets seemed to run out of stock quickly and there soon developed an underground sales momentum; e-Bay became the place to buy your iPod as well as other online retailers like Amazon.

All these elements have been important in the growth in popularity of the iPod but, if we keep in mind our definition of marketing, it might not have had the success it has had if it had not have taken initial notice of customer needs and tried to anticipate those needs. Those customer needs might have been functional things like a small, good-sounding personal music device. It might

have been the need to have something a little less intrusive and bulky than a personal CD player. It might have been ease of use or the ability to access a wide range of music – that is where the iTunes music store became so vital a part of the whole product offering. It may also have been that the style and design of the product was important in consumer minds. It is all very well having a personal music player, but it might also have to be something that reflects an image that the user wants to associate with. These are all factors that Apple would have considered in developing the iPod.

If we continue to refer back to our definition of marketing, we remember that marketing is also a process. Steve Jobs, the founder of Apple, recognises this very clearly. The feedback about the first iPods from customers (and prospective customers who may not have bought the first versions of the iPod) would have told him important things about how to develop and amend the product to better meet customer needs. Customers may have wanted improved battery time, smaller, more powerful units, different colours to allow greater personalisation of the product and better quality sound reproduction. Jobs will have been able to feed all that information back to his designers and production staff as the life cycle of the iPod developed.

Activity

Discuss the implications of integrating the four elements of the marketing mix for Apple's iPod.

For example...

SSL International – Durex

The iPod was a new development; MP3 players have only been around for a short time. Other products face the same issues but we may take some of them for granted. Take a product like a condom. One of the largest brands of condom,

Durex, is made by a company called SSL International. SSL also make Marigold gloves, own the Dr Scholl footwear range and a host of other fast-moving consumer durables (FMCs) such as Meltus cough medicine and Syndol painkiller.

cont...

For example...

The marketing mix is just as relevant to Durex as it is to any other product, but the influences on the mix may be different. For a start, the very nature of the product presents different challenges. Durex has been around a long time – the brand name was registered in 1935 although the product was originally developed around 1915. The marketing mix for Durex now is very different from that which existed 40 years ago. One of the important elements of the mix is the product itself – it has a function to perform and the quality of the product must therefore be high in the mix. In addition to its role as a birth control measure, it also has to take into consideration user experience – the emphasis the promotion places on how the use of a condom does not detract from sexual pleasure is an important message, but also a difficult one to balance.

The price has to be another consideration – SSL will be hoping it will sell large volumes, and so margins may be relatively low. The total market for condoms is estimated at around 4 billion; Durex is sold in 150 countries and has a market share of 26%. Because of what the product does, it has to be priced so that consumers can afford it. 40 years ago the availability of the product was relatively limited – chemists, machines in pub toilets and barbers' shops were often seen as being the main route to market. However, changing social attitudes along with changes in the way supermarkets have developed mean that they are now far more widely available. 40 years ago, the idea of promoting Durex would have had severe limitations – adverts for the product were unheard of. Today that is quite different.

One of the key factors that has driven the growth in the condom market has been the development of HIV Aids. One way of helping to reduce the spread of this disease is through practising safe sex – using a condom. From being a product that was secretive and associated with guilt, condoms became socially acceptable. A whole new market was created when women took on the responsibility of also carrying condoms, not to mention the expansion into overseas markets that might not have existed prior to the HIV Aids outbreak: Africa, the Middle East, and because of the changes to political systems, Eastern Europe. This allowed companies like SSL to market their products in quite different ways. Despite the change in social attitudes which changed the relative importance of elements in the mix, SSL has had to be sensitive to the views of those who believe that such methods of birth control are ethically wrong. Now there was a different balancing act to be carried out in getting the mix right.

Without doubt, social attitudes and technology have had a massive impact on the marketing mix for Durex but the changes in technology and market research have also helped the company to be able to develop, change and innovate the product to meet market needs better and improve their business.

Activity

Discuss how changes in society have influenced the relative importance of the different elements of the marketing mix for SSL International.

The two examples above show how the different elements that influence the mix can all be present at the same time.

In the case of Apple

- The finance it had available will have some impact on the extent to which it is able to fund product development and continued product innovation.
- Its skills and expertise in technology in related production areas might have helped them to develop smaller, more

powerful units and in so doing, did not sacrifice the quality of sound reproduction (the introduction of the iPod Nano being an example here). In addition, the technology changed to enable people to download music, and as a result, there has been a change in customer needs.

- The market research that would have been ongoing would have also informed the mix. Market research may have told them that consumers were not willing to pay £200 for an iPod, but that £149 would draw in a whole new group of consumers.

In the case of SSL

- Changes to social attitudes affected the way in which the business was able to market the product and how they were able to diversify the product range.
- Market research will have helped them to be able to look at what customers wanted from the product, to know how they wanted to buy it, when and where.
- Market research will also have enabled the business to be able to introduce new products into the portfolio.
- SSL is likely to have used the changes in the market to change their objectives – this is likely to have involved moving into new markets: in countries in Africa, for example.

The importance of an integrated marketing mix

The different elements of the marketing mix have to be drawn together in the same way that the ingredients in a cake are mixed together. Once the cake has been baked, all those ingredients are still there, but it is not easy to identify them individually as to which was the key ingredient. So it is with the marketing mix.

An integrated marketing mix can be seen as the way in which the different elements complement each other. The price of a product needs to be closely related to the product itself. The price has to convey value to the consumer to encourage them to part with their money. Choosing the appropriate price that reflects the product itself is a key decision therefore. However, setting an appropriate price for the product will then need to be supported by the decisions on the way in which the product is promoted and the type of distribution network that is used to get the product to the consumer. Some products may be offered for sale through online routes only, whereas for other products the need to get the product into as many different retail locations as possible may be an essential part of the mix.

Chocolate bars, for example, have to be priced competitively. Many are of similar size and with similar ingredients to their competitors. The price that is charged not only has to reflect the product itself and what customers expect of such a product but also to bear in mind how the product might perform against its competitors against whom it is going to sit on the retailers' shelves.

The method of distribution therefore, is informed by the need to get the bar in as many retail outlets that are known for selling chocolate bars, and many that are not, as possible to maximise potential sales. Pubs, for example, now regularly stock chocolate bars! The decision on the promotional support for the bar might not just include advertising but the point of sale display stands and support that is provided to the retailer to help that particular product stand out against its competitors.

It may be, therefore, that one element of the mix is deemed to be more important than the others, depending on the product, but without the support of the others the product is not likely to be as successful. The final 'baked cake' therefore represents a value that is more than the sum of the ingredients used.

However, successfully integrating the marketing mix requires input and effort from everyone in an organisation. Marketing is not just the responsibility of the marketing team (which may not even exist in a small business); it is the responsibility of everyone in the organisation. We can see this more clearly when we go back to our definition of marketing: 'the management process that identifies, anticipates and satisfies customer requirements profitably'.

If we think about this definition in relation to the other business functions – production, accounts and finance, administration, sales, IT and human resources – we can see how the marketing function relies upon and feeds the other functions in a business – big or small.

Production

Marketing is about 'satisfying customer requirements profitably'; the production department will need to look closely at how it operates to identify where efficiencies can be made. If costs can be cut then it either allows the firm to increase margins or allows them greater flexibility to use price as a means of competition. The work of the production team, therefore, is essential in maintaining competitive advantage in the marketplace. The production team also have the responsibility of ensuring that the quality of products produced is of the required standard – who needs an iPod that keeps breaking down?

In turn, the marketing function provides information to the production team. If market research has identified that customers are not happy with a particular aspect of a product, then the production team can work on trying to change the product to better meet those needs.

Accounts and finance

Accounts and finance will monitor the monies coming into and out of a business, as well as giving information to all functions in the business about budgets and variances. They can report to the other functions about just how profitable a particular product or service actually is. They can identify where costs are being incurred, whether particular areas are having greater problems meeting targets or budgets than others, and all this information helps to identify whether the business is carrying out the marketing process satisfactorily.

In turn, marketing can feed back into the accounts and finance function. It may be that a gap in the market has been identified. Before a product or service is developed to meet that market need, there will be discussions with accounts and finance to see whether meeting that need could be carried out by the business profitably. The accounts and finance team might have information on other product developments the firm has carried out that can inform the decision-making process and ensure, as far as possible, that the development of the new product is based on a sound financial footing and is as risk-free as possible.

Administration

One of the important functions of administration is to ensure the efficient flow of information through a business. Often, an administrator will be the first point of contact with customers. Creating the right impression at the outset and making sure that customers are treated appropriately is important in gaining and keeping customers. The administration department will also be responsible for making sure that appropriate records are kept, that individuals and groups within the business remain informed about developments within and outside the business, for ensuring the smooth organisation and running of events such as training events, meetings, conferences, and so on.

Sales

The sales team are often the ones at the sharp end of the business. They have to know the product or service inside out and in many cases have to believe in the product or service they are selling. As sales teams will be talking directly to customers and will mostly know their customers very well too, they will be an invaluable source of information to the marketing team. In many businesses, sales are not just 'real time'; many sales forces are working in B2B and will be selling products that will not be in the hands of the final consumer for many months ahead. Being able to read the market, and to anticipate and identify consumer needs, are important skills in the sales team. Marketing can, in addition, seek out the expertise of the sales team when developing new products or researching amendments to existing products.

IT

The vast majority of businesses rely on the use of information technology (IT) systems – whatever their size. IT systems might range from simple accounting packages that record the daily costs and sales information in a small business, through to highly sophisticated software packages that track data flow in large organisations with different plants in different parts of the world. The use of e-mail, BlackBerries® and the Internet are now an accepted part of many business operations – again large and small – and many businesses rely on these systems to improve effective communications and facilitate the flow of information across a business.

IT can inform marketing about customer needs (maybe through collating and analysing market research data), can run speedy and regular updates on costs and sales to help provide information about whether consumer needs are being met profitably, and can also help speed up the regularity and accuracy of customer feedback. Many customers might be happy to provide feedback on the service or products they have received through simple online surveys. Loyalty cards such as the Tesco Clubcard or the Nectar card can also provide valuable information to a business about consumer spending habits.

Point-of-sale systems can also provide information that helps to plan stock levels and deliveries. All this information is driven by IT and can be used by the marketing department in their ongoing analysis of the market.

Human resources

At the heart of any business is people – most businesses, especially those in the service sector, simply would not exist without its people. The human resources department not only has the responsibility of recruiting staff, it is also responsible for maintaining their needs, for providing the framework for motivation, for identifying and managing their training needs, and so on. Well-trained, well-qualified and motivated staff are more likely to be in sympathy with the mission of a business – again, whatever its size – and in so doing be in a better position to help meet customer needs. The bored receptionist who cannot be bothered to greet customers on the telephone or in person appropriately is not going to create the right impression to recruit and keep those customers.

Further material and resources relating to this section can be found at **www.collins.bized.co.uk**. Keep checking for updates.

Designing an effective marketing mix:
Summary

- The marketing mix is the combination of price, product, promotion and place that a business uses to meet the needs of its customers and implement a marketing strategy.
- There are a number of factors that influence the relative importance of the factors in the mix. These include social changes, the availability of finance, technological changes and feedback from market research activities.
- An effective marketing mix is based around the integration of activities of all aspects of the business – marketing is everyone's responsibility.

Summary questions

1 What are the four elements of the marketing mix?

2 Give a short definition for each of these elements.

3 Identify and explain three factors that influence the marketing mix.

4 Identify and explain two factors that might influence the marketing mix for a pen manufacturer like Parker pens and an insurance broker.

5 State two different marketing objectives that a business might have.

6 Suggest a suitable marketing objective for each of the following:
   - Cadbury
   - a small-town hairdressing salon
   - Amazon, the online retailer.

7 Why might limits on finance have an effect on a successful marketing mix?

8 Why is accurate information important to the success of the marketing mix?

9 What is meant by the phrase 'integrated marketing mix'?

10 Explain why it is said that 'marketing is a whole approach to doing business'.

Points for discussion

Using either the case study of the iPod or Durex, discuss how changing market and social conditions might affect the balance of the marketing mix for these products.

Exam practice

In the summer of 2007, the nation seemed to hold its breath in anticipation of the release of the final Harry Potter novel – *Harry Potter and the Deathly Hallows*. The publishers of the *Potter* series, Bloomsbury, have clearly had a hit on their hands. Little might they have realised just how successful the series would turn out when they originally commissioned the first book. We might expect bookshops like Waterstones, WH Smith and Ottakers to have stocks of the book as well as the many smaller independent bookshops. However, buying the book is now far easier than it ever was because of the sheer amount of businesses who are offering it for sale. Amazon, for example, had the book available on pre-order for months and it is also available at supermarkets.

Herein lies the problem. Organisations like Tesco and Asda sold the book at a heavy discount; Amazon is also selling it for less than the cover price. Bloomsbury set the cover price at £17.99 but those of you who

have bought it already are unlikely to have paid that amount. In some outlets the book is selling for as little as £7.99. What this means is that firms like Tesco and Asda are not making any money out of selling the book.

For independent booksellers, the competition is stifling; they simply cannot afford to sell the book at such a heavy discount, and as a result they might only have limited numbers and decide to avoid getting involved in selling the book. This seems a pity given that it is clearly one of the publishing events of the year and it might be expected that booksellers would be the main group to benefit. Some independent booksellers have suggested that they will make as little as £1.30 on the sale of each book and that if they buy copies from their local supermarket and then re-sell them they can make slightly more! Some are deliberately publicising the fact that they are going to go to Tesco and buy several dozen copies not, they say, because of the money they can make but to highlight the situation they find themselves in.

Source: Biz/ed In the News: http://www.bized.co.uk/cgi-bin/chron/chron.pl?id=2895

1 Describe the advantages that a business like Tesco and Asda might gain from discounting the book *Harry Potter and the Deathly Hallows*. (4 marks)

2 Consider the possible marketing objectives for Tesco and Asda in marketing *Harry Potter and the Deathly Hallows*. (6 marks)

3 What do you think is the most important element of the marketing mix for a firm like Bloomsbury in marketing the *Harry Potter* novels? (8 marks)

4 Explain how changes to the way consumers buy books have affected independent booksellers. (8 marks)

5 Assess the factors that might have influenced the marketing mix for books like the *Harry Potter* series. (14 marks)

Total: 40 marks

Chapter 30   Using the marketing mix: product

This chapter will help you to understand the role of the product in the marketing mix. It will look at how new products are developed, how businesses try to make their products unique, how they analyse the position of the range of products they offer, and how the life cycle of a product is assessed.

Product

A product is a good or service produced by a business or organisation, and made available to the public for consumption. 'Product' incorporates a range of features that the firm could focus on:

- technical specification: the capacity of the iPod, for example
- features: colour, design, texture, functionality, and so on. An armchair may be made of leather, have swivel and tilt capabilities, be black, have a rosewood frame, be classed as 'luxurious', for example
- packaging: either designed to appeal (such as the cover of a CD), or for health and safety purposes – the packaging of food, for example.

Influences on the development of new goods and services

The product is a fundamental part of the marketing mix. It is, after all, the part of the mix that customers will use, eat or drink, etc. For B2B businesses, the product might be essential. The dynamic nature of the market means that it is forever changing; many factors will work together to create a constantly changing market landscape, and firms must be in a position to be able to respond to these changing conditions. Existing firms may be dominant in a market at this moment in time, but that position will not remain indefinitely and if the firm does not change and keep abreast of the myriad changes in the market then it will quickly fall behind. New products are developed, new ways of using products and services are found, new technologies that allow consumers to access products and services differently, social change affects what we want to buy and why, and consumer spending power is constantly changing in response to economic conditions.

The place of product in the mix will have to reflect these changes if a firm is to continue to have some competitive advantage. We can see examples of this in the fortunes of some very high-profile businesses.

<div class="key-terms">

Key terms

Brand image The personality given to a product through marketing activities.

Cash burn The rate at which a product or business uses up the cash available to it.

Extension strategy Marketing strategy to prevent sales from declining.

Market growth The rate at which the entire market is growing over time.

Product portfolio The range of products at different stages in the life cycle that a business has for sale at any one time.

Unique selling point A feature of the product, its image, its price, its promotion or its distribution that is different from and superior to the competition.

</div>

For example...

HMV is a music retailer. It has been around since 1921 and is a major presence in many high streets around the country. In the 1980s, HMV faced growing competition from new music retailers like Virgin. It also faced a changing market; the demand for vinyl records started to decline as first cassette tapes and then CDs came to dominate the market. CDs became the dominant product in HMV's sales because technology had changed and allowed the development of CD players which were affordable. In combination with CDs, video was a major source of income for firms like HMV. The more compact format of a CD meant that smaller retail units could exploit this – firms like MVC, Music Zone and Fopp sprang up, providing yet more competition for HMV.

In the late 1990s, video began to be overtaken by the developments in DVD technology and at the same time the developments in computer technology meant that many more people could access music through their PCs and through MP3 players. The whole nature of the music landscape changed in the first decade of the 21st century. People were buying their music in different ways – no longer did they have to buy a whole album to get the one song they liked, they could now pick and choose and even swap with their friends (illegally for the most part!). On top of that, developments in online retailing meant severe competition from firms like Amazon.

HMV found its profits falling, sales declining and was being lumbered with very expensive overheads in the form of retail outlets across the country. To survive, therefore, HMV is having to make significant changes to its 'product' – not the CDs or DVDs it sells (although they will still have an important role) but in the way it provides for the needs of its customers – customers who now have greater choice and greater power within the market. How it does that is a massive challenge to the company.

Currys and Currys.digital are two major high-street electrical retailers. They sell cameras, hi-fis, TVs, PCs, video and DVD players, etc. Within these broad product definitions huge changes have taken place that have provided challenges to the way they do their business. Cameras are still popular but changing technology means that traditional cameras that take photographs using film are fast becoming a niche market. Customer needs have changed as technology has changed. The use of digital cameras is growing. Customers find them easier to use, more convenient, faster, more flexible and more creative.

Similar issues are happening in the market for TVs and video. Video recorders and players are now virtually non-existent and both companies have had to take decisions about whether to stock such products anymore. In addition, DVD players are now being superseded by DVD recorders, cathode ray tube TVs have now been replaced by flat screen TVs and the technology is continuing to change. There is now a huge range of TV programmes that can be accessed by viewers, and digital television will continue to evolve and create changing market conditions.

Because of situations like those described above, firms – whatever their size – have to look at ways that they can adjust the product element in the mix to cater for changed consumer needs – however those changes came about. This means that new goods and services are constantly appearing. These new goods and services may be the result of new firms entering a market or existing firms looking to develop new ways of doing business – for example, HMV having to change the customer experience in response to changed market conditions in the music industry.

Why develop new goods and services?

There will be a number of reasons for the development of new goods and services. These include:
- changes in the way we live
- social changes

- changes in technology
- the actions of competitors
- entrepreneurial skills of business owners and managers.

For many larger firms the decision as to the exact product or service to be sold or when a new product will be developed and launched will be a strategic one. As such, product strategy is determined in relation to corporate and marketing objectives. Use of strategic models will inform the way that product is used as part of the marketing mix.

In addition, several product-specific models exist to help a business decide how best to use the marketing mix based on a market analysis of its current products. This is part of what is called '**product portfolio analysis**'. Many large firms have more than one product in many different markets and it has to monitor how each of those products are performing and what role the product is playing in meeting the overall strategy that has been decided. This is discussed in more detail later in this chapter.

Changes in the way we live

At the time of writing, life for many people in the UK is very much different from that which we experienced 10, 20 or 30 years ago. Many things have some element of consistency – we have schools, we have colleges and universities, people have to work to earn a living and we have to buy food, clothing and have a need for entertainment. We have to sleep, get to places, have holidays, and so on. Despite these consistencies in the way we live, the subtleties about how we go about these daily routines or habits, there are massive underlying changes that have occurred and which continue to occur.

For example...

A sketch of a typical middle aged person circa 2008!

My parents used to work and shop to buy food and clothes to feed me and the rest of my family. Now I am a working parent, I have to do those same things. The way I go about doing these everyday things, however, has changed dramatically. I can go to supermarkets that are larger and have a much wider choice than ever before, many of which are open 24 hours a day. I can buy fresh fruit all year round – not just at certain times of the year. I can get virtually everything I need in one retail outlet. If that is not enough then there are massive shopping complexes that combine not only retail but leisure and entertainment – going out shopping can be seen as a day out! If I really hate shopping I can get my groceries and most of the shopping needs I have delivered directly to my door via online ordering. The choice of products I have available as a result of this is extensive. I can easily go onto

Amazon Japan and buy CDs or DVDs that are not available in the UK and have them arrive at my door within days.

I am more likely not to be the only car owner in my family, I will almost certainly have more than one TV in the house, and the leisure and sporting opportunities available to me have changed beyond recognition. I can still go to a football match on a Saturday afternoon (although the number of

cont...

For example...

Saturday matches might be fewer in the highest leagues) or I can subscribe to a satellite provider and watch in the comfort of my own home. I might prefer some atmosphere when watching my football – no problem; there will be a pub somewhere with big screens and any amount of people to share my passion. However, there are now many more things that I could do on a Saturday afternoon other than watch football.

I don't have to play a sport now to keep fit; I can join a gym and have access to a wide range of machines and equipment to help me keep in shape. When I go on holiday it is unlikely to be to places in the UK. Spain and France are now becoming a bit boring and we are looking for more exotic forms of ways to spend our hard-earned holidays. Trips to the Arctic Circle, South America, Eastern Europe and Asia are now more easily within reach and there are any number of companies who can promise me a holiday experience of a lifetime. I still go to places in the UK of course, but it tends to be for weekend breaks rather than two-week holidays, and when I go I don't just want to sit on the beach – I want to be involved in some sort of activity.

I am more likely to have more flexibility in the way I work, how I work and where I work. I may use a variety of types of public transport to get to work, have to pay for the privilege of taking my car to work, be bombarded by free newspapers both on my way to work and on the way back, buy my lunch from a sandwich bar or any of the range of specialist shops that have opened up to cater for my needs or the offshoot of major supermarkets that have sprung up on the high street to also vie for my custom.

I am more likely to be aware of the threat of climate change, healthy foods, the value of eating organically, the foods from India, China, Indonesia, Thailand and a host of other exotic places, drink wine from all over the world – not just France – prefer my beer to be in a bottle, like drinks that are colourful and fruity and spend more time drinking at home than in pubs or clubs. I might be more likely to be vegetarian or even vegan; I have a concern that the average big business does not behave as ethically as I would like but still patronise them.

In short, our lives are far more complex but have greater opportunities than ever before. For businesses, keeping up with the way we live our lives, trying to anticipate changing trends and fashions, developing products to meet the needs of consumers, needs that might often create conflicts (for example, wanting free newspapers but having a concern for the amount of litter, pollution, trees that are used in the paper industry, etc.) is a major challenge. Firms simply cannot stand still.

The sketch above highlights some of the ways in which the way we live our lives have and continue to change. As changes occur, new opportunities arise to fulfil needs that are not being met or are perceived as not being met. The marketing function is to keep on top of these changes and to try and find ways of developing new products and services to meet those needs.

Social changes

Society is constantly changing. Our views, attitudes and the way we live together in groups is a shifting mass of complexity. Social changes may manifest themselves in concerns over our health, over how we view the actions of firms, individuals and groups, violence, crime, how we spend our leisure, and so on. The development of concerns over the effect of business activity on the environment has led to growing pressure on businesses to account for their actions. We are now told by many firms that they are changing how they do things to reduce the impact on the environment of their actions – their green credentials. The increase in the number of people being diagnosed with obesity has led to changes in the way in which we are approaching what and how we eat. Schools have now been forced to make changes to the food they provide, vending machines have been removed or the products available from them changed.

Social changes also manifest themselves in the way we dress. Youth groups referred to as 'chavs' and football hooligans have hijacked a brand for their own – this is not what Burberry wants to be associated with. The range of acceptable forms of clothing are now far wider – we no longer get too worked up about people who dress outrageously, although there are some places where this is still the case. For example, the fashion for wearing 'prison style trousers' that are too big and hang round our hips displaying the branded boxer shorts that we are wearing has created offence in some US states. Atlanta has considered fining youngsters who display their underwear to the public!

The public perception of smoking has now changed. Many people, even smokers, accept that the habit is not good in lots of ways – it affects the smoker's health, it affects non-smokers' health through passive smoking, leaves clothes smelling and makes the atmosphere in enclosed spaces unpleasant. The law banning smoking in public places covers the whole of the UK. Pubs, clubs and other public places, as well as tobacco companies, have had to adjust to the change.

Social changes can manifest themselves in many different ways. Changing trends and fashions can affect a wide variety of different types of business but also provide new opportunities for other businesses to find ways of exploiting new customer needs. The case of the smoking ban in the UK, for example, has created opportunities for businesses who are finding ways of providing shelters for smokers in pubs and clubs whilst also meeting the new legislation. Social change therefore provides both threats and opportunities for the place of the product in the mix.

Changes in technology

The massive advances in technology over the past twenty years have seen opportunities for new products and services grow at an almost exponential rate. The ability of manufacturers to pack in computing power into minute chips means that the potential for developing new devices and gadgets that exploit this new technology is almost endless. In addition, technology is allowing us to be able to communicate faster, more effectively, in different ways and 24 hours a day. The growth of the information economy means that the main 'product' for many businesses is information. Finding ways to transmit that information quickly and efficiently has spawned a whole new industry. In addition to this, improved computing power means that data can be identified, collected, processed and analysed in ever more sophisticated ways. This not only provides increased business opportunities for new product development, but also gives marketers access to more sophisticated ways to segment the market to ensure that products are being targeted at the right people.

The actions of competitors

One of the features of the market system is that there are always opportunities to be exploited to gain competitive advantage and enter new markets. Competitors can take the form of existing rivals in a market and new firms entering that market. To maintain competitive advantage, a firm will have to constantly have in mind the marketing process and to review its existing product offering in the light of the rest of the market and from feedback from market research. Changes to the product, therefore, might be necessary to be able to maintain or regain competitive advantage. A car manufacturer, for example, might be outflanked by a rival who has introduced satellite navigation systems or a more efficient fuel system into a new model. The manufacturer will have to respond to this. It might not be sufficient to simply copy their rivals; they may have to find a way of dong the same thing – but even better – in order to capture back competitive advantage.

Entrepreneurial skills of managers and owners

As the marketplace gets more crowded, so the apparent opportunities for capturing a market seem to diminish. What this means is that to maintain competitive advantage, the way of looking at the product in the mix has to be viewed with ever more creative approaches. In recent years there has been a growth in TV programmes highlighting entrepreneurial skills. These programmes highlight the importance of such skills in a modern economy. It is not just a case of thinking about new products and new ways to exploit existing products; it is also about how to bring these products to market. The development of such techniques as guerrilla marketing, for example, has been one example of how new entrepreneurial skills are being utilised.

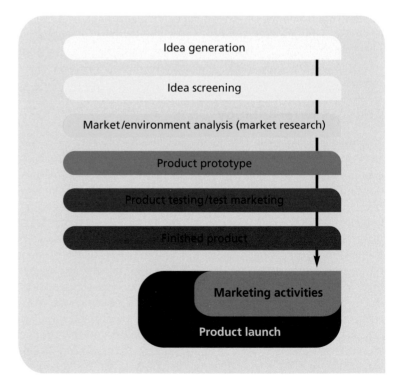

Figure 30.1 Product development and innovation

Product development

There are many reasons why new products are important to businesses. Some of these reasons include:

- to counter competitors' actions
- to smooth out seasonal fluctuations
- to spread risk through diversification into new markets
- to increase or maintain market share
- to replace old, unpopular or discontinued products.

The stages necessary to bring a new product to market are shown in Figure 30.1.

Fewer than one in seven (or one in ten for food) product ideas ever make it successfully to market (see Figure 30.2). Some, despite all the testing and checking, fail once they reach the market.

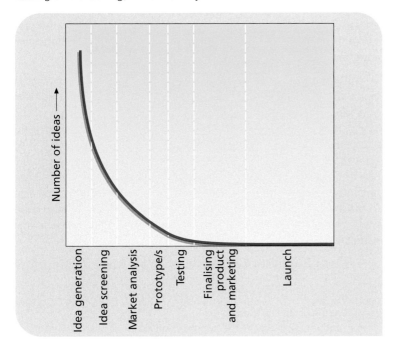

Figure 30.2   New product fall-out rate

Unique selling points or propositions

The drive to gain and keep competitive advantage might mean that firms look to find ways of differentiating their product or service. Competitive advantage is the way in which a firm appeals to its consumers through adding value which makes the firm unique in some way. This uniqueness can be both defended and is distinctive, and means that it is difficult for its rivals to be able to imitate or replicate these features. Key sources of competitive advantage come from cost advantages or through differentiation.

One way of doing this is to find what is called a '**unique selling point**' (USP) or unique selling proposition. This is not easy! The term 'unique' gives some clues as to what a business might be looking for in building competitive advantage through their product. They will be looking for something that makes their product totally different from any competitor's product. Not only that, but it will have to be something different that fulfils a customer need.

Returning to our example of the iPod, the design of the shuffle wheel was something that was not found on any other MP3 player at the time. It was not sufficient, however, for it to be some sort of clever gadget; it had to be functional and customers had to feel that it added value to the product.

Online provider Amazon was able to differentiate its product (a service in this case) by utilising the technology of cookies to help improve its understanding of its customer needs. A cookie is a device that tracks an individual user's movements through a website. This meant that Amazon could build a picture of its users and use the data to target other products which might interest those same users more effectively. The addition of this service to the product offering was something unique to Amazon at the time and gave them a competitive advantage.

Mobile phone manufacturers are also good examples of ways in which the product is manipulated to try to build in USPs. It might be how slim the phone is, it might be the colour range, the style of the casing, the functionality of the phone, the fact that it has a swivel head, a big megabyte camera, a built-in MP3 player, bigger keypad, and so on. What has to be remembered, and mobile phone manufacturers have found this out, is that USPs have a limited shelf life. If the USP can be protected by some form of patent or trademark then it may be able to maintain its USP for some time. However, this does not stop rivals from finding other ways of emulating or even improving on the particular USP.

The following could all be ways in which a business could establish a USP:

- design
- technical specification
- functionality – what the product can do
- colour
- size
- weight
- efficiency – in energy use, for example
- environmental impact
- comfort
- degree of customisation
- taste
- durability
- quality
- aesthetic qualities.

Product portfolio analysis

Many of the large corporations that we are familiar with have a wide range of products, often arranged as different businesses, which they often sell in a range of different markets. Keeping track of the contribution these products are making to the businesses' overall strategy is an important part of the business process. Data from such analysis provides the firm with the information to enable them to change the mix and to perhaps change the relative weighting of an individual item, like product within the mix.

Product portfolio analysis is the term used to describe this process. One of the major ways that have been devised to analyse the position of products within the portfolio of products a firm has at any one time is called the Boston Matrix. It was developed by the Boston Consulting Group in 1968 and has become widely known and used. When looking at this sort of technique, we do have to be aware of limitations in the analysis. Firms who use such an analysis will be acutely aware that it is not always easy to simply classify a product and in addition, it might be very difficult to see exactly what is happening to the market as a whole.

The Boston Matrix

The Boston Matrix is often shown in the form of a diagram – see Figure 30.3. The matrix links together market share and market growth – make sure you understand the difference between the two (see the definition on pages 292 and 311). Products are placed in different quadrants according to their perceived position in relation to their share of the market and their position in a growing market – that market could be growing quickly or slowly. Given the position, the importance to the business can be gauged. This importance will relate to the effect of the product on the cash flow of the business and the investment in resources needed to support it. These four quadrants are described as 'dogs', 'cash cows', 'problem children' and 'stars'.

DOGS

These are products with low market share in low-growth markets. A low-growth market may be a market which is in decline or which is so specialised that it is unlikely to grow with any sort of rapidity. Dogs do not generate cash for the company; rather they tend to cause cash to flow out of the business at a high rate – sometimes referred to as a 'high **cash burn** rate'. If a product is identified as a dog, a business may have to take some very serious decisions about its future. The most common strategy for dogs is to divest – this involves selling off the product if a willing buyer can be identified, or ceasing production altogether and pulling out of that particular market. There are a number of current examples of low-growth markets: video recorders, sports utility vehicles (SUVs) and certain types of beer. The decision of what to do with a dog is not always easy. Vinyl records could have been seen as a dog a few years ago and many in the music industry predicted its demise. However, vinyl is making a bit of a comeback – certainly not at sales levels that it enjoyed in the 1960s and 1970s, but it is refusing to go away nevertheless!

CASH COWS

These are products with a high share of a low-growth market. These are often products that have been in existence for many years and are at the mature stage of their life cycle (see below). Products like Kit Kat, Mars, Walkers Crisps, spectacles and certain types of fizzy drink are examples of such mature markets with well-established products. They might often be mass markets with high volumes of sales for the firms within them, but relatively low-profit margins. Cash cows, as the name suggests, can be milked for cash; what this means is that they generate more income for the business than is invested in them. The products are invariably at a stage where much of the up-front investment in developing and promoting them has now been made and they are big enough and powerful enough to survive in the market with more limited resources being used to support them. This surplus cash can be milked to support stars or problem children.

This is not to suggest that the firm can simply sit back, relax and expect the cash to continue to roll in. As we have seen, if a firm does this it will soon be taken over by the changes in the market. Kelloggs, for example, relied on its major brand, Corn Flakes, for many years, but then found that entry of new competitors into the market, including own-brand products, along with the greater variety in the market for breakfast cereals saw the position of Corn Flakes start to fall. It needed a promotion campaign to remind consumers that the product was still there – 'Have you forgotten how good they taste?' it urged. Some cash must, therefore, be spent to help hold the product in its cash cow position. Cash cows may find their market positions frequently challenged by competitors.

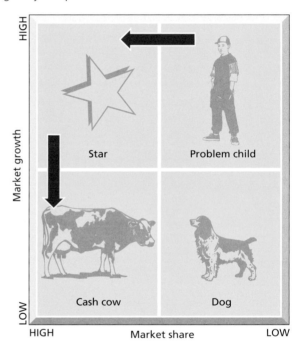

Figure 30.3   The Boston Matrix

PROBLEM CHILDREN

Products with a low share of a high-growth market are referred to as problem children. They might have just been launched, or for some reason are having trouble making headway in the market despite the fact that the market is growing strongly. To support them and try and boost their profile they consume marketing resources but generate relatively little income in return. They may, because the market is growing, become the stars or cash cows of the future if they can gain greater market share. Increased marketing expenditure and attempting to build product awareness and **brand image** may be needed.

Microsoft's X-Box proved to be a problem child when it was launched in 2001. It struggled to make headway against its more established rival – Sony's PlayStation. However, Microsoft persisted and the product has now gained ground on the PlayStation, capturing 15% market share by the middle of 2007. It is expected that Sony's current market share of 70% will decline by as much as 20% in the face of competition from the X-Box and the other main console unit from Nintendo. However, compare this to the proposed competitor to Apple's iPod, the Zune. At the time of writing, this is also a problem child but it is by no means certain that this product will make it in the way that the X-Box has. By January 2007, Zune managed a 3.2% market share compared to 72.7% of the iPod in the share of music player sales.

STARS

These are products in high-growth markets with a relatively high market share. Stars often generate high amounts of income, but may need protecting from competitors. Market leadership may not have been established in these markets, giving the business the opportunity to really exploit its dominant position, and companies will be fighting for market share and brand loyalty.

Balancing the portfolio

A business is likely to be looking to achieve a balance within its product portfolio. Whilst a business might wish to avoid dogs, stars and problem children might need to be developed and invested in to maintain their competitive position in the marketplace. It might also be hoped that such products become future cash cows. The importance of cash cows is the fact that they use relatively small amounts of resources in relation to the cash they generate, meaning that they provide funds for product development, new product launches and for supporting problem children and stars. Ideally, a business would have a product development cycle that follows the path indicated by the arrows in Figure 30.3. Examining its product portfolio allows a business to consider whether it has got this balance right and adjust its strategy accordingly.

Criticisms of the Boston Matrix

- Some have argued that the Boston Matrix is too simplistic a structure to represent what are increasingly complex market structures and complex product portfolios of many large corporations. To an extent this is valid, but we might also point out that few firms would rely solely on this information in its decision-making. The analysis of the portfolio using the Boston Matrix may help to clarify understanding and offer a clearer picture to all workers than some more sophisticated methods of portfolio analysis. However, it remains the case that management experience and intuition remain important.
- There is an implied assumption that profit is directly related to high market share. This may not always be the case – when Boeing launch the new Dreamliner with predicted sales of around over 600 aircraft, it might achieve a high market share in that particular market – the market for medium-sized

aircraft. Despite gaining market share quickly, it will have to sell an estimated 250 aircraft to break even. This is because the development costs of such a product are vast – estimated at between $10 and $12 billion. It may be some time before it makes sufficient sales to start to generate a profit.

- The strategic responses suggested by the models will not suit all business situations. Many marketers argue that 'milking' a cow is likely to hand competitive advantage to other firms in the market.
- Conducting a product portfolio analysis is of little use if it is not done in conjunction with a plan of action as to how to deal with the situation the business might find itself in as a result of the analysis. In reality, most businesses will recognise this!

The product life cycle

What do you know about the following products: Junglies, Aztec, Prize bar, 4-track tape cartridges and Betamax videos? The answer is probably 'not a lot' and for good reason. They are products that made brief and sometimes spectacular entries to the market, only to be withdrawn some years later. Most products have a lifespan – the time from when they first appear on the market to the time when they are withdrawn. This lifespan is represented by what is called the product life cycle. Whilst every product has a life cycle, the length of that life cycle will vary enormously from product to product (the term 'product' also includes services).

The traditional representation of the product life cycle goes through initial development of the product and its introduction to the market. Hopefully, its sales will grow and eventually the market will stabilise and become mature. Then, as new products are launched and competition grows, sales for the original product will start to decline. This process is shown in Figure 30.4.

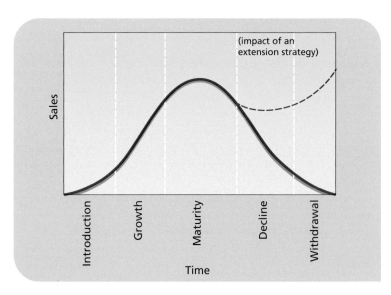

Figure 30.4 A typical product lifecycle

Stages of the product life cycle

RESEARCH AND DEVELOPMENT

This is where many products start their lives. The R&D might be planned in relation to a targeted gap in the market that the firm wishes to exploit. Some products may take many years to research and develop – pharmaceutical products in particular, can easily take ten to fifteen years to develop; many cars are years on the drawing board and test circuits before being introduced; and aircraft can take even longer – the Airbus A380 Super Jumbo has been 10 years in development and is due to go into service in 2008.

INTRODUCTION

After research and development, which may include test marketing, the product will be launched onto the market. Costs incurred in launching the product will be high and sales may be low. The product is unlikely to make any profit at this stage.

GROWTH

Sales begin to grow and competitors enter the market. The extent to which competitors will enter the market depends on a variety of factors; the cost of development, the technological sophistication of the product, access to resources (not least human resources: specific highly valued skills, for example) and the extent to which the business can protect the product. This might be done through the use of patents or other legal restrictions such as licences. The growth stage will start to see cash being generated which will begin to pay off the development costs. There will be a stage where sales are sufficient for the revenues generated to more than cover the development costs and the product may become profitable. At this stage, the product may well need significant resources to help it achieve its sales potential.

MATURITY

Sales grow at a decreasing rate and then stabilise. The maturity stage in the product life cycle can last for many, many years and will depend on the nature of the product. In other cases, the maturity period may only be a few weeks or months. Products like Polo mints and Kit Kat, for example, have managed to maintain relatively high levels of sales for decades; some fashion clothing may only have a maturity stage of two months before new products come out to replace them. You may also see reference to another stage of the product life cycle after the maturity stage – saturation. The market becomes saturated when there are lots of competing products all servicing the same consumer needs. Differentiation between them is difficult and as a result sales of all products may start to fall or interest in the product starts to wane.

DECLINE

Sales, for most products, eventually fall. New, more innovative products may be introduced or consumer tastes might change. Products that reach the decline stage are often withdrawn from sale. The market for personal CD players is slowly declining, the market for video recorders and players has now all but ended and most firms are now not producing any more cathode ray tube TVs or computer monitors. Products like Aztec and Prize – both chocolate bars – have long since departed. (It is interesting to note, however, that Cadbury did bring out a limited edition of the Aztec bar during the Millennium celebrations in 2000).

Knowledge and awareness of the product life cycle concept allows managers, in theory, to adjust marketing strategy accordingly. Of course, in reality, the difficulty is often identifying which stage the product is in or how long the stage will last. The producers of the Aztec chocolate bar may well have hoped that it would become a cash cow like the Mars Bar, its direct rival, and last for many years. It proved not to be the case. Any changes to marketing strategy as a result of analysis of a product life cycle might, therefore, be seen as being reactive rather than proactive. To counter this, firms may well employ other techniques and strategies in addition to product life cycles in the marketing function, for example, futures thinking.

	Introduction	Growth	Maturity	Decline
Features of stage				
Sales	Low	Growing	Slow growth	Declining
Profits	Small	Highest	High but declining	Low
Cash flow	Negative	Positive	Positive	Positive, but falling
Customers	Early adopters	Early majority	Mass market	Laggards
Competitors	Few	Growing	Many	Falling
Marketing strategy				
Marketing expenditure	High	High (cost per sale falling)	Falling	Low
Price	Skimming or penetration strategy	Price cut/increase demanding on introduction strategy	Going-rate or competitor-based	High
Product	Basic	Improved	Differentiated	Basic
Promotion	Focus on awareness	Generate brand preference	Retain brand loyalty	Targeted promotions
Place (distribution)	Few outlets	Increasing	High number of outlets	Falling

Figure 30.5 The features and marketing implications of the product lifecycle

We also need to consider the following when looking at the life cycle theory: many products fail, some have very short life cycles and others enjoy extremely long lives – Bisto gravy, for instance, has been on shop shelves since 1908. In reality there are very few products that follow the classic life cycle shown in figure 30.5.

Figure 30.6 shows some of these different life cycles.
- The length of each stage varies enormously between products.
- It is difficult to identify where a product is in its life cycle.
- It is impossible for mangers to know with any degree of certainty when a product will enter the next stage of its life.

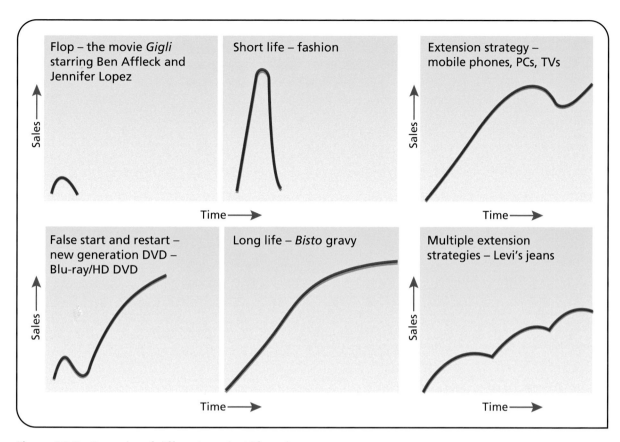

Figure 30.6 Examples of different product life cycles

- Usage of the product life cycle, like all business tools, needs to be balanced against management experience, personal intuition and a sound analysis of the market.

Extension strategies

As markets change and evolve, businesses may look to respond by also changing or allowing their products to evolve. The base product may stay the same, but somehow the business will manage to breathe new life into it to prevent sales from declining. One good example is the mortgage market. A mortgage is a loan primarily designed for the purchase of property. It is different from most other loans because of the size of the loan and the long-term nature of the repayment period. Acquiring a mortgage prior to the early 1980s was a challenging affair for many people. Mortgages were only available from building societies and these organisations had limited funds – dependent on the number of people they had saving with them. A mortgage may only have been granted to couples who had been saving for a number of years.

The deregulation of the financial services industry in the early 1980s changed the whole market. Banks joined the market and other firms also entered the industry. Competition for customers grew and the boom in the housing market meant that there was no shortage of customers for these new businesses. As the 1990s and the first decade of the 21st century has progressed, mortgages as a product have evolved to take account of the changing needs of customers. Firms used to ask for a deposit but as competition grew, the size of that deposit required started to shrink. As prices in the housing market rose rapidly,

Activity

Look at the different types of product life cycles. Try to think some some actual examples for each one. An example of a short product life cycle might be clothes that are in fashion for only a few months – sales peak for a short period of time.

the plight of first-time buyers grew more difficult. Firms in the mortgage industry were not slow to respond to these needs. Products were developed that would lend more than the standard 3.5 times income – four times, five times and even more than this. Fixed interest mortgages, 100% mortgages (and more), mortgages in foreign currencies, discount rate mortgages – all were extensions to the basic mortgage.

A variety of **extension strategies** (see Figure 30.6) can be used to prevent sales decline.

ENCOURAGE INCREASED USAGE

Doritos tortilla chips were marketed under the slogan 'friendchips' in an effort to encourage people to buy more of the product.

FIND NEW USERS

Mobile phone companies have developed phones and airtime packages designed to appeal to younger children and pensioners.

FIND NEW USES FOR THE PRODUCT

Helly Hansen managed to increase brand awareness and extend the life of its sailing clothing by selling it as fashion items. Fruit juice producers have packaged their product in lots of different ways to appeal to different target markets – small cartons for children's lunches and for people on the move, for example. Mars, Cadbury and Nestlé have managed to take a number of their 'countline bar' products and move them into the ice cream market.

CHANGE THE PRODUCT

This may involve tangible changes to the product (Dyson launched its vacuum cleaners in a range of different colours) or intangible changes to the product's image (Pepperami was re-launched under the slogan 'a bit of an animal'). Kit Kat releases limited edition products – Kit Kat Orange, Kit Kat Mint and white chocolate Kit Kats, for example.

Product life cycles and the Boston Matrix

We can see close links between these two ideas. The diagram in figure 30.7 summarises this relationship. Putting the two things together, a business can get a good idea of where its various products are in the life cycle and what sort of products these are. A cash cow, for example, may be in the maturity stage in the life cycle. The firm might exploit this by using the cash generated to invest in its problem children and stars to try and boost their progress through introduction and growth. At the same time, the business might be very aware of the position of the cash cow in that mature market – how long has it been there, how close to decline might this stage in the life cycle be? The firm can also see the extent to which it has a balanced product portfolio with products at different stages of the life cycle and in different quadrants of the Boston Matrix. Such an analysis will contribute to its decision-making.

Many well-known pharmaceutical companies might well make use of such an analysis. Some have products that are in the mature stage of the life cycle; they are cash cows by virtue of the protection that patents might have afforded them, but these patents might well be starting to run out. If they then look at other products in the pipeline, they might see that some products are proving very difficult problem children; some products might have gone through many years of expensive research and development only to fail clinical trials. They might be asking where the funds are going to come from to maintain their market position in the future!

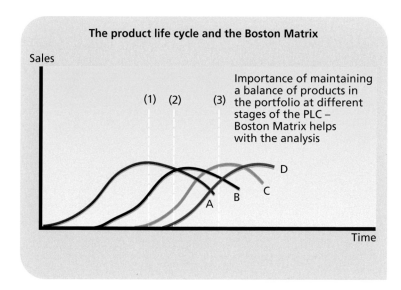

The product life cycle and the Boston Matrix

Importance of maintaining a balance of products in the portfolio at different stages of the PLC – Boston Matrix helps with the analysis

Figure 30.7 The product life cycle and the Boston Matrix

A business has four products, (a), (b), (c) and (d) in its portfolio. At time period 1, product (a) is in the maturity stage, product (b) in the growth stage, product (c) has just been launched and product (d) is still in development. By the time we reach time period 2, product (a) is in decline, product (b) is reaching maturity; product (c) is growing slowly and product (d) has just been launched. The use of the Boston Matrix may be useful for a firm in this situation to help analyse its portfolio and aid decision-making. In time period 3, for example, has product (a) become such a dog that it needs withdrawing? Is product (b) proving to be a problem child? Is product (c) a cash cow and product (d) a star?

Further material and resources relating to this section can be found at **www.collins.bized.co.uk**. Keep checking for updates.

Using the marketing mix: product: **Summary**

- The product is one of the key elements of the marketing mix.
- The term 'product' can refer to a physical product or a service.
- Goods and services are developed in response to customer needs and from an anticipation of those needs.
- New goods and services are developed because of the following reasons:
    - changes in lifestyles
    - social changes
    - changes in technology
    - the actions of competitors
    - the entrepreneurial skills of business owners and managers.
- Product development often takes place against the backdrop of a product portfolio.
- Products will be at different stages in the life cycle and this portfolio needs managing.
- The Boston Matrix is one way in which a business might analyse its product portfolio. This allows them to be able to amend the product element of the mix to cope with market changes and perceived changes in the portfolio.
- The product life cycle describes the typical stages a product goes through during its life.
- A product can have this life cycle extended through the use of extension strategies.

Summary questions

1   List the main stages in a product's development.

2   Describe an example of a recent, successful new product launch of which you are aware.

3   Identify the main stages of the product life cycle.

4   Explain how the promotional support given to a product might differ in each stage of its life cycle.

5   Sketch product life cycles for the following:
    - a failed product
    - a successful extension strategy.

6   Explain two ways in which a firm might use product life cycle analysis.

7   Using real life examples, state and explain three product life cycle extension strategies.

8   Explain how the use of the Boston Matrix can help a business to manage its product portfolio more effectively.

9   Explain, with reference to portfolio analysis, what is meant by a 'dog' product.

10 What strategies might a firm use with a product identified as a 'problem child'?

Task

1   Read through the sketch on pages 313–314 and think about how the changes described might affect firms in the following markets:
    - banking and mortgage

- farming and agriculture
- supermarkets and grocery stores
- pubs and clubs
- the housing market.

2 Prepare a portfolio analysis for a mobile phone manufacturer.

- Pick a mobile phone manufacturer (Nokia or Siemens, for example). List all the mobile phones that they manufacture. Take a look at the manufacturer's website or, if you need to, go to a mobile phone provider's website, such as Carphone Warehouse.

- Draw a large version of the Boston Matrix on a sheet of paper and place a cut-out of the name of the different phones the company has on the Matrix. Discuss your judgements with the colleagues in your class. Do you all agree? If not, why not?

Exam practice

The Easter holidays mark the start of an upsurge in sales for many businesses with the summer season offering the opportunity to boost sales. One such example is the cider industry. There has been a change in the cider industry in recent years. The product has been repositioned. It is now not seen as a cheap and rather grubby drink, but as cool, refreshing, fashionable – possessing different qualities. The challenge is to build on this and maintain sales growth not only during the summer months but in the years ahead.

The main drive behind this repositioning has been the brand Magners. The brand is owned by Irish-based C&C group. The group also owns other well known brands, such as Carolans Irish Cream, Irish Mist, Bulmers Original, Britvic and Ballygowan. The success it has had with Magners, however, is the real eye-catching story for the company. Not only has it had an effect on C&C's fortunes, but also the cider industry as a whole.

Turnover for the C&C group rose from €750.4 million in 2005 to €816.6 million in 2006. Magners had been sold in Ireland and was also retailed in Scotland from 2003. It was available in the London area but not in England as a whole. In 2006, the company launched a £25 million advertising campaign to launch Magners in England and this led to sales rising by 225%.

The campaign attempted to appeal to the younger market that had been used to drinking sweeter drinks, such as alcopops. The marketing focused on how the drink could provide a refreshing and cool antidote to the heat of the summer. The background of apple orchards bathed in a warm amber glow further emphasised the summer theme. The drink itself comes in a pint bottle and the adverts show it being served with lots of ice.

There is a range of brands available covering the whole spectrum of the market. At the top end there are companies like Thatchers, based in Somerset, the traditional home of cider making. Thatchers produce a range of ciders including 'speciality' ciders that have high alcohol content. Its main thrust has been to rely on the origins of the drink – the use of different English apples for different products, and where and how the drinks are made.

2007 *Magners* advert

Source: adapted from Biz/ed 'In the News': http://www.bized.co.uk/cgi-bin/chron/chron.pl?id=2820

1 Explain what USP you think Magners might possess. (4 marks)

2 Consider how changes in lifestyles, society and the competition might have affected the cider industry. (10 marks)

3 How might a firm like C&C use product portfolio analysis to manage its product portfolio? (12 marks)

4 It has been suggested that Magners is fast becoming a cash cow. Evaluate the strategies open to C&C in managing the future for this product. (14 marks)

Total: 40 marks

Chapter 31 Using the marketing mix: promotion

In this chapter you will learn about promotion as an element of the marketing mix. You will learn that promotion is more than just advertising, but is about making the consumer aware of the existence of a business's products and services through a variety of means. Finally, you will come to understand how the choice of promotional method used is determined.

What is promotion?

Promotion is about communicating with customers and potential customers. Through promotion a business communicates:

- who they are (developing a corporate image)
- what they sell (informative promotion)
- why consumers should buy their products (persuading)
- the brand image of a product (reminding and reinforcing)
- where customers can get the product (informative)
- how much the product costs (informative).

Consumers are faced with so much choice that it is often the business that 'shouts the loudest' about its products that gets noticed. Promotion is essential to:

- increase demand for products
- establish a price for products
- create, enhance or maintain a brand image
- raise awareness, emotion or concern for an issue or product
- maintain, protect or increase market share.

How important is promotion?

The extent to which promotion is important, relative to other aspects of marketing, depends on:

- the degree of competition in the market
- the extent to which promotion is the norm in a particular market
- the market segment (a niche product may need little promotion)
- the marketing emphasis (if the product is differentiated, whether this difference is tangible or intangible – intangible differences may require heavy promotional support)
- stage in the product life cycle (established products may need little promotion)
- the extent of supply (a product that is widely available may need little promotion).

Key terms

Above-the-line promotion
A paid form of promotion where a commission is paid by the media to an agency. This includes promotion through media such as TV, radio, posters, the press and cinema.

Below-the-line promotion
A range of promotional techniques, such as personal selling, direct marketing and PR, over which firms direct (some) control; usually led by the firm and not involving payment to independent agencies and so does not involve a commission to an agency.

Elements of the promotional mix

There are many ways that a business can promote its products or services. A distinction is often made between **above the line** and **below the line** promotion (see Key terms).

Above-the-line methods

Above-the-line promotion involves the use of advertising media over which a firm does not have direct control and where it invariably uses an agency to which it pays a commission. The following are examples of some above-the-line methods of advertising.

Television

Television is the most familiar face of advertising. Because of its wide reach, most mass-market consumer goods are advertised on television. Television is a relatively expensive medium, but on a 'per viewing' basis is very cost effective. This is because the cost can be spread over so many people. On ITV, one of the main commercial television networks, advertising is seen as a commodity. The price paid for an advertising slot (sold in 30 second bits) is dependent on supply and demand. Each hour of TV air time has around seven minutes allocated for commercials. TV companies sell advertising time in line with the number of people viewing programmes – so-called TVRs – television ratings. Popular programmes will have higher TVRs, measured as the percentage of people watching a TV commercial. A TVR of 20% means that 20% of people watched a particular commercial. TVRs tend to be highest during popular programmes. The ITV soap *Coronation Street*, for example, regularly commands 10 million viewers and will reach highs of 15–20 million depending on the storyline. Getting a slot during this programme could be highly economical for some companies – but it will be priced highly.

At other times of day, adverts can be relatively cheap. Slots at different times of the day will be priced differently and might range between £8,000 and £45,000. This is small change compared to the cost for a business wanting to purchase advertising time during major events like the NFL Super Bowl in the United States. For the 2007 Super Bowl between the Indianapolis Colts and the Chicago Bears, a 30-second slot might cost as much as $2.6 million!

What has to be remembered is the average cost per target viewer; if, for example, a business paid £500,000 for one advertisement during a key episode of *Coronation Street*, that advertisement would potentially have reached 15 million people. The cost of reaching each person is therefore only 3p per person reached which, in advertising terms, is good value for money – despite the artificially high-cost example used. For the 2007 Super Bowl, it was estimated that TVRs reached a household level of 42.6 and there was an average of 93 million viewers. For companies commanding ad slots during Super Bowl that comes out at less than 3 cents per viewer!

Television commanded the second highest share of advertising spending in 2005 at 25.4%.

*(Data source on TVRs :
http://www.itpmag.demon.co.uk/Downloads/Rough_Guide_to_Costs.pdf)*

A billboard goes up for the film Casino Royale

Outdoor advertising

Outdoor advertising includes advertisements at bus stops, on the sides of buses and taxis, billboards (above) and posters. This accounts for 5.5% of all advertising spending.

Newspapers

Newspapers are the most popular medium for advertising. In 2006, The Advertising Association published its latest figures on the share of advertising accounted for by different media. Newspapers, magazines and directories accounted for 45.3% of an industry worth £19 billion. This media is popular because it reaches so many people. In addition, newspaper publishers are able to clearly define their target audiences, making newspapers attractive to advertisers looking to reach specific market segments.

Magazine publishers, like newspaper publishers, also have a clear idea of who their readers are and use this information to attract advertisers seeking to target specific market segments. Magazines are useful for building brand image – clothing seen in Vogue or FHM gains fashionable status almost by default!

Cinema advertising

Cinema advertising depends, to some extent, on the success of the movie industry. Big blockbuster films have helped to boost cinemas' popularity over recent years. In January 2007, Pearl and Dean, who are synonymous with cinema advertising, reported that total advertising spending in 2006 was £154.5 million and in the first six months of 2007, was £91.8 million. Cinema advertising is often used to reach young audiences who are difficult to communicate with via other mediums. The sorts of companies who make use of cinema advertising include Orange, Apple, Ford, Red Bull, Sony, BSkyB and Microsoft. Cinema advertising accounted for 1% of total advertising expenditure in 2005.

Radio

Radio has the advantage of low cost, and the ability to target specific regions. However, commercial radio accounts for only 45.5% of total radio listening – the rest being made up by BBC stations (where advertising is not allowed). As digital radio becomes more popular, the number of commercial stations (and the promotional possibilities) should, however, increase). Radio accounted for 3.1% of total advertising spending in 2005.

Internet advertising

Internet advertising blossomed during the dotcom boom of the late 1990s. Expenditure on Internet advertising was growing faster than for any other media type. When the dotcom bubble burst, so did the bubble surrounding Internet advertising. However, after the shake-up in the industry, Internet advertising is now growing. The Advertising Association reported that spending on Internet advertising now accounts for 7.2% of the total compared to 4.5% in 2004.

(Source of data: Advertising Association's Advertising Statistics Yearbook 2006)

Below-the-line promotion

Below-the-line promotion involves use of promotional media over which the firm has control, such as direct mail and trade fairs.

Personal selling

This involves an individual making personal contact with a client and discussing particular solutions which meet the needs of the client. It often involves five main stages.

PROSPECTING

This means finding out who potential clients might be. Such information might come back from word-of-mouth recommendations, market research feedback or from the research carried out by the sales individual. An important part of prospecting involves trying to weed out the likely prospects from the unlikely, and pre-plan solutions that might meet their needs before the next stage.

MAKING INITIAL CONTACT

The initial contact can be crucial. Make the wrong impression and you can lose the customer. Planning out the meeting to try to gain maximum return from the visit is also vital; neither the client nor the sales person wants their time wasted.

THE SALES PRESENTATION

This is where the sales 'pitch' is made. Experienced sales staff are aware of their clients' needs and know when to introduce different ideas and how to do these to maximum effect.

OBJECTION HANDLING

Many clients might decide that the offering is not for them or present all sorts of reasons why they do not want to buy – the job of the salesperson is to anticipate these objections and know how to deal with them, to make the path between presentation and sale as smooth as possible for all parties.

CLOSING THE SALE

Getting the client to actually put pen to paper and agree the order.

Sales promotion

These are methods employed that do not usually involve personal contact initially. They include such familiar things as free samples, coupons and vouchers, competitions, special discount days (for example, the Blue Cross sale days), free gifts, point of sale displays. and special offers, such as 'BOGOF' (buy one, get one free).

Public relations (PR)

This involves creating and maintaining awareness with the public of the product, service brand and so on. Getting a product or service into the public eye and keeping it high profile is a particular skill, especially if the message and relationship that you build with the public is intended to be a positive one. What is said/shown/released, when, where and how, might all be crucial in the building of a successful PR campaign. In some cases, negative publicity can be of benefit but relying on bad publicity to build awareness can backfire!

Direct marketing

This involves sending information to customers directly without any intervening media. As a direct result of the promotion, consumers are immediately able to purchase the product. Typical examples include direct mail (often called junk mail), leaflets enclosed in magazines and newspapers, telemarketing, e-mail marketing, banner ads on the Internet, and so on. Figure 31.1 highlights the advantages and disadvantages of direct marketing.

> ## Guru's views
>
> 'The codfish lays ten thousand eggs; the homely hen lays one. The codfish never cackles to tell you what she's done. And so we scorn the codfish; while the humble hen we prize – which only goes to show you, that it pays to advertise.'
>
> *–Anon*

Advantages	Disadvantages
• Accurate targeting of potential customers.	• Direct mail often seen as intrusive and a nuisance ('junk mail').
• Message can be personalised.	• High initial costs (market and data is expensive).
• Easy to measure customers' responses.	• Often low response rates to direct mail.
• Competitors less aware of marketing activities.	• Gives poor results if market data is out of date or incorrect.

Figure 31.1 Advantages and disadvantages of direct marketing

Trade fairs and exhibitions

These are usually specialist means of promotion and are often focused on B2B marketing.

Sponsorship

Being involved with another business can often be a valuable source of promotion. Sponsorship involves a business paying to be associated with a particular event (such as the 2012 Olympics), individual star or even TV programme. Whatever the size, the aim is the same – to help raise awareness about the business. Nike's sponsorship of Tiger Woods has helped Nike to become one of the leading suppliers of golf clothing.

User testing/trials

If you have wandered through some of the larger music retail outlets, then you will have seen examples of this type of promotion. Microsoft, Nintendo and Sony will often provide consoles, large screens and different games to entice the user to 'have a go'. Such methods are often very successful in turning interest into sales and in some cases might be essential to persuade the customer to make the purchase decision.

Merchandising

Using other products to help raise the profile, and also sell more of the businesses products, is known as merchandising. This has been used extensively by the film industry with spin-off products associated with major film releases such as *Star Wars*, *Harry Potter*, *Transformers*, *Batman*, *Spiderman*, and so on.

Branding

Branding refers to the use of a name, symbol, design or other medium to identify or create an association with a particular product. Popular brands include Nike, FCUK, Sony and Heinz. It is often thought that branding relates to high-priced fashion products, such as Hugo Boss, Louis Vuitton and Armani, for example, but any firm will be looking to develop a brand. Poundstretcher and Primark are two examples of brands but they are certainly not high priced. Read about the importance of branding on the next page.

Others

Other forms of below-the-line promotion include:
- money-off coupons
- competitions
- free gifts (for example, a free music video with an album download)
- introductory offers (for example, buy Sky TV and get a free installation)
- tasting sessions and demonstrations.

The importance of branding

What a brand does is succeed in creating an association in the consumer's mind. This association may be a mental image, a sound, a slogan, a logo, a thought, a feeling, a smell, a touch, a memory, taste – some connection. The intention is that if we associate a particular brand with a particular product or service, we are more likely, when faced with choices, to plump for the branded item that we associate with. Branding is a long-term strategy and many firms spend millions not only building the brand, but also protecting it.

In recent years, our understanding of the brain and how it works has grown exponentially. It is not surprising that marketers have looked at the research to see how it can be exploited to build and maintain product awareness. The use of so-called neuromarketing uses developments in magnetic resonance imaging (MRI) techniques to identify how the brain reacts to particular stimuli associated with different products. It is thought that advertising, for example, may work in quite different ways from that originally thought. Firms can use these developments to refine their product and also their branding techniques.

Brand image is often referred to as the 'personality' given to a product through marketing activities. This brand image will be deliberately created to appeal to a specific market segment; for example, the fizzy drink, Tango, has been given a 'wacky' image to appeal to younger people. Branding is also used to do the following.

CREATE AND MAINTAIN BRAND LOYALTY

When Kit Kat, at great expense, changed its packaging by removing the silver foil inner wrapper, loyal customers were outraged. The brand loyalty generated by the ritual of opening a Kit Kat was immense. Brands create familiarity and encourage long-term repeat purchasing.

EXPAND PRODUCT RANGES

Consumers are more likely to try a new product if they trust the brand. Boots was able to enter the beauty treatment market because customers trust the Boots brand.

DIFFERENTIATE PRODUCTS

A brand may be the only thing that makes one product different from another. This was, in fact, the original purpose of brands. The Cadbury brand was borne out of the need to distinguish itself from other chocolates on the market.

AID RECOGNITION

The presence of a distinctive brand logo can help products to stand out on supermarket shelves. Coca-Cola bottles have a distinctive colour and shape, both aiding recognition.

GAIN PRICE FLEXIBILITY

The fact that the product is 'different' and has established brand loyalty or has a desirable brand image allows firms to charge higher prices.

Influences on the choice of promotional mix

Bearing in mind the distinction between above-the-line and below-the-line promotion, the choice of promotion method may well depend on a variety of factors:

THE TARGET MARKET

What they read, their hobbies, their leisure activities, what they watch on TV, what type of music they listen to, what films they watch, how often they go out, and so on.

WHETHER THE MARKET IS LOCAL OR NATIONAL

A local market might be targeted through the use of local newspapers or at a regional level through regional television and local radio advertising or leafleting and so on. Care will need to be taken that the target market is reached though the most effective promotional channel for the market targeted.

THE ADVERTISING BUDGET

Smaller firms with a limited advertising budget will have to think carefully about how they choose to allocate their funds and what sort of advertising media they need to use to hit the target audience most effectively. Larger firms may have a greater range of choices open to them because they have a larger budget and as such may have some advantages over smaller firms.

WHERE THE PRODUCT IS IN ITS LIFE CYCLE

Products at the maturity stage of the life cycle may not need to spend as much on promoting a product in comparison to the budget that will have to be allocated at the launch stage. Decisions will also have to be made about the extent to which resources are devoted to products at the decline stage of the life cycle.

THE TYPE OF PRODUCT BEING ADVERTISED

Some products will tend to be associated with certain types of promotion and advertising. Perfumes, for example, tend to be associated with sexy and seductive types of advertising and the promotion of these types of products needs to give the air of sophistication and exclusivity that manufacturers will want the product to be associated with. Food, for example, will need to be advertised in colour to enhance its appeal and convey the right message to consumers.

ANY LEGAL CONSTRAINTS

For example, the Tobacco Advertising & Promotions Bill regulates tobacco advertising in the UK; the advertising and promotion of alcohol is subject to a number of restrictions which a firm needs to consider when devising the promotional mix.

WHETHER THE METHOD CHOSEN WILL COMPLEMENT OTHER ELEMENTS OF THE MARKETING MIX

In the example above with regard to perfumes, a promotional package of display box, free gifts, the design of a highly sophisticated container and use of high profile celebrity will imply that the price needs to reflect the exclusivity that is being suggested. In addition, the business might be concerned about the sort of outlets that the product is going to be sold in, focusing on specialist outlets where staff might be available who are trained to meet customer needs more effectively.

Control of promotion

The Office of Communications (Ofcom – www.ofcom.org.uk/) takes principal responsibility for regulating advertising in the broadcast media. Within this, promotion is controlled and regulated by the BCAP (British Code of Advertising Practice). The code states that all promotions must be:

- legal, decent, honest and truthful, and prepared with a sense of responsibility to consumers and society
- produced in line with the principals of fair competition.

These rules are enforced by:

- the Advertising Standards Authority (ASA – www.asa.org.uk/asa/) – controls all advertisements except TV and radio
- the Independent Television Committee (ITC) – controls advertising on TV
- the Radio Authority – controls radio advertising.

These bodies are industry-funded and self-regulatory. Where an advertisement is deemed unacceptable, the advertiser must withdraw or amend it.

> Up-to-date links to these websites can be found at **www.collins.bized.co.uk**.

Is promotion ethical or desirable?

The increasing sophistication of promotional techniques has given rise to some criticism of this element of the marketing mix. Terms like 'pester power', 'junk mail' and 'spam' have come into common use and are linked in some way to the changes in the way companies promote their products, not just in a particular country, but increasingly on a global scale.

Criticisms of advertising include:

- it raises costs without adding tangible product value
- it is used as a way of maintaining monopoly power
- it can be misleading
- it stimulates wants that cannot be met (creating a materialist society)
- the benefits of advertising (higher prices) are not passed on to product manufacturers (a Nike factory worker in Indonesia might earn $2 a day for producing $120 Nike trainers).

Guru's views

'If advertisers spent the same amount of money on improving their products as they do on advertising then they wouldn't have to advertise them.'

–Will Rogers

The regulation of the way businesses promote their products is largely self-regulation. Many people suggest that self-regulation does not always work and would like to see stricter regulation of how firms promote and advertise their products and services. The ASA does handle a large number of complaints about advertising every year. In 2005, it handled over 26,000 complaints and in 2006, nearly 22,500. The ASA looks at each complaint in relation to the British Code of Advertising Practice (CAP Code). Complaints might include: people finding an ad offensive because of its religious, sexual or cultural suggestions; adverts that are seen as being misleading or providing false information, or implication (that a certain type of alcoholic drink might improve your sexual prowess, for example); adverts that are seen as insulting, suggesting inappropriate claims or that the advert is irresponsible and could encourage inappropriate or illegal behaviour amongst others.

Further material and resources relating to this section can be found at **www.collins.bized.co.uk**. Keep checking for updates.

For example…

In August 2007, Ann Summers, the high-street sex shop chain, launched a new advert to promote the opening of a new store in Exeter, Devon. The ASA investigated the complaint that the advert was offensive and could be seen by children. The advert was placed on a van which drove around between 10am and 5pm on weekdays. The ASA ruled that although the advert made use of innuendo and the use of a model might be seen as being distasteful to some, it was unlikely to cause widespread offence and was not likely to be seen by children as they would be in school at the time. The complaint was dismissed.

For example…

Kraft Foods were reported to the ASA for an advert for its 'Lunchables' product which had the strapline 'Packed with good stuff'. The ASA received complaints that the product contained high levels of salt, and after investigation, the ASA concluded that the product implied it was healthy and nutritious when in fact it contained high levels of saturated fat and sodium. The complaint was upheld and the ad deemed misleading. The relevant part of the CAP code in this case was truthfulness and substance.

Using the marketing mix: Promotion: **Summary**

- Promotion is an element of the marketing mix which involves making customers aware that a product or service exists, and making a purchase of that good or service more desirable.
- Promotion is important but is only one element of the mix – no amount of promotion will, on its own, make a success of a product or service that does not meet customer needs.
- There are a number of factors making up the promotion mix. These include user testing, advertising, free gifts, direct marketing, public relations and sponsorship.
- The choice of promotional method is important. Promotion can be either 'above-the-line' or 'below-the-line'.
- There is an ethical dimension to promotion. Attempts to encourage consumers to buy one good or service over another can have important consequences for the firm.
- Regulators are set up to monitor the behaviour of firms' promotion methods.

Summary questions

1 Distinguish between above-the-line and below-the-line promotion.

2 Give three examples of above-the-line promotion and three of below-the-line promotion.

3 Examine the costs and benefits of TV advertising. (Don't just think of the costs in terms of money!)

4 Discuss the relationship between promotion and market segmentation.

5 Give two arguments against advertising.

6 Is any PR good PR?

7 What factors might influence the success of a promotional campaign?

8 What is direct mailing?

9 Which independent body controls TV advertising?

10 What does the British Code of Advertising Practice state that all advertisements must be?

Activity

In small groups, prepare a presentation on the advantages and disadvantages of two contrasting media types. (Others groups could present different media types.) You may want to prepare a handout to support your presentation – these handouts can be distributed to the whole class to support your course notes.

Exam practice

For many young people in the 1960s and 70s, the Hammer horror films were staple viewing. They brought traditional characters to the big screen and attempted to introduce true horror to the movie genre. Many of these films became cult classics – Dracula, The Mummy, Frankenstein and werewolves were all subject to the Hammer treatment. Some of the films were in black and white but this seemed to merely enhance the horror effect. The films also made stars out of Peter Cushing and Christopher Lee, who seemed to take turns in playing the lead character and were either the 'goody' or the 'baddy'.

Whilst in modern film terms Hammer films were not that scary, they did encapsulate a changing approach to film-making and the name 'Hammer' became synonymous with horror. In recent years, the films have seemed to disappear from our TV screens and the studio stopped producing films in 1979. There used to be a time when a Hammer film was almost guaranteed to be playing in the early hours of a weekend morning – an ideal antidote to *Match of the Day*. As a brand and a going concern, however, it seemed to quietly slip away.

Christopher Lee as Count Dracula

However, it is now likely that the films will once again be seen on the big screen as well as TV after Hammer Film Productions was sold to a Dutch group, Cyrte Investments. The man behind this group is the creator of *Big Brother*, John de Mol. The purchase includes all the back catalogue of around 300 films.

The private equity group now plans to spend $50 million on the films, bringing them back to cinemas and also onto new media like mobile phones and the Internet. There are also plans for a Hammer Horror TV series and negotiations are reported to be underway with a UK broadcaster. The £25 million investment will also see new Hammer productions although it is not clear as yet what these will be.

The new owners have made it clear that they are aiming to develop the brand for a 21st century audience and want to exploit its global potential. For many film fans and late-night TV viewers, the resurrection (excuse the pun) of Hammer will be good news. Some of the back catalogue can be purchased on DVD for less than £10 but this might mean that the complete range of Hammer output will soon be available to fans and new viewers alike.

Source: Adapted from Biz/ed 'In the News': http://www.bized.co.uk/cgi-bin/chron/chron.pl?id=2847

1 Explain the meaning of the term 'brand'. (4 marks)

2 Analyse possible elements of the promotion mix that the new owners of Hammer films might use in bringing the product to the notice of consumers. (12 marks)

3 Assess the use of above-the-line and below-the-line promotion methods in promoting the return of Hammer Films. (10 marks)

4 Given Hammer Films reputation for horror, assess the ethical considerations that the new owners of the brand might need to consider in devising its promotional activities. (14 marks)

Total: 40 marks

Chapter 32   Using the marketing mix: pricing

In this section you will learn about the range of ways in which a business can manipulate its prices in order to increase sales and gain competitive advantage. You will learn that changing price has costs associated with it and also consequences which the firm needs to consider carefully. You will also learn about the variety of **pricing strategies** that firms might use.

Price – an outline

The price of a product is dependent on a variety of factors. Theory tells us that price is determined by the interaction of supply and demand. Supply and demand form a model that helps us to make predictions about and understand how markets work. There are a lot of assumptions about markets in such models. In reality, some or all of these assumptions

Fans queuing for the Wimbledon Championships

may not hold, but the model provides us with the basis for helping us to analyse what is happening and why it might be happening.

For example, every year there are massive queues to get tickets for the All England Tennis Championships at Wimbledon. How does a model of demand and supply help us to explain this? A queue invariably means that demand is greater than supply. The theory tells us that in such cases, the price will rise until the shortage is competed away. However, in the case of Wimbledon tickets, official prices do not rise – the result is that the shortage remains; hence the queues. If the All England Club wanted to get rid of the queues, then all they have to do is raise the price of tickets!

The fact that they do not do this tells us something important. One of the reasons why they maintain prices at the level they do is because they do not want to exclude 'ordinary' fans from getting to see games. If prices were five times higher then there might not be so many queues, but only certain people would be able to afford the tickets. The All England Club would rather set prices so that some 'ordinary' people get to see games rather than set prices which would exclude them. However, the model also tells us that when there are shortages that persist, black markets will tend to arise – which is exactly what happens. The model is very powerful!

Whilst the model can tell us a great deal about how markets work, don't think that individual businesses will be sitting down drawing supply and demand diagrams – they don't. When deciding on price they will be thinking of a variety of factors that might influence the price they set. For example:

- the cost of production
- the target customers (market segment)
- marketplace competition
- the business's overall objectives, marketing objectives and marketing strategy
- where the product is in its life cycle.

However, having taken some or all of these factors into consideration, there is still no guarantee that the price set will be the 'right' price. Businesses will have to constantly monitor market changes and may have to adjust prices accordingly. It is important to remember that whilst a business might try and estimate how the consumer might react to price, they are not in a position to determine demand. The decisions of consumers and producers are, to all intents and purposes, entirely separate.

Pricing strategies and tactics

Before we look at pricing in more detail, it is important to have a clear understanding of the difference between pricing strategies and **pricing tactics**.

A pricing strategy represents the way in which an overall goal is identified and the establishment of a set of principles for reaching that goal. The long-term goal might be something like raising profit margins, achieving a certain market share for a product, repositioning a product in a new market, rebranding a good or service, or expanding into new markets.

Tactics, on the other hand, are the actions taken to fulfil the strategy – the means to an end. Tactics tend to be specific responses to particular situations that arise.

Strategic objectives

The following might all be strategic objectives in which price has a role.

PROFIT MAXIMISATION

Firms may seek to maximise the profit they make either in the short-term or the long-term (or both) and pricing is set so that either goal is achieved.

REVENUE MAXIMISATION

Revenue maximisation is different from profit maximisation. Revenue is found by multiplying the number of items sold by the price. The pricing method therefore would be carefully planned to achieve this objective. Revenue maximisation may not always mean profitability!

PRICE LEADERSHIP

A firm may be seeking to become the dominant firm in the industry. This may allow it to take the lead in prices that are set and which others in the industry have to follow. This might arise because the firm has some degree of market power.

PRICE TAKERS

In some markets, there are many relatively small firms who have little or no market power. These sorts of firms have to take the price that is dictated by the market. Examples might include businesses in agriculture. The behaviour of the firm in such a case will be influenced by their position in such a market.

SALES MAXIMISATION

The aim is to increase sales volume and prices can be set to achieve this goal. The price would be set to encourage maximum sales and get customers to buy.

PROFIT MARGIN MAXIMISATION

Price is set in relation to the unit cost in order to maximise the difference between the two. In such cases, sales volumes might be less than with other strategies, but this might suit certain types of market.

QUALITY LEADERSHIP

Price is used to signal to the market that the product or service is high quality.

PARTIAL COST RECOVERY

Prices may be set not to cover all costs but only part of the costs. In effect, other products or services the business has might be used to subsidise the price in this particular market.

SURVIVAL

Ultimately, many firms will have a goal of simply surviving – not always an easy task! In such circumstances, prices may be set to enable the firm to remain in the market, to make a profit that allows them to do so but which does not maximise profit.

STABILITY

A firm might set its prices in relation to competitors in the market to maintain some element of stability in the market. In such cases, price wars may be seen as being damaging and to be avoided.

Pricing strategies

Cost plus pricing

The most commonly used pricing method is cost plus, which forms the basis of all pricing decisions – after all, if a business does not cover its costs in the long term, ultimately it will be forced to close.

The average cost of one item is calculated (total cost ÷ number of units) and then a mark-up is added to give the final selling price. Mark-up is found as follows:

$$\text{Mark-up} = \frac{\text{Profit}}{\text{Cost}} \times 100$$

For example, if the cost of producing a can of Coke is 30p but the sale price is 60p, then the profit on each can is 30p. The mark-up is therefore 100%.

For example...

Part one

A business produces headphones for personal music players. The total production costs are £500,000; the business produces 100,000 units.

$$\text{Average cost} = \frac{£500,000}{100,000} = £5 \text{ per unit}$$

If the business then decides its mark-up will be 150%, the selling price will be:

£5 + (£5 X 150%) = £12.50 selling price

Tip It is important to remember to add in the original cost when calculating mark-up.

Penetration pricing

When a product is launched into an established market, its price may be set low to attract customers. *Front* magazine was launched at just a £1, to encourage young males to trial it. You may see a number of adverts on TV for magazines that contain models or CDs based around popular films or pop stars, such as Elvis Presley, *Star Wars* and *Harry Potter*, by a firm called de Agostini. The first issue of the magazine is usually offered at a very low price to encourage initial take-up. Subsequent parts of the 'collector's edition' tend to be higher. Many firms who adopt this strategy may well increase the price once market share has been gained and established.

Price skimming

Where a product is first to market, a high price is often charged. New technologies are often launched at a high price to recoup development costs as quickly as possible, and to benefit from the high profit margins available when a product is new and desirable. Plasma TV screens were a price skimming strategy.

Contribution

The price is set at a level that covers the direct costs of making a good (variable costs) and adds (contributes) an amount to paying other costs.

For example...

Part two

The total cost (£500,000) is made up of fixed costs plus variable costs. If the variable cost of making one set of headphones was £2, the fixed cost would be £300,000. (It follows that 100,000 units produced at £2 per unit cost £200,000; as the total cost of production was £500,000, the fixed costs must be £300,000.).

If the business charges £4 for the headphones, it would cover its variable costs of £2 per unit, and each unit sold would contribute £2 towards fixed costs – a total of £200,000.

In this case, if this were the business's only product, it would make a loss of £100,000. In practice, the business is likely to have a range of goods and the profits from other sales may offset this loss.

Pricing tactics

Captive product pricing

Companies are able to charge a premium (or higher) price where the consumer is 'forced' to use complementary products. For example, Gillette recently introduced a new battery-powered razor called the Fusion Power. To buy the razor itself is relatively cheap – around £9.99 at the time of writing. If you then want to buy replacement blades, these are priced much higher. A pack of eight blades can be priced up to £20.

Destroyer (or predatory) pricing

Prices are set deliberately low (and even in some cases zero or negative) in an attempt to force other producers out of the market. Microsoft, for example, gave away its Internet Explorer and its Windows Media Player for free in order to establish dominance over other Internet browsers and media players in the market. Some supermarkets actually offered money-back vouchers on their own brand tins of beans – an example of a negative price.

Discriminatory pricing

Different prices are charged to different groups of people at different times. For instance, cinemas charge different prices for daytime and evening showings; train companies charge different prices for the same journey at different times of the day; airlines charge different prices for the same flight; energy and mobile phone companies operate different tariffs.

Geographical pricing

Prices vary according to the location of the store or outlet – petrol pricing is an example. A BP station at a motorway service area might charge a higher price that a station situated in a supermarket.

Going rate or market price

The price charged is set at the same level as other products in the market, and at such a level that customers either expect or are willing to pay. The current 'going rate' for the average hobby magazine, for example, is about £4.99 regardless of whether it is for photographers, guitar players, gamers, anglers, hi-fi buffs, model aircraft enthusiasts, digital music fans, train spotters or mountain bikers.

Loss leader

Certain products are sold at below cost price in order to provide 'headline grabbing' prices that encourage customers to visit a particular store. Supermarkets often sell their 'own brand' basic foodstuffs as loss leaders but at certain times of the year may also use major branded items in the same way. Some supermarkets have sold bottles of Gordon's Gin, for example, at way below cost in order to promote their wines and spirits department just before Christmas. They hope that once customers are in the store the 'loss' will be made up as customers purchase other, higher profit margin items.

Premium pricing

This approach is used where a product has significant competitive advantage, or is clearly differentiated from the competition. It might also be used where a strong brand image has been developed. A number of car manufacturers have premium prices associated with certain models; the brewer, Peeterman, has fixed a relatively high price on its Stella Artois brand and Nokia might set a high price on its latest N series mobile phone.

Psychological pricing

The price is set, for example, at £39.99 rather than at £40. This relates to perceived price barriers that customers may have – £40 may seem too expensive for the product in question. Most retailers use this strategy.

Discounting

This refers to cases where firms will reduce prices for relatively short periods of time. The aim might be to clear out stock, offer discounts on additional items to encourage multiple purchases, encourage large orders or to encourage customers to shop when they might not necessarily be inclined to do so. Examples are Blue Cross days and the use of such pricing tactics by B2B firms like Viking, the stationery firm.

Influences on pricing decisions

Pricing decisions will be influenced by a variety of factors. We will look at one in particular in more detail in this section – price sensitivity. However, some of the others include:

- marketing objectives
- finance

- the action of competitors
- the other elements of the marketing mix.

Price sensitivity

In 2007, Microsoft announced that it was reducing the price of its Xbox 360. Why do you think it did this? What do you think happens to the sales of a product if a business reduces its price? Logic would suggest that people will buy more of the product. That is what Microsoft may have hoped would happen to sales of the Xbox. If you sell more products then that is generally seen as a good thing. We might conclude from this that reducing prices is a good thing. Why don't firms do it more often if this is the case? The opposite would occur if prices were raised – sales would be expected to fall. In such a circumstance, why bother to increase price?

Changes to prices are not as straightforward as you might think. Two important questions have to be considered when changing prices:

- How much should the price change by? Should the price be reduced, for example, by 1%, 5%, 10%, 25%, 50%, etc.?
- How will consumers respond to the change in price? Will sales rise, for example, by 2%, 7%, 15%, 30%, 250%?

The way that consumers respond to changes in price is called price sensitivity. When making purchasing decisions, price will be one factor that consumers will consider. The question for businesses is: how important is price in that decision? Take a business selling boxes of matches. A box of matches is priced at around 20p. Is price a really significant factor in the decision to buy a box of matches? Probably not. If a business selling matches decided to increase its price by 50% to 30p, the effect on sales is not likely to be that great. In this case, consumers are not very sensitive to the change in price.

Compare this to a business selling HD flat screen TVs. Assume that the average price of such a product is £500. If the business decided to raise the price by 50%, what do you think would happen? The new price would now be £750. It is highly likely that this might put off a large amount of potential customers and sales might fall off dramatically. In this example, we would say that customers are highly sensitive to price changes.

When considering price as a strategy in the marketing mix, therefore, a firm has to think about how much they might raise or lower a price and also the extent of the effect on sales as a result. This concept is also called the price elasticity of demand.

> Elasticity of demand measures the responsiveness of demand to a change in price or, in simple terms, a measure of the extent to which sales of a product are affected by a change in its price.

Percentages and percentage changes

There are many different ways of calculating percentage change. If you have been taught a different method, you may wish to stick with that.

PERCENTAGES

One way to remember how to work out percentages is to 'divide what you have by what you could have and multiply by 100'. For example, in a test, you get 80 out of 125: 80 is what you have, 125 is what you could have. Your score as a percentage therefore is 80/125 x 100 = 64%.

PERCENTAGE CHANGES

To work out percentage changes, take the difference between two numbers, divide by the first number you started with and multiply by 100. So, using one of the price elasticity examples: if a firm increases price from £10 to £12, the difference is £2. The first or original price was £10 so we get: $2/10 \times 100 = 20\%$. If the percentage is less than 100, then the percentage change is a minus value. So $80\% - 100 = -20$ change.

A product that is very price sensitive might see demand fall by, for example, 20% if price rose by as little a 5%. A product for which sales are not very price sensitive might see a fall in demand of only 5% despite a 10% price increase.

The price elasticity of demand is normally expressed as a number which is derived from the following formula:

$$\text{Price elasticity of demand} = \frac{\text{Percentage change in quantity demanded}}{\text{Percentage change in price}}$$

If the percentage change in price was a rise of 10% and this was met by a fall in demand of 20%, then substituting this into the formula gives us an elasticity coefficient of $20/10 = 2$.

If the coefficient is between 0 and 1 we say that demand is **price inelastic** and if it is greater than 1 then it is described as being **price elastic**.

In the example above, demand would be elastic or very sensitive to a price change. If a firm has a product with a price elasticity of 2, it means that any change in price will lead to a change in price that is 2 times the change in price. If price was reduced by 5%, demand would be expected to rise by 2 times this amount: 10%.

A business must know how price sensitive or responsive their products are to price changes so that they can analyse the potential impact of, say, special offers or a price increase. We will now look in a little more detail at the degree of elasticity of demand of different products and the effect of this.

Price inelastic demand

Despite heavy taxation by the government, smoking is still a popular habit. The purchase of cigarettes is, therefore, not very sensitive to price changes (price inelastic).

As Figure 32.1 shows, when the price of a packet of cigarettes is increased from £5 to £6, demand falls by 7,000 packets. In this example, the demand has fallen by 5% but the price has increased by 20%.

If the percentage change in quantity demanded is less than the percentage change in price we say that a product is price inelastic.

In this example, demand for cigarettes is price inelastic, indicating that any percentage change in price results in a proportionally smaller percentage change in demand.

What is important to notice is the effect of the price rise on revenue. Revenue is found by multiplying price by the number of products sold. (TR = P X Q). In this example, revenue (total income received) has actually risen as a result of the price increase (from £700,000 to £798,000).

We can state that if a product is price inelastic a rise in price will lead to a rise in total revenue whilst a drop in price would reduce total revenue.

It is important to realise that there are also different degrees of price inelasticity. A product can be very price inelastic which means that demand is hardly affected by or is not very sensitive to price at all.

Price per pack	Quantity demanded	Revenue
£4	150 000	£600 000
£5	140 000	£700 000
£6	133 000	£798 000

Figure 32.1 The price inelasticity of the demand for cigarettes

Price elastic demand

While cigarettes have a price inelastic demand, Figure 32.2 shows that perfume has a price elastic demand.

In this example, an increase in price from £25 to £30 (+20 %) results in a fall in quantity demanded from 20,000 to 10,000 units (-50%).

Here the percentage change in quantity demanded was greater than the percentage change in price. Such a product would be said to be price elastic. This means that demand is highly sensitive or responsive to a change in price.

Notice that in this case revenue falls by £200,000 (from £500,000 to £300,000).

We can state that if a product is price elastic a rise in price will lead to a fall in total revenue whilst a fall in price would increase total revenue.

Price per pack	Quantity demanded	Revenue
£20	30 000	£600 000
£25	20 000	£500 000
£30	10 000	£300 000

Figure 32.2 The price inelasticity of the demand for perfume

Influences on the degree of price sensitivity or elasticity

Several factors affect how price elastic or inelastic a product is.

AVAILABILITY OF SUBSTITUTES

The more choice consumers have, the greater the price sensitivity. Breakfast cereal is likely to be price elastic as so many alternative brands are available.

BUYERS' KNOWLEDGE

The more aware buyers are that alternative products exist, the more price sensitive a product will be.

SWITCHING COSTS

If the cost of switching to a substitute product is high, demand may be relatively price inelastic. On the other hand, where customers can switch easily, the product may be price elastic.

The effect on revenue and profit

Price changes, as highlighted, can have a significant impact on revenue. The extent of this impact will depend on price elasticity. It is important to also consider the impact on profit (revenue minus costs).

For example, cutting prices where only a small amount of profit is being made on each unit, will require significant price elasticity to make the price change worthwhile in profit terms (that is, a large increase in demand will be required).

Further material and resources relating to this section can be found at **www.collins.bized.co.uk**. Keep checking for updates.

Branding
Create brand loyalty through promotion, service, etc. For example, Dell Computers.

Product
Make the product as individual as possible. For example, Dyson.

Place
Make the product available in unique or monopoly locations. For example, food at concerts.

To reduce price elasticity a firm might ...

The key is substitutability

Remove competition
Takeover or merge with the competition, reducing customer options. For example, Microsoft.

Price fixing
Form a price cartel with competitors and set artificially high prices. For example, the oil industry.

Barriers to exit
Make it difficult for customers to switch brands. For example, mobile phones and banks.

Figure 32.3 Strategies to reduce price elasticity

Problems involved in measuring elasticity

Whilst the theory of price elasticity is fairly straightforward the reality is somewhat different. Getting accurate measures of the price elasticity of demand for different products and services is not easy. A business might be able to draw some tentative conclusions about price elasticity based on the data generated from its own activities when it has changed prices in the past. For new businesses just starting up, this sort of information will not be available.

There will be a number of secondary sources of information available generated by research organisations and universities that attempt to use sophisticated statistical and mathematical models to estimate elasticities. Firms can gain access to this sort of research data and it can prove useful but may not be specifically related to the businesses particular product.

Where estimated price elasticities are available the business needs to use the data with caution since the reliability of the methodology used to estimate the elasticity may be flawed and in some cases, its limitations may not be understood by the reader who may not be familiar with the econometric techniques used to gather and interpret the data.

Using the marketing mix: pricing: **Summary**

- Price is the amount consumers are asked to pay to acquire a certain good or service.
- Prices are determined in part by the cost of the factor inputs that go into production and by the interaction of demand and supply.
- The model of supply and demand (the price mechanism) is a powerful tool for analysing how markets work.
- Firms have long-term objectives and price can be used to achieve those objectives.
- A pricing strategy refers to the range of pricing tools used by a business to achieve a long-term goal.
- Tactics are the actions taken to fulfil the strategy – the means to an end. Tactics tend to be specific responses to particular situations that arise.
- The consequences of changing price must be considered – what will be the impact on sales and revenue as a result?
- The concept of price elasticity of demand is a measure of price sensitivity in a market.
- A product that is not very sensitive to price changes is referred to as being price inelastic.
- A product that is sensitive to price changes is referred to as being price elastic.

Summary questions

1 Describe three factors that will affect a firm's pricing decision.

2 When might a firm use price skimming?

3 Using the model of supply and demand, what would you expect to happen to the price of tickets for England if the team reached the next football World Cup final? Why might this model not fully represent what might happen in reality?

4 What is meant by the term 'loss leader'? When might this pricing strategy be used?

5 What pricing strategy might a firm use when trying to gain a foothold in a competitive market?

6 What is price elasticity a measure of?

7 Comment on the following price elasticities:

- 0.2
- 6
- 1.1
- 0.89

8 What types of good might be price inelastic?

9 How might a firm attempt to reduce a product's price elasticity?

10 If a product's sales have risen by 30% after a price cut from £5.99 to £5.49, what is its price elasticity? What type of product might it be?

Price	Demand
£14	36 000
£16	28 000
£18	20 000
£20	6000

Figure 32.4 Demand for DVDs

Activity

1 Using the guide to calculating percentages, the formula for price elasticity in this chapter and figure 32.4 calculate the price elasticity of demand for an increase in DVD prices from:

- £14 to £16
- £16 to £18
- £18 to £20.

2 In the light of your calculations, comment on the relevance of the price elasticity of demand for firms setting prices for DVDs.

Exam practice

Low-priced airlines

The no-frills airline market has been at the forefront of an explosion in the number of flights around Europe. The ease and convenience of flying both to other parts of Europe and within the UK is matched by a fiercely competitive pricing structure between the airlines that have set themselves up specifically to capture the market: companies such as BMI Baby and Ryanair being two of the most well known. Established airlines like British Airways have also had to find ways of competing to stay in the market.

One of the markets that the likes of British Airways have been able to maintain has been the so-called long-haul market. These are the flights to destinations in the Far East that take many hours. Keeping customers satisfied on flights that last such a long time requires significant customer service. The business model of the low-cost airlines has so far not been transferred to the long-haul market.

A new business is looking to change that. Oasis Hong Kong Airlines is attempting to provide a lowcost long-haul service from Hong Kong to London – a 12-hour flight under normal circumstances. In such a business model, the idea of packing in customers and giving them a no-frills cheap ride is not really an option. To compete, however, it does have to find a way of offering prospective passengers a price that is highly competitive, plus the opportunity to be able to make a profit.

For customers, the price of a flight on Oasis is certainly cheaper. The price is well under a half of that which the established airlines charge and with a business class cabin, in-flight entertainment, hot meals and free drinks, the company seems to have all the ingredients of a business proposition that is going to be a success with customers.

On the other side of things are the costs of operating. Profit margins, the difference between the price charged and the cost of production are very narrow, and delays and problems can very quickly eat away at those margins.

Source: Biz/ed 'In the News' http://www.bized.co.uk/cgi-bin/chron/chron.pl?id=2711

1 Explain the meaning of the phrase 'fiercely competitive pricing structure' in the context of the airline industry. (6 marks)

2 Analyse the likely price elasticity of demand for any ONE of the budget airlines and justify your analysis. (10 marks)

3 Explain why BA might not have been in a position to be able to compete on price with the budget airlines when they first entered the market. (6 marks)

4 Is the pricing method adopted by budget airlines such as easyJet and Ryanair a pricing strategy or a tactic? Explain your reasoning. (4 marks)

5 Evaluate the likelihood of success of a budget long-haul airline such as Oasis. (14 marks)

Total: 40 marks

Chapter 33   Using the marketing mix: place

In this section you will learn about the role of place in the marketing mix. You will learn that place is concerned not with physical location, but getting goods and services to where customers want them in order to help maximise sales potential. You will learn that improving the efficiency of the **supply chain** can have a significant effect on costs, whilst at the same time improving the opportunities for increasing sales revenue.

What place is not!

Place (or more properly distribution strategy) refers to the way in which a product is distributed – how it gets to the end consumer. The product must get to the end consumer at the right time, in the right quantities and in the right condition (that is, not broken or perished). If products are not available for consumers to buy when they want to buy them, the business can quickly get into difficulties. This was made very clear in the case of one of the major supermarkets. Sainsbury's invested £1.8 billion in a new automated distribution system and associated IT facilities. The investment was meant to improve the supply chain and reduce costs whilst improving efficiency. Unfortunately, the systems hit problems and the result was a lack of goods on the shelves in their supermarkets. Sainsbury's lost market share as customers went elsewhere.

New chief executive Justin King took control of the company in 2004 and set about trying to solve the problem he had inherited. He recognised that if products were not on the shelves, Sainsbury's position would simply get worse. Over the next few years, the distribution system was improved and with it, Sainsbury's fortunes. This is a simple but very important lesson in the importance of place in the mix.

Distribution channels

A **distribution channel** includes a number of intermediaries (stages in the distribution chain) through which a product passes before it reaches the end consumer. These **intermediaries** (sometimes called middlemen) might include wholesalers, retailers and import or export agents.

Choosing appropriate outlets/distribution channels

A product's distribution channel will be determined by a number of factors.

Marketing aims

A business aiming to increase sales volume will try to secure as wide a distribution as possible. In some cases, a business might want to limit the distribution channels to deliberately position its product/service in the market. For example, some golf clubs in the UK are not necessarily

Key terms

Disintermediation A move towards direct distribution – reducing the stages a product must pass through to reach the consumer by 'cutting out' intermediaries.

Distribution channel The method used by a business to get its product/s to consumers.

Intermediary The different stages in the distribution channel are known as intermediaries, that is, the stages a product must pass through in order to reach the end consumer (retailer, wholesaler, and so on).

Supply chain The whole network of activities, people, other organisations and systems that work together to get a product or service from the supplier to the consumer.

concerned about selling large numbers of memberships but in limiting the number of members they have. In this case the distribution channel might be very narrow.

Product characteristics

The cost of the product, its shelf life and product type all affect how it is distributed. For example, a product with a short shelf life needs to get to customers quickly. Products that are very bulky might be limited in how they get from supplier to consumer – often this will be a B2B operation.

Market coverage

The number of outlets where a product is sold affects the distribution method. Getting Walker's crisps into newsagents or Mars bars into motorway service stations, for example, requires many different stages in the distribution channel.

Cost considerations

The longer the distribution channel, the more costly distribution will be. Short channels can increase stockholding costs because the same amount of stock is shared among fewer intermediaries.

Special services

Some intermediaries offer specialist purchasing advice (DIY stores) or specialist storage conditions (for example, industrial chemical distributors).

Degree of control required

The longer the channel of distribution, the less control the original producer has.

Customer expectations and brand image

Customer perceptions about retail outlets and a desire to create or maintain brand image may affect distribution. Levi's managed to stop Tesco selling its jeans at discounted prices and a number of perfume companies have attempted to stop discount retailers like Superdrug from selling their perfumes. They argue that specialist retailers offer additional services to customers, such as advice and guidance, that discount retailers do not offer.

Product life cycle

Different channels can be used at different points in the product life cycle. For example, mobile phone 'top-up' cards were once available in just a few outlets; now they are available almost everywhere. Stamps are now available to buy online – the customer is able to print off the stamps for postage.

The choice of distribution channel reflects a balance between these considerations. Essentially, this means that a business must balance its own needs (a desire for cost efficiency, for instance) against the needs of the consumer. This balance is shown in Figure 33.1.

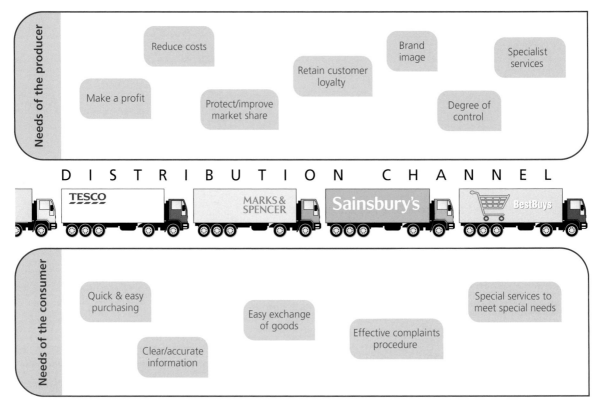

Figure 33.1 The distribution balance

Types of distribution channels

Figure 33.2 shows the main channels of distribution, listed below.

Direct distribution

The producer sells goods directly to the end consumer – no intermediaries are used (small local bakers and Mesh Computers plc are examples). An important part of direct distribution is the idea that no one else takes ownership of the product on its journey from product marketer to final consumer. The main advantage of direct distribution is that, by cutting out these intermediaries (who add their own mark-ups), the product can be sold to the consumer at a competitive price. The producer is also able to develop a relationship with consumers and benefits from direct product feedback. Producers are able to react much faster to consumers' needs and changing market conditions. Many firms now operate this sort of system through their own website or through owning their own retail outlets (Starbucks, for example).

Direct selling

Direct selling has become popular in recent years due to the introduction of Internet and TV shopping. Products traditionally sold through long distribution chains have undergone a process of **disintermediation** ('cutting out the middleman'). Producers can sell directly to large numbers of consumers and reduce the costs that normally would have been paid to intermediaries for their services. Niche products can be sold to wider audiences. For example, specialist skateboard equipment can be easily purchased from the USA via the Internet.

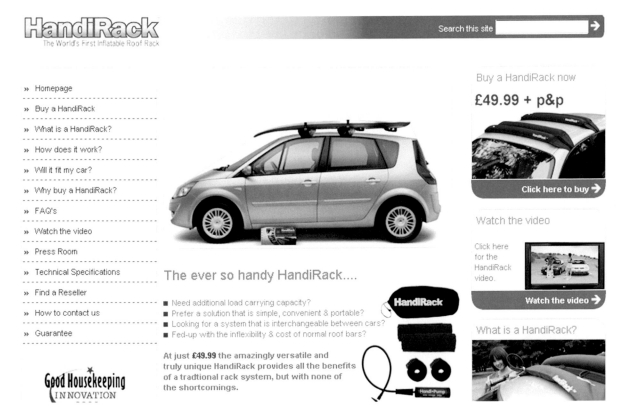

HandiRack website

HandiRack is an example of a product that may not have traditional distribution channels. You might expect to find such a product in stores like Halfords. However, it is only available via the Internet.

The Internet has also changed the way that many bands and artists are getting their music to the public. Bands are using channels such as MySpace to market their music. This is cutting out the traditional route of manager, record company, radio airplay and retail store as a means of distributing music. Online PC businesses, such as Mesh and Dell, have become successful by exploiting the advantages of direct selling.

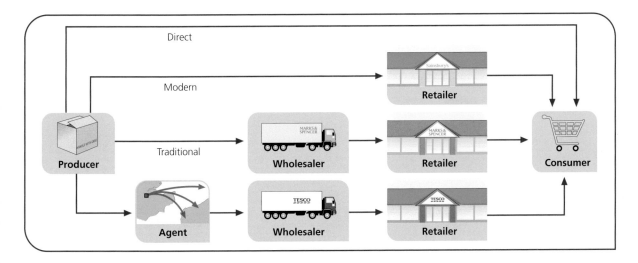

Figure 33.2 The main channels of distribution

Retailers

Even though direct selling is becoming more popular, the majority of consumer products are still sold via retailers.

Retailers allow producers to achieve wide distribution and can help to support or develop brand image (designer clothing is usually sold in small boutiques). Some retailers, such as Harrods or Fortnum and Mason, have strong brand images themselves, helping to boost the image of products sold there. Retailers can help to promote and merchandise products, for example, by point-of-sales displays or special offers. Retailers, such as Currys, offer credit to customers for high-price purchases such as HD TV screens, which might not be within reach for some customers otherwise. However, products sold via retailers usually have to fight with the competition for precious shelf space. Currys, for instance, sells several different brands of televisions. It is this wide choice that attracts customers to retailers, but draws attention to other elements of a product's marketing mix (for example, the factors that differentiate Sony from JVC televisions).

Wholesalers

In many markets, wholesalers act as a link between producers and consumers. Where a retailer does not have the purchasing power to buy directly from a manufacturer, they will buy from a wholesaler. Wholesalers break down 'bulk' into smaller quantities for resale by a retailer. An independent grocer may use this method. Examples of this type of operation include Spar, Costcutters and Londis. In addition, wholesalers provide a range of other important functions:

- Wholesalers provide a means for small producers to get their products into retail outlets. A large supermarket chain may be unwilling to buy directly from the manufacturer until certain production volumes are reached or until sufficient demand has been established – wholesalers provide an alternative route to market.

- When a business sells many products, it may use a wholesaler to bear the distribution costs of shipping those products to thousands of retailers.

- Wholesalers can provide storage facilities and can reduce producers' stockholding costs. Wine merchants (wholesalers) often buy 'young' wine relatively cheaply (taking the storage cost away from the wine producer); the wine is then stored until in reaches maturity and sold to retailers at a profit.

- Some producers want to limit direct contact with customers (reducing the need for a large customer service department). Wholesalers can act as a buffer between producers, retailers and consumers. Faulty goods are returned in bulk via the wholesaler making the process more efficient. JBL (a speaker manufacturer) uses this strategy.

Agents

In contrast to wholesalers, agents never actually own a product. Agents usually connect buyers and sellers and manage the transfer of the good. Agents usually take a commission on sales, or charge a fee for their services. Estate agents and travel agents are good examples.

Agents are often used by businesses trading overseas. Agents specialise in managing complex import and export procedures, and can provide a range of advice services. Differences in local product laws and customs procedures can, among many other things, make exporting goods very challenging. Businesses with little experience of foreign trading often find that agents offer a relatively safe way of entering new markets.

Establishing distribution

Establishing effective distribution can be one of the biggest challenges facing small businesses. A great new product idea is unlikely to be successful if distribution cannot be secured. Retailers are often very reluctant to give valuable shelf space to new products.

Convincing a major national supermarket chain to stop selling an established product in the hope that the new product will generate higher sales represents a significant barrier to success. Many new products are sold via smaller, specialist retailers, where a brand image and customer demand can be established before supermarkets are approached. Häagen Dazs took this approach when it entered the competitive ice cream market in 1989.

Further material and resources relating to this section can be found at **www.collins.bized.co.uk**. Keep checking for updates.

For example…

Maria Difolco has come up against similar problems in trying to get her product to market. Maria came up with the idea of gift bags for wine (see page 6). The bags have an identifiable cartoon character on them called Squiffy and have various messages appropriate to the purpose of the gift. Since she came up with the idea of 'Stupid Bags', Maria has been working on ways to get greater exposure of her product to a wider market. A deal with one of the supermarket giants, Morrisons, was one step along the way, but the involvement with Morrisons took time and helped Maria to learn many lessons.

Using the marketing mix: place: **Summary**

- Place is an essential (and often overlooked) element of the marketing mix. Effective distribution will be a major factor in a product's success. An excellent promotional campaign is useless unless supported by the distribution needed to meet demand.

- Place must complement all other elements of the marketing mix and marketing strategy.

- Increasing market share might require a significant increase in distribution; establishing a premium price suggests restricted distribution.

- More is not always better. Not all products require wide distribution: for example, designer brands closely control distribution to maintain brand image and exclusivity. Consumers do not expect Bose hi-fi equipment to be widely available and are willing to travel to buy it.

Summary questions

1   What is an intermediary?
2   State and explain three factors that influence the choice of distribution channel.
3   What is the role of a wholesaler?
4   What do distribution agents do?
5   Examine the role of the Internet in changing distribution options for a business.
6   State and explain two benefits of using direct distribution methods.
7   Examine the impact of the Internet on distribution.
8   Explain the role of agents in distribution.
9   Examine the relationship between cost of distribution and product price.
10 Suggest, and justify, a suitable method of distribution for the following products:
    - a breakfast cereal
    - books
    - computers
    - motorbikes.

Points for discussion

The MP3 revolution

The development of the online music business has changed the face of the global music industry. Direct selling facilitated by the Internet presents a growing threat to traditional music retailers. The choice facing consumers in the way they buy their music has widened dramatically and some argue that the established music industry has been slow to adjust to the changes that disintermediation has generated.

- What is meant by 'direct selling'?
- Examine why the Internet facilitates disintermediation.
- Discuss how traditional music retailers might respond to the 'digital threat'.

Exam practice

Confectionary producer Cadbury launched a new brand of chewing gum in 2007 in an attempt to enter a market dominated by Wrigley. The UK spends around £240 million on chewing gum, and the market leader by a long way is Wrigley with a market share of 98.5%. The global chewing gum market is worth $15 billion and is currently experiencing growth of around 8% a year. Globally, Cadbury has a 26% market share whilst Wrigley has 36%. In the UK, the picture is not quite so rosy with the market shrinking by 4% in each of the past two years.

It is against this background that Cadbury has spent years and over £20 million developing a new product in the United States where the gum has been planned, tested and tweaked during the product development stage. The launch will be backed by a £10 million marketing campaign. The product is called Trident.

In a sense, the launch is a bit of a gamble for Cadbury; the market does have a degree of brand loyalty and the dominance of Wrigley in the UK might be seen as being too strong for rivals to really break that monopoly. Cadbury will have the job of convincing customers to try its new juice-centred and long-lasting gum and then to continue to buy it in the future. It believes that the gum market in the UK has become stagnant in recent years because of Wrigley's dominance and the lack of innovation in the market. It hopes that it will have significant advantages in terms of an effective and efficient distribution network that will enable it to get the product into shops, petrol stations, supermarkets, newsagents, and so on, where gum is sold. Expect to see the product taking high-profile spaces in these outlets; if Cadbury get the marketing right you will be aware of the product.

Source: Adapted from Biz/ed 'In the News': http://www.bized.co.uk/cgi-bin/chron/chron.pl?id=2776

1 Discuss THREE of the factors that Cadbury might have considered in deciding how Trident would be distributed. (4 marks)

2 Describe the likely distribution channels for a product like Trident. (10 marks)

3 Analyse the possible response to this new market entrant by the market leader Wrigley. (12 marks)

4 To what extent will distribution be the key element of the marketing mix in the long-term success of Trident? (14 marks)

Total: 40 marks

Chapter 34 Marketing and competitiveness

In this section you will learn that firms face different competitive conditions and that this can affect the relative importance of the elements of the marketing mix. You will learn that firms have to find non-marketing methods of improving their competitiveness in the face of different market conditions.

Market conditions and the degree of competition

There are many different types of business and each operates in a very different competitive environment. The type of competitive environment is determined by the following factors.

The number of firms in the industry

Some industries (for example, agriculture) are made up of hundreds of thousands of relatively small firms. Farmers in the UK producing wheat, for example, are not only competing against farmers in the rest of the UK, but also farmers in Europe, Canada, the United States, China, and so on. In such cases they have to accept the market price that is determined by global commodity markets. In this case they are price takers. Other industries have a relatively small number of firms producing goods or services. The manufacture of aircraft engines, for example, is highly specialised and technical and there are not many firms that produce such products. Oil exploration is similarly, a highly technical and expensive operation and only a relatively small number of firms are able to do this.

Market power

It is not just the number of firms in the industry, but the extent of the market power that they are able to exert on the market. The grocery market in the UK is worth £128.2 billion in 2007. It is made up of 99,134 grocery stores. However, the industry is dominated by four companies who account for around 73% of all sales in that sector. These four companies, Asda, Tesco, Sainsbury's and Morrisons, have a considerable degree of market power compared to a small village grocery store. Many industries these days have very big firms who have a great deal of market power. Banking, pharmaceuticals, music and entertainment (for example, cinemas), electrical goods, and financial products like insurance and pensions, are all examples of industries where a relatively small number of firms account for a large proportion of the total sales of the industry.

The nature of the product

Products take on different characteristics. For example, could you tell which producer was responsible for the production of eggs, milk or potatoes? Probably not. These products tend to be very similar regardless of who or where they were produced. Such products are called 'homogenous' goods – they are to all intents and purposes identical to each other. However, it is very likely that you would be able to tell the difference between different cars, different games consoles, different chocolate bars, and so on. These products are capable of being differentiated – made to look, feel, function or taste differently and thus stand out amongst the **competition**. The extent of the homogeneity or **differentiation** between products and services will have an impact on the way the mix is developed.

Entry and exit into and from the market

To gain entry into some markets requires huge amounts of capital, expertise, access to raw materials, and so on. This makes it difficult for some firms to be able to enter markets. Equally, exiting a market can be very costly, especially if massive investments have already been made over a number of years. The factors that prevent firms from entering a market might include the existence of some form of legal restriction such as a licence or a patent. Many pharmaceutical companies will apply for a patent for new drugs they are developing. If the drugs are successful then other firms are legally prevented from copying the product for a specified period of time. There have been legal restrictions on who could send mail through a postal system using stamps – only the Royal Mail had the licence to be able to do this. In such cases the firms who operate in that market may have certain advantages that allow them to adapt the marketing mix in different ways from how things might be if there was the threat of competition.

The amount of information available to buyers and sellers

For markets to work effectively, buyers and sellers have to have access to adequate information. The more information a consumer has, for example, the greater the choice they have. In such markets where information on the product, its price and so on, is widely available and high quality, the marketing mix might be adjusted differently from one where the information available to consumers is less clear. There has been considerable interest in the idea of asymmetric information in markets. This is where one party to a transaction has knowledge or information that the other does not have. For example, if you go to an electrical retailer to enquire about a new HD plasma screen TV and the assistant tells you that brand A is better than brand B and then proceeds to tell you why in technical language, how do you know that what he or she is telling you is accurate? It may be that the assistant has sales targets for that particular brand to reach; it may be that the product really is superior – the problem is, you, as the seller might not know whether it is accurate or not!

These factors will affect the **market structure** that the firm operates in and in turn this will have an influence on the nature of the marketing mix. It is usual to classify the different types of market structure as follows.

HIGHLY COMPETITIVE

- many small firms
- homogenous product
- high level of information for buyers and sellers
- firms tend to be price takers.

COMPETITIVE

- many small firms
- capability of differentiating the product
- the existence of asymmetric information
- some barriers to entry.

OLIGOPOLISTIC

- the market is dominated by a small number of large sellers
- may be many firms in the industry however
- products highly differentiated, for example, branding
- price may not be a weapon of competition but price wars can break out.

MONOPOLY

- market dominated by one firm
- firm may be the price leader and cost leader
- may be legal restrictions on entry
- firm may be able to exert control over price or output (but not both)
- demand for the product tends to be price inelastic.

Depending on which type of market structure the firm is operating in, the marketing strategy and the use of the marketing mix can be different. It should be noted that in some cases, market power does not always equate to large size. It may be that a fish and chip shop, a plumber or an electrician, for example, might all have a local **monopoly**. There may not be other firms offering those products or services in the locality and as a result, the firm may enjoy some market power.

The impact of different market conditions

Operating in different market conditions will affect how a business uses the marketing mix. This may also be reflected in the marketing objectives that the firm has.

Corporate objectives

Marketing objectives must directly reflect overall corporate objectives. Orange may have the corporate objective to increase its total global sales revenue; this might translate as a set of marketing objectives relating to awareness of Orange products in different countries. Increasing sales revenue could be done through some pricing strategy or tactic, but Orange will need to be mindful about what its rivals might do in response. Orange operates in an **oligopolistic** market and as such, any price strategy it follows might be copied by its rivals and thus renders the strategy ineffective in the long run. In such a case, Orange may well have to adjust its objective or think of another way of increasing its sales revenue, through more aggressive promotion, improving its product portfolio, securing more effective distribution methods (acquiring its own stores, for example).

The market

Highly competitive markets demand flexible marketing strategies. Music companies, for example, constantly adjust their strategies to cope with new music trends and new music formats, such as MP3. In such cases distribution methods are having to be reviewed and changed, pricing may be an important element of the mix and the product itself may even change (consumers are buying fewer physical CDs and instead buying downloads).

Competition

One of the most important determinants of marketing strategy is competition. Businesses constantly seek to attain or maintain market leadership and will introduce strategies accordingly – a price cut or special offer by the market leader just as a competing product is about to be launched might help to maintain market position. Which strategy or tactic that is used, however, will be highly dependent on the extent of the competition. In the face of competition from the opening of a large supermarket, a local greengrocer is unlikely to be able to use price as a means of competition. Farmers may have to rely on diversifying their product as a means of ensuring long-term survival; PC manufacturers might have to focus on the quality and technical superiority of the product as a primary focus of the marketing mix.

Design of marketing mix

B2B goods and services are likely to require different marketing strategies from B2C goods and services. Industrial markets are often characterised by small numbers of buyers and sellers, and products can often be highly specialised. Increasing market share may well be difficult, therefore a business might concentrate on cost reductions or developing new products in related markets (for example, Rolls Royce's entry into the marine engine market).

The mantra 'high volume to low price versus low volume to high price' is a basic business principle. This may seem a little simplistic, but it is a good starting point for considering marketing strategies. Businesses must choose their strategy based on one of these two market positions and so determine all other aspects of their marketing strategy. It might well be that mass markets are associated with highly competitive markets whilst niche markets might have less competition. Niche markets might also be associated with highly differentiated products, whereas mass markets such as that for certain types of foodstuff like sugar, potatoes, wheat, barley and vegetables, will be associated with markets that are highly competitive and have largely homogenous products.

In niche markets it may be the case that promotion will be very specific; the product needs to be clearly differentiated and the outlets it is sold in must reflect its image. If a business sells a truly undifferentiated product, then it may pursue a strategy of cost leadership. As we have seen earlier, it may be that there is only room for one cost leader in a market – if a business is not the cheapest then it must offer some form of differentiation to attract customers and this might affect the balance of the mix. In other cases prices may be forced so low that it is difficult to make a profit. American farmers growing potatoes to sell to fast-food chains face this problem and it has also been an accusation levelled at the big supermarkets in the UK that they have put undue pressure on farmers to force prices down to the point where it almost becomes unprofitable to continue in business. Once again, in such cases, price may cease to be an element in the mix that a firm has any control over.

Methods of improving competitiveness

Introduction

Given that firms will be operating in different competitive environments, some elements of the marketing mix might become more important than others in helping the firm to compete. For example, a firm in a highly competitive market may feel that competing on price is not an option, so they may try to find ways that they can differentiate their product to improve competitiveness. By successfully differentiating their product, the business may then be in a position to set a different price. Firms in an oligopolistic market structure might feel that promotion is vital to keep customers aware of what it is doing and persuade them to buy their products or services. Price, in such cases, might be relatively stable and not seen as the key element of the marketing mix.

Few firms are ever immune from competition. If there are profits being made in an industry, it is highly likely that at some point another firm will come along to take advantage of the profits that can be made and begin to challenge existing firms. Intel is the market leader in microchip production, but Advanced Micro Devices (AMD) has come on the scene to challenge that dominance. The threat from AMD necessitated that Intel defend its market share. In 2004, Intel had just over 64% of the US retail PC market, but this fell to just over 53% by 2006. Part of the reason was the rise in the number of PCs using AMD processors rather than Intel ones.

As the competition grew more intense, both companies have been investing in research into new, faster chips. These new products have flooded the market and as a result, prices of these processors have fallen. Again, the focus on product has meant that there has been less opportunity to use price as a key part of the mix. In addition, AMD, as a market challenger, pursued a strategy of directly attacking Intel's leadership position. AMD claimed its microchips to be faster than Intel's, and significantly cheaper. This was something they wanted the computing industry to know about and so they placed an emphasis on promoting this point.

Firms may improve competitiveness in the face of increasing competition or changing market conditions in the following ways.

Differentiated marketing

Cost leadership is difficult to achieve and can result in low profitability, so most businesses differentiate their products – that is, they offer customers something different or superior from what the competition offers. Whilst many products might appear to be identical, there are ways that firms will try and show the consumer how the product is different in some way and as a result, give them the ability to charge different prices. For example, milk is differentiated with different treatments – pasteurised, filtered, semi-skimmed and so on – which helps milk producers to compete. Potatoes are now classed as baby new potatoes, suitable for roasting, baking, mashing, making chips, and so on. Eggs are differentiated by size, colour, whether they are organic, free range (or both), barn eggs or caged. Restaurants will differentiate themselves by the quality of the service, the ambience, the type of food they serve, whether it is take-away or eat in, served at the table or a carvery, and so on. By differentiating a product in a competitive market, a business can reasonably justify charging a higher price.

Differentiated restaurants

Some products rely on perceived differentiation (how customers see the product) rather than actual tangible (physical) differences. For example, a branded shirt or a pair of trainers may be identical to an unbranded one in quality (it may even have been made in the same factory!), but the presence of a well-known logo and brand name helps to differentiate the branded shirt or trainers and justify a higher price.

Reducing costs

Finding ways to reduce costs may include rationalisation and reorganisation programmes where a business restructures its business to make it more efficient or streamlined. This may involve moving production to other plants, shifting the emphasis of service to online media, making staff redundant, sourcing manufacturing or raw materials abroad, outsourcing certain types of business function or activity to low-cost countries, investing in methods to improve productivity, and so on. In some cases it may not be the total costs that the firm is trying to reduce as much as the average or unit costs. This is found by dividing the total cost by the amount produced (output).

Improving quality

Improvements in quality might relate to reliability, the quality of the raw materials and components used, longevity of use, efficiency of use (particularly important in these days where customers may be sensitive to environmental considerations), the speed and courtesy with which customers are dealt with, after-sales service, the level and quality of customer advice and information and so on. Improving quality can not only be a means of differentiating a product or service but might also be a way in which the firm can charge a premium price. If quality is improved then it may require investment in promotion to make sure that consumers are aware of it.

Staff training

As mentioned above, the quality of the customer experience is in part dependent on the interaction that the customer has with staff. If staff appear knowledgeable, confident, helpful, courteous and reliable, it may well be an important source of competitive advantage. To get staff to this level it is not only the recruitment process that is important, but also the ongoing training that staff receive when they are with the company. Investment in improving the abilities and competencies of staff can be vital, particularly given that so many businesses in the UK are not necessarily selling a physical product but might be selling a service or information.

 Further material and resources relating to this section can be found at **www.collins.bized.co.uk**. Keep checking for updates.

Marketing and competitiveness: **Summary**

- The marketing mix will be influenced by the nature of the market that a business is operating in.
- Markets are usually classified according to the degree of competition in them.
- Market structure will be determined by:
  - the number of firms in the industry
  - the nature of the product: the degree of homogeneity of the product
  - the extent to which firms possess market power
  - the ease of entry to and exit from the industry
  - the extent and quality of the information possessed by buyers and sellers.
- The marketing mix will also be informed by the nature of the corporate objectives set by the firm.
- Firms can increase competitiveness by:
  - reducing costs in some way
  - improving quality
  - improving the effectiveness of staff in the firm: some people argue that P for people is a fifth element of the marketing mix.

Summary questions

1 State what type of market structure you think the following firms operate in:

   - Microsoft
   - GlaxoSmithKlein
   - The *Financial Times*
   - Your local Spar
   - The Balti Restaurant in Anytown High Street.

2 Explain how globalisation and the Internet are changing the nature of competition for many firms in the UK.

3 Identify and explain three ways in which a firm might be prevented from easily entering a market.

4 Explain how improved information helps a market to work more effectively and competition to be improved.

5 What would you expect to happen to prices and profits in the medium- to long-term of firms who operate in highly competitive markets?

6 Why do you think that firms in an oligopolistic market structure would rather compete through differentiation of product or brand than price?

7 Explain how the balance of the marketing mix for a B2B firm might differ compared to a B2C firm.

8 Explain how a firm producing a homogenous good might differentiate its marketing.

9 Explain two ways that a firm like Virgin Rail might improve its competitiveness.

10 Should there be more than 4 Ps in the marketing mix? (You might want to consider people, process and packaging.)

Points for discussion

'For years we thought of ourselves as a product-orientated company, meaning we put all of our emphasis on designing and manufacturing the product. But now we understand that the most important thing we do is market the product. We've come around to saying that Nike is a market-orientated company, and the product is our most important marketing tool.' (Nike CEO, Phil Knight)

Source: Naomi Klein, No Logo, Flamingo (2001)

- What type of market structure is Nike operating in?
- In what ways do Nike attempt to differentiate their products?
- Suggest and explain three ways that Nike might seek to improve competitiveness.

Exam practice

The Glastonbury Festival began in 1970. One and a half thousand people paid £1 – including free milk – to attend to see the likes of Mark Bolan of T Rex and Quintessence. Since that time, the festival has gone through a huge number of changes to become a mammoth undertaking requiring year-round planning and execution, with up to 150,000 attending. It is the most famous music festival in the world. It can be argued that the festival has become a victim of its own success; demand for tickets is so great, that within hours of them going on sale tickets are sold out.

Glastonbury as a business relies on a great many partners involved in the staging of the event. The organisers have gone some way towards ensuring that the event does not have any overt commercialism.

'Although we get a huge number of companies wanting to be involved, we are not open to sponsors in the same way other events are. We could make millions but we choose not to, and we never will. We would rather not have the festival. We don't allow any branding on site – Orange, for instance, removes all its logos – and we try to make sure sponsors are giving something back to the people at the festival. Any involvement is low key

A view from the air of the Glastonbury festival

rather than in your face. It's better from a marketing point of view because, in this environment, over-branding would work against you. The people who come here are very media-savvy and don't like to be told what to buy.'

Source of quote: the festival's commercial manager Hannah Rossmorris accessed via http://www.virtualfestivals.com/festivals/article.cfm?articleid=173 and reproduced with permission.

Source: Biz/ed 'Mind you Business': http://www.bized.co.uk/current/mind/2003_4/081203.htm

1 Comment on the view that Glastonbury has a monopoly position in terms of music festivals. (6 marks)

2 Analyse the ways that Glastonbury can differentiate its offering to consumers. (6 marks)

3 Discuss the possible marketing objectives that the organisers of the Glastonbury festival might have. (6 marks)

4 There have been complaints that the Glastonbury festival has become too middle class and been taken over by middle-aged adults who have the best access to the Internet and are able to access tickets through the chosen distribution networks. In addition, there have been criticisms that the festival is becoming more commercial. Discuss possible ways that the organisers could amend their distribution to improve access to younger people, and whether it is inevitable that it will become more commercial. (10 marks)

5 Given the undoubted success of the festival, comment on the view that Glastonbury does not need marketing any more. (12 marks)

Total: 40 marks

Index